RELIGIOUS AFFECTS

RELIGIOUS AFFECTS

Animality, Evolution, and Power

DONOVAN O. SCHAEFER

Duke University Press *Durham and London* 2015

© 2015 Duke University Press
All rights reserved
Printed in the United States of America on acid-free paper ∞
Typeset in Arno Pro by Westchester Publishing Services

Library of Congress Cataloging-in-Publication Data
Schaefer, Donovan O., [date]
Religious affects : animality, evolution, and power /
Donovan O. Schaefer.
pages cm
Includes bibliographical references and index.
ISBN 978-0-8223-5982-1 (hardcover : alk. paper)
ISBN 978-0-8223-5990-6 (pbk. : alk. paper)
ISBN 978-0-8223-7490-9 (e-book)
1. Animals—Religious aspects. 2. Affect (Psychology)—
Religious aspects. 3. Theological anthropology. I. Title.
BL439.S34 2015
156—dc23   2015021376

Cover art: Skunder (Alexander) Boghossian, *Night Flight
of Dread and Delight*, 1964 (detail). Collection of the North
Carolina Museum of Art, Raleigh. Purchased with funds
from the North Carolina State Art Society (Robert F. Phifer
Bequest). Courtesy of the estate of Skunder Boghossian.

To my parents

CONTENTS

ACKNOWLEDGMENTS

This book is the product of a very long thought process that has been instructed by countless other bodies over the past decade. Financially, *Religious Affects* was made possible by grants from the Mellon Foundation, which sponsored first a dissertation fellowship in the Humanities Center at Syracuse University, then a postdoctoral fellowship in the Hurford Center for the Arts and Humanities at Haverford College. The final round of revisions was made after taking up a departmental lectureship in the Faculty of Theology and Religion at Oxford.

Intellectually, it owes its greatest debts to my teachers, who have patiently struggled with me throughout all my interventions in their classrooms, welcome and unwelcome. This long list would start with Jack Caputo (Jed Bartlet to my Leo McGarry) and Gail Hamner (who pushed me to find ways to always make intellectual labor matter), Lorraine Weir, Masako Nakatsugawa, and John Simmons. My other mentors at Syracuse, including Linda Martín Alcoff, Zachary "Zeke" Braiterman, Joanne Waghorne, Patricia Cox Miller, Jim Watts, William Robert, Gustav Niebuhr, and Gregg Lambert, are all distinctly present in this conversation.

Religious Affects was written during a two-year Mellon postdoctoral fellowship at Haverford, during which time I was a participant in the Hurford Center's Faculty Seminar on

Affect Theory, led by Gustavus Stadler. Gus and Jill Stauffer became my two most committed and engaged mentors at Haverford, coaching me through and way beyond the writing process. Other members of the seminar, Tina Zwarg, Raji Mohan, Lisa McCormick, and Deep Ghosh, added their own impresses to this project. Laura McGrane, director of the Hurford Center, deserves special mention for her patient mentorship in pedagogy, which inevitably found its way into this book. I am also deeply indebted to the people who make the Hurford Center into the finely calibrated machine for producing intellectual community that it is—Emily Cronin, James "Zilla" Weissinger, and Kerry Nelson. My other colleagues in Haverford's Religion Department, especially Ken and Naomi Koltun-Fromm, have been unfailingly generous with their guidance and friendship.

This book is, in part, about the ways that intellectual and political circuits are informed by relationships between bodies that are invisible to discursive analytics. Syracuse is remarkable for the rich collegiality of its graduate program in religion, and my friendships there inspired much of *Religious Affects*. Nell Champoux, Jill Adams, Wilson Dickinson, Francis Sanzaro, Dan Miller, Mariam Parekh, and Sangeetha Ekambaram were some of the strongest voices at my side while I wrote this book. Others include Alyssa Beall, Emma Brodeur, Jenny Caplan, Dan Cheifer, Melissa Conroy, Wendy DeBoer, Juliana Finucane, Seren Gates Amador, Kandace Geldmeier, Tanushree Ghosh, Airen Hall, Peter Katz, Craig Martin, Paul Morris, Dan Moseson, Prea Persaud, Jessica Schoolman, Fumi Showers, Christa Shusko, Cordell Waldron, and Holly White. I also want to thank the spouses and partners of many of these folks for generously loaning their counterparts to us for our intellectual experiments—especially Galen, John, Carly, Pedro, Christy, and Ariane.

While at Haverford, I was extremely fortunate to find myself in a similarly generous, vibrant, and welcoming community. My thanks go to everyone who brought so much joy and intellectual energy to the arboretum, especially Jon Wilson and Sara Arnold, Sorelle Friedler and Rebecca Benjamin, Andy Cornell and Ellie Shenker, Lindsay Reckson, Jamel Velji and Chloe Martinez, and Zainab Saleh. This extends to everyone at Turtle Island—Emile, Lou, Meg, Berg, the Sea Creature, and the rest of my friends with shells. It was also during this period that I was privileged to be involved with the intellectually charged circle that founded the Religion, Affect, and Emotion group in the American Academy of Religion. My thanks to everyone in that community, especially Abby Kluchin and Jenna Supp-Montgomerie. From an earlier period, no less formative of this project, I need to thank Eric Pedersen, Kelly Henderson, Charlie Demers, Julian Hou, Dylan Godwin, Mark Rosini, Trevor Shikaze, and especially Shazah Sabuhi.

This book is also about pedagogy, conceptualized as a set of multilateral, overlapping networks that make up the affective pulse of social-political worlds. In light of this, I need to thank many of my students, first from my Animal Religion class at Syracuse—especially Emily Romano and Jonni Stormo—as well as from Religion, Emotion, and Global Cinema at Haverford: Dominique Caggiano, Simone Crew, Michael De Wolf, Mowie Freeman, Ian Gavigan, Edward Gracia, Lauren Hawkins, Siobhan Hickey, Gebby Keny, Laurie Merrell, Lindsey Palmer, Juliette Rando, Waleed Shahid, Sarah Wingfield, and especially David Roza, my indispensable and inventive student research assistant, who helped with the preparation of this manuscript. It is a platitude that our students teach us, but perhaps we underattend the uncountable other ways in which they shape us and enrich our lives and thought.

Aaron Gross looked at several versions of this manuscript and provided an extraordinarily generous set of reflections that are largely responsible for what I consider some of the best parts of *Religious Affects*. Three anonymous reviewers at Duke pointed out several flaws I had missed in the first draft and prompted crucial rewrites that have made the manuscript immeasurably stronger. Nonetheless, I must take responsibility for the many weaknesses that remain. My editor at Duke, Miriam Angress, has been a tireless and passionate supporter of this project from the beginning, and the editorial staff at Duke have improved the finished product immensely. My thanks to Lisa Guenther for generously sharing her manuscript for *Solitary Confinement* in advance of its publication, and to Ludger Viefhues-Bailey and others who helped with the book proposal. A number of people helped me think through the title; most I've already mentioned here, but Anna Gade and Mary-Jane Rubenstein deserve special thanks. Extra thanks to Sondra Hausner for suggesting the final version. Dave Aftandilian and Paul Waldau helped with reading lists and other guidance early in the project.

I must also thank my new colleagues in the Faculty of Theology and Religion at Oxford, Sondra Hausner, Joshua Hordern, Justin Jones, Philip Lockley, Joel Rasmussen, Graham Ward, Bill Wood, Stefano Zaccheti, and especially Johannes Zachhuber for their extraordinarily generous efforts to acquaint me with the faculty and Trinity College, my new students at Trinity, and Alister McGrath, Andrew Pinsent, Ignacio Silva, and the other members of the Ian Ramsey Centre for Science and Religion for creating one of the most welcoming, open, and generative spaces for the discussion of religion and science I've been privileged to join.

My thanks, finally, to Allison Covey, for the generosity, patience, and passion of her mind and spirit; to my brother, Gavin, for his confidence and endless, uncanny brilliance; and to my companion creature, Job. This book is dedicated to my parents. I hope they see in it the commitment to the arts of making the world richer in compassion and dignity that they taught me.

SPECIES, RELIGIOUS STUDIES,
AND THE AFFECTIVE TURN

What is the highest nature? Man is the highest nature. But I must
say that when I compare the interpretation of the highest nature
by the most advanced, the most fashionable and modish [?] school
of modern science, with some other teachings with which we are
familiar, I am not prepared to say that the lecture-room is more
scientific than the Church (cheers). What is the question now placed
before society with a glib assurance the most astounding? The
question is this—Is man an ape or an angel? (loud laughter.) My
lord, I am on the side of the angels (laughter and cheering).
—**Disraeli,** *Church Policy*

What is the trajectory of a newly considered humanities, one that
seeks to know itself not in opposition to its others, the "others" of
the human, but in continuity with them? . . . What kind of intellectual revolution would be required to make man, and the various
forms of man, one among many living things, and one force among
many, rather than the aim and destination of all knowledges?
—**Elizabeth Grosz,** *Becoming Undone*

The Side of the Apes

In *Reason for Hope,* the primatologist Jane Goodall describes
a scene she witnessed many times in the forests of Gombe.
Goodall's subjects, the chimpanzees of the Kakombe valley

community, arrive at a particularly lush and magnificent waterfall—an eighty-foot tower of rushing water. They stop walking and begin to, in Goodall's account, "dance." This dance involves a sequence of "displays" in the direction of the waterfall. The animals swing through the spray on hanging vines, lift up and hurl heavy rocks and branches, and rhythmically stamp their feet in the water—sometimes for more than ten minutes—though they usually prefer not to get wet.[1]

In her entry "Primate Spirituality" in the *Encyclopedia of Religion and Nature*, Goodall identifies these "elemental displays" as possible early variants of religious ritual.[2] Goodall's account of the chimpanzees' embodied response to a feature of their world as religious is not hers alone. Similar "elemental dances" have been observed by other primatologists among other groups of chimpanzees, reacting not only to waterfalls but to rain, heavy winds, and blazing wildfires.[3] Even veteran chimpanzee researchers describe these dances as startling. As primate expert Frans de Waal writes of witnessing the chimpanzee rain dance for the first time, "I had trouble believing what I saw."[4]

These observations open the gates of the zoo, allowing other behaviors we witness in animals to hover on the edge of forms of behavior that, in humans, get called religion, including complex forms of sociality, ritual, and responses to death.[5] But is it possible for an animal to have religion? The history of Western thought on the animal is studded with instances in which animality is defined precisely in opposition to the capacity for religion. For British member of Parliament Benjamin Disraeli, speaking at Oxford in 1864 in the early aftermath of the shock of the Darwinian revolution, animal religion remained unthinkable: religion was the exclusive property of humans, an index of our participation in the divine fabric of the universe. Humans, for this nineteenth-century politician, sitting uneasily at the apex of the most powerful European Christian empire, were better understood as angels, rather than apes.[6] But even in contemporary religious studies—a century and a half after Darwin, when almost every other presumed indicator of human uniqueness has fallen apart (cognition, language, tool use, morality)[7]—we don't think of animals as religious. If religion in the Protestant key that underpins the Enlightenment axioms of Western culture is a matter of belief—the cognitive manipulation and the autonomous affirmation of a set of propositional assertions about the nature of reality—how could animals, who are prelinguistic bodies who don't fit the mold of speaking, reasoning, choosing subjects, be religious?

Religious Affects proposes that if we are to attempt to understand the chimpanzee waterfall dance, we must allow for the possibility that what gets called religion may not be predicated on the uniquely human property of language. This approach not only asks what it would mean for animals to have religion; it explores the possibility that a turn to affect can help us better understand human religion as animal. What would happen if we subtracted the framework of human exceptionalism from religion, following the Darwinian turn to an animalist understanding of human religious expression? What if religion is not only about language, books, or belief? In what ways is religion—for humans and other animals—about the way things feel, the things we want, the way our bodies are guided through thickly textured, magnetized worlds? Or the way our bodies flow into relationships—loving or hostile—with other bodies? How is religion made up of clustered material forms, aspects of our embodied life, such as other bodies, food, community, labor, movement, music, sex, natural landscapes, architecture, and objects? How is religion defined by the depths of our bodies—our individual and species histories that we know only by their long shadows but that shape the contours of our everyday experience? How is religion something that puts us in continuity with other animal bodies, rather than something that sets us apart? How is religion something that carries us on its back rather than something that we think, choose, or command?

In *Reason for Hope*, Goodall speculates on the sources of religious behavior among great apes: "Is it not possible," she writes, "that the chimpanzees are responding to some *feeling* like awe?"[8] In a later interview with Kimberley C. Patton and Paul Waldau, Goodall takes her proposed etiology of the elemental displays even further. She distinguishes the performance of the waterfall dance from chimpanzees' known mating and intimidation routines, linking it instead to her observation of chimpanzees staring in fascination at objects in the world—a response that she describes as "over and above just play; over and above mere curiosity."[9] For Goodall, an affective reaction to the waterfall—an emotional transport, "over and above" a rationally organized response or an evolutionarily implanted cost-benefit calculation—compels an embodied response, no less among animal bodies than among human bodies. "Was it perhaps similar feelings of awe," she asks, "that gave rise to the first animistic religions, the worship of the elements and the mysteries of nature over which there was no control?"[10]

Goodall's assessment of the chimpanzee waterfall dance is especially interesting in the context of a book that is markedly concerned with the question of how the things that bodies do *feel*. Whether Goodall is describing her own religious experiences in the cathedral of Notre Dame or her discovery of empathy as a scientific technique for studying chimpanzees, *affect*, the flow of forces through bodies outside of, prior to, or underneath language, is a crucial theme.[11] We could ask the same question of Disraeli's speech. As the transcript records, the audience did not simply nod their heads in studied, silent agreement at Disraeli's assertions: they filled the halls of the Sheldonian Theatre with their laughter and cheering. As Janet Browne writes, this was exactly Disraeli's hope: his objective in resolving the academic question of human origins in favor of a traditionalist biblical account was consummately political, an attempt to corral a religious constituency in service of his ambition to rise through the Tory Party ranks.[12] Affect shapes this intersection between knowledge, religion, and power. The location of affect as a determining element of religion—as well as other productions of embodied life such as knowledge, politics, language, economies, and relationships—is not confined to chimpanzees.

A number of scholars of religion—especially those in conversation with evolutionary biology—have raised the possibility of animal religion, ranging from passing mention in Darwin, Teilhard de Chardin, Johannes Maringer, Mircea Eliade, Walter Burkert, and E. O. Wilson to longer essays by Goodall, Kimberley C. Patton, Stewart Guthrie, Barbara J. King, Lionel Tiger and Michael McGuire, and James Harrod.[13] But animal religion has not yet been systematically explored through the lens of emotion.[14] *Religious Affects* develops Goodall's intuition that starting with animals in the study of religion prompts us to think about emotion and, as a corollary, that thinking about animality and emotion together gives us new ways of exploring human religion. This begins with articulating affect theory to the materialist shift in religious studies.

The Side of the Angels: Religion and the Linguistic Fallacy

In the inaugural lecture of his chairship at the College of the University of Chicago in 1974, Jonathan Z. Smith, the most prominent theorist in the field of religious studies of the last forty years, recounted a story from his youth, when he worked on a dairy farm in upstate New York. The farmer, his employer, had Smith draw a bath for him every morning. After bathing and eating breakfast, the farmer would step outside, then immediately plunge his arms into the soil, scoop it up, and rub it over his hands. One day, Smith, overwhelmed by curiosity, asked his boss, "Why do you do that?" The farmer studied him, then responded, "Don't you city boys understand anything? Inside the house it's dirt; outside, it's earth. You must take it off inside to eat and be with your family. You must put it on outside to work and be with the animals."[15]

In the lecture, later published as *Map Is Not Territory*, Smith frames this explanation using the terms of Mary Douglas's *Purity and Danger*, proposing that the act of picking up the earth instantiates a mental division of the world into different spaces, distributing a set of conceptual properties across a cognitive landscape: outside it's earth; inside it's dirt. For Smith, the farmer's action was a cosmological compartmentalization—a way of thinking a cosmic architecture into being. The farmer's body drew a map of the world, an epistemic regime that divided the cosmos into meaningful parts.

In this explanation, Smith is explicitly repudiating a range of ahistorical, metaphysical systems that had dominated the field of religious studies up to the 1970s, what are now called sui generis understandings of religion that saw religion as a distinct (human) undertaking that could not be reduced to political or epistemological concerns. Smith replaced these explanatory strategies with an epistemic orientation that viewed religion as a way of thinking and labeling certain features of the world—and thereby as inextricable from history and power. Smith prompted religious studies to move past a set of earlier methodologies that tended to orbit some version of experience—such as William James's description of the varieties of religion as private, solitary experiences, Rudolf Otto's phenomenology of holiness as an encounter with the "numinous," or the history of religions school's emphasis on "hierophanies of the Sacred" plunging into the mundane or profane world of human time. For Smith, and almost all who came after him, these earlier methods—which I will call, following convention in religious studies, "phenomenological" or "relating to the way things feel"—presumed that religion was an ahistorical phenomenon, a transcendent source of meaning arriving from beyond human circumstances (or ineluctably bound to a sacrosanct individual religious subject) and therefore disconnected from systems of power. For Smith, the phenomenological approach to religion was a depoliticizing analytics that, like all attempts to mask the motions of power and history, risked sinister outcomes.[16]

To counter these earlier approaches, Smith devised the first linguistic turn in religious studies, insisting that religion is best understood as a category manufactured within human histories through the devices of human representation and cognition. Religion, for Smith, is a creative intervention in an existing conceptual field, an "occasion for thought . . . a rational and rationalizing enterprise, an instance of an experimental method."[17] Robert Sharf defines the supersession of earlier phenomenological approaches along the same lines: "it is ill conceived," Sharf writes, "to construe the object of the study of religion to be the inner experience of religious practitioners. Scholars of religion are not presented with experiences that stand in need of interpretation but rather with texts, narratives, performances, and so forth."[18] When J. Z. Smith, farmhand, asked the farmer, *Why do you do that?*, he inaugurated a new approach in religious studies—a linguistic-conceptual method that primarily engages in "reading texts, in questioning, challenging, interpreting and valuing the tales men tell and the tales others have told about them."[19] What gets called religion after Smith's linguistic turn has been a network of linguistic nodes to be deciphered in terms of their efficacy within ideological regimes.[20] Religion, Smith would write in a later essay, is "the relentlessly human activity of thinking through a situation."[21]

Religious Affects is best understood as one long argument against both the adjective ("relentlessly human") and the gerund ("thinking through a situation") of this claim: religion, I argue, is best understood neither as exclusively cognitive nor as exclusively human. In spite of this critical frame, however, I see this firmly as an extension of Smith's project of insisting on religion's correspondence with history and power. Smith's corrective to the early phenomenological approaches was indispensable for the growth of religious studies as a field. It unshackled the study of religion from a model that sequestered religion away from human history—a model that suppressed local differences (Religion is what we say it is), paved the way for deadly colonial hierarchies (Who has religion?), and masked the imbrication of religion with networks of power (Religion is "private"). The conceptual-linguistic strand of Smith's work that redefined religion as "worldview" even made possible later work such as that of Russell McCutcheon, Bruce Lincoln, and Tomoko Masuzawa, which focused on the politics of how the word *religion* is used.

But although this line of inquiry has been extraordinarily fruitful for the project of religious studies, it opens onto a set of strictly epistemological and linguistic questions that do not offer resources for understanding why chimpanzees might dance at the base of a waterfall. Some interpretations of Smith's cognitivist orientation risk constraining religious studies inside the linguistic fallacy: the presupposition that the medium of power—the answer to the question, Why did you do that?—can only ever be a linguistic formation. By contrast, affect theory offers resources for charting maps of power that are not limited to the plane of language. It proposes that—contra earlier phenomenologists of religion who saw religion as sui generis—the phenomenological is itself political. *Religious Affects*, following an animal turn past the grid of signification, explores affect theory as a supplement to what Michel Foucault has called the "analytics of power," a set of tools for analyzing power in its multidirectional engagements with bodies, within and without language.[22]

The Materialist Shift

In the early 1990s, building on Smith's conviction that an analytics of religion must be in conversation with an analytics of power—but departing from his emphasis on religion as a form of thought—scholars in postcolonial anthropology of religion developed a new set of questions based on a template of religion as a network of bodily practices. In parallel with Smith, Talal Asad's seminal critique of the symbol-oriented analytics of Clifford Geertz showed how a Protestant model of religion as "faith"—a set of propositional beliefs—had been smuggled into the study of religion.[23] Still more recently, a number of scholars have built bridges into different subfields within brain-mind science to explore a variety of questions surrounding the cognitive, neurological, and evolutionary factors affecting religion.[24]

These projects have been collectively labeled the "materialist shift" by another anthropologist of religion, Manuel Vásquez. Vásquez's starting point is the assertion that the religious studies canon is not adequate for understanding lived religion, religion as it is practiced by bodies, especially under the circumstances of increased hybridization, migration, and mediatization advanced by accelerating globalization. Inverting the Enlightenment parameters of Disraeli's triumphalist confession, Vásquez describes the materialist shift as examining "religion as it is lived by human beings, not by angels."[25] *Religious Affects* seeks to advance this materialist shift in religious studies by bringing the field into conversation with another set of critical resources emerging out of queer theory, feminism, postcolonial critique, and post-structuralist philosophy—what has come to be called affect theory.

How can we return to embodied experience outside of the productions of language—what I am here calling the phenomenological domain—within religious studies without lapsing into the ahistorical metaphysical essentialism of Eliade or the politically detached individualism of James? The critique of the "private affair" tradition within religious studies—whether it be as belief or experience—is entirely correct in its suspicion toward a depoliticized vision of religion as the self-contained property of self-contained subjects. But this critique also risks fleeing so far from these experiential accounts that it lapses into the linguistic fallacy—the notion that language is the only medium of power. More recent work within religious studies has renewed attention to religion in its emotive dimensions,[26] but these forays have not had the benefit of a systematic, interdisciplinary account of affect.

Affect theory addresses both of these concerns. It emerges out of a critical tradition (queer theory/feminism/postcolonial theory) that has produced formidable critiques of the public-private binary—precisely by thematizing the way that private, local, or individual actions have ramifications for broader regimes of power. Affect theory is about showing the multidirectional vectors of influence between embodied emotions and politics, not about consigning emotions to a private domain. Through interdisciplinary engagements between literary theory, anthropology, and political science, it has produced the groundwork for a flexible account of the relationship between affect and power. The affect theorist and anthropologist Kathleen Stewart locates power firmly within the body's affects. "Power," she writes, "is a thing of the senses."[27] *Religious Affects* develops this insight, highlighting the many modes in which religion, like other forms of power, feels before it thinks, believes, or speaks. The phenomenological is political.

Moreover, this book contends that adding perspectives from critical animal studies (including new resources from evolutionary theory) to affect theory has implications for religious studies and other accounts of the relationship between power and bodies. Affect theory, in this reading, is about thematizing power outside of language. Animal bodies—our bodies—are invested in fields of power that are not mediated by language. Although language is an important feature of human bodies, it is only one of many channels for the operation of power. Where concepts and language are part of the religious matrix, they, too, must be considered as part of an embodied complex that loops through the material forces of affect that direct bodies. Affect theory is a necessary tool for mapping religion, not just because it adds to our inventory of descriptive tools, but because affect constitutes the links between bodies and power.

Take Smith's employer, the dairy farmer, thrusting his hands into the soil. In Smith's telling, the farmer's action is a cosmo-logy, a way of thinking through a situation that writes a formation of the cosmos. For Smith, this thing that a body does is a kind of text—the conceptual inscription of a grid on the world. *Religious Affects* opens up a line of inquiry that is invisible to this analytics: it enables us to propose (as one hypothesis among many) that the farmer didn't start with a cosmology, a need to write the world differently, but with a complex of material sensations emerging out of an affectively driven, embodied practice. What if the practice starts before the concept? What if his body started by rubbing earth on his hands, and only stopped to explain it when J. Z. Smith, farmhand, came along and asked why? The farmer's explanation may or may not be correct, but either way, affect theory offers the suggestion that the explanation did not come first.

Religious Affects explores a perspective that sees bodies moving through worlds under the pressure of a complex welter of affects, with language weaving between and reshaping those pressures only sometimes—and even then only haltingly and unevenly. Affect theory—examining the mobile materiality of the body—thematizes the ways that the world prompts us to move before the interventions of language. It calls attention to embodied histories that precede the advent of language—as well as moments when language is bound with other thick, embodied forces. Before language, before cosmology, even before "thought," understood as a way of converting a situation into an explanation, the farmer's body moves, interacts with the world, and produces a field of sensations through that interaction. The linguistic fallacy misunderstands religion as merely a byproduct of language, and misses the economies of affect—economies of pleasure, economies of rage and wonder, economies of sensation, of shame and dignity, of joy and sorrow, of community and hatred—that are the animal substance of religion and other forms of power.

Affect, the Postsecular, and the Posthuman

One of the many achievements of the linguistic turn in religious studies was Smith's continuation of the dismantling of nineteenth-century colonial hierarchies of the primitive and the civilized. Like Eliade before him, Smith showed that there was no essential difference between the beliefs and practices of the Christian empire and the non-Christian lifeways beyond that empire's ever-expanding, bloody horizons. But where Eliade proposed an ontological continuity that cast "primitive" religions as drawing on the same transcendent religious resources as Christianity, Smith suggested that we view all religion as a formation of human thought.[28] Where Eliade made all bodies yearn for primitivity, Smith's approach was to keep a Kantian framework of rational subjects intact (while subtracting Kant's racism): he promoted all religious bodies to the level of Kantian rationalizers—linguistic subjects thinking through their situations.

This effects an important corrective to racist colonial logics. But the move to enshrine the Kantian logic that traffics in the linguistic fallacy also comes with a cost: by establishing language as the medium of power and the primary analytic locus of religious studies, this strand of Smith's project locks religious studies into an Enlightenment prism that tends to reduce religion to a series of cognitive appraisals of the world. This approach is of no value, therefore, for theorizing what scholars are coming to call postsecularism—those moments when religion flows over the boundaries of language or thought. It can write a conceptual history of how Benjamin Disraeli and the heavenly host of upperclass white male Christians at the Sheldonian in Victorian Oxford came to believe that humans were better understood as angels rather than apes, and it can write a conceptual history of how we came to call that religious. It cannot address what, to me, are the equally interesting questions of why those men laughed and cheered when Disraeli spoke their beliefs back to them, or how those affective reactions activated a configuration of power that consolidated and transformed the landscape out of which it emerged. Nor can it address moments when bodies without language move in ways that seem religious.

Smith's work focuses on what I would identify as the dawn of texts. He is interested in the cosmologically rich epics of the ancient Near East (*Gilgamesh, Enuma Elish,* Hesiod's *Theogony*). By raising up these linguistic artifacts as exemplars of religion, Smith established a template by which it was possible to see the farmer's act of plunging his hands into the soil as itself a sort of text—a cognitive operation that writes a worldview into reality, a book of the world. In this strand of his expansive and complex body of work, Smith proceeds under the neo-Kantian assumption that power is directed by language. He relays an interest in a model of religion that, although shot through from the beginning with the striations of power and history, starts and ends with books, ideas, and beliefs—the concretizations of religion as a linguistic system.

Religious Affects, by contrast, is interested in histories that start before texts: phylogenetic histories originating with prelinguistic bodies— including nonhuman bodies—driven by forces outside of language. This move is not designed as a way of retrieving some sort of authentic or nostalgic essence of religious experience, but of vastly expanding the toolkit of religious studies—and other contemporary critical projects focusing on the intersection of bodies and power—to enfold a plurality of historically embedded practices, images, objects, and affects. I contend that prelinguistic bodies, too—animal bodies—may well have stepped outside of their homes and plunged their hands into the earth, with not a cosmology in sight.

Language produces late-stage explanatory frames for what now gets called religion, but neither the dancing of the chimpanzees in the waterfall nor the farmer scooping up the earth nor the cheering of the diocesans in the Sheldonian can be reduced to language. Accounts of power that reduce all of these phenomena to "language-like systems" return to the logic of Enlightenment secularism, in which religion is always and only a way of thinking. *Religious Affects* supplements Smith's ardent opposition to the divide between "savage/emotional" and "civilized/ rational" in a different way: by firmly locating even those bodies that have demanded the right to hold themselves immune to affect—white bodies, Christian bodies, secular bodies, American bodies, male bodies, even scholarly bodies—within the field of animality.[29]

Disraeli's ape or angel speech also suggests the friction between what might be called the humanities and the natural sciences: the categorical refusal of human beings to allow their bodies to be framed by science.

There is an insistence, in the repudiation of the connection between the material forces studied by science and the subjects of the humanities, on reserving a special ontological status for humans—a consubstantiality with angels, the Kantian subject as "free and not determined through any [prior] causes."[30] As Aaron Gross writes, "to shift the study of religion from divine to human may really be little more than a shift from one understanding of divinity prevalent before modernity to a more modern conception of the divine that ascribes attributes once considered exclusively divine, such as infinity, to the human—as in, for example, the idea of the infinitely open human that can never be fixed."[31] This is why Vásquez's materialist shift enfolds approaches from evolutionary biology and the brain-mind sciences: understanding religion means pulling humans out of the domain of the angelic—which means out of the domain of self-determination through sovereign reason—and into the bodily, the material, and the animal.[32]

At the same time, following the affective turn means putting to rest some of the misconceptions that circulate within scientific accounts of religion, particularly the varieties of determinist reductionism. Understanding human bodies as confluences of material processes (affects as well as language) complicates bodies, rather than rendering them transparent. Only bodies understood as fundamentally light, uncomplicated, shadowless, and floating—in a word, angelic—can be controlled for and predicted with the degree of precision boasted by classical scientific determinism or its contemporary iterations, the more staunchly reductive forms of sociobiology and evolutionary psychology. This work, then, dovetails with contemporary feminist science studies and research into embodied cognition that have insisted on understanding the operations of knowledge production as driven by bodies, rather than transcendent, immaterial "reason."

Religious Affects also attempts to fill a gap in contemporary affect theory: although there is already a formidable library of books on religion and emotion, some of which glance at affect theory,[33] and although several affect theorists have begun to think through the implications of their work for religion,[34] there is no full-length work critically engaging affect theory from a religious studies perspective. This book is designed to build a bridge between conversations in affect theory and religious studies by thinking about species. To this end, it considers three concepts derived from current conversations in affect theory and animal studies—intransigence (chapter 2), compulsion (chapter 4), and accident (chapter 6)—and explores each with a corresponding case study, building up to a comprehensive theory of the chimpanzee waterfall dance in chapter 7.

INTRANSIGENCE

The linguistic fallacy assumes that the medium of power is language—that depth, complex responses, experiences, and decisions cannot take place without the machinery of a linguisticized reason. One of the features of this model is that depth is sculpted out of the sedimentation of linguistic processes. *Historicization,* in this context, means excavating the linguistic regimes that have accumulated within a particular body to produce subjectivity—what Michel Foucault has labeled the complex of power-knowledge. Animal subjectivity—subjectivity without language—by these lights, can only be a contradiction in terms. Religious bodies, according to the linguistic fallacy, move because a particular textual regime has directed them to do so.

The notion of *intransigence* complicates this model, deploying the resources of affect theory to show how a textured, postessentialist account of bodies helps us to understand the interface between bodies and power. Chapter 2 defines intransigence by examining the tension between the Deleuzian and phenomenological branches of affect theory. Deleuzian modes tend to underline *plasticity,* the fundamental reconfigurability of bodies under the influence of the overlapping systems of forces within which they are embedded.[35] Phenomenological affect theory retains this interest in the politics of reconfigurability, but also thematizes the intransigence of emotions persisting across bodies and creating species-specific, embodied universals imprinted at birth. Rather than a 3D-printed body produced by layers of liquid plastic, bodies are constituted in part by an array of intransigent shapes embedded within them. Bodies are neither carvings pared out of formless blocks, nor plastic shapes created ex nihilo: they are complex, chunky genealogies, bricolages of existing forms.

Building a conversation between affect theory, evolutionary theory, and material feminist philosophy of science, intransigence provides a new way of thinking about the relationship between power and history. This means looking not only at the history of language systems within which a body emerges, but at embodied history—a lineage of intransigent, semistable forms emerging out of an evolutionary history and a local confluence of social, political, economic, and cultural contexts. This approach answers the question of whether or not emotions—such as shame, fear, or happiness—exist before or after language. Intransigence suggests that emotions are built into our bodies—that they are artifacts of an embodied evolutionary history. Connecting the analytics of species to the "onto-epistemological" project of Karen Barad, *Religious Affects* suggests a new attention to the onto-phenomenology of bodies: the way it feels to be the kind of bodies we are.

These onto-phenomenological shapes become the raw material of religion and are key to understanding how animal religion unfolds—especially, I argue, in a globalized world where the mediatized forces that can build religious bodies are becoming increasingly complex. Chapter 3 explores this approach by considering globalization as a matrix that redistributes certain affective forms through an assemblage of media and pedagogical practices. Heidi Ewing and Rachel Grady's 2006 documentary film *Jesus Camp* illustrates this network by calling attention to how religious bodies embedded in particular formations of nation, race, and gender teach one another how to feel, and in the process produce political subjectivities made up of reticulated affective forms. This allows for new ways of examining the intersection of religion with global mediascapes and new ways of typologizing religions according to their affective configurations, rather than their propositional beliefs.

COMPULSION

Chapter 4 explores compulsion as a way of naming forms of power outside of the network of sovereign, speaking subjects—the things that make bodies move without being told, either by another body or by an angelic "self." In a queerly Cartesian move, chapter 4 starts with a body at a sort of phenomenological zero point: a prisoner in solitary confinement. But contra Descartes, solitary confinement shows that starving bodies of their affective points of contact with their worlds does not liberate them, but drowns them in profound suffering, leaving sustained traumatic effects. As the philosopher Lisa Guenther points out, where the sovereign self would be immune to solitary confinement as a form of torture, mapping bodies according to their compulsions depicts bodies as animal—as radically dependent on their affective relationships with the world. Affectivity is not optional, but compulsory.

The linguistic fallacy affirms that depth can't exist without language—that we can't want things without being told that we want them, without deciding that we want them, or without learning to want them. This is the presupposition of classical psychological behaviorism as much as textualism. But affect theory suggests that our animal intimacy with the world precedes constitution inside a linguistic frame—that there are "Proustian nooks" that pull us into the world without the application of language. The relationship between affect and power moves bodies transversally through and across the grids of language, consciousness, or cognition. The compulsions of affect are better understood as addictions, as thick passions for bodies, objects, and relationships.

Chapter 5 turns to the example of contemporary American Islamophobia, in particular the Park51 controversy of 2010, to demonstrate that these compulsions guiding bodies off the grid are signally important for understanding relationships between religion, bodies, and power. Where anti-Muslim discourse often presents itself as a patient, reasoned discourse (and its opponents as bestial), locating the power of affect to move bodies outside of language highlights how the very practice of inscribing and electrifying racialized social boundaries is an eminently animal process. Rather than a discourse, Islamophobia's mobilization of an *us-them* divide is predicated on a cluster of affective forces working through bodies and coalescing into religious forms.

At the same time, this prelinguistic animal sociality is implicated in an antithetical affective process: the cultivation of religious practices of compassion. Both the production of quasi-racist discourses and the attempts to demilitarize those boundaries can be understood according to animal sociality. *Religious Affects* suggests that embodied religious practices are often found proliferating at social boundaries—what critical race theorist Sharon Patricia Holland calls "feasts of difference"— whether through the thrilling disdain or the compassionate embrace of bodies felt to be other. These affective forms merge into the global complex of animal religion.

ACCIDENT

Affect theory takes place in the wake of Jacques Derrida's deconstruction of traditional Western metaphysics, particularly the fixation on sovereign human rationality. In *The Animal That Therefore I Am*, Derrida writes that his work can be understood as a philosophy of *animalism*—a situation of language, reason, and experience against the background of a field of traces operating according to contingency, contamination, and difference rather than an overarching rationality—locating metaphysical artifacts within the frame of species. For Derrida, metaphysics—a correspondence between human bodies and the transcendent *logos*—is impossible because every word, concept, or object is susceptible to accident, to the collisions of meaning brought about by the play of traces. By stepping outside of what Derrida calls the *carno-phallogocentric* regime of discourse—the rational, linguistic, nonanimal grid of meaning making that underpins the linguistic fallacy—affect theory opens up an analytic strategy that is invisible to Enlightenment humanism and conventional ideology critique: the way that regimes of power are composed not by a closed network of rational actors, but within a spiraling current of accidents.

The invocation of animalism helps to advance the incipient conversation, begun by Elizabeth Grosz, between deconstruction and evolutionary biology. Chapter 6 explores how a Darwinian, post-adaptationist position—what in contemporary evolutionary biology is called the "pluralist" approach—can be brought into dialogue with the theme of accident. Classical evolutionary biology was beholden to a positivist adaptationism, an orientation Stephen Jay Gould and Richard Lewontin define as focusing on "the near omnipotence of natural selection in forging organic design and fashioning the best among possible worlds."[36] Contemporary evolutionary biology does not presuppose that evolution produces perfect fits, but instead looks at the residues, the remainders, the collisions, and the dead zones within phenotypes—the lingering accidents of embodied histories.

Like these post-Darwinian biologists, affect theory is also interested in sidestepping the idea that bodies can be comfortably fit into rationalized economies. What Sara Ahmed calls affective economies are queer economies marked by "sliding" motions—relationships between bodies and power that twist the arithmetic of rational self-interest.[37] Affect theory repudiates the presupposition that bodies, especially our human bodies, are best understood according to a rationally arranged grid of calculations, propositions, and decisions, reorienting the study of religion to the thematics of accident—the way bodies splash and splatter across the balance sheet of costs and benefits.

This move is particularly important for reframing functionalist (crypto-adaptationist) and ideological accounts of religion—such as are found in some evolutionary psychological approaches or the social-rhetorical approach. Affect theory suggests that economically tinged analytics of religion that analyze complex behavioral forms in terms of how they facilitate the accumulation of material or political assets, what the primatologist Frans de Waal calls "a cardboard version of human nature," is limited in that it cannot account for how affects dissolve the priority of the economic and become, in Sedgwick's word, "autotelic"—out for themselves rather than aiming toward ulterior purposes.[38] Affects are queer because they are ends in themselves: they frustrate the insistence on a chain of intelligible *whys* at the heart of carno-phallogocentric metaphysics and lead to more complex accounts of the operation of power.

In chapter 7, *Religious Affects* returns to the chimpanzee waterfall dance and analyzes it as just such an affective economy—a flow of forces producing movement at the knotty contact point between bodies and worlds. The dance is not to be construed in functionalist terms—as a device for advancing rational self-interest—but as part of a slid-ing play of affects linking bodies to systems of power. Even though it emerges out of a spiral of articulated embodied histories driven in part by evolutionary mechanisms (including natural selection), the queer iterations of these histories are better understood as accident-driven, af-fective economies rather than balanced budgets. The dance is a dance in the way that it recapitulates and replays the affective ligaments tying bodies to worlds. Drawing lines between a set of interlocking but non-streamlined embodied elements, religion traffics in a network of effects better understood as a regime of accidents than an icon of rationally or-ganized *logos*. This template allows religious studies to consider human and nonhuman animal religion side by side.

If, as Derrida writes, "nothing risks becoming more poisonous than an autobiography,"[39] then the story that we are angels is the ultimate narcotic, distorting our understanding of our own bodies and the bodies with which we share this world. If a dairy farm is a world where animals are kept in their proper place—violently separated from us by the bar-riers of language, religion, and reason—then the emphasis on language in the contemporary humanities risks turning us all into farmhands, patrolling the fences between human and nonhuman animal bodies. As the critical animal studies theorist Kari Weil has noted, where "post-structuralism insisted that we humans can never get outside of our linguistic frameworks and that we have no knowledge and no experience that escapes language . . . the turn to animals may be seen as an attempt not only to escape from post-structuralism's linguistic trap but to reexamine its confines."[40] The figure of the religious animal roils the discourses of Enlightenment humanism, prompting us to ask Elizabeth Grosz's posthumanist question: "What kind of intellectual revolution would be required to make man, and the various forms of man, one among many living things, and one force among many, rather than the aim and destination of all knowledges?"[41]

Reading affect theory and critical animal studies together allows the posthumanities to draw more detailed maps of ecosystems of bodies and power by reversing the fiction that depth, phenomenological complexity, and embodied histories cannot exist without words—making palpable the plural flows of power outside of language. Lingering with the chimpanzees dancing in the waterfall—reassessing the set of differences and proximities that link and divide us—helps us dismantle the fences separating human bodies and animal bodies. This opens up better understandings of the shared worlds spiraling around, through, and between us, as well as new modes of interspecies community.

ONE

RELIGION, LANGUAGE, AND AFFECT

Power is a thing of the senses.—**Kathleen Stewart,**
Ordinary Affects

In *God Is Not One*, Boston University professor Stephen Prothero places religion on the dissection table and finds it to contain four parts: there is a problem, then a solution (the "goal"
of any religion); there are techniques for reaching this goal and
exemplars who lead the way. In Christianity, for instance, the
problem is that the world is sinful; grace through Christ or
faith or works is the solution and the practice; Jesus the mythological figure is the exemplar. Although Prothero acknowledges
the usefulness of Ninian Smart's model of religion as constituted by multiple "dimensions," of which belief is only one, it
is difficult to escape the conclusion that assessing all religions
as beginning with problems fundamentally orients religion to a
cognitive-linguistic axis. In such a scheme, language and power
form a smooth, hydraulic system without remainder: "people
act every day on the basis of religious beliefs and behaviors
that outsiders see as foolish or dangerous or worse," Prothero
writes. "*Allah tells them* to blow themselves up or to give to the
poor, so they do. *Jesus tells them* to bomb an abortion clinic
or to build a Habitat for Humanity house, so they do. Because *God said so,* Jews, Christians, and Muslims believe that

this land is their land, so they fight for it in the name of G-d or Jesus or Allah."[1] Religion, for Prothero, is a grid of linguistic commands, a current of force from concepts and beliefs to moving bodies.

This model is no doubt useful in many contexts,[2] and Prothero is exactly right to push back on the tendency to extract religions from a historical frame by flattening their conceptual differences. But the problem-based model is also an illustration of the linguistic fallacy: Prothero locates power within symbol systems, of which religion is one example. In this, he builds on a linguistic template developed by religion theorist Jonathan Z. Smith that is in the background of several contemporary projects in religious studies. For Smith, the "human sciences"—including religious studies—become "conceptually possible largely through the acceptance of the argument that their objects of study are linguistic and language-like systems."[3] This comes across in Smith's analyses of the zone of overlap between power and religion, which highlight how systems of power are led and maneuvered by symbol systems. Smith argues that religion is best understood as a worldview—"a culture's or an individual's symbolization of the cosmos and their place within it"—that is shaped by social processes.[4] Smith imagines a speaking, thinking-knowing subject as the indivisible unit of systems of power. In Smith's model, to change power, one must only change the thinking subject's symbolic milieu—the transcript of what is said to us and by us.[5] For Smith, culture, religion, and society are texts inscribed in minute detail by systems of power.

In addition to being in the background of popular offshoots like Prothero's book, this template is also a precursor to the social-rhetorical approach in academic religious studies. Contemporary scholars such as Russell T. McCutcheon, Timothy Fitzgerald, and Bruce Lincoln have developed the social-rhetorical approach as an adaptation of neo-Marxist ideology critique to religious studies. In this model, *religion* is functionally synonymous with *ideology*—a set of lies designed to mask certain material interests in accumulating what McCutcheon calls "social benefits."[6] "Religion" is a discursive strategy, a linguistic move made in a multidimensional chess game played by bodies embedded within an economically arranged, zero-sum social landscape. Smith's work lays out the contours of this template for religious studies by focusing on religions as text-like technologies of social control.[7]

Affect theory does not seek to interrupt the hypothesized link between language and power, which has been well established in neo-Marxist and post-structuralist critiques. Affect theorist Lauren Berlant notes that "affect theory is another phase in the history of ideology theory," and that "the moment of the affective turn brings us back to the encounter of what is sensed with what is known and what has impact in a new but also recognizable way."[8] Ann Pellegrini writes that culture critic Raymond Williams's notion of "structures of feeling" is not designed to abandon "worldview" or "ideology" as categories of analysis, but to "push us to take seriously how 'formal or systematic beliefs' are embedded in, and arise out of, concrete relations and experience."[9] Smith's linguistic turn in religious studies dispatched earlier metaphysical approaches to religion that mystified the relationship between religions, the category "religion," and systems of power. This paved the way for the historically and materially grounded (nonangelic) approaches to religious studies on which *Religious Affects* is built. The social-rhetorical method and other linguistic models of religion are indispensable components of the religion theorist's toolkit. Affect theory adds to the critique of power by supplementing the linguistic turn, not erasing it.

And yet, the affect theorist Eve Kosofsky Sedgwick expresses a weariness toward the hot pursuit of approaches deriving from the hermeneutics of suspicion. In her extraordinary essay "Paranoid Reading and Reparative Reading," she argues for attentiveness to what she calls the "queer possibility" that the things bodies make and do—relationships, cultures, texts, religions, regimes of knowledge, gestures—might not always be sinister or cynical acts of dissimulation, but loving, joyful, or healing.[10] For Sedgwick, the exact equation of language systems with regimes of power risks lapsing into a practice of endless accusation that suppresses other ways of diagramming culture and politics. Just as Thomas Tweed suggests that every theoretical approach is a "sighting" that entails its own vistas and its own blind spots,[11] the critique of the phenomenological tradition in religious studies launched by Smith—in successfully pushing back against the ahistorical, sui generis tradition in religious studies that insisted that religion as a private feeling could never touch or be touched by the political—could be said to overlook the ways that the phenomenological can be recruited into a political analytics.

Affect theory, then, opens onto new ways of framing religious studies. Religion understood affectively illuminates a much more complicated picture than the "paranoid" vantage offers, a picture in which bodies move in a variety of directions at a variety of odd angles that cannot always be cashed out in terms of "social benefits" like financial or political gain. The social-rhetorical approach attributes a level of cohesiveness to language—and a level of forethought to human bodies and institutions—that is unsustainable in the wake of the materialist shift: it elevates us to the status of far-sighted angels. Affect theory's project is to question the extremely tight fit between language and power—the flawless symmetry without remainder—that has become the orthodoxy of some offshoots of the linguistic turn. Knowledge is embedded in fields of power, but it is by no means the only form of power. Complicating the social-rhetorical approach by exploring affect is one of the subplots of this book, developed especially in chapter 6.

In superseding the linguistic fallacy—the myth that the medium of power is language—affect theory is a continuation of the materialist shift outlined by Manuel Vásquez in *More Than Belief.* Vásquez is also wary of the overemphasis on social constructionism and the "suffocating textualism that approaches religions as essentially systems of symbols, beliefs, narratives, and cosmologies, ignoring other important material dimensions of religious life."[12] Instead, Vásquez proposes materialist phenomenology as a working model for religious studies: an interdisciplinary exploration of the way that religion is lived and experienced within and without the limited domain of language. For Vásquez, traditional phenomenological approaches from philosophy and religious studies have been too much in the thrall of transcendentalist—and anthropocentric—models of subjectivity. But, at the opposite end of the critical spectrum, social constructionist approaches that overemphasize the linguistic model fail, for their part, to "acknowledge our embeddedness in nature . . . and our continuities with nonhuman animals."[13] Materialist phenomenology, for Vásquez, retrieves "alternative phenomenological currents [that] stress historicity, facticity, enfleshment, and embeddedness in everyday life."[14] In developing a model of power that is not reducible to language, affect theory helps to map the contours of animal religion as a materialist phenomenology enfolding human and animal bodies.

This chapter serves as a survey of contemporary affect theory, with an eye to developing a set of conceptual tools useful for religious studies in subsequent chapters. Following recent genealogies of affect theory such as those created by Ann Cvetkovich, Jasbir Puar, and Melissa Gregg and Gregory J. Seigworth, *Religious Affects* proposes that affect theory is best understood as emerging in two currents, what I call its Deleuzian and phenomenological modes.[15] This work charts the similarities and divergences of these currents and begins to indicate their relevance for thinking a materialist phenomenology in religious studies that sidesteps the "suffocating textualism" of the linguistic fallacy. Affect theory in all its forms is designed to profile the operations of power outside of language and the autonomous, reasoning human subject. Affect theory asks: what if power was not a symbol system, but something enfolding and exceeding language in the ways it plays across bodies—a "thing of the senses," in Stewart's phrase?

Affect Theory: A Dual Genealogy

Material feminist theorist Karen Barad opens her essay "Posthumanist Performativity: Toward an Understanding of How Matter Comes to Matter" with a line that could serve as a miniature manifesto for affect theory: "Language has been given too much power."[16] Affect theory is a cluster of interrelated but not always commensurate theoretical approaches that take affect or affects (the distinction is important for some, as discussed below) as their objects of study. These approaches draw on different theoretical lineages in bringing forward the notion of affect, and so there is a hazard in venturing a single definition of their shared terminology. But as a provisional locus, affect or affects can be understood as the propulsive elements of experience, thought, sensation, feeling, and action that are not necessarily captured or capturable by language or self-sovereign "consciousness."

Affects, then, are forces that exceed the classical liberal thematics of self-sovereignty. *Liberalism* here refers to an intellectual lineage emerging out of Western modernity that places the *liber*—the free man, the singular, rational, autonomous, speaking agent—at the center of its understanding of culture, politics, reason, knowledge, and religion. The liber is auto-nomous—both self-lawed and self-sovereign—and therefore is the node (either the origin or the target) of systems of power.

Affect complicates this picture. Berlant calls affect "sensual matter that is elsewhere to sovereign consciousness but that has historical significance in domains of subjectivity."[17] Bruno Latour identifies the turn to affect as the reformulation of bodies as processes rather than entities.[18] The shapes and textures that inform and structure our embodied experience at or beneath the threshold of cognition are affects.[19] To study affects is to explore nonsovereign bodies, animal bodies, bodies that are propelled skittering forward by a lattice of forces rather than directed by a rational homunculus.[20] The liberal topoi of language, cognition, will, and free choice are layered on top of these stormy affective climates. "Where has logic originated in men's heads?" Nietzsche asks: "Undoubtedly out of the illogical, the domain of which must originally have been immense."[21] Affects are the deep, recalcitrant textures of our embodied animality.

For some affect theorists, such as Brian Massumi, Patricia Clough, and Erin Manning, the term *affect* rigidly excludes what are called emotions—felt experiences that are the pieces of our personhood. But others, such as Silvan Tomkins, Eve Kosofsky Sedgwick, Sara Ahmed, Teresa Brennan, and Ann Cvetkovich, suggest that the consideration of emotions falls under the purview of affect theory. This work will consider both of these perspectives in exploring the prelinguistic and prepersonal dimensions of religion—not exactly noncognitive but extra- or paracognitive, *coassembling* with the cognitive (Silvan Tomkins's word) to shape the contours of thought, action, and experience. I suggest that at the emotional and preemotional levels, affects are the flexible architecture of our animal lifeways, the experiential shapes that herd together and carry religion on their backs. Affect theory makes available a set of approaches to religion that work through animality by probing the thick forms moving outside of the narrow lighted circle of language.

To develop the dual genealogy of affect theory, we turn to two of the starting points for contemporary affect theory and their ramifications for the study of religion: Brian Massumi's 1995 essay "The Autonomy of Affect" and Eve Kosofsky Sedgwick and Adam Frank's edited volume of the same year, *Shame and Its Sisters: A Silvan Tomkins Reader*.[22] What I see as the constitutive tension of affect theory and its potential for building bridges into the study of religion emerge out of the interplay and the null zones between these early entries, which inaugurate the Deleuzian and the phenomenological streams of affect theory.[23]

Massumi's essay is·an effort to crystallize a particular intellectual lineage—from Spinoza to Nietzsche to Deleuze to contemporary neuroscience—around a single analytic locus: Spinoza's notion of affect. In the Spinozistic sense of affect, all aspects of embodiment are understood as the effects of a matrix of micrological forces. Spinoza in his *Ethics* writes that his study of affects "shall consider human actions and appetites just as if it were a question of lines, planes, and bodies."[24] Departing from the Cartesian notion of the human subject as an undifferentiated pocket of self-mastery, Spinoza finds in affects a multitude of forces that are the plural, heterogeneous materials of subjectivity. Deleuze characterizes this as the ethological approach, in which bodies are understood as a compendium of crisscrossing lines of force.[25] For Spinoza and Deleuze, affect dislocates the anthropocentric perspective, opening up onto a multiplicity of animal ways of being organized around the variety of "natures" making up the bodies of different organisms.[26] The ethological approach explores the variety of animal life streams by mapping our affective makeup as heterogeneous networks, rather than undifferentiated "subjects."

Massumi updates Spinoza by bringing his model of affect into conversation with contemporary neuroscientific frameworks. "The Autonomy of Affect" is structured around three different neuroscientific investigations, one in which German test subjects were shown a short film about a melting snowman with different narrative voice-overs, a second in which it was demonstrated that the minimum threshold of awareness of a stimulus for the human brain was a one-half-second duration, and a third in which the psychologist Oliver Sacks described the reactions of aphasic hospital patients to a speech by Ronald Reagan: watching the disjuncture between Reagan's facial expression and his speech, the patients would laugh wildly.[27]

Massumi uses the German film experiment to explore the divergence of language and affect. Reacting against the critical tradition in humanistic scholarship that defines cultural artifacts exclusively in terms of their linguistic content, Massumi insists that the point of contact between images and bodies is more heavily charged by affect than by text. What we name a cultural text or how we react to it on the level of the person is superseded by its affective potency. Massumi suggests that there is often a perpendicular relationship between explicit emotional content and affective force: the sad scenes of the film were the most preferred—"the sadder the better."[28] The circuitry made up of "semantic wires" is scrambled by affect: according to the register of prelinguistic intensity, "sadness is pleasant."[29] What this study will term *compulsion* invokes this set of affective properties that pull bodies independently of the linguistic index.

In this desire for sadness, Massumi defines the charge that attaches itself to affect as *intensity*. (Since the affective charge of an intensity is what the affect is, affect and intensity are effectively interchangeable in Massumi's work.)[30] But affect/intensity is methodologically distinct, in Massumi's vocabulary, from *emotion*. This is where Massumi's interest in the "missing half-second" at the granular level of perception comes in. Citing the neuroscientific experiments of Benjamin Libet, Massumi notes that we can be affected by forces that we do not perceive. At the personal level, we may find something "sad," but that response in the register of awareness does not dictate our preference—whether our bodies move toward or away from that object. Massumi finds in this missing half-second a trope for thematizing the imperceptible register on which affect plays out. Massumi follows the early twentieth-century philosopher Henri Bergson (also a favorite of Deleuze) in seeing "consciousness" as subtractive: consciousness carves out perception from a plenitude of sensory information rushing into our senses at each moment. The missing half-second is missed because it is "overfull, in excess of the actually-performed action and of its ascribed meaning."[31] Conscious awareness is structurally incongruent with the overwhelming intensity of affect in this plenum of intensity.

Along these lines, Massumi insists that affect and emotion must be separated. Deleuzian affect theorist Eric Shouse fleshes this out by suggesting that feelings (which are "personal and biographical") and emotions (which are socially expressed feelings) sit at the level of the stable, the structured, and the detectable.[32] Erin Manning writes that affects, by contrast, "exceed the realm of the modal, tending toward the edge of experience where amodality takes shape."[33] Affect is "as stable as electricity," circulating beneath the threshold of perceptibility and between bodies.[34] For Massumi, this is the *autonomy of affect*: its escape from structures of capture and control, its formal indiscernibility to "conscious" awareness.[35] Massumi sees affect as that which is ontologically incompatible with the structuring grid of personal experience.

Massumi's interpretation of the study of the aphasics' reaction to Reagan's speech merges Deleuzian affect theory with an analytics of power. He argues that Reagan was "not a political mastermind nor a charismatic figure": his ability to manipulate a political landscape derived from affective methods. Instead of providing a cohesive ideological frame, the perpendicular relationship between Reagan's ideological platforms and his body—the twitches, the spasms and "veers," the discrepancies that left Sacks's aphasics rolling in the aisles—allowed him to maneuver his way into the interstices of America's affective fabric and so achieve transformative political effects.[36]

Although the particulars of Massumi's analysis of Reagan may be somewhat underdeveloped, his overall point that we need to recognize how ideological effects are instigated by affective means, that the substantive precursor of ideology is not a rationalized matrix of concepts, data, and argument, but prediscursive compulsions circulating heavily within bodies, is a vital corrective to the linguistic fallacy—the humanistic notion that language is necessary for depth, complexity, and power. Moving beyond the linguistic domain that is the traditional province of the humanities, the affective turn is an *animalization* of theory—a version of the materialist shift that expands the range of questions that can be asked. Massumi suggests that we move beyond the humanistic definition of the human as "the chattering animal"—the contradictory creature for which animality is, in fact, erased and obscured by a scribbled thicket of words.[37]

This Deleuzian sense of affect has already begun to be deployed in the context of religious studies in the groundbreaking work of Johns Hopkins political theorist William Connolly. Connolly argues for a methodological approach to religion that emphasizes precognitive, affective dimensions—what he calls "Proustian layers, nooks, and sparks"—rather than the primacy of texts.[38] To take one of many compelling examples, in *Capitalism and Christianity, American Style,* Connolly proposes that the contemporary alliance between right-wing evangelical Christianity and corporate capitalism should not be viewed as a coalescence based on a shared set of articulated creeds or propositional beliefs, but as a "resonance machine," an affectively glued-together contraption "in which heretofore unconnected or loosely associated elements *fold, bend, blend, emulsify, and resolve incompletely into each other,* forging a qualitative assemblage resistant to classical models of explanation."[39]

Contra the linguistic approach, Connolly's Deleuzian sense of affect is more akin to Vásquez's materialist phenomenology, in which embodied forms—affects, habits, practices, dispositions, and beliefs—become the textures of religious life that shape the interface between religion and power.

The anthropologist of religion Kevin O'Neill also invokes a primarily Deleuzian understanding of affect in his "Beyond Broken: Affective Spaces and the Study of Religion." O'Neill rejects accounts of religious space (such as J. Z. Smith's) that understand it in terms of a "neutral grid" onto which thinking subjects project meaning.[40] For O'Neill, following Massumi, bodies do not arrive in neutral: they are "yelping" creatures that move to form space rather than waiting to create networks of mechanical meaning. Bodies are "excitable," rather than docile.[41] Moreover, these spaces, for O'Neill, are the loci of frames of power: "as a religiously managed and politically manipulated sensation," he writes, affect "makes legible a series of spaces that are not necessarily territorial but that are nonetheless deeply political. These include, for example, the felt distance that exists between *us* and *them*, between *high* and *low*, and between the *sinner* and the *saved*."[42] For O'Neill, affect in this Spinozistic/Deleuzian sense helps produce genealogies of how American religious spaces are "felt into existence" by affective bodies.[43]

But the Deleuzian vocabulary of affect represented by Massumi and others is only one current within contemporary affect theory. A second strand begins with Eve Kosofsky Sedgwick and Adam Frank's retrieval of psychologist Silvan Tomkins's theory of *affects*. Tomkins describes the affects as an ensemble of psychological engines—as emotions that rise to the level of the personal, even if they are not reducible to language. This model—concerned with what I here call *phenomenological affects*, affects woven into the textures of experience, hovering around, rather than beneath, the line of "conscious" awareness—gives religious studies resources for studying the named (shame, happiness, fear, anger, etc.) and the as-yet-unnamed emotions of embodied affective palettes.

Tomkins's career trajectory serves as a helpful backdrop for charting this approach. Tomkins started out studying drama as an undergraduate at the University of Pennsylvania in the late 1920s, an experience that set him on the path to thinking about the dynamic of motivation underpinning language.[44] The labor of theater—a recurring subject of interest among queer theorists[45]—is the injection of meaning into a diorama of bodies by attaching layers of emotional interpretation to a script, transforming a text into a living, breathing, embodied scene.

When Tomkins switched his academic attentions to psychology, he quickly became frustrated with the dominant cognitive paradigms of his time. Cognitive theory, Tomkins wrote, is too close to folk psychology in its view of affects as triggered by a singular organ of rational appraisal: "There are today," he wrote in a 1981 essay, "a majority of theorists who postulate an evaluating, appraising homunculus . . . that scrutinizes the world and declares it as an appropriate candidate for good or bad feelings. Once information has been so validated, it is ready to activate a specific affect."[46] For Tomkins, this model cannot adequately explain the emergence of affects from bodies: "But what is the cognitive appraisal when one is anxious but does not know about what; when one is depressed or elated but about nothing in particular? Even more problematic for such theory is infantile affect. It would imply a foetus in its passage down the birth canal collecting its thoughts, and upon being born emitting a birth cry after having appraised the extrauterine world as a vale of tears."[47] Bodies, for Tomkins, are not determined by a cognitive-linguistic regime that authorizes the rational appraisal of the world and then the rote deployment of a reasoned emotional response. Like Massumi, Tomkins is interested in the possibility that we may be motivated and directed by affective forces that exceed the cognitive or conscious.

In his multidecade, multivolume magnum opus *Affect Imagery Consciousness*, Tomkins combines Darwinian evolutionary biology, cybernetics, developmental psychology,[48] and psychoanalysis to diagram this complex theory of affects. Key to Tomkins's innovation is his simultaneous displacement of the Freudian model of drives and the cognitive model of appraisal with a framework in which affects have priority in the production of action, knowledge, and experience. This priority is nonetheless a picture of continuity, rather than (as with Massumi) a separation of domains: the title *Affect Imagery Consciousness* is designed to be printed without commas because the three zones are, in Tomkins's view, inseparable.[49] "Reason without affect would be impotent," Tomkins writes, and "affect without reason would be blind."[50]

Tomkins's affect theory is also marked by a theme of *configurability*. Tomkins suggests that bodies are always orienting themselves toward the attainment of particular "images," which are themselves assembled out of a heterogeneous conglomeration of "diverse sensory, affective, and memory imagery."[51] These images are not necessarily assimilable to structured economies of survival. Affect often runs against the grain of what contemporary economists call the "rational choice" model of decision making in which far-seeing actors pursue thoughtfully chosen goals to maximize wealth and longevity. "One can frighten the soldier out of cowardice," Tomkins muses, "by making him more afraid of cowardice than death."[52] Tomkins's affect theory, then, diagrams a complex and transitory landscape, in which language and embodied histories interface with evolutionary, affective, and cognitive structures—the shifting material repertoire of embodied life of interest to the materialist shift in religious studies. Tomkins's phenomenological approach to affect, then— rather than recapitulating the transcendental phenomenology spurned by Vásquez and Smith—spotlights how the way we feel has a complex, heterogeneous history.

This multilayered understanding of affects is what draws Sedgwick and Frank to Tomkins's work. Sedgwick writes that she turned to Tomkins while searching for intellectual resources to understand the phenomenology and the generativity of shame—to trace shame as something other than a lash of repression and despair.[53] But the excerpts from Tomkins's work comprising *Shame and Its Sisters* include much more than just a new set of resources for theorizing shame: they explore fear, anger, joy, and interest itself, among other emotions. Tomkins, in Sedgwick and Frank's hands, becomes a resource for prompting a new set of critical reflections on the textures of a range of embodied affective forms (a category that seems to be functionally interchangeable with the heading of "emotion"), the felt substance of motivation.

These critical reflections also prompted Sedgwick and Frank to reevaluate the map of contemporary "theory" itself. Sedgwick insisted on bringing to the fore Tomkins's sophisticated sense of the plasticity of affects, the possibility that emotions could be reshaped and redistributed through the embodied histories of individual bodies: "Affects can be, and are," she reminds us, "attached to things, people, ideas, sensations, relations, activities, ambitions, institutions, and any number of other things, including other affects. Thus, one can be excited by anger, disgusted by shame, or surprised by joy."[54] The medium of this transformation and the redistribution of affects across bodies—primarily human bodies—is often language, making linguistic analysis an indispensable critical tool.

But Sedgwick and Frank's opening essay in the volume, "Shame in the Cybernetic Fold," is unusually polemical (certainly in comparison with Sedgwick's other work) in its aggressive destabilization of the orthodoxies of contemporary theory, leading off with a sarcastic recitation of "what theory knows today," and lambasting the "reflexive antibiologism" within theory circles that dismisses features of embodied life that are situated outside the domain of constitution by discursive regimes. Like Massumi, Sedgwick and Frank want to create spaces for the discussion of affect as something that is not determined by linguistic effects. They effect a shift from epistemic histories, or the archaeology of how we think, to phenomenological histories—the sedimentation of how we feel.[55]

At the same time, this orientation to the phenomenological seems to be the crux of Sedgwick's departure from Massumi. She and Frank dismiss the "hygiene of current antiessentialism" in which, "insofar as they are 'theorized,' affects *must* turn into Affect"—sweeping up the title of Massumi's essay in their critique.[56] Meditating on the value of Tomkins's work on biologically ingrained affective textures for contemporary theory, Sedgwick and Frank suggest that it is a mistake to consider affect to be a homogeneous domain outside the perimeter of the sphere of representation, the binary antithesis of the linguistic. "We don't want to minimize the importance, productivity, or even what can be the amazing subtlety of thought that takes this form," they write, "but it's still like a scanner or copier that can reproduce any work of art in 256,000 shades of gray. However infinitesimally subtle its discriminations may be, there are crucial knowledges it simply cannot transmit unless it is equipped to deal with the coarsely reductive possibility that red is different from yellow is different again from blue."[57] Of course, on a microscopic level, colors are actually all the same thing: waves of light oscillating at different frequencies. But Sedgwick and Frank's metaphor indicates the way that rising from the ontological to the phenomenological level—from what they "are" in their "molecular" structure to how we encounter them at the level of bodies—opens up a new set of analytical tools: the panoply of embodied phenomenological reactions, felt affects.

Sedgwick and Frank's poststructuralist reading of Tomkins is a major foundation of the phenomenological branch of affect—a canon more or less coextensive with the subfield Sara Ahmed has called "feminist cultural studies of emotion and affect": her list includes Sedgwick, Teresa Brennan, Elspeth Probyn, Ann Cvetkovich, Lauren Berlant, and

Kathleen Stewart.[58] Unlike Massumi, this phenomenological branch insists on tracing affect as something felt, something that rises into embodied spheres of awareness. It is telling that in the reissues of the two 1995 introductory essays, Massumi in 2002 and Sedgwick and Frank in 2003—both from Duke University Press—neither author's name appears in the other's index. Two books, both looking at affect, from the same publishing house and landing in contiguous fields (queer theory and post-structural philosophy)—yet their use of the same vocabulary belies their theoretical divergences.

This divergence is perhaps best explained by Ahmed, who writes in her 2004 essay "Collective Feelings" that she finds herself "departing from the recent tendency to separate affect and emotion, which is clear in the work of Massumi. . . . This analytic distinction between affect and emotion risks cutting emotions off from the lived experiences of being and having a body."[59] For Ahmed, and perhaps Sedgwick as well, the overemphasis on Deleuzian affect—subphenomenological affect[60]—risks contravening a certain feminist imperative to connect scholarly work to lived experience. Cvetkovich also allows a blurrier sense of affect, calling the Deleuzians (such as Massumi) "intimates and fellow travelers" but rejecting the confinement of affect to the prephenomenological sphere—the hard typologization of affect, feeling, and emotion.[61]

Religious Affects, in keeping with the emphasis on affects plural, trends more toward the approach of Ahmed, Cvetkovich, and Mel Y. Chen in viewing with some suspicion the attempt to compose a hard line between affect and emotion. From my perspective, to divide affect and emotion using a rubric of "structure/antistructure" or "awareness/nonawareness" presupposes in advance that structure and awareness can be comfortably set aside from the prestructured or preconscious forces that make them up. As William Mazzarella notes, the "reductive binary opposition between (in Deleuze and Guattari's terminology) 'molar' structures and 'molecular' potentials continues to inform Massumian affect theory today in a way that undercuts its considerable power."[62] Cvetkovich's note, echoed by Chen, on the value of the imprecision in terms like *feeling* and *emotion*—an imprecision that spans different understandings of affect—seems to me a compelling and insightful starting point for this conversation.[63] At the same time, the Deleuzian approach to affect is particularly helpful in thinking beyond the framework of liberal sovereignty by focusing on the agency of nonhuman forces, what Erin Manning calls the "pulsions" of the body and Jane Bennett calls "vital materiality."[64] These terms offer valuable resources for conceptualizing animal religion.

Like scholars of religion and emotion such as Virginia Burrus, John Corrigan, Janet R. Jakobsen, and Ann Pellegrini, the phenomenological current within affect theory stresses the urgency of including emotion in any account of embodied life. This is not merely to enrich description, however: attending to affects helps to produce more detailed analyses of how bodies are moved by systems of power. Pellegrini, for instance (who describes herself as "promiscuous" in her movement back and forth across different definitions of affect, feeling, and emotion), assesses instances of American religion such as Hell Houses or the Westboro Baptist Church's protests and anti-WBC counterprotests according to a typology of affective spaces in which feelings of rage and indignation are either exercised or dissipated. She describes how the "joyful vengeance" of the WBC was deflected, at the picketed trial of Russell Arthur Henderson, by a group of counterprotesters dressed as angels, who "countered with a highly theatricalized emotional display that worked on multiple levels—aesthetic, political, spiritual, and affective—to create a literal space between hate and love, vengeance and forgiveness."[65] For Pellegrini, the different affective modes represented by the two groups are not simply symmetrical processes of "affect," but typologically distinct varieties of affect instrumenting different regimes of power.

Pellegrini's approach seems to correspond to the definition of religion offered by Thomas Tweed in his *Crossing and Dwelling*. Tweed sees religion as a set of techniques to "intensify joy and confront suffering."[66] Arguing against earlier definitions of religion that appealed to an intellectualized "ultimate concern" or "concern with death," Tweed suggests that religion's efficacy is located in procedures for eliciting particular affective reactions in bodies: "Religions provide ways for humans to imagine and enhance the joys associated with the encounter with the environment and the transitions in the lifespan. Humans want something to say and do in the face of wonder. Religions provide that idiom and transmit those practices. . . . Religions are about enhancing wonder as much as wondering about evil."[67] Tweed sees religion as a repertoire of procedures for pushing around and evoking specific affects, rather than an undifferentiated "affect."

In spite of this dual lineage, other writers working on affect, such as Lauren Berlant and Kathleen Stewart, draw on both currents, bringing a seemingly irreconcilable set of conceptual tools into a single, pluripotent jumble. This jumble is the shape of contemporary affect theory, a collection of texts trying to understand where bodies go by studying experiential and preexperiential shapes that do not take linguistic form. What unites these undertakings—however much they may diverge— are a pair of performative questions diagramming affect as the space where power operates outside of language: What do affects do? What do we do for affects? This book explores the usefulness, for the study of religion, of affect theory's tools for mapping the ensemble of affective processes that give depth and shape to experience at the same time as they articulate bodies to power.

Affective Religion: Power and Animality

Affect theory works inside the materialist shift by addressing a gap that has been overlooked by textualist scholarship: how power relations touch and move bodies. Affect theory suggests that power is more expansive than discourse—that it choreographs bodies on registers that exceed the linguistic. As Pellegrini writes, "at the end of the day, the ability to win over converts or spark spiritual rededication does not rise and fall on fact checking of biblical hermeneutics. It is a matter rather of affective congruences. . . . The process of conviction may engage preexisting beliefs—such as the notion that homosexuality is wrong, abortion is evil, or Satan is real—but for conviction to take hold something more is required. The participant is invested (or reinvested) in a deeper structure of religious feeling that can tie together disparate, even contradictory, experiences, bodily sensations, feelings, and thoughts."[68] Without affects, power—even and especially discourse—is inert. Recognizing that language is one small subset (or feature) of the migrating system of forces running between bodies and worlds, we can set it against the backdrop of animality and entertain a more expansive, transspecies understanding of religion.[69]

Affect theory is a multidimensional coalescence of theoretical concerns. In this sense, it is like a body—a heterogeneous compendium of organs, tissues, cells, limbs, and other artifacts of evolutionary history. Religion, viewed affectively, takes the same form: a bulging mass rather than a pristine dictionary entry that dispatches its subject matter in a few sentences without remainder. Sedgwick calls the affective responses that choreograph our bodies in relation to power—phenomenologically perceptible but hovering beyond the threshold of the sovereign self—our "queer little gods."[70] In this phrase lies a wealth of potential for thinking through the plural relationships between affect and religion, from the named affects to the thick interstices connecting bodies to worlds erupting beneath and between the links of language.

Religious Affects argues that understanding the political effects of religion—the cables between religion and bodies—and drawing up taxonomies productive for scholarly labor can be advanced by mapping affects, perhaps more so than the propositional content of worldviews. Affect theory points to a flaw at the heart of traditional ideology critique, which takes as given that language is a sort of computer program, an intrinsically compelling system of information/force—because God said so. The linguistic fallacy presupposes that language is an apparatus of command that effortlessly articulates with bodies. It has no sense of how discourses attach to bodies and get them to move, and is baffled when bodies sincerely "believe" one thing and do another. Affect theory maps the deeper embodied formations by which power makes bodies move. In this way, it updates Foucault's formula *power-knowledge* to *power-knowledge-affect*: it details the ways affects link bodies to systems of power and to regimes of information.[71]

To reduce religion to a contraption of beliefs disrupts our ability to grasp how religion produces politically engaged religious bodies, but also makes invisible religion's profile against the backdrop of species. As Donna Haraway writes, species "is about the corporeal join of the material and the semiotic in ways unacceptable to the secular Protestant sensibilities of the American academy and to most versions of the human science of semiotics."[72] Along these lines, this book proposes a pluralist approach to religious studies that develops a range of theoretical tools, including linguistic, cognitive, and affective methods. Reframing religion as animal offers new techniques to explore religion's imbrication with the flows of power running between bodies and worlds.

TWO

INTRANSIGENCE: POWER, EMBODIMENT,
AND THE TWO TYPES OF AFFECT THEORY

In a 2008 article, the historian Pamela Klassen describes a retreat she took at a Theravada Buddhist monastery in Thailand
shortly after college. The twenty-six-day cycle incorporated sitting and walking meditation on a fixed schedule, interspersed
with daily conversations with the monastery's abbot. Klassen
describes how, after two weeks of meditation, her dreams were
taken over by ghastly images that lingered during her meditation, scaring her and disrupting her focus. When she recounted
her concerns to the abbot, she was reassured that her nightmares were "right on schedule." Rather than sharing Klassen's
sense of alarm, her teachers told her that her nightmares were
themselves part of the "schedule" of the meditation regime, and
that they would pass with further meditation. Eventually, as the
abbot predicted, the horrific mental images dwindled away and
Klassen finished the rest of her retreat undisturbed.

As Klassen notes, the confidence of her teachers that her
meditation experiences would follow a particular psychological itinerary surfaces profound questions for the study of religion. If the evocation of emotional and religious states through
bodily practice follows a track that is shared across bodies
emerging out of different cultural histories, we are confronted
with a set of methodological concerns that the contemporary
humanities after the linguistic turn are not equipped to deal

with. Klassen maps these concerns out as a series of questions, asking, "What is the relationship between physiology and culture in the practice of religious ritual? Does physically choreographed ritual engender universal emotional responses? What is the role of culture in the evocation as well as the expression of ritually produced emotion?"[1] These questions can also be phrased using the vocabulary of affect theory: How do material bodies insert themselves into cultural-intellectual landscapes mediated by discourse? How do the thick, quasi-stable shapes of affect circulating heavily within and between bodies condition and drive the phenomenological geography of religion? And how do these phenomenological textures condition encounters between bodies and power?

From the standpoint of the linguistic turn, questions like these are difficult to address: they suggest a bodily orientation prior to (not to say untouched by) determination by language and culture. A body determined by language—a deanimalized body—is a blank slate without preexisting affective dispositions. The phenomenological stream of affect theory, however, offers resources that provide a way through this problem. Rather than viewing bodies entirely in terms of a highly plastic set of sculpted dispositions—a sort of phenomenological sand castle—affect theory is interested in the ways that the shapes of emotion express intransigence. Intransigent structures are susceptible to reconfiguration without being so flexible as to lack consistency. Moreover, these forms are shared among bodies in ways that step across local cultural histories.

These questions also map the tense formations structuring the interface between the humanities and the life sciences. This relationship has a fraught history, with the humanities traditionally expressing suspicion toward biologistic accounts of the formation of political subjectivities. This suspicion is rooted in part in an Enlightenment-era model of disciplinary domains—*Geistes-* and *Naturwissenschaften*—and partly in an entirely justified lingering mistrust of the use of Euro-American biologistic models, authorized with the imprimatur of science, in the propagation of racist, imperialist, heteronormative, and sexist regimes of power-knowledge.[2] But as a number of scholars of religion have suggested, the imperviousness of the humanities to dialogue with the sciences is producing an artificial barrier to interdisciplinary conversation.[3] The humanities after the linguistic turn have erected for themselves a cloudy comfort zone in which our primary objects of study are held to be linguistic artifacts determined by local circumstances of culture and power—and subtracted from the domain of biological inflexibility.

As Klassen shows, these tools alone are not enough to study the dynamic force of bodies as they project themselves into religious spheres. The question of the universal sources of what gets called religion have been part of the agenda of religious studies since Durkheim and James, but have been obscured as the field developed a new set of valuable theoretical tools in the wake of the linguistic turn. Klassen's questions point beyond the arcs of the linguistic turn to the animality of religion, religion's entanglement with bodies prior to the register of discourse or culture, opening out onto the plain of biology. This opening—where biological materiality can be methodically explored—is a way of reconsidering the relationship between religious bodies and power.

Klassen's argument is that the analysis of emotion and religious practice must consider a combination of physiological and cultural factors, to "attend to embodiment and physicality, as well as to the social, historical, and cultural networks within which ritualized emotions 'make sense.'"[4] She reflects, here, Thomas Tweed's understanding of religions as a "confluence of organic cultural flows,"[5] and anticipates Manuel Vásquez's call for a materialist phenomenology of religion that "would explore how religious meanings are created and experienced by specific embodied individuals endowed with sensorimotor and cognitive capacities and limits, as they encounter the world praxically, as they shape and are shaped by the natural and social environments, and as they enter into power relations with other individuals with whom they share spaces of livelihood."[6] This chapter makes the same argument, returning to the dual genealogy of affect theory outlined in the introduction to deepen its contours.

Affect theory also stages a conversation between biologistic and post-structural versions of embodiment in its phenomenological and Deleuzian currents. In Deleuzian affect theory, bodies are fundamentally plastic. In phenomenological affect theory, experiencing bodies are hybrid systems of locally devised power relations and semiplastic biological structures—intransigent affects. Routing this trajectory through a deeper exploration of Silvan Tomkins's relationship to Darwin as well as material feminism, I suggest that phenomenological affect theory is particularly well suited to exploring the emergence of intransigent emotional forms out of embodied histories. This convergence helps to map the onto-phenomenology of animal bodies: the ways the kinds of bodies we are feel, or the blueprints for our species-specific religions.

This synthesis suggests that affect has a particular relevance for the study of religion. This is because affects are not simply to be understood as passive channels activated by the play of language hovering over them. Rather, affects surge through bodies, producing semistable structures that become the tough, raw materials of religion. Tracing these embodied affective templates advances the understanding of religion not only as a set of private experiences but as an engine that penetrates systems of power and produces widespread, subdiscursive effects within those matrices. If the phenomenological is political, the way things feel is not the window dressing of power, but the substance of its material dimensions.

Affect Theory, Biology, Sand Castles

Affect theory is interested in the animality of embodied experience, the aspects of experience that circulate beneath and outside of linguistic determination. This focus on the prelinguistic domain has led a number of affect theorists into conversation with biology, psychology, and the life sciences—approaches that do not start from the presupposition that the forms of human experience are determined exclusively by culture. These resources turn affect theory into a valuable set of tools for rethinking problems in religious studies orbiting emotion, universality, and species. At the same time, the phenomenological and Deleuzian branches of affect theory tend to view biology differently, and to deploy it for different purposes.

At a conference in Milwaukee in 2012, I saw Brian Massumi engage in a short debate with media theorist Richard Grusin on migratory birds. Massumi had just finished a lecture on how evolution could be understood in terms of Deleuzian affect, as a sort of improvisational flow made up of endless becomings.[7] Grusin mentioned the songbirds that returned to his backyard year after year, often nesting in the same tree. Massumi was doubtful, proposing that the birds actually changed their location every year. Where Grusin wanted to underline the stable patterns embedded in the durable relationship between the animals and their material worlds, Massumi emphasized the granular modulations of behavioral forms.

In this exchange we see the contours of a controversy at the heart of affect theory, a controversy that also maps onto a broader field of questions within the humanities itself surrounding species, embodiment, and language. On the one side are theoretical approaches that emphasize difference as a field of infinite gradation. In these Deleuzian/Spinozistic models, affects are the molecular forces that coalesce to form soft structures—sand castles—always subject to erosion and mutation. On the other side are perspectives rooted in psychological (Silvan Tomkins) and phenomenological traditions that focus not only on variation and transformation, but on sustained attachments—the firm shapes of experience that emerge out of embodied histories. Whatever called the migrating birds back to Grusin's yard year after year was not a "becoming," but an enduring, sustained relationship with space. In this section, I want to explore the dynamic between these perspectives by examining their interactions with the life sciences and draw out the implications of this dialogue for a materialist phenomenology within religious studies.

The interest in the life sciences emerges in both the Spinozistic and phenomenological strains of affect theory, but with different disciplinary and experimental emphases. Massumi deploys a series of scientific experiments to scaffold his Spinozistic imaging of affect as prepersonal forces. For Massumi, affect is a sort of finely granulated field of vital energy sifting through bodies. Spinoza's vision of God/nature as a being made up of an "infinity of attributes" is in the background of this model.[8] But Massumi draws this out further, emphasizing that for Spinoza bodies are nothing more than conglomerated relationships between movement and rest, susceptible to infinite gradation and variation.[9]

The upshot of this is that affect comes to be defined as the space of becoming—a register of nanological change, first and foremost a process that is "ontogenetic" rather than merely ontological.[10] Massumi's reading of Spinoza articulates a sense of affect as the "elusively ongoing qualitative activity (*becoming*)" posed against the "manipulable objectivity" of the world.[11] This is why Michael Hardt writes that Spinoza's sense of affect offers "an ontology of the human that is constantly open and renewed."[12] Spinozistic affect suggests the constant making and remaking of bodies through the ongoing, mixing waves of becoming.

For Massumi, this ontogenesis of affect is essentially counterposed to structured "feelings," or "emotions," which subsist at the level of the "person"[13]—a constituted entity that is many stages downstream of the production of bodies by affects.[14] Affect is not perceived directly—it rises into the living circuitry of awareness only as it escapes, precisely at the moment when it is converted into structured feelings.[15] What Massumi calls "impersonal affect"—autonomous affect, formally incompatible with structured patterns—is a principle of connection generating infinite gradation and variation, sensed only as it dissipates by assembling the architecture of experience.[16] Massumi's analysis of the success of Ronald Reagan works inside this model: by trafficking in political "spasms," Reagan converted the flow of affective becoming into a channel of political power. For Patricia Clough, the affective substance of memory is best assessed as a "block of becoming" that "allows lines of flight, of inventiveness, through transversal communication, that is, communication without any fidelity to genus or species, or a hierarchy of forms."[17] The focus of Spinozistic or Deleuzian affect is always flux, the plasticity and endless reshaping of substance through the reformation of its infinite attributes.[18] Affect in this sense images bodies as sand castles, granulated conglomerates that are susceptible to radical reformation by the action of multidirectional waves washing over them.

This strain of affect theory, and particularly its deployment of scientific research, has not passed without criticism. Constantina Papoulias and Felicity Callard, for instance, in "Biology's Gift: Interrogating the Turn to Affect," criticize what they see as the move toward "afoundational biologism" in affect theory.[19] Afoundational biologism, as Papoulias and Callard describe it, is a sort of overcorrection in humanistic scholarship, a sharp swing of the pendulum from biological determinism to biological hyperplasticity—what Massumi calls "fluidifying" theory. Affect "is seen as proceeding *directly* from the body—and indeed *between bodies*—without the interference or limitations of consciousness, or representation": a prepersonal, unstructured, mobile contact zone.[20]

The heart of Papoulias and Callard's critique is that reading "prepersonal" affect as fluid runs directly against the grain of several key thinkers in affective neuroscience, including some who are favored by Deleuzian theorists. The Deleuzian "aleatory bio-logic" is fundamentally out of step with, for instance, Antonio Damasio and Joseph LeDoux, who argue that "the body's non-cognitive dimension is at least in part pre-adapted to initiate very precise, constrained courses of action.... Crucially, such a pre-adaptation is possible because of what LeDoux sees as the *intransigence* of emotional conditioning: for LeDoux, once the amygdala has been habituated to respond to a stimulus, no amount of effort can extinguish that response."[21] Rather than a "version of nature with no fixity," affective neuroscience traces structural features of the brain that yield intransigent emotional textures: neuroanatomical structures, neuro-hormones, and deeply embedded, durable behavior patterns installed by sculpted evolutionary trajectories or resolute patterns of attachment.[22]

The Spinozistic doctrine of affective plasticity at the level of embod-ied sensations and behaviors is more like the behaviorist orthodoxy of mid-twentieth-century American psychology, in which organisms, through training, could be "conditioned" to undertake any behavioral configuration. Affective neuroscientist Jaak Panksepp writes that although "a certain amount of output flexibility is a design characteristic of most brain operating systems," there are also domains of inflexibility—in par-ticular the emotions.[23] Rather than a sand castle, Panksepp sees behav-ior as built from chunks of psychological texture—a compendium of preexisting shapes that project their own potentials and limitations into the behavioral field. Behavioral and emotional configurability is real, he argues, but no one has yet managed to train a laboratory rat to run backward through a maze.[24]

Papoulias and Callard steer their discussion toward a cautious con-clusion warning of the danger of using science as an unimpeachable field of factual information for corroborating theoretical work in the humanities—rather than as an unsettled network of conversations that can be brought into dialogue with humanistic inquiry.[25] Ruth Leys goes further in "The Turn to Affect: A Critique," insisting on the rejection, *tout court*, of "anti-intentionalist" affect theory. Although I think her case is overstated,[26] where I concur with Leys is in her overall sugges-tion that the distinction between affect and emotion as it is advanced in Massumi and some other Spinozistic affect theorists cannot be taken as the only template for affect theory.[27] In turning to the domain outside of language, affect theory must be sensitive to not only the micrological but the higher-order dynamic of affects rising and falling and reshaping the threshold of perceptibility. There is, in the architecture of feeling, a dynamic between structure and flow, between form and flux, between stability and change, between the global and the local. An ontology of affect as pure becoming is unfaithful to scientific perspectives that focus on the intransigence of affects, their circulation as nonplastic elements rather than their hyperflexibility, and inadequate to explain how an affec-tive itinerary attached to a bodily practice—including the timely arrival of a pervasive, sticking fear during meditation—could exist across bodies or track the semistable patterns of species.

The Color Wheel of Difference:
Evolution and Phenomenological Affect

Phenomenological affect theory offers an alternative strategy for mapping the dynamic between bodies and emotions, one emerging out of Sedgwick and Frank's reading of the work of Silvan Tomkins in "Shame in the Cybernetic Fold." Part of what Sedgwick and Frank draw out of Tomkins in 1995 is a set of methodological strategies for thinking about complex systems with variable zones of stability and instability. One of their first accusations in the sarcastic litany of "what theory knows today" at the outset of "Shame in the Cybernetic Fold" is that theory "has become almost simply coextensive with the claim . . . *it's not natural*."[28] What they call the "hygiene of current antiessentialism" insists on language as "the most productive, if not the only possible, model for understanding representation."[29] By the same token, contemporary theory makes it impossible to countenance biological approaches because biology is opposed to linguistic analysis's "potential for doing justice to difference (individual, historical, and cross-cultural), to contingency, to performative force, and to the possibility of change."[30] "Theory" in Sedgwick and Frank's formulation has become a field so committed to the conceptual repertoire of becoming—the way discourse changes everything—that it has no room to think about condensed biological features.

There is a connection between Massumi's antiessentialism and the antiessentialist "theorists" that concern Sedgwick and Frank: even though Massumi defines himself in opposition to linguistic constructionism, both camps chart a space of essential contingency, where the stuff of subjectivity can be molded and remolded into an infinite number of perfectly pliable forms. This is a sandbox ontology: bodies and the political systems within which they are embedded are highly plastic nonstructures of pure becoming. The forms we find in bodies—returning to the same location on a migration route year after year, for instance—are no more than sand castles, ready to collapse with the influx of a single wave. Both groups are, in a sense, heirs of American behaviorism, which emphasizes the total plasticity of behavior. The theoretical episteme that Massumi operates within sees behavior, emotion, and culture as a sandbox, a field on which an unlimited number of shapes can be created out of the granular units of prepersonal affect.

But Sedgwick and Frank find in Tomkins a way to conceptualize a set of parameters of meaning that are neither binary nor infinite. Tomkins's approach to affect traffics in what has been called the basic emotions paradigm, which suggests that there are a limited number of affective channels biologically inscribed in bodies.[31] In this, Tomkins is more akin to Charles Darwin than Spinoza: like Darwin, he sees emotions as emerging in semistable forms within evolutionary histories. This paradigm, Sedgwick and Frank point out, is not a binary system—a play between a digital on-off or the two poles of a spectrum—nor is it infinite: it maps out a limited number of "finitely specified dimensions," along which there exist ranges of gradation.[32] Sedgwick and Frank express this model with the formula "finitely many $(n > 2)$." Building on Tomkins, they posit a noninfinite system that is nonetheless multiple, a plurality that is not reducible to an oscillation between binary poles.

Sedgwick and Frank also have an original strategy for dealing with the charge of essentialism: they preemptively argue that discursive plasticity—the presupposition of a flat landscape on which identity can be sedimentally constructed by language and culture—is, in fact, its own form of essentialism. "There is not a choice waiting to be made," they write, "in evaluating theoretical models, between essentialism and no essentialism. If there's a choice it is between differently structured residual essentialisms."[33] Edward Slingerland calls this crypto-essentialism the "High Humanist stance": an "approach to the study of culture that assumes that humans are fundamentally linguistic-cultural beings, and that our experience of the world is therefore mediated by language and/ or culture *all the way down*."[34] To grant language or undifferentiated affect sole power to determine the structure of subjectivity or experience is itself a form of essentialism.

The essentialism of discursive plasticity can be seen, in a sense, as importing a distinctly liberal ontology (and a liberal strategy for analyzing the distribution of difference) into contemporary theory. Although Deleuzian affect theory is not interested in the agency of individuated subjects, like classical liberalism, it does see bodies as starting from a uniform position of epistemic and experiential neutrality: the body is not an animal, fused to a biological history, but a *liber*, a free man, a blank slate. Variation, in both classical liberalism and Deleuzian ontology, is introduced through the interface of mobile, nanological grids of influence. The ontology of classical liberalism corrected hierarchical ontologies in which human groups were taken to be organized vertically along an axis of superiority that, further down the pole, also enfolded the remainder of the animal world—what Mel Y. Chen calls an "animacy hierarchy." Liberalism as an ontology of homogeneous configurability dismantled the vertical hierarchy of monarchist ontologies determined by preoccupations with bloodlines and genealogies[35] by replacing it with a flat plane in which all bodies were taken to be clones of the same free, linguistic, reasoning subject. This angelic subject eludes the sticky, uneven, bestial textures of biology, animated instead by an abstract, reasoning potential that is held in common by all human beings.[36]

But phenomenological affect theory points to a different ontology altogether. Neither hierarchical nor homogeneous, Tomkins's understanding of affects acknowledges the intransigent animality of bodies, the reefs that subsist below the level of rational control, linguistic sedimentation, or affective flux but nonetheless shape our encounters with power. As Sedgwick and Frank point out, the "digital" model of configurability is a way of distancing subjects from species, a "reflexive antibiologism" that peels us away from animality and liquidates the ability to trace biological forms embedded in bodies.[37] This criticism seems to include the Deleuzian/Spinozistic sense of affect in its scope, a digital model in which "insofar as they are 'theorized,' affects *must* turn into Affect."[38] As Elspeth Probyn writes in recapitulation of Sedgwick's argument: "let A-ffect rest (in peace), so we can put our energies into motivated analyses of the constitution, the experience, the political, cultural and individual import of *many affects*."[39]

The digital model of affect produces dichotomous pairings in which affect is one of two terms, either on or off: that is affect/affect that is not. It is possible, for instance, within this binary picture, for writing (or politics, or religion) to be *nonaffective*. But in Tomkins's framework, this would be unthinkable: affect saturates experience, cognition, and behavior at every level. Language never even begins to diverge from the liquid seams of affect that stick meanings to words.[40] It's not that Reagan beat his opponents by mastering *affect*—it's that he used the right *affects* in the right time and place to launch a political movement. From Tomkins's work, Sedgwick and Frank extract a new emphasis on a nonbinary model of affects, emerging in plural forms out of bodies. Rather than a dyad of affect or not-affect, they find in this approach a "color wheel of different risks, a periodic table of the infinitely recombinable elements of the affect system, a complex, multilayered phyllo dough of the analog and the digital."[41] Finitely many, but $(n > 2)$. Where Deleuzian affect points to the plasticity of affect, Tomkins points to the catalog of affects, the semistable phenomenological structures of embodiment.[42]

Tomkins develops his version of the basic emotions hypothesis out of a biological model: Darwinian evolutionary theory. Darwin, too, in *The Expression of the Emotions in Man and Animals*, proposes biologically established channels of emotional expression for shame, surprise, disgust, anger, reflection, joy, and despair.[43] Tomkins and Darwin draw on several of the same methods: like Darwin, Tomkins studies his own children's development and enfolds those observations into his work.[44] And like Darwin, whose *Expression* was one of the first English-language academic studies to make significant use of photography,[45] Tomkins's work is linked to a history of imaging technologies and methods of scholarship that step outside of the domain of discourse analysis. To study the details of the physiological trajectories of embodied affects, for instance, Tomkins once constructed a custom-made camera capable of capturing facial expressions at 10,000 frames per second.[46] Both scholars brought bodies to the surface of their research to record their intransigent emotional textures.

Applying these methods to his field of psychology, Tomkins developed a Darwinian account of the evolution of the affects: affect systems emerge, in deep time, out of a variety of evolutionary processes, as the preferred method for bodies navigating the ambiguity of information-rich environments. They prioritize effective survival strategies by intensifying their motivational force.[47] The finite catalog of affects—in Tomkins's case, disgust-contempt, shame-humiliation, distress-anguish, anger-rage, surprise-startlement, enjoyment-joy, interest-excitement—represents an unlearned phenomenological matrix that emerges in bodies out of this evolutionary dynamic and operates prior to language and acculturation.[48]

However, Tomkins also emphasizes that, from the Darwinian perspective, organisms in their need to affectively sift through the textures of the world did not emerge out of a unilinear or streamlined process. In evolving an affect system, bodies were required to develop multiple channels of sensitivity defining a pluriform set of relationships with their worlds. This gives the tapestry of affects the form of "a patchwork thrown together," a living multiplicity of diverging emotional drivers rather than a unified economy.[49] Rather than a pristine set of interlocking gears, the finitely many $(n > 2)$ set of basic emotions is a system in tension.[50]

Finally, these semistable phenomenological forms emerge out of a dynamic evolutionary history, but they occur at the organismic level—the level of individual bodies within a species—reliably and predictably enough that they resemble an ahistorical essence. It is with an eye to this historicized sense of *essence* that the evolutionary biologist Stephen Jay Gould writes that it is "high time that we repressed our aversion to this good and honorable word."[51] For Gould, essences need not be Platonic in cast: we can rehabilitate "essence" as a concept by viewing it as a long-term pattern expressing a slow-motion trajectory of change within an expansive evolutionary dynamic. Basic emotions have histories, but these histories move at a time scale that vastly exceeds human experience, let alone human history. The varieties of animal affect fall into this category of semistable forms emerging out of shapeshifting embodied histories.[52]

Tomkins's basic emotions hypothesis diverges from Massumi's sense of affect as what Papoulias and Callard call "afoundational biologism." Sedgwick and Frank's formula of finitely many $(n > 2)$ is, in a sense, a reversal of the hyperflexible, antistructural essentialism of Massumi, an openness to the intransigence of certain phenomenological forms—such as birds returning to the same spot in their migrations, or the cross-cultural emotional impact of a regimen of meditation. But, crucially, Tomkins's version of affect theory by no means abandons the motif of plasticity. The versatility of this approach is amplified by the extraordinary flexibility of affect in its recirculation and redistribution across other objects inhabiting a body's phenomenological world. Affects are highly configurable in their varied bonds of attachment.

As Sedgwick points out, Tomkins's affects, unlike drives, can be invested in any object at all: they "can be, and are, attached to things, people, ideas, sensations, relations, activities, ambitions, institutions, and any number of other things, including other affects. Thus, one can be excited by anger, disgusted by shame, or surprised by joy."[53] Whereas drives suggest a set of rigid ligatures between bodies and worlds, affects, as members of a physiological amplification system rather than a fixed set of relationships, can be recalibrated and rewritten. Affects drive bodies from within, rather than working as a set of extendable, mechanical arms that reach out to retrieve preprogrammed objects from the world. Quoting Tomkins, Sedgwick and Frank point out that "unlike the drives (e.g., to breathe, to eat), 'Any affect may have any "object." This is the basic source of complexity of human motivation and behavior.' "[54] Affects are propulsive—pushing bodies into worlds—but not teleological.[55]

This is why, Sedgwick and Frank suggest, Tomkins's writing style is so often in the genre of the catalog or list—a set of propositions strung together by a connective tissue of possibilities, a serial array of "if . . . may . . ." sentences: "If I wish my work to be in the mainstream of contemporary efforts, I may be ashamed if my work is judged to be somewhat deviant. If, however, I wish to be creative, I may be ashamed if my work is judged to be in the mainstream of contemporary opinion. . . . If I am a bright housewife, I may be ashamed because too much of my work is too exclusively muscular. If I am a mesomorphic academic, I may be ashamed because my work is too much cerebral and too little somatotonic."[56] The *may* is, for Tomkins, a discursive technique for sorting the complex pluralism of embodied affects. The effect of these catalogs of possibilities is to suggest "the possibility of random, virtually infinite permutation, some of it trivial, some of it highly significant," creating what Sedgwick and Frank name as a consummately "postmodern" syntax: an architecture of shifting possibility and transformation composed out of complex forms.[57]

Although discourses of biology are often caricatured in the humanities as oriented entirely toward fixity and inflexibility, Tomkins's approach is consistent with the interpretation of Darwinian theory developed in the work of the affect theorist Elizabeth A. Wilson, reading Darwin as a resource for exploring the dynamic between stasis and change within embodied histories. Like Sedgwick and Frank, she is critical of the antibiologist strain in theory that has foreclosed "the particularities of the muscles, nerves, and organs."[58] This is why Wilson writes that "projects that interrogate the heterodox character of the body's organs—projects that lean on and amplify biological data—can break new, vital ground for feminism."[59] Rather than viewing biology and the organic structures of biological models as an intrinsically reductive set of analytical tools, Wilson takes them to be assets in reinscribing feminist attention to relations between embodiment and power.

Turning to Darwin, Wilson maps this interest onto the question of species by turning to *The Expression*, in which Darwin elaborates on the intransigent and involuntary dimensions of affective response. From the title of the book—*The Expression of the Emotions in Man and Animals*—and throughout, Darwin animalizes human affective responses, disputing "the detachment of emotive capacities from reflexive behavior."[60] The figure of the animal becomes a way for Wilson to connect intransigent embodied response and embodied transformation, a hinge between affect as transformation and affect as stable reaction pattern. Animality draws out what Wilson calls the complex "bio-logic" of the body, interrupting the equation of biologism and reductionism.

For Tomkins, then, named affects such as shame or fear are like "a letter in an alphabet, or a word in any sentence," elements on a felt periodic table that are reassembled within embodied histories into living particularities.[61] Or affects are like Lego bricks: hard shapes that can be moved around, combined, and rearranged in the life span of an organism but that will only be seen to fundamentally transform in the macroscopic frame of evolutionary deep time. Like a Lego sculpture, bodies are a hybrid system of functionally intransigent pieces that are nonetheless highly configurable, detachable, and reworkable. This is similar to Thomas Tweed's view in *Crossing and Dwelling*, that religions "provide the lexicon, rules, and expression for many different sorts of emotions, including those framed as most positive and most negative, most cherished and most condemned."[62] But where Tweed images biology as the "channel" and culture as the "current" flowing through that channel, phenomenological affect theory sees culture more as a current flowing over and between the reefs of physiologically inscribed affects—a much more intimate relationship.[63] The encounter between bodies and formations of power such as religion is difficult to theorize precisely because of this hybrid complexity—neither essentially plastic nor static.

This is why embodied histories always need to be understood in a double sense, as the accumulation of a complex genotype in deep time and as the cascade of accidents that affect the phenotype during an individual body's life span. That ongoing simultaneity of biological and cultural processes is what it means to think the dissolution of the barrier between nature and culture, to view them as contiguous and interwoven systems of force moving at different speeds, what Donna Haraway calls "naturecultures."[64] This offers an alternative to the "tug-of-war" mentality

in the debates over nature and nurture within the humanities, recon-
ciling "context-sensitive" and "comprehensive" theories of religion and
embodiment.[65]

Onto-Phenomenology: The Shape of How Things Feel

Phenomenological affect theory can also be placed in conversation with
material feminism, which is instrumental in Vásquez's formulation of
the materialist shift in religious studies.[66] In the introduction to their edited volume *Material Feminisms*, Stacy Alaimo and Susan Hekman echo
the concerns of Sedgwick and Frank that theory has become reflexively
antibiological, relying exclusively on the register of language as the only
possible zone for critical work.[67] Although post-structuralist models
after the linguistic turn have been successful in mapping relationships between knowledge and power, Alaimo and Hekman point out, they risk
excluding "lived experience, corporeal practice, and biological substance
from consideration."[68] The material feminist method re-animalizes
theory, turning to experiential shapes existing prior to or outside of
language, thematizing "the co-extensive materiality of humans and non-
humans" as interlinked embodied histories.[69]

Karen Barad uses this framework to develop an analytic of what she
calls *onto-epistemo-logy*. Building on the work of Niels Bohr, Barad rejects epistemological accounts that view knowledge production as a set
of neutral, immaterial tools of measurement applied to the world.
Instead, she argues, knowledge is made when a particular set of intransigent, species-specific embodied practices—such as language, technologies of measurement, and patterns of sensation—imprint their
own distinctive shapes on experience. Framing bodies in terms of onto-
epistemo-logy—"the study of practices of knowing in being"—attunes us
to the ways in which we know via our emergence within embodied histories.[70] Knowledge is generated in particular configurations out of particular onto-epistemo-logical forms. Certain kinds of knowledge happen to
certain kinds of animal beings experiencing worlds in particular ways.

But where material feminism has been primarily concerned with
rethinking epistemology, or the way we know, affect theory in the Tomkins lineage has taken special interest in the relationship between embodied histories and phenomenology, or the way things feel.[71] For what
Ahmed terms feminist affect theory, embodied histories are a convergence between biological histories and the lived experience of bodies

navigating systems of power.[72] Embodied histories, viewed through the lens of affect theory, are about the intransigent, shifting, feeling shapes of animal life. If material feminism points to an onto-epistemology, embodied histories diagram an onto-phenomenology—the way things feel for the kinds of animals we are.

Just as the materiality of knowledge practices projects into ways of knowing, the materiality of feeling practices—intransigent affects—projects into the phenomenological fabric of animal worlds. Emotions have their own architectures, their own interests and profiles, their own shaping influence on the lived worlds of the bodies through which they move. Following David Wills, I suggest we label these affective shapes *technologies*—bodily technologies that emerge in semistable patterns that then condition formations of power—including religion.[73] As Dominic Pettman writes, "definitions of *technology* should not be limited to industrial infrastructure and other 'machines that go beep,' but should extend to specific relationships involving power, knowledge, and discourse (often based on the biomechanics of natural organisms and processes)."[74] Not just passive artifacts, these technologies are living agents that make possible the multilateral textures of power wrapping up our bodies. Onto-phenomenology diagrams these moving, overlapping, bodily technologies.

Religion, Fear, and Power

Phenomenological affect theory helps map the lines linking biologically grounded emotional responses—for example, fear—to religion and other systems of power. Darwin identifies fear as a universal emotional response found across human cultures and nonhuman animal bodies,[75] and Jaak Panksepp concurs that fear is the least controversial item on any neurobiologist's list of the basic emotions, since it is in evidence early in infant development across human cultures and in other animal species.[76] Fear, in other words, is a universal aspect of embodied experience, an onto-phenomenological structure shared by all humans and most, if not all, animals. Panksepp rejects the behaviorist model of fear that emphasized conditioned plasticity—a set of learned associations accumulated through classical conditioning—insisting instead that "the potential for fear is a genetically ingrained function of the nervous system." Fear, Panksepp suggests, was so evolutionarily important—an indispensable bodily technology—that it could not be left in the hands of learning mechanisms alone.[77] Klassen fretting in her meditation room feels an emotional potential latent in every animal body on the planet—a global network of sensitivity linked by our shared genomic plane.

But this grounding of fear in cross-species biological mechanisms does not make fear rigid or uniform. For one thing, on the genomic plane, the variety of animal species means a variety of inborn fear triggers across bodies. Neuroscientists consider the intransigent starting forms of fear to be species specific: where humans, for example, are afraid of "dark places, high places, approaching strangers (especially those with angry faces), and sudden sounds, as well as snakes and spiders," laboratory rats fear illuminated areas, open spaces, and the odors of predators, such as cats and ferrets.[78] Embodied histories unfolding back into evolutionary time produce different distributions of fear—different onto-phenomenological architectures that incline fear to attach to different objects in the world or emerge out of different practices—such as a sustained course of solitary meditation.

But fear also varies from body to body within species. Sedgwick and Frank go back to Tomkins precisely because of the way that he maps the dynamic between the intransigence and the configurability of affects. Affects—including fear—coassemble with different cognitive, imagistic, and affective forms in the time scales of memory and experience to produce the striking breadth of emotional responses found among bodies: "One can frighten the soldier out of cowardice by making him more afraid of cowardice than death."[79] Affects can be attached to anything, fusing with objects in worlds and reticulating them to networks of power. Always the playwright, Tomkins sees the distribution of the affects as the ongoing unfurling of a set of narratives fashioning thick, semistable response patterns.

Feminist affect theorists use this double sense of affect (as both intransigent and configurable) to illustrate how the phenomenological is political. Sara Ahmed, for instance, calls our attention to how fear constitutes religious-political identities and shapes regimes of power.[80] In "Affective Economies," she focuses on anti-immigrant discourses—such as an Aryan Nations website and a speech by conservative British politician William Hague—as discursive technologies arranging fear to produce a shared sense of an *us* that is in danger. Affect builds networks of power structuring social forms: fear, the pressure of a threat to *us*, "does not involve the defense of borders that already exist; rather, fear makes those borders, by establishing objects from which the subject, in fearing, can stand apart, objects that become 'the not' from which the subject appears to flee."[81] Ahmed's examples—antiblack and Islamophobic racism—are not neutral ideological positions that occasionally find themselves dancing with affect. The affective chemistry itself is the politics: racism consumes and desires fear in the same way that we stand in line to buy tickets for a horror movie. Robert C. Fuller suggests that the genre of religious apocalyptic fulfills the same function. The Christian book of Revelation, Fuller writes, "by linking emotional experiences of fear, anger, and resentment with culturally elaborated eschatological hopes, forged lasting communal and theological bonds among early Christians."[82] These mechanisms, piggybacking on the bodily technology of fear, continue to reverberate through contemporary Christian contexts, offering the durable raw materials for new regimes of political solidarity 2,000 years later.[83] Religious affects, then, are not cosmetic: they are the material substance of power, enticing bodies into political regimes. "Fear," Ahmed shows, "*does something*."[84]

In a related move, Harvey Whitehouse takes an anthropological perspective on rituals involving the production of fear in participants, what he identifies as an "ancient and cross-culturally recurrent feature of religion."[85] For Whitehouse, fear becomes an integral element of certain religious rituals, triggering affective mechanisms that exceed their conceptual or cognitive frameworks.[86] Whitehouse suggests that these experiences of terror provoke states of heightened arousal, etching deeply rooted "flashbulb" memories, "distinctive episodes" that continuously resurface in memory.[87] The "wounds" of the fearsome ritual are constantly retrieved in later life, accumulating new strata of meaning as they do so and ensuring "that participants will always recall who else was present during a given ritual ordeal, thereby establishing enduring and cohesive bonds between those who went through the experience together."[88] The embodied capacity for fear becomes, in other words, the condition of possibility for a certain technology of religious identity formation.

Whitehouse's sense of fear as the substance of the efficacy of certain rituals converges in interesting ways with Darwin's own remarks on fear and religion in *The Expression of the Emotions in Man and Animals*. Darwin, too, points out that "fear often acts at first as a powerful stimulant," and suggests that this affect coassembles—along with other emotions—with the bodily practices of devotion.[89] A parallel understanding is in the early twentieth-century work of phenomenologist of religion Rudolf Otto, who identified the core religious feeling as the *mysterium tremendum*—wonder combined with what he calls "tremor." In the religious encounter, our bodies "recoil in a wonder that strikes us chill and numb."[90] Otto's model of religion, then, is a confluence of two intransigent affective forms: fear + wonder. Affect theory allows us to reexamine these older phenomenological models of religion—swept away by the linguistic turn—with a twist: where Otto (and likely Darwin) saw religious emotion as transcendent and apolitical, affect theory prompts us to ask how these embodied affective potentials form and accelerate systems of power.

One of the most provocative correlations of fear with the analytics of religious power comes from the late writings of Eve Sedgwick. In "Pedagogy of Buddhism," Sedgwick offers a way of rethinking Buddhist practice as an intervention in a particular affective situation: the human body nearing death. Sedgwick starts the essay with a rehearsal of Donald Lopez's argument in *Curators of the Buddha: The Study of Buddhism under Colonialism* that the version of Buddhism transmitted to the West from the nineteenth century onward is an artifact of European Orientalism. Rather than an authentic Buddhism, Lopez suggests, the "hypostatized object, called 'Buddhism'" was an "adaptation," a set of traditions manipulated to conform to a colonialist vision—and to serve as an expedient instrument to authorize colonialist violence.[91]

Sedgwick proposes that, without abandoning the critical force of this analysis—particularly its usefulness in elaborating a clearer picture of the damage wrought by Western colonialism—we can consider other approaches to the global dissemination of what gets called *Buddhism*. "What if," she suggests, "an equally canonical topos such as *recognition/ realization* describes some dynamics of Western Buddhist popularization better than does the one-directional topos of adaptation?"[92] Rather than understanding transmission as the hostile takeover of a tradition and its manipulation and forced confinement in an alien cultural field, Sedgwick suggests that transmission may be multidimensional, a process of coalescence driven in part by a recognition between bodies that a particular bodily practice has meaning across cultural and historical contexts.

As an example, Sedgwick turns to the American Transcendentalists of the nineteenth century, such as Elizabeth Palmer Peabody and Henry David Thoreau, suggesting that their encounter with Buddhism may have amounted to more than a "tautology"—"the projection of Western commonplaces, our already-known, onto the glamorizing screen of a fantasied Orient."[93] Instead, Sedgwick proposes that the transcendentalists recognized a set of truths in Buddhist thought and practice through a resonance within their bodies. The transcendentalist encounter with Buddhism was not, in Sedgwick's proposal, purely an act of violence that mutilated an existing tradition to fit a set of predetermined cultural forms. Rather, the forms it evoked were "already inside the listener[s]."[94] This field of potential recognitions is created within the scope of a species-specific onto-phenomenological blueprint, through practices evoking semistable, species-wide, embodied reactions.

The writing emerging out of Western encounters with Buddhism need not be merely "distorting or appropriative. Instead, its very ways of being 'Western' locate it in an ongoing, palimpsestic, but very dynamic conversation with, among, even within a variety of Asian teachings."[95] Traditions of bodily practice, texts, conversations, observations, mutations, accidents of communication, optimistic distortions, cynical manipulations, bloody colonial encounters, and the rich panoply of bodily technologies layer on top of one another, producing a mobile contact zone for the flowing tributaries of religion on an uneven, intrusive bodily landscape. This contact zone is shaped not only by adaptation, but by embodied recognition.

Given the cautious tone of Sedgwick's chapter, I would suggest that she is well aware that her claim is controversial, but she nonetheless proposes that, rather than viewing religions purely as artifacts of discourse, we see them as submerged in bodies, composed out of a suite of embodied forms that, at least in part, precede discursive determination. Along the same lines, Slingerland writes that "we can recognize the importance of culture and history while remaining open to the possibility that, for instance, we are motivated to apply the common word 'mysticism' to a variety of experiences from different times and places because they share certain features—a commonality that is both the product of human cognitive universals and recognizable because of those universals."[96] David Morgan makes a similar point in examining the commonality of "behavior that might be reasonably said to represent a recurrent set of concerns designated by [the] term *religion*" across times and places.[97] Religious practices tap embodied histories, activating coalitions of bodily technologies that have been shaped by long evolutionary timescapes. They are recognized at the level of intransigent, onto-phenomenological features of our animal bodies at the same time as they are spun and maneuvered by systems of signification. Sedgwick puts forward a proposition that many Buddhists would find unobjectionable, and one that is consistent with the materialist shift in religious studies: that Buddhist practices have effects on bodies that are not reducible to the discursive vehicles by which those practices are transmitted.

Where does the impetus for this reorientation to recognition—to an embodied resonance with a foreign teaching—come from? There is no question, to my mind, that it is motivated by a particular dynamic in Sedgwick's own life between fear and healing. Sedgwick, writing in the early 2000s, had already been diagnosed with breast cancer, the disease that would take her life at the age of fifty-eight. In keeping with the method of all her work, she used writing as a venue to explore this experience and turn it into a source of healing for herself and others. In "A Dialogue on Love," Sedgwick describes in detail the process of going through therapy to help her deal with her renewed sense of mortality. Weaving poetry, narrative, and academic prose together to capture the way her affective life muscled its way into her intellectual frameworks, she writes, "I fear and hope, I burn and freeze like ice."[98] But she also writes, in "Pedagogy," that her exposure to Buddhism, as she began to confront the possibility of her death, "rearranged the landscape of consciousness that surrounds, for me, issues of dying." Buddhist thought and practice enabled her to slit the knots of the painful circuits of thought emerging from the landscape of her fear.[99]

Rather than trying to decisively establish the accuracy of Sedgwick's assessment, affect theory only elevates the provocative hypothesis underneath it to the surface. What if religions were not simply sand castles made out of symbols, but were systems of practice that engaged with, explored, and choreographed human bodies—the intransigent evolutionary forms that delimit our animality? Bodily practices, by this understanding, might have semistable effects across cultures—at least as stable as discursive regimes. Moreover, if, as Ann Cvetkovich argues, healing and hope are themselves extraordinarily important political processes, these religious practices that reconfigure affects must be considered in the analytics of power.[100]

Do all human bodies fear death in the same way? No, but we all fear or have feared, and the reconfiguration of that fear can be accomplished using a set of practices that can span historical epochs, in the same way that we can find a carving transplanted from a different culture evocative and compelling even if we are not invested in the discourses of aesthetics of that time and place. Discursive practices of religious traditions intersect with animal embodied histories—because discourse is no less a bodily technology, an accident of embodied history—and the systems of affect that have been carried forward by those trajectories to form complex, powerful linkages.[101] For Sedgwick, Tibetan and Japanese Buddhist practices and discourses are affectively powerful for her, a white, American, middle-class woman with cancer in the process of "learning to unbe a self."[102] Affect theory proposes that we need to consider the possibility that although the distribution, significations, and permutations of bodily practices (including discourses) are varied, they nonetheless can yield more or less consistent effects and affects across bodies. Religious discourse is not the only mechanism by which religion articulates bodies to power.

This understanding also helps us to make sense of Klassen's experiences in the meditation chamber. Klassen's body shares an onto-phenomenological makeup with all the other meditators who have come before her. Out of a long-developed understanding of the intransigent landscape of this constitution, the abbot is able to anticipate her fear and counsel her through it, to recognize that this is something that happens to the kind of bodies we are. At the same time, Klassen sits in a local history, both of traditions of Buddhist practice stretching back thousands of years and of contemporary global networks of knowledge production, imagery, desire, commerce, and migration that bring her body into contact with these practices, allowing them to transform her individual body and its situation within a global network of power.

Conclusion

The impetus for this chapter emerges out of a worry that the humanities do not have adequate vocabulary for thinking about the animality of bodies—whether our own or those of other animals. The linguistic fallacy implicitly creates a binary frame, in which nonhuman animal bodies lack any history, and our own histories are composed only out of the sedimentation of language. The humanities are only just beginning to devise tools to respond to Jacques Derrida's call to think the "hetero-geneous multiplicity" of animality—the multidimensional spectrum of richly textured, feeling bodies emerging out of a branching array of deep evolutionary histories.[103] Animal religion, then, approaches bodies in terms of a complex set of continuities and differences across species—onto-phenomenologies, the ground plans of what gets called religion. Vásquez's materialist phenomenology works in tandem with the real-ization that different species may configure religion in different ways. Religious affects are not merely zaps of novelty or the microphysics of transformation: affects are better understood as semistable, complex formations of embodied sensation that have coalesced through the ad-vance of ancient evolutionary processes operating in deep time.

Intransigent features of bodies—such as basic emotions—are not unchanging, but they are things that we, in our individual histories, can't necessarily push against. Intransigence is not determinism or physiologi-cal uniformism: it stands in support of Eve Sedgwick's foundational axiom, in *Epistemology of the Closet*, that "bodies are different from each other."[104] It indexes resolute features of bodies, but these features, by virtue of being embedded in long-range embodied histories, are them-selves always fuzzy, always producing outliers—which in turn become the starting points of new trajectories of transformation within deep time. Intransigent things are semistable: their patterns are detectable but never perfectly replicated. And intransigent features can them-selves be rearranged. Affect always maps these dynamics between form and movement, structure and change. The materialist shift, especially thought through in conjunction with affect theory, means we can talk about religious bodies as material things that are not determined from top to bottom by regimes of discourse (or even learning) without being essentialist. It is the only way to talk about animality.

Religious studies has always been concerned with the transaction between the local and the global, the particular and the universal. This interest has paralleled the fascination, within religious studies, with the affective. "However complex the outward manifestations of religious life may be," Durkheim wrote in 1912, "its inner essence is simple, and one and the same. Everywhere it fulfills the same need and derives from the same state of mind."[105] Religious studies begins in a constellation of theoretical moments—James, Durkheim, Otto—in which prelinguistic affect was put forward as the cradle of religion as such. Affect theory turns back to these resources, but, building on the linguistic turn, radically redraws the map of theoretical engagements between religion and emotion by explicitly linking affects to frames of power.

At the same time, religious studies as a field recognized by the latter decades of the twentieth century the risks of making phenomenology the only analytical paradigm for defining religion: phenomenology, history of religions, and related approaches tended toward inflexible understandings of religion as an ethereal, sui generis phenomenon that visited bodies from above—a metaphysical property unscathed by questions of power, authority, and place. The linguistic turn in religious studies destabilized the rigid phenomenological architecture of these early attempts to define religion in the vein of affect, displacing discussion of religion's points of origin in bodies to the field of semantic meanings. As Klassen writes, "any theory of religious ritual and emotion that does not take into account gender, race, class, and other socially formative categories—categories with profound effects both at cultural and individual levels—will only answer very limited questions, for a very limited audience."[106]

Affect theory opens up ways of understanding religion's traffic with all of these as well as systems of power outside of discourse. Switching from the model of a *construction* to an *assemblage* helps to map power flows as shaped by material phenomenological textures rather than emerging through a plastic dynamic of discursive sedimentation. The shapes of affect, the finitely many $(n > 2)$ of Sedgwick and Frank's reading of Tomkins's basic emotions hypothesis, are the components of political subjectivity—an animal subjectivity far upstream of the sovereignty of the self—structuring power relations and shaping the durable textures of what gets called religion. Affect theory gives us resources to think of religion set against the backdrop of onto-phenomenology: the way that the kinds of bodies we are and are becoming in the swaying currents of our living and evolutionary embodied histories feel.[107] By reanimalizing bodies, we can see how affects connect political, religious, and cultural spheres to bodies. Animal religion emerges out of the shapes—what Tomkins calls the new "alphabet"—of these intransigent, onto-phenomenological forms.

THREE

TEACHING RELIGION, EMOTION,
AND GLOBAL CINEMA

Is it true that we can learn only when we are aware we are being taught?—**Eve Kosofsky Sedgwick,** *Touching Feeling*

The title of this chapter is borrowed from a class I taught in the Religion Department at Haverford College in spring of 2013—Religion, Emotion, and Global Cinema (REGC). Through the theoretical resources of affect theory, the class explored how four films we screened together over the course of the semester—Heidi Ewing and Rachel Grady's *Jesus Camp*, Kim Ki-Duk's *Spring, Summer, Fall, Winter . . . and Spring*, Nina Paley's *Sita Sings the Blues*, and Alfonso Cuarón's *Children of Men*—documented, imaged, and enacted globalized religion. Taking film as our case study, we examined the production of religious formations of power through the circulation of affects along transnational media networks.

The class was new, and I was anxious over how well the different materials would fit together. But over the course of the semester, my students assuaged my concerns, drawing lines and points of connection inside the textual-filmic assemblage of the class that I had only dimly perceived as it was coming together in my sketchbook. I came to learn that the set of films, clips, images, and texts I had brought together for the course—as always in a zone of uncertainty and indecision that students never see—were enfolded in a thick web of convergences, not all of which were apparent to me when I had selected them. Students, through their own ongoing conversations about the materials, color-stained those transparent but durable nodes of contact. The seminar turned into a multidimensional pedagogical space, where the impressions of images, affects, and bodies were cycled between participants.

This process highlighted Eve Sedgwick's question—used as an epigraph to the class syllabus and to this chapter—"Is it true that we can learn only when we are aware we are being taught?"[1] In Sedgwick's essay "Pedagogy of Buddhism," this question indexes an insight of affect theory that is consonant with her reading of Buddhist epistemology: that knowledge production consists of an ensemble of material processes—practices of understanding flowing through bodies on multiple levels—rather than the digital transcription of data from text to body. Sedgwick articulates this in terms of the difference between knowing and realizing: different corners of the body, different channels and buried cisterns, can know a thing in different ways and at different times. Sedgwick calls this the phenomenology of knowing. "In modern Western common sense," she points out, "to learn something is to cross a simple threshold; once you've *learned* it you *know* it, and then you will always know it until you *forget* it. . . . In this model, learning the same thing again makes as much sense as getting the same pizza delivered twice."[2] But for Sedgwick, pedagogy is about circulation, opening up the possibility of repetition, reiteration, mutation, and transformation as a field of experiences intersects with the concealed and submerged layers of bodies.

Sedgwick's essay is also about globalization, the way that Buddhist epistemology was transmitted to the West and reconfigured through multilateral processes of cultural reconfiguration and embodied recognition. The American Transcendentalists, for instance, saw their own thought as already formed by Asian influence.[3] As discussed in chapter 2, Sedgwick posed the possibility that this global unfolding was better understood as a dynamic of what she called recognition of intransigent affective forms across contexts rather than a unidirectional distortion of a religious tradition in order to fit it into a new market. The process of globalization is, in a sense, a bricolage, a surge of elemental forms that swirls between bodies through technologically mediated channels.[4]

Bricolage is not collage. Where collage presumes an open field of materials, bricolage assembles an artwork out of a limited set of objects available in the environment. French sculptor Hubert Duprat has, since the 1980s, carried out experimental art projects illustrating this technique with caddis fly larvae. These trichopteric worms gather materials—plant matter, sand, mollusk and crustacean shells, small fruits, coniferous needles—from their environment and glue them together with silk emissions in order to create sturdy, tube-shaped carapaces.[5] Duprat collects the worms from rivers, gently removes their existing carapaces, and replaces them in artificial ecosystems containing precious stones and metals. In this in vitro environment, the larvae harvest this new palette to construct glittering, polymorphous carapaces.

I argue that this process is best understood as a sort of pedagogy. The caddis fly larva is taught by its environment. The forms available to it become part of the repertoire of a self-formation. Each animal is a magnetic vector constituting a material history, an accumulation of intransigent shapes configuring a distinctively textured body. But the bricolage method is not entirely composed by the world around it: the bodies at the core of it also have preferences and variations.[6] The entomologist Irina Soukatcheva writes that this variegation of capacities and tastes emerges against the backdrop of an evolutionary history, an unfolding panoply of bodily intuitions.[7] Duprat noticed that even discarded carapaces themselves become features of the environment, provoking new reactions and configurations.[8] The pedagogical process, the protocol of globalization, is a dynamic of bodies and worlds, a history formed by the collision of material and embodied histories operating not in the fluid space of discursive plasticity, but a repertoire of intransigent elements.[9]

This chapter illustrates how the phenomenological branch of affect theory models global religion. In addition to the economic, ethnic, nationalist, technological, and historical forces shaping its cross-currents, global religion emerges from the arrangement of affects along relays formed by intersecting bodies and media technologies. This web of religious forms is not a sand castle, a perfectly plastic nanocreation: it is a circulation of intransigent embodied affects—bodily technologies created by evolutionary forces in deep time. Rather than a top-down design or even a collage that gathers from an unlimited range of materials, global religion is a bricolage, a compendium of locally available forms resonating with textured bodies.[10] Any religious artifact could help to illustrate this animal patterning, but the premise of REGC was that contemporary cinema is a particularly effective medium of globalization because of the intimate overlap it stages between bodies, technology, globalization, and affect.

To this end, I rehearse the close reading of the 2006 documentary feature film *Jesus Camp* that emerged out of the multidirectional conversational flows of REGC. This film, focusing on the transformations experienced by children's bodies through exposure to international networks of media, practices, and affects, draws out the theme of pedagogy I want to develop here. Furthermore, I suggest in the conclusion that an examination of the white American evangelical context provides a valuable lens for repudiating a set of intertwined presuppositions about white religion. Rather than seeing white religion and American Protestantism as the triumphant radio frequency of civilization—as the culmination of an angelic human subject's separation from animality—this approach draws these forms within an animalist frame, highlighting how they are constituted by affects, embodied histories, and the accidental global regimes diagrammed by new media technology.

The interpretation presented here was created by the conversations of my REGC class. Where a particularly salient point was brought forward by another participant in the seminar, I have attributed it accordingly. However, in many respects this chapter should be considered as a coauthored work between me and fifteen students, both a recapitulation and an extension of a field of conversations that emerged in a shared pedagogical space.

Combinatorium: Religion, Globalization, and Intransigence

Manuel Vásquez has suggested that the materialist shift in religious studies is particularly helpful for thinking religion in the context of globalization—"the constant movement, contestation, and hybridity involved in what has been called popular religion—religion as it is lived in the streets, workplaces, and schools, for example, by poor Latino immigrants as they settle in small towns in North Carolina or Nebraska."[11] But Vásquez has also suggested that to overemphasize mobility—what he calls "excessive fluidism"—loses sight of how religious forms are sustained in the process of distribution.[12] To begin our seminar's conversations about globalization, we read from Srinivas Aravamudan's *Guru English*, an exploration of the relationships between language, religion, and the global dynamic of cosmopolitanism. Aravamudan's project starts by tracing the history of English on the South Asian subcontinent through the intertwined channels of religion and empire. English was adopted by certain classes of Indian society, producing a fusion with local linguistic and inflectional forms. This new creation eventually emerged as a hybrid intellectual voice with its own ability to play the strings of the global network of English-language speakers.[13]

From the late nineteenth century onward, this voice interfaced not only with seemingly secular English-based domains such as politics, literature, and academic research, but with religion. Through skilled, novel redeployment of the English language by Indian religious figures— transnational gurus from Swami Vivekananda to Deepak Chopra—in conjunction with selected elements of Indian religious traditions, what Aravamudan calls Guru English emerged as a heterogeneous set of discursive forms and practices with global reach.[14] Guru English transformed Indian religion into a global power apparatus by piggybacking on preformed imperial language networks. Aravamudan calls Guru English a theolinguistics, a flexible, heterogeneous register of discourses out of which religious meaning can be manufactured.[15]

In class, we discussed the imagery of fluidity in Aravamudan's work as a heuristic for understanding Guru English as a sort of cultural liquid: Aravamudan encourages us to think of language as flow—as "mutant, recombinant, and morphing under the conditions of globalization."[16] But the fluid metaphor of Guru English only takes us so far. Guru English, Aravamudan makes clear, isn't just a vapor, but a chunky, heterogeneous cascade, a living, mobile assemblage not of droplets but of parts, semistable forms that are replicated, recombined, and mutated over the course of their ongoing global dissemination.[17] Guru English, Aravamudan writes, is an ensemble, a "set of images, representations, and vernacular expressions and colloquialisms" that attach themselves to local cultural forms using English as a global distribution system.[18] Guru English produces a postsecular "free-floating *combinatorium*" within which elements of global religious repertoires are folded together under a supererogatory Hindu triumphalist frame.[19] As a global network, it produces meanings through a circulation and recognition (in Sedgwick's vocabulary) of intransigent shapes rather than through an undifferentiated liquid.[20]

Students pointed out that although the Guru English model provided a useful template for understanding globalization, it remained within a linguistic orbit that focused on religion as a literature rather than as a suite of embodied affects. They noted that although Aravamudan has moments when he seems to map the attachment of linguistic forms to affects, he focuses most on the intersection of discursive forms with economic dimensions, Guru English as a "commodifiable cosmopolitanism" flowing over and reshaping global conceptual archives.[21] This is where, as the anthropologist Kevin O'Neill has suggested, a turn to contemporary affect theory can productively supplement existing understandings of globalization, setting the stage for the reading of cinema as imaging and performing globalized religion in this chapter.[22]

Contingency: The Pedagogy of Affect

From the account of globalization offered in Aravamudan, we began to look for ways to connect his pedagogical approach to affect. Pedagogy has been addressed by a number of affect theorists,[23] but here I focus on the work of Teresa Brennan and Sara Ahmed, who helped our class adapt Guru English as a model for the global rotation of affects. Brennan's *The Transmission of Affect* is structured around a disruption of what she diagnoses as a delusion at the heart of Western thought: the "foundational fantasy" of the subject's autonomous self-containment. Rather than being secured within solid borders, Brennan suggests, we must return to an understanding of bodies as interlaced with other bodies and spaces surrounding us. Rather than individuated subjects, bodies are radically interconnected—global—constituted by a dynamic of transformative affective flows enfolding us in intimate proximity with other feeling bodies.

The memorable opening image of Brennan's book illustrates this: the moment when a body walks into a room and "feels the atmosphere." This universal experience of feeling the atmosphere, Brennan writes, is not merely observational, but transformative: the affects of the room are incorporated. What Brennan calls the transmission of affect (TOA) materially "alters the biochemistry and neurology of the subject," subtly reshaping the embodied circuits of the body.[24] In agreement with many affect theorists, Brennan believes that bodily habits are accumulations of these affective compounds, spirals of thoughts, sensations, images, words, and other affects instilled with deep dimensions of affective resonance.

This reshaping takes the form of entrainment—the transmission of an affective state felt by one body to another body through proximity. The channels of TOA can be olfactory (the wafting of hormones through the air), tactile, sonic (tones of voice, volume, rhythm), or visual (images, bodily postures, facial expressions).[25] These transmissions produce physically transformative effects—mutations sedimented within embodied histories.[26] TOA slits the foundational fantasy by highlighting the cumulative, constitutive rotation of affective impressions between bodies.

The particulars of Brennan's work have had an inconsistent reception among contemporary affect theorists,[27] but the basic blueprint of TOA is widely accepted in phenomenological affect theory. In class, we followed Brennan's work with Sara Ahmed's *The Promise of Happiness*, in which Ahmed builds on Brennan's interest in the "atmospheres" that surround and shape bodies. But Ahmed also modifies Brennan's emphasis on entrainment by refocusing on what she calls "conversion points," moments when an affective transmission is redirected rather than replicated.[28]

For Ahmed, reception of affect is an active process. In Ahmed's TOA, bodies are impressed by the shaping currents of the world, but intransigent features of bodies also exert their own influence to pattern that reception. "If bodies do not arrive in neutral," she writes, "if we are always in some way or another moody, then what we will receive as an impression will depend on our affective situation. . . . *To receive an impression is to make an impression.*"[29] The pedagogical space is not constituted simply by a passive field of receptors, but by a recursive dynamic of embodied histories receiving impressions, marking, scoring, and reshaping them, then rebroadcasting them to other bodies.[30] TOA is not only a unidirectional broadcast—a signification—but a queer recursion, a dynamic of spiraling transmission and reconfiguration.[31]

For Ahmed, the starting point for the study of affect must be what she describes in *Promise* as the drama of contingency, the "messiness of the experiential, the unfolding of bodies into worlds . . . how we are touched by what comes near."[32] This motif appears at least as early as Ahmed's 2004 *Cultural Politics of Emotion*, where she emphasizes "the 'press' in an impression."[33] Impressions transform us, in-struct our bodies in an ongoing pedagogic encounter with the world. We are always in dynamic relations with objects leaving their mark, things in the world—including emotions—shaping the horizons of our experience. Intransigent emotions create the surface of the self by absorbing an endless series of intersecting, broken, but resolute waveforms from the world. The globalized self is a living contact zone of sensations, a felt embodied history.[34]

Ahmed insists, then, on the performative dimension of affects, their ability to do things, to instrument a set of relationships, to in-struct or in-form (rather than merely reflect, record, or document) the felt sense of reality that structures our encounters with power. If the phenomenological horizon of the body is constituted by a tissue of affectively charged objects, then not only do bodies change, but the horizon of political awareness itself evolves.[35] Pedagogy is about transforming the way the world feels, rather than simply absorbing knowledge: the body "learns by *switching affections*."[36]

This capacity for in-struction, though, means the drama of contingency is played out in a field of intransigent forms. The pedagogic contact zone is an accumulation of shapes rather than a purling of liquids. Ahmed describes the phenomenological horizon of experience as the interior of a sphere constituted by the dense accumulation of affective objects. Objects stud what Ahmed calls our "near sphere," the "world that takes shape around us . . . a world of familiar things." Our "likes," Ahmed suggests—the concrete shapes of desire—"establish *what we are like*."[37] Our embodied history corresponds to the bricolage of one's affectively collected objects, our "biographies of likes and dislikes."[38] Rather than a liquid, the force of affect binds us, like the silky glue of a caddis fly worm, to an assemblage of hard objects.

The chunky raw materials making up the contact zone between bodies and worlds—the membrane between bodies and power—include not only a range of unnamed forces, but the named affects or emotions. For instance, what Ahmed describes as "economies of hate" function through the correlation of certain bodies with specific, intransigent affects—especially fear and hatred.[39] Subjectivities are constituted within fields of superimposed, globalized relationships informed by these affective structures. The same could be said of happiness, an affective element with a distinct power to compose near spheres and also horizons of future promise. These promises are passed around between bodies, creating durable global networks of power.[40] The raw materials of globalization, then, are not a pool of liquid, but a combinatorium, a zoo of forms, the finitely many ($n > 2$) textures proposed in Sedgwick and Frank's reading of Tomkins.

In the remainder of this chapter, I want to restage our conversations from REGC on Grady and Ewing's *Jesus Camp*. Through these conversations, we explored how the film not only imaged but enacted the spin cycle of globalized religion. Cinema—an iconography of movement and bodily forms—is a media technology uniquely capable of redrawing regimes of power by rotating emotions between bodies. As M. Gail Hamner writes, "the viewing of film can function as an ethical 'pedagogy of self'" that fashions affective structures into political networks embedded in bodies.[41] Through global media, a collection of images, texts, religious traditions, and affects are inserted into a combinatorium that connects bodies to a heterogeneous global register, against the backdrop of which religions and other durable formations of power are devised.

Kids on Fire: *Jesus Camp*, Pedagogy, and Affect

Churches our God likes to go to . . . our churches are jumping up and down, shouting His name and just praising Him. They are not acting. They are not quiet—"We worship you." They are "Alleluia! God!" You know, and . . . and depending on what . . . how they invite Him, He'll be there or not.
—**Rachael Elhardt,** *Jesus Camp*

Our discussions of Heidi Ewing and Rachel Grady's *Jesus Camp* as a recursive image of globalized religion drew on two strands of thought: we concluded that the film was both a documentary text that explores the spread of global religion in America during the presidency of George W. Bush and a performative iteration of globalized religious sensibilities that resediments affectively circumscribed postsecular communities. The film accesses and recharges the affective landscape of the mid-2000s culture wars in the United States, at the same time as it traces the ways that contemporary globalizing technologies have plugged the heterogeneous U.S. cultural reservoir into a transnational economy of image and affect flows that is reshaping local configurations of religion.

The documentary tracks a group of white American children from their homes in the Midwest through their attendance at a series of evangelical Christian youth events, with a long middle section focusing on the Kids on Fire School of Ministry (KFSM) summer camp in North Dakota. The KFSM camp, led by the organization's director, Becky Fischer, is depicted as a space where extraordinary emotional reactions are elicited in children's bodies. Children weeping, wailing, entranced, scornful, fearful, speaking in tongues, preaching, awestruck, and transported by joy form some of the most stunning images of the film. The documentary is framed by excerpts of a Christian radio program, *Ring of Fire*, in which the liberal Christian Mike Papantonio expresses his alarm at the coalescence of religion and politics in contemporary American society.

One of the most striking features of the documentary's release in 2006 was its bifurcated pattern of reception. The film came out against a backdrop of American cultural polarization, in which the loose left-right divide that characterized twentieth-century American politics had evolved into a much deeper and more expansive set of binary cultural coordinates—red state versus blue state, "retro" versus "metro," "makers" versus "takers"—mapped onto a highly complex landscape of class, race, geographic, and gender parameters. The 2001–2009 Bush presidency—the outcome of a disputed election in which Bush lost the popular vote but claimed victory through the electoral college—accelerated this national fission.

Of particular concern to many of Bush's detractors was the twenty-first-century Republican Party's campaign to increase the representation of evangelical Christianity in civil and public life. This included the appointment of religiously conservative Supreme Court judges such as Justice Samuel A. Alito Jr., whose confirmation battle is reported in snatches of radio broadcasts in the opening and closing sequences of the film. The documentary's most controversial image shows the children of KFSM praying over a cardboard cutout of President Bush. Although the ABC network report that described this as children "worshiping" Bush was an unaccountable error,[42] the image is emblematic of an alliance between a politicized Christianity and an increasingly ideologically extreme Republican Party, what William Connolly labels the "evangelical-capitalist resonance machine" in his landmark analysis of twenty-first-century American politics, *Capitalism and Christianity, American Style*. It is this machine that is imaged by this film.

Against this polarized background, *Jesus Camp* spoke a double language—both entraining affect and producing affective conversion points, with commensurate political effects. As a record of the emotional intensity elicited and transmitted by evangelical Christian youth groups, it was viewed favorably by many conservative Christians, especially charismatic evangelicals, but with horror and alarm by many on the political left and center. Tory Binger and Rachael Elhardt, two of the film's young Christian protagonists, writing a few years later on a website created by Fischer to promote a book Fischer published to manage reactions to the film, describe how they initially did not understand why the film was contentious. Rachael states that "for the first several years after it was released, I didn't understand all the controversy surrounding it. For me I was watching great memories in high definition."[43] Fischer went on tour in support of the film,[44] and on her website and in her book republishes letters she has received from around the world documenting transformative experiences other Christians have had after viewing it. "This is why I did not denounce the movie, cry 'foul,' or fight the filmmakers for what I felt was the inappropriate political slant," she writes. "I knew there was enough really good stuff in the movie that if the right people saw it, it would impact lives."[45]

For Fischer, the film itself is a religious vehicle. Although she is dismissive of Grady and Ewing's decision to frame the film according to the political controversy surrounding the Alito nomination, she points proudly to a specific scene in which the children are filmed passionately chanting for "righteous judges" to overturn *Roe v. Wade* two weeks before Justice Sandra Day O'Connor announced her resignation, an event that opened the door to the eventual appointment of Alito to the Supreme Court:

> So while [the filmmakers] were seeing political overtones through secular eyes, we believe we captured a spectacular moment on camera where these children's prayers were answered! You might say, yes, but thousands of Christians everywhere have been praying for the overturn of *Roe vs. Wade*. You can't give all the credit to those children! . . . Correct. But look who God chose to spotlight! "The least of these"—Children! You can't help but say the sequencing of these events was very interesting just at a time when this film was being made to be shown on TV and in theaters across America![46]

Fischer understands the film as a divine tool, an instrument of God plugged into a U.S.-Christian media assemblage.

At the same time, the reception was overwhelmingly negative from other quarters—what Fischer collectively refers to as "the secular market." Fischer was forced to shut down the camp almost immediately after the film's release after incidents of vandalism and harassment of the campers. The film was nominated for an Academy Award in the Best Documentary category (along with Al Gore's *An Inconvenient Truth*), suggesting an affinity with the liberal Hollywood establishment that had by 2006 already mobilized in opposition to Bush. Watching the film in class at Haverford, a predominantly left-liberal college, I asked students to reflect on how their own affective positions within this political-cultural matrix were activated and reinforced—or redirected—by the film. Most reported that they felt discomfort or horror at the events depicted in the film, though some complicated that affective response by adding that it also helped them to better understand the skein of motivations that made this particular iteration of religion possible. Becky Fischer writes that Heidi Ewing told her, "'It was like people were watching two different movies. They either loved it or hated it.' That's been my experience exactly."[47] The disparity between how the film was viewed by insiders and outsiders of the community mapped and intensified the network of the mid-2000s culture wars, reflecting the highly complex, postsecular affective landscape of early twenty-first-century America.

What Does *Us* Feel Like? Globalizing Felt Boundary Markers

God . . . I'm here to be trained.—**Becky Fischer,** *Jesus Camp*

What is fascinating about *Jesus Camp*, however, is that the binary frame its critical reception highlights—between insiders and outsiders—is shown, within the film, to be the composite product of a multidimensional global media network—a set of images that have been assembled into religio-political formations. As Melani McAlister writes, "it is no longer possible to understand US evangelical politics or culture without understanding its border-spanning investments."[48] For instance, Becky Fischer mentions several times throughout the film that she sees KFSM as a reaction to the training of children by "our enemies," by which she seems to mean something like a militant, politicized Islam. "Where should our focus be placed?" she asks in an early interview, as images of children from KFSM events flicker on the TV screen of her living room, then continues:

> I'll tell you where are our enemies are putting it. They are putting it on the kids. You go to schools. . . . You go in Palestine—and I can take you to some websites that would absolutely shake you to your foundations, and show you photographs of where they're taking their kids, camps like we take our kids to Bible camps—and they're putting hand grenades in their hands. They teach them

how to put on a bomb belt. They teach them how to use rifles. They teach them how to use machine guns. It's no wonder, with that kind of intense training and discipline, that those young people are ready to kill themselves for the cause of Islam. I wanna see young people who are as committed to the cause of Jesus Christ as the young people are to the cause of Islam. I wanna see them as radically laying down their lives for the Gospel as they are over in Pakistan and Israel and Palestine and all those different places, you know, because we have—excuse me! But we have the truth![49]

Fischer's project does not emerge ex nihilo. It is constituted through her contact with a technologically mediated global network of highly affectively charged images. Specifically, by consuming pictures of militarized Muslim bodies, Fischer's body entrains a global current of felt boundary markers—from media-savvy Muslim militants, through the transnational digital transmission of images, to a set of pedagogical practices in American Christianity. These labile nodes of power are constituted by a complex of affects including not only fear, defiance, and rage, but also a subtler, unnamed affect corresponding to the embodied sense of group solidarity: what *us* feels like. Fischer's body is a relay, the locus of a global pedagogy, patching in a swirl of religious imagery and intransigent emotional textures and producing a new configuration of power.

This pedagogy of felt boundary markers is not limited to the transnational scale: *Jesus Camp* also calls attention to the ways that media networks circulate perimeter-making affects even within national borders. For instance, the right-wing Christian radio broadcasts skirmish with Papantonio's *Ring of Fire* program in the soundscape of the film. The right-wing broadcasts are first heard over a bricolage of Midwestern American highway scenes: God Bless USA signs, intertwined Christian and American flags, strip malls, and sprawling church complexes. Over this compilation we hear President Bush's affected Texas drawl announcing the search for a new Supreme Court justice, then a battery of blaring talk radio preachers declaiming in tense, seething voices:

- I believe as Christian citizens of this country we should be actively involved in this historical moment.

- And if the churches across this country, believers can come together and take a stand, I think it's gonna have a powerful, powerful impact on this process.
- We dare not sleep through this decision because frankly, future generations depend on us!
- We are engaged today in what they call a "culture war." We did not start it but, we, by his grace, are going to end it!
- And we should say: Yes, we want to reclaim America for Christ![50]

Thick, vivid boundary markers are transmitted through voice in these broadcasts. There is an acute sense not only of a felt *us*, but of a particular affective configuration of *us*, a carapace made out of a particular set of affective materials: rage, fear, righteousness.[51]

The liberal Christian radio broadcaster Mike Papantonio has a different affective orientation. This is transmitted to us through his facial expressions and speech patterns, which express an appeal to shared values rather than focused, lashing rage. These affects create a different pattern of boundary making, a differently textured perimeter. "None of this really makes any sense for me," he starts, incredulously.

So there is some new brand of religion out there. It's somehow that things have changed since Matthew, uh, wrote . . . uh . . . wrote about Jesus's Sermon on the Mount where Jesus told us to be peacemakers. And right now they . . . everything they do, they say, they do it in the name of God. That we need to go to war in the name of God. They are being told, by George Bush, of all people—he is the holy man who has been anointed with the job of . . . of creating a Christian society not just in America, but all over the world. You and I know that's false. This entanglement of politics with religion. What . . . what kind of lesson is that for our children?[52]

The word *children* is assigned two different affects by these jousting speeches: in the right-wing broadcasts *children* becomes a hypervulnerable object that must be protected at all costs, a vector of fear making. In Papantonio's speech, *children* is a reservoir of shared hopes, a field of promise. The printed text only captures one fixed plane of this heterogeneous, three-dimensional affective landscape. An interplay of vocabulary, imagery, and rich vocal registers defines this intranational globalization, a technologically mediated suite of affectively distinct boundary-making strategies.

These intranational globalizations animate other spaces documented within the film. At the house of Levi O'Brien and his family in exurban Missouri, Levi's mother walks her son through a homeschooling curriculum, teaching an itinerary of talking points against global warming: "What if you have to go to a school where you were told that creationism is *stupid*? And you're *stupid* if you believe in it?,"[53] she asks her son. The word *stupid* is almost spat, invested with acute poignancy. It is heavy with anger, reflecting an embodied history of epistemic marginalization and shaming now liquidated by blazing defiance. Levi repeats his mother's talking points with conviction, absorbing not only the propositional content but the affective valences of her speech. Discussing the importance of homeschooling her children, Levi's mother states confidently that "our nation was founded on Judeo-Christian values," and "our firm belief is, there are two kinds of people in the world—people who love Jesus, and people who don't."[54] The zeal not only against external threats, but against putative internal threats such as liberalism and secularism, is mobilized using a ring of affective technologies that fuse bodies and media in affectively determined power formations. As McAlister writes, "evangelical hearts have enabled evangelical political commitments."[55]

These affective boundary-making technologies are deployed within Christianity, as well. When Rachael Elhardt is interviewed at a campground, for instance, she describes how churches are divided into "dead churches" and "churches in motion." "Churches our God likes to go to," Elhardt continues, "our churches are jumping up and down, shouting his name and just praising him. They are not acting. They are not quiet—[stilted voice] 'We worship you.' They are 'Alleluia! God!' You know, and . . . and depending on what . . . how they invite him, he'll be there or not."[56] For Rachael, boundary markers distribute religious bodies according to a set of affective bodily practices. Her miming of the different worship styles of Christian churches establishes a boundary that has nothing to do with propositional beliefs, and everything to do with affective orientations. These political boundaries are made not by doctrines, but by exclamation points.

A fascinating coda that ties together the intranational and extranational processes of felt boundary making comes at the very end of the film, during the closing credits: Rachael in Washington begins witnessing to a group of older black men engaged in conversation in a park: "If you were to die right now," she asks the nearest man, "where do you think that you would go?"

"Heaven."

"Really? Are you sure?"

"Yeah."

"Okay."

She returns to her friends, unbowed, and dismisses the encounter, saying, "I think they were Muslim."[57] Here, the parameters of race and religious otherness (why does a nine-year-old white girl from exurban Missouri know what a Muslim is, except that she has been taught an affectively charged vocabulary of who she is not?) shuffle together. The failure of her witnessing is read through the prism of racial alterity and then coassembled with a broader discourse of religious alterity. The intersection of global and local maps of alterity is redeployed in a visceral game of border making. A set of perimeter-forming affects define this process, driving the mechanisms of global community formation and rejection.

What Does It Feel Like to Be *Us*? The Materialist Phenomenology of White American Evangelicalism

The affects linked to border making are only one facet of the globalized network of religion depicted in *Jesus Camp*. American evangelicalism draws on a rich repertoire of embodied affective technologies that become its stable material components: what get circulated by evangelicalism are intransient feelings, which are repurposed and repackaged for different formations of power. The felt sense of *us*—an esprit de corps—is one such affect, as well as the fear and drama of militarized displays that reverberate through the global network of images and form the emotional textures of borders. (Your children are fearsome? Then our children are fearsome, too.) But other affects emerging out of globalized, material embodied histories are also embedded in this complex.

The opening assembly at the camp in North Dakota offers a panorama of the affective technologies deployed by this religious community. The session begins with music and dancing; the children's faces are smiling and joyful as they clap and bob in place. Tory Binger, who was earlier interviewed about her passion for dance, takes to the rhythm like a fish to water: this is her thing. When Fischer emerges (after we see her backstage, carefully coiffing her hair), she starts her sermon off with a joke—"How do you guys like the hair?"—patting her curls.[58]

But the emotional timbre of the sermon moves on quickly, taking on a succession of different shapes. Fischer begins a section on temptation using a pair of toy lions. Terror is etched on the children's faces as Fischer describes the grave power of sin. "The devil goes after the young," she warns heavily, her voice and sharp facial expression conveying the impact of her meaning far more than her script.[59] What Rudolf Otto calls *grue*, "the ensnaring attraction of the ghost-story," spills out of Fischer's speech, amplifying the ambient, horror-movie atmosphere she has already created in the room.[60] The tenor of the room resembles Ann Pellegrini's description of evangelical Hell Houses, which "draw upon even as they move to recode experiences of 'safety' and 'fear,' 'reality' and 'unreality,' in the service of a fundamental spiritual transformation."[61] Fear is deployed not to repulse the congregation, but to ensnare it in a new religio-political regimen.

Suddenly, her discourse takes a hard turn. She begins stabbing the air with her finger and her cadence becomes punchy, staccato: "And while I'm on the subject, let me say something about *Harry Potter*. Warlocks are *enemies of God*! And I don't care what kind of hero they are: they are enemies of God, and had it been in the Old Testament, Harry Potter would have been *put to death*! You don't make heroes out of warlocks!" Like Disraeli's audience in Oxford, her congregation cheers their assent.[62] The violence of Fischer's remarks is all the more shocking for the abruptness with which they break into her discourse. It feels like an ad lib, an actor's playful improvisation designed to thrill the audience as she descends deeper into the affective simulation of her character. This time the affect resonates with Pellegrini's description of the Westboro Baptist Church's music videos and the "gleeful enthusiasm" they express as they outline their vindictive fantasies.[63] There is a sense in which Fischer, through her body and tones of voice, is singing a song to her audience, gilding them with rage.

Fischer changes gears again, beginning an eerie ritual of condemnation and penitence with the children. "There's some kids here that say they're Christians," she admonishes passionately. "They go to church all the time, but you're one thing when you're at church, and another thing when you're at school with your friends. You're a phony, and a hypocrite. You do things you shouldn't do. You talk dirty just like all the other kids talk dirty. And it's time to clean up your act. Come up here and get washed. Because we can't have phonies in the army of God. If that's you, put your hands up here."[64] The performative force of her accusation activates a vivid collective expression of shame among the children, who raise their hands and weep while a woman wails in the background. One boy falls to the ground and plants his face against the floor. Teresa Brennan's observation that the transmission of affect within a group can have recursive and cumulative effects that are greater than the sum of its parts—that the "emotions of two are not the same as the emotions of one plus one"—is on full display in this scene.[65] A felt alchemy of shame circulates diametrically from body to body in the space, gaining momentum as it jumps.

This embodied sense of shame enfolded into religion recurs a few minutes later, when an unnamed blond boy with a book in his hand takes the microphone and begins an impromptu speech. "Uh . . . I . . . uh . . . haven't got much to say," he begins, his eyes pulling downward, his vocal inflection declining, and his head softly shaking from side to side, expressing a subtle shame or uncertainty:[66]

> I just wanted to talk about belief and God and . . . I've had a hard time doing it and . . . it's just really hard to do this . . . just to believe in God is really hard because you don't see Him. You don't . . . you don't . . . really know how much. Sometimes I don't even believe what the Bible says. It makes me *a faker*. It makes me feel . . . guilty and bad 'cause God has always talked to me about that and I kinda . . . rejected Him.[67]

The entire monologue is a rich, embodied performance of shame—neither inauthentic nor spontaneous—a set of postures, vocal tones (the word *faker* is subtly stressed in such a way as to almost suggest a savoring of the deep cut it inflicts), and narrative fragments that concentrate the felt shame of the speaker and display it for the audience—what Sedgwick calls the "blazons of shame."[68] The boy is then shown seated on the floor of the stage, slumped, raising his palms and his face up to the sky, the other members of the assembly studying him carefully (figure 3.1).

In class, students debated whether the boy was making a confession that could be viewed as resisting the parameters of the space—the presumptive spiritual and moral fortitude of children—or was in some

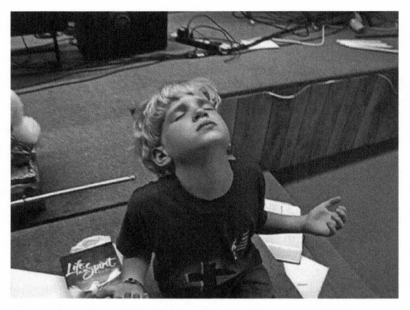

3.1 Religious shame. Screen captures from *Jesus Camp*, directed by Heidi Ewing and Rachel Grady.

way reinforcing the existing regime of embodied desires by putting his shame on display. I can see both sides of the argument, but my own inclination is to read the performance as a display of an affect that is part of the living religious architecture of the space.[69] His bodily postures and the tones of his voice take priority over the propositional content of his speech in casting the meaning of the miniature sermon. Crucially, rather than portraying shame as an aversive emotion, shame is being picked up and plugged into a religious power grid. As Sedgwick writes, shame, understood queerly, is not merely repressive, but can be generative and even pleasurable in the play of identities, expressing "its own, powerfully productive and powerfully social metamorphic possibilities."[70] The blond boy's shame becomes a focal point for the group, a thick, pulsing strand shaping the transmissive atmosphere of the space. Brian Massumi's interpretation of the melting snowman film is productive here as well: what are consumed are not "happy" or "sad" emotions, but dimensions of intensity: the more shameful the better.[71] We see the impressions of a pedagogical regime not only in the conceptual content of all these moments, but in their presentation of a particular arrangement of intransigent affects. These children are being taught not only what *us* feels like, but a specific configuration of what it feels like to be *us*.

We see this pedagogy of affective instruction in action again on the closing night of the camp, when a guest preacher, Lou Engle, spontaneously calls Levi up out of the audience and prophesies over him in a husky, resonant voice:[72]

> ENGLE: Here's the deal. Before you were born, God knew you. *Extraordinary*. He said this. He said He formed you in your mother's womb. You're not just a piece of protoplasm—*whatever that is*! [Engle mugs to the audience and Levi smiles broadly.] Not just a piece of *tissue* in your mother's womb. You were created intimately by *God*. Is that incredible? God wrote a book about your life and He wrote, "Levi . . . Levi would be a God seeker from an early age, and he would become a voice that touched America. And he would not sell out in his teenage years. He would go for God all those days, and he would be a man of prayer. And in his twenties, he began to shape things real strong for God and in the nation." God's dream: *The Novel of Levi's Life*. Signed: God. What do you think of that?
>
> LEVI: 'S pretty cool! [smiling and nodding excitedly]
>
> ENGLE: Pretty cool, huh? You're pretty cool![73]

Here, an entwining of religion and affect is passed from the older man to the younger. A thrilling, affectively charged narrative—a prophecy—is recited in awed tones to impress on Levi the passion, dignity, and excitement of their shared faith. This is the pedagogy of global religion: the transmission not of knowledge, but of affective shapes between bodies. Through a display of affects, Engle is instructing Levi, singing him a song to teach him what it feels like to be *us*.[74]

These swinging political borderlines also intersect with an affectively crafted gender binary. In a late scene, Engle is shown applying red strips of tape with the word LIFE printed on them to the mouths of the KFSM campers and asking for their names as he passes them. Addressing two boys, he says: "[Who's this] young man, Gideon? Gideon? You'll be a mighty warrior for God. There you go, son. . . . Here you go, Joseph. Someday you might be the leader of the government. You never know, Joseph." And then, to a young girl: "What's your name? Allison? You look great with that tape on your mouth."[75] What we see in this scene is a pedagogy of gender, a way in which adults provide children with sex-specific instruction in religious affects: boys are encouraged to think of themselves as ambitious, powerful, and dynamic, girls as visible and passive.

The affective ramifications of this gendered pedagogy are played out in an interview toward the end of the film, in which Rachael and Levi are asked about the concept of "spiritual warfare." The gendered dimorphism of their answers is instructive of the ways that gender coassembles with affect and religion in American evangelicalism:

> LEVI [focused, concerned]: We're being trained to go out and train others. Train others to be God's army and to do God's will. What *He* wants you to do.
>
> RACHAEL [excited, eager]: I feel like we're kinda being trained to be warriors, only in a much funner way. We don't like . . . I don't feel the sense of like afraid to die in battle or anything like you would when you're actually going off to a war in the physical. There's a peace with it all too. There is an excitement yet peace at the same time. It's really cool!
>
> LEVI [cool, reserved]: You know . . . a lot of people die for God and stuff, and they—they're not even afraid. They don't get afraid of it or anything.
>
> RACHAEL [excited]: And it is like . . . I heard Dad told me like when their dads are like missionaries and stuff and they had to go to somewhere really dangerous and stuff they jumped around them and yelling: "Martyr! Martyr!" It's really cool [nods].[76]

Levi and Rachael are speaking the same vocabulary, but they diverge so sharply in the affective meanings that they use to flesh out this single concept that they are, in fact, talking about two different things. Rachael understands God's army metaphorically, as an index of the excitement and passion of faith. But Levi feels the religious meaning of the concept using a very different set of affective forms: for him, it is about nobility, command, and sacrifice—possibly even violent self-sacrifice. It is an open question whether *warfare* for Levi is a metaphor at all. For both, the meaning of the concept—the way it links their bodies to power—emerges out of a gendered ensemble of affects produced by a pedagogical apparatus, rather than by abstract propositional content.

The deployment of the word *war* in this film is a fascinating subject for an examination of globalized American religion in its own right. It begins with the invocation of the culture war in the collage of right-wing Christian radio broadcasts in the opening sequence. Military imagery appears as early as the conference at Mission Church where Fischer first meets O'Brien. During the service, children perform a militaristic marching dance in camouflage costumes and face paint while a speaker declares, "There has never been a generation like this one. The Earth is filled with dead and dying . . . in spirit and body. But now is the time for the glory of the Lord to cover the Earth as the water covers the seas."[77] Later, Fischer's male campers will also wear military-style costumes (while the girls dance in leotards). Fischer chants, "This means *war*! This means *war*!" during a KFSM song about sin. And Ted Haggard cheerfully announces, "It's massive warfare every day!" with reference to the upcoming Supreme Court confirmation battle. The most fascinating moment in this process comes when a camp counselor has the children pray over the cutout of Bush, instructing them to "do some warfare over him."[78] The film assembles a miniature narrative depicting how the word *war* becomes a sort of magnet, attracting multiple configurations of affect—entrainments and conversion points—that are then cycled over into new semantic registers. The meaning of the word *war* indexes a global sedimentation of affective attachments rather than a dictionary definition. It turns into an affective invocation that is then creatively— even playfully—redeployed in new contexts.

Children's bodies have a special status in the religious network of KFSM. Fischer explains this in an interview at the outset of the film, describing how children's bodies are highly susceptible to the affective intensity of religious pedagogy: "I can go into a playgrounds [*sic*] of kids that don't know anything about Christianity, lead them to the Lord in a matter of . . . just . . . no time at all and . . . and just moments later they can be seein' visions and hearing the voice of God because they're so open. They are so *usable* in Christianity." Their religious "usability," Fischer explains, is because of their affective hypersensitivity.[79]

At the same time, children's bodies in this matrix are not just passive recipients but active components building a field of globalized religion. Fischer is seen on several occasions watching video clips of her KFSM campers. In a late scene, Fischer is seen in her living room at night, viewing especially emotionally vivid footage, her mouth hanging slightly

3.2 Watching images of religious affects. Screen captures from *Jesus Camp*, directed by Heidi Ewing and Rachel Grady.

open, her eyes wide and her head shaking back and forth softly in wonder (figure 3.2). A box of tissues sits next to her on the sofa. It is difficult to tell if she is at work or at play. Plugged into a network of electronically disseminated images, Fischer's embodied, affective technologies are drawn out by the children's bodies on screen. Their religious affects become a new religious entertainment for grown-ups around them. Children's bodies themselves—imaged in global media technologies—are gathered into the bricolage of religion.

And for us as well, I realized—our postsecular bodies build affective systems out of the embodied practices of scholarship and media consumption. In the seminar, we discussed the ways that we were made particularly uncomfortable (or not) by the transmission of images of highly affective children's bodies. The film would not have had the impact it did in either the evangelical or "secular" markets if it had been about an adult evangelical camp: the liberal-left students at Haverford consumed it as a sort of horror movie/call to action because of the age of the bodies depicted. This is not a conceptual horror or an impassive affirmation— a cool reflection on the ways children's bodies are enfolded into religious projects in contemporary white-dominated American evangelical spaces. The children's bodies become the vector of the steep emotional impact of the film for viewers because they are children's bodies, no matter whether that emotional impact is read as disgraceful or inspirational. The political impact of the film, for both audiences, is effected by the capacity of children's bodies to amplify affective transmission.

A double layer of embodied histories—deep-time histories crafting a set of intransigent affects, and pedagogical histories directing those affects into local configurations of power—collide in the production of religious and postsecular bodies. As Levi O'Brien writes in his reflections a few years after the release of the film: "It wasn't anything anyone ever said or did that convinced me to serve God with all my heart. It was when I experienced Him at the altars in those meetings, when I felt the God of the universe rushing through me as I prayed, or when I felt heat pulse in my hands as I watched someone get healed by the power of God."[80] Religious bricolage is created out of this dynamic stitching together of powerful affective technologies embedded in bodies and distributed through pedagogical practices. The film shows how a catalog of affective technologies—a finitely many $(n > 2)$ range of felt textures—becomes the raw, durable materials of religion transmitted through recursive global networks.

"What Really Is Brainwashing?"

So while the public schools [are] telling them they're animals, they're the product of natural selection, we tell 'em God loves you. God's created you. You have a purpose in life! I mean, the kids are . . . just lovin' it!
—Ted Haggard, Jesus Camp

Jesus Camp evoked two regimes of interpretation among viewers: while some found the extreme expressions of religion alarming, others experienced them as inspiring and godly. Jesus Camp, I found, is difficult to teach to some undergraduates because it provokes such visceral currents of rage that the unraveling operation (and the analytical affects such an operation demands) I want them to perform on it is pushed to the background. These regimes of interpretation were not passive sets of hermeneutical coordinates, but pedagogical practices in their own right, practices that continue to rewrite and quicken the dynamic global network of religious bodies. In short, this analysis would not be complete without asking a question that came into sharp focus for the class over the course of a semester's worth of conversations: what does this film do to us?[81]

The double audience of the film is reflected in a decision made by the filmmakers to frame their narrative inside Papantonio's radio broadcast criticizing the politicization of U.S. Christianity. For a certain audience of the film—an audience largely, but not entirely, reflected in our classroom[82]—this broadcast reflected their own concerns about the elicitation of extreme emotions in children as part of a religio-political training regime. The Papantonio segments gave voice to this secular-progressive Christian perspective, articulating a classical liberal argument against "chipping away at separation between church and state."[83] This point of view gave voice to the left-wing backlash against Bush and the influence of evangelical Christians in U.S. politics in the mid-2000s—a backlash that was still palpable and intelligible to my students at a northeastern liberal arts college in 2013.

The traditional mode of film analysis that explores how directors use camera work and mise-en-scène to generate cinematic meaning is provisionally helpful here. Unlike the right-wing Christian radio broadcasts that are heard only in a pastiche of overlapping truncated soundbites, Ewing and Grady give Papantonio a sustained platform to articulate a liberal vision of religion dutifully extracted from politics. Papantonio's radio booth seems lukewarm, measured, and calm—perhaps reflecting what Rachael Elhardt called the "dead church" sensibility—a tranquil oasis within the cinematic maze of highways, roadside advertisements, and religious signs of the rural Midwest and the affectively flooded scenes at KFSM in North Dakota. Directorial decisions help to create this enclave of liberal testimony within the filmic space, and so set the stage for the production of a bifurcated regime of interpretation.

But this conventional approach only carries this analysis so far, because it cannot be said that there is a substantial difference in how Becky Fischer and Mike Papantonio are shot by the directors. In terms of framing and composition—the decisions made by directors—they are more or less isomorphic, with a mix of full-face close-ups and medium-range body shots while they speak. One could make the argument that Papantonio is never directly interviewed by the filmmakers and therefore is denied an accessible platform to present his ideas: since Papantonio is never given a chance to directly address the camera (unlike Fischer, Levi, Rachael, Tory, their parents, and Haggard), the case could be made that his perspective is objectified in a way that makes him more distant to the viewers. But I think this is a dead-end analysis. Instead, to understand what the film does to us, how it teaches viewers to feel, we need to look at the bodies moving onscreen—not only their words, but their repertoires of intransigent affects.

Like Fischer, Papantonio's language traffics heavily in an *us–them* binary, but with a different affective sheen: his face expresses concern and humility; he comes across as pleading, rather than angry and denunciatory.[84] The way this *us* feels is different from the *us* shaped by the white/conservative Christian radio broadcasts and Fischer's ministry in North Dakota. This divergence comes into sharpest relief when Fischer calls in to *Ring of Fire* to discuss her work. Even when Papantonio launches into what seems like a strident condemnation of Fischer, saying, "God is watching us, and God has a very special place for those people who mess with our children," there is a strangely friendly core to his accusation.[85] The printed text almost shows this with the way that Papantonio uses the collective *we* and *us* rather than a bitter and accusatory *you* or *them*. But the most important pedagogical work is done in the vocal tones of the dialogue: Papantonio transmits a very subtle, nuanced affect to his conversation partner. He is trying, I would suggest, to gently shame her, to reteach her by illuminating a different affective orientation, a different way for her body to fit into *us*. This conversation, relayed into the global mediascape, is itself a religious micropedagogy.

The dialogue between the two Christians is a face-off between rival pedagogical regimes—different distribution patterns for the affects studding religious worlds. Papantonio and Fischer are trying to teach other bodies around them by rearranging affects through words:

PAPANTONIO [bemused, incredulous]: Ehhhhh you can tell a child *anything*. Just like I say you can tell a child, ah, you can make a child into a *soldier* that carries an AK-47.

FISCHER [slightly exasperated]: You can call it brainwashing, but I am radical and passionate in teaching children about their responsibility as Christians, as God-fearing people, as Americans if you wanna take it there.[86]

The most glaring difference here is in how the two factions use the word *soldier*. For Lou Engle, Rachael, Levi, and Fischer, the language of militarism is a dynamic and vital mode of religious expression—a lexicon heavy with pride and a trace of threat.[87] Papantonio, by contrast, attaches horror to the word *soldier*—especially the child soldier. With his voice, he tries to rearrange the affective shapes around this index of bodily practices. In her countermove, Fischer taps into and enhances the palpable sense of pride and dignity shaping the perimeter—what Ahmed would call the skin or the near sphere—of what she sees as her community: "Christians . . . God-fearing people . . . Americans." Through their exchange, they are mutually shaping each other's affects—in addition to the affects of the multiple audiences tapped into their cat's cradle of superimposed digital broadcasting technologies.

Papantonio summarizes his argument against Fischer's indoctrination of children by launching into a passionate articulation of liberal orthodoxy,[88] demanding that religion be confined to the private sphere: "I respect your right as a fundamentalist to teach your children whatever you wanna teach 'em, but don't let that bleed over into the public sector. Don't let that bleed over into the schools."[89] While Fischer disputes that Christianity should be kept out of the public sphere, she also insists that her project is not political. She affirms that she is "not going after [her] kids politically," a sentiment she immediately follows up by stating, "At the same time I wanna say, and I don't have any problem saying to my children, we are pro-life."[90] Where Papantonio maintains a liberal optimism toward the line of separation, Fischer neatly indicates the complexity and the porosity of the religious-secular divide.

In our end-of-semester discussion, one of the seminar participants asked whether or not affect theory fatally complicated the presuppositions of liberalism: does the liberal model of the separation of church and state dissolve when we imagine bodies as fluid systems of force? Where Papantonio wants to draw a sharp line between the religious and the political, we concluded that the affective approach to globalization means not only the sharp complexification of nation-state borders, but the washing-out of liberal private/public sensibilities.[91] Affect theory is not compatible with classical secularism. It suggests that affective residues cannot be confined to the political or the religious spheres, that public and private are a Möbius strip of intertwined power relations rather than walled gardens. In this sense, affect theory is postliberal and postsecular. Religion, as Connolly writes, "surges into the pores and pulsations of politics."[92] Affect theory indicates animal political actors—moving, interlocking bodily economies—rather than autonomous, rational subjects. Papantonio's claim that his brand of Christianity is not a politics, just as much as Fischer's, is unintelligible from this perspective. Both build formations of religious power by drawing together specific affective clusters.

This is why Fischer's question, "What Really Is Brainwashing?"—posed as a section title on her blog—is apt. Fischer understands that her pedagogy competes on an affective rather than a theoretical game board for the hearts and minds of her pupils. She defends herself against the accusation of brainwashing not by reinscribing the public/private distinction, but by pointing out that the concept is incoherent, that "brainwashing" is everywhere. "Brainwashing," she writes, "is the deliberate, systematic bombardment of ideologies and concepts aimed at a group of people to sway their beliefs. Based on that definition, the American children and youth are being brainwashed every day through books, movies, television, the internet, the music they listen [to] and our school systems."[93] From the perspective of the affective turn, Fischer is correct. Affect theory, in emphasizing the animality of bodies, points to the way that we are crosscut by striations of force recorded in multiple, articulated embodied histories. Brainwashing is a form of pedagogy,[94] and pedagogy is always happening: bodies are always wrapped up in the folds—the overlapping rings of impressions—of globalization. The medium of brainwashing is the avalanche of affect cascading through global media networks and everyday embodied encounters.

How, then, does the film train us, if we are slotted into separate pedagogical regimes by our patterns of reaction at the outset? Are the parallel affective-interpretative regimes of *Jesus Camp* two onanistic, self-contained circuits? Is there a sense in which *Jesus Camp*, although it has the unique feature of landing happily in two different postsecular folds, can only ever be an inert pedagogy, a "preaching to the choir"? Lauren Berlant encourages us to ask a different question—a question emerging from an analytics of affective pedagogy: *What does preaching to the choir do?* "When an intimate public is secreted in its own noise," she writes, "it rehearses affectively what the world will feel like when its vision gains mass traction. At the same time, though the strength of any political movement depends on persevering in the face of the inevitable kinds of internal dissent that will put at odds people also bonded through critique. But perhaps reinforcing intimate binding is the main function of avant-garde counternormative political work."[95] As Pellegrini writes,

"Conversion is never a finished process, and [evangelical religious theater] is as much about reconfirming the individual participants in their faith commitments as it is about spreading the Good News to others."[96] Political affects can operate as a pedagogy even when transmitted within "ideologically" uniform global networks.

This postsecular pedagogy reinforces and expands a set of affectively sculpted perimeters, an embodied history of what it feels like to be *us*. The rehearsal of love, of consonance, of outrage, or of loathing is nonetheless a pedagogy, no less than practicing a musical instrument, a martial art, or a dance. *Jesus Camp* is both a documentary ethnography and a reinscriptive pedagogy. The seemingly secular audience, too, is fascinated by children's bodies contorted by mind-bending religious affects. We, too, in the seminar, absorb the play of boundaries. We, too, repeat and recalibrate how it feels to be us. No matter what interpretation my students walk away from the film with, they are being affectively instructed by it in ways that always and of necessity bleed across the public-private boundary.

Conclusion

For Vásquez, globalization is about the "portability of religion today, the videotaped sermons, ritual objects, traveling spirits, self-help New Age paraphernalia, architectural patterns, liturgical styles, sacred music, and missionary subjectivities that enter transnational and global networks."[97] But affect theory takes the materialist shift even further, exploring not only the circulation of material forms, but the distribution of intransigent affects across global networks. Ann Pellegrini writes that religious realms are constituted not by linguistic operations, but by the transmission of affect, "points of contact that can jump across theological differences and even the differences religious/secular."[98] Pedagogy swirls affects into bodies, creating sedimented, animal subjectivities that cannot be carved at the joints into political and religious modes, but travel through fields of power. Global media networks move these intransigent affective forms from place to place and body to body.

Cultural and religious texts are technologies for the distribution of affects. Film is distinctive within this field because it brings not only language but bodies and voices into the global register of religious meaning making. Where Guru English is a theolinguistics, film is better understood as a theokinematics: it animalizes religion by offering a repertoire of embodied responses as the material of global religion. The pedagogy of affect theory is about teaching students to trace meanings that are outside of propositional content, attuning them to the play of affects both contingent on and exterior to language. Studying films only by reading their scripts misses how they participate in an embodied dynamic of globalization. As some students in the seminar insisted, watching *Jesus Camp* helped them better understand how religion happened. The ligaments of power activated by affect had been felt for them, not merely read or conceptualized.

This focus on attunement to a combinatorium of animal religious affects has an antecedent in Alphonso Lingis's *Dangerous Emotions*. Lingis imagines a global relay system through which emotions flow between animal and human bodies.[99] In the chapter "The Religion of Animals," Lingis diagrams how affect and animality coassemble into shapes that inform human religious worlds.[100] Animal affects supply the raw material for the ongoing bricolage of embodied histories. Other bodies instruct us in the composition of religious affects using a combinatorium of shared affective technologies.

The decomposition of the assumption that religion is unaffected by animality, emotion, and global history also destabilizes a set of background coordinates surrounding European/settler religion—namely, the myth that white Protestantism is uniquely self-governed and self-lawed, that it represents a pinnacle of convergence between religion and reason, that it calls out stage directions while the rest of the world dances. Affect theory highlights how the production of white religion is itself a global, animal process. Globalization is not something that happens only to the colonized. It is not only brown bodies that have their religious worlds reconstituted by the emergence of a global affectscape: the global networks of power, capital, media, imagery, and affects also impress, reshape, rearrange, and spin Euro-American bodies. White Protestantism, too, is ecological—albeit an ecology that is wrapped in the veneer of what Brennan calls the "foundational fantasy" of insularity, autonomy, and inner destiny. By analyzing the ways that white religion is constituted by affective histories, we can reanimalize whiteness, setting it against the backdrop of a global pedagogical network within which it is immersed and by which it is produced.

On the first day of Religion, Emotion, and Global Cinema, we discussed a still image from *Jesus Camp*. It shows Tory Binger, holding a

3.3 Transmission of affect as circuit of power. Screen captures from *Jesus Camp*, directed by Heidi Ewing and Rachel Grady.

microphone in her hand (she is reciting Bible verses) as tears stream down her grimacing face (figure 3.3). At the same time, her free hand is raised skyward. Students quickly pointed out that there is a strange tension in the composition of the image: Binger is weeping, suggesting sorrow or shame, while her hand is elevated, suggesting authority, control, drama, power. Students also noted that Binger in this image is at the center of a circle of bodies, all facing her. Some of those bodies—including adults—have their arms raised as well, imitating her gesture.

This image captures the complex work that *Jesus Camp* does in documenting and performing the correlation of religion and affect—the global field of multilateral power relations that affect theory helps to map out. The shot of Tory is an image of embodied power: holding a microphone that broadcasts her voice throughout the room, she becomes the center of a system of embodied flows of religious attention, making bodies move. Her microphone is also plugged into a global network of identity, status, religious practice, entertainment, consumption, hope, and scholarly attention. Her intransigent affects are magnified, replicated, inflected, converted, and reversed across this global mediascape. This is how affect theory encourages us to think globalization: not just as a proliferation of connections, but, like a caddis fly worm, as a field for the distribution of intransigent affects—as a pedagogy mediated by technology and structured by colliding layers of embodied histories moving at different speeds. Religion circulates images and affects, composing a global dance of imitation, repetition, reconfiguration, and transformation. The effect of this dance is a living, glittering, polymorphous carapace, a textured material interface between bodies and power.

FOUR

COMPULSION: AFFECT, DESIRE, AND MATERIALITY

Everywhere Proust contrasts the world of signs and symptoms with the world of attributes, the world of pathos with the world of logos, the world of hieroglyphs and ideograms with the world of analytic expression, phonetic writing, and rational thought. What is constantly impugned are the great themes inherited from the Greeks: *philos, sophia, dialogue, logos, phone.*—**Deleuze,** *Proust and Signs*

In Henri Charrière's autobiographical novel *Papillon,* a prisoner pursues a series of escapes—known as *cavales* ("horse runs") in his jailhouse slang—from the pre–World War II penal colonies in French-dominated South America. The book's narrative tension is created by the abrupt oscillations of the story, from the sun-drenched travelogues and joyful camaraderie of the cavales to the increasingly brutal punishments inflicted on Papillon and his fellow prisoners when they are recaptured; the eight-inch centipedes climbing the cell walls; the ocean-side jail in Santa Marta, Colombia, where the rising tide brings a wave of black sewage into the dungeons; and the sadistic guards, who escalate their torture of the prisoners after each escape.

But none of these images actually express what, for Papillon, was the most devastating punishment inflicted on him: his years of solitary confinement. The image of a body held inside a cell—uninjured but isolated, its basic needs for food, water, and shelter satisfied—can't compete with the gruesome visuals we associate with torture. Like a weapon that leaves no bruises, solitary confinement as a form of torture is selected not least because its damaging effects elicit no sympathetic response on the part of onlookers. And yet Papillon insists that solitary confinement was so painful, he preferred the sewage of the jail. Rather than mutilating bodies, solitary confinement mutilates affects.

If the horrific suffering that this torture by subtraction inflicts cannot be rendered in imagery, it also cannot be easily expressed in language. We feel no twinge of horror when reading about a body punished in time rather than space.[1] This limitation betrays a critical failing of the linguistic fallacy: the inability to explain how a body can be bored to the point of torture is a function of a mistaken understanding of bodies as autonomous, reasoning, speaking subjects who operate within a fundamentally linguistic medium of power. Solitary confinement shows up the lie of what Jacques Derrida calls "auto-affection," the myth of our own sovereignty over our emotions.[2] This carno-phallogocentric discourse denies bodies our animality, our attraction to the world independent of a set of linguistic maxims. It sees us as angels hovering above the fray, only voluntarily choosing to run into the world.

Affect theory offers an alternative model, in which affects have their own capacity to articulate bodies to systems of power—what this chapter calls compulsion. The compulsion of affects can be drawn out by starting with a simple question: Why is solitary confinement torture?[3] Although the body looks like a physical object with a fixed location in time and space, affect theory proposes that bodies are anticipating things, compelled to form relationships with worlds. A body is always pulsing in currents of affect formed by a biological footprint configured by the finely grained, sedimented strata of an embodied history. To extract animal bodies from the buzzing, blurry sources of meaning that surround us is to violently sever the ligaments of our affective economies. Bodies cannot be switched on or off by sovereign selves.

Lauren Berlant writes that to study affect is to "think about sensual matter that is elsewhere to sovereign consciousness but that has historical significance in domains of subjectivity."[4] Where traditional poststructuralist critiques of the coherent liberal subject exerting sovereign will over its body have been strictly negative—telling us what bodies are not—affect theory supplies vocabulary for mapping these nonsovereign selves, diagramming bodies as heterogeneous economies of pulsing, intransigent forces. Affects are not passive receptors of inconsequential feeling that serve as window dressing on the linguistic architecture of power; power moves bodies through the pulsing of mobile, uneven affective systems. The linguistic *I* is a figurehead monarch in this field of recalcitrant attachments.

This chapter moves through three illustrations highlighting how compulsory affects articulate bodies to networks of power outside of the intervention of sovereign consciousness. The first is solitary confinement, analyzed in terms of Lisa Guenther's critical phenomenology. The liberal model of the autonomous self cannot explain solitary confinement: sovereign subjects are not vulnerable to isolation because they have no intrinsic relationship with their worlds. Only if we start from the assumption that bodies are affectively dependent on worlds rather than self-lawed does the capacity of solitary confinement to inflict pain make sense. A second image of compulsion is presented in Berlant's notion of cruel optimism. Berlant cycles through a series of case studies in which affects tether bodies to worlds, overwhelming the material or psychological priorities of selves. Affect theory sees these compulsions as the productions of attachments that move at cross-purposes with "what is good for us"—cruel optimisms. Finally, Marcel Proust's exploration of the desire for objects, bodies, and affects brings affect theory into conversation with contemporary work on material religion. Thinking affect as compulsion thematizes the sovereignty of affects over selves, the ways affects surge through bodies to produce formations of power, including religion.

Papillon

THE DRY GUILLOTINE: WHY IS SOLITARY
CONFINEMENT TORTURE?

The intellectual historian Caleb Smith has argued that the development of solitary confinement—the extreme isolation of bodies as a mode of punishment—reflects an understanding of the self that tracks the advances of Western modernity. In *The Prison and the American Imagination*, Smith charts how shifting theories of the subject produced a new approach to punishment in which prisoners were obliged to confront their crimes by being placed in a space of radical introspection: solitary confinement.[5] The inventors of modern solitary confinement believed that the "radically individuated citizen-subject's" isolation would produce a self-disciplinary, therapeutic effect that would rebirth criminal bodies as virtuous, autonomous members of society.

But Smith documents how, from the very beginning, experiments in the use of solitary confinement in the nineteenth century rapidly turned into "a notorious massacre," with many inmates committing suicide or going mad.[6] As Beaumont and Tocqueville wrote in their discussion of these experiments in the United States, "absolute solitude, if nothing interrupts it, is beyond the strength of man; it destroys the criminal without intermission and without pity; it does not reform, it kills."[7] As Frans de Waal, developing an evolutionary theory of sociality puts it, "Next to death, solitary confinement is our most extreme punishment."[8] Papillon and his fellow French prisoners nicknamed the solitary confinement chamber "the dry guillotine": not merely a deprivation, but a mind-destroying torment.[9]

Charrière describes the experience of solitary confinement as excruciating. In an environment designed as a vacuum of stimulation—lightless and soundless, guards and prisoners wearing slippers to muffle their footsteps—the *reclusionnaire* begins to suffer from an "intolerable pressure in his head."[10] Charrière corroborates Smith's descriptions of prisoners deranged by the isolation: "Suddenly a cry, a horrible anguished cry of despair, penetrated the door of my cell. What was it? It sounded like a man being tortured.... No doubt someone had gone mad. It was so easy in these cells where nothing happened."[11] The prompt for this torment is not physical torture, but absence itself—the frustrated compulsion for contact. Bodies in solitary confinement are not subjected to violence. Instead, the breaking of the affective links to the world produces suffering.

Prisoners are driven so far in their need for an affective portal into the world that they provoke confrontations with their guards—"Just to hear voices," Charrière writes, "just to have somebody speak to you even if he only said, 'Go ahead and croak, but shut up.' "[12] As this cycle unfolds, the prisoners are subjected to retaliatory violence. But even this, Charrière insists, is preferable to the suffocating void of their cells, hence the prisoner's defiant cry to the guard trying desperately to control him with threats and intimidation: "What's worse than this silence? Punish me as much as you like, cutthroat, beat me if it makes you happy, you'll never think of anything worse than this silence."[13] *Reclusionnaire* bodies subtracted from their phenomenological matrixes are suffering bodies, bodies thrashing to create new affects.

Papillon survives this slow, invisible torture by creating devices that give exercise to his body's compulsions rather than allowing them to be extinguished: "What matters," he realizes, "is that I have to furnish these days, hours and minutes with something, all by myself, alone."[14] Realizing that his sovereign consciousness is not in charge, Papillon finds ways to produce affects by, for instance, marching in rhythm "like a pendulum," or allowing himself to indulge in vivid, hallucinatory fantasies.[15] Papillon's body, twisted by absence, fills up his sharply contracted world with "furniture," giving run to compulsions rather than pretending to be inert.

Like the eponymous butterfly tattooed on his chest, then, Papillon must "fly." But this is not to succumb to the gleeful but simplistic romanticism of his memoir—to lapse into a metaphysics of "freedom" that rejects *tout court* the body's radical relationality. Such a naive libertarianism could not explain the torture of solitary confinement because it fails to grasp the body's dependency on other things. Papillon must fly, must drift off into garish hallucinations, must move in his cell like a living pendulum, not because of a romantic destiny, but because his affects are sovereign: his body gives him no choice. It is not his human dignity that makes him fly, but the compulsions that are the substance of his animality.

AMPUTATION: INTERANIMALITY AND THE BEHAVIORIST FALLACY

Our own body is in the world as the heart is in the organism: . . . it breathes life into it and sustains it inwardly, and with it forms a system.
—**Merleau-Ponty,** *Phenomenology of Perception*

The acute suffering inflicted by solitary confinement suggests more, then, than a set of shifting discursive frameworks for understanding subjectivity. No one taught or told Papillon to suffer in *la mangeuse d'hommes*—even though local histories can lend their impress to the experience. Papillon as swinging pendulum is an ontology—an intransigent, onto-phenomenological structure of animal life—that diagrams the moving architecture of feeling bodies. This is the approach taken by philosopher Lisa Guenther in her *Solitary Confinement.* Guenther points out that "while penal codes, theories of criminal justice, and psychologi-cal terminology have all changed over time, the symptoms of solitary confinement have remained strikingly consistent."[16] It is on the basis of the intransigent efficacy of solitary confinement as a technique of torture—the way that susceptibility to solitary confinement emerged as an essential feature of mammalian life[17]—that she builds her argument.

For Guenther, human bodies need to be in relationship with other bodies. Solitary confinement "works by turning the prisoner's *consti-tutive relationality* against herself, turning her own capacities to feel, perceive, and relate to others in a meaningful world, into instruments of her own undoing. *This self-betrayal is only possible for a being who is complicated, whose subjectivity is not merely a point but already a hinge*, a self-relation that cannot be sustained in absolute solitude, but only in relation to others."[18] The excruciating effectiveness of solitary confine-ment reveals human bodies' compulsory relationality, our connection by skeins of animal affect to the worlds in which we are embedded.

Guenther fleshes out the detail of her project through a critique of behaviorist psychology, a school of thought dominant in the American academy throughout the mid-twentieth century. Behaviorism under-stands bodies as free-standing stimulus-response machines—detached "black boxes" that produce outputs according to associational program-ming. Emotions, in this view, are unnecessary explanatory tools that had been eclipsed by the discovery of conditioning. Like the antibiologist school of high humanist "theory" critiqued by Eve Sedgwick and Adam Frank,[19] depth and complexity, behaviorists believed, could not exist without a sedimentation of cultivated associations best understood on the model of language.

This framework led to the classic behaviorist question: What happens if you extract a body from its world? Which behaviors would be shown to be innate to the organism, and which learned? This question created an extraordinary regime of violence written on the bodies of animals in-volved in lab work: cats with amputated forepaws or atrophied optical nerves, rats kept for the entirety of their natural lives in total isolation, then subjected to a blitz of light and sound, monkeys with surgically de-stroyed eyes.[20] These images encapsulate the behaviorist model, ampu-tating the body from its environment by extinguishing its relationships with its world.[21] Along the same lines, behaviorists saw no intrinsic harm in removing human beings from their relationships with others.[22] Behaviorism offers a portrait of bodies unscathed by isolation.

But while behaviorism was thriving in the United States, a rival school had emerged in continental Europe. Known as ethology, this approach from the biological sciences—focused on studying animals in their natural habitats—would have a major influence on the development of twentieth-century phenomenology.[23] "We no longer regard animals as mere machines," wrote Jakob von Uexküll, the founder of ethology, in his 1934 essay "A Stroll through the Worlds of Animals and Men," "but as subjects whose essential activity consists of perceiving and acting."[24] Rather than solitary or detached, animals for the ethologist are essentially active, essentially interwoven with their worlds. The medium of this essential activity, for von Uexküll, is the *Umwelt*, the lifeworld of individual animals determined by a set of intersecting embodied histories. Von Uexküll describes, for instance, the tick, for which the physiological markers of its food source—a nearby mammalian body—"shine forth from the dark like beacons."[25] These beacons make up the lifeworld of the tick, the vivid channels of its compulsion and desire. More complex organisms, von Uexküll suggests, inhabit more complex lifeworlds, from the spider to the astronomer.[26]

Crucially, for von Uexküll, these relationships must not be understood in terms of detached perceptual transmissions. An Umwelt is a field of connections, a mobile, thrumming phenomenological relay system. "As the spider spins its threads," he writes, "every subject spins his relations to certain characters of the things around him, and weaves them into a firm web which carries his existence."[27] The Umwelt is itself an organism, a living thing that cannot be decomposed without torturing the body. From the ethological perspective, animal bodies form intractable affective economies linking them with their lifeworlds.

This phenomenological understanding becomes the basis for Guenther's analysis of solitary confinement.[28] Guenther follows mid-twentieth-century phenomenologist Maurice Merleau-Ponty's critique of behaviorism as a model that artificially divorces organisms from the web of meaning-making processes that enfolds them.[29] The Umwelt is not just a neutral field of survival, but a richly necessary space in which animals "struggle to maintain a *meaningful*, integrated and open-ended relation to [their] environment as a whole, including the other living beings with whom [they share] a common Umwelt."[30] Behaviorist procedures of knowledge production—such as confining animals in cages or disabling their sensory organs—do not discover a truth about bodies as isolated stimulus-response agents: they manufacture radically disrupted bodies by immersing them in pathological situations in which their lifeworlds are ripped apart.[31] The laboratory cages, the solitary confinement cell, and the abstract, rationally calculating subject are all echoes of the same liberal model of bodies with no necessary relationship to the network of affects holding their worlds together.

For Guenther, the phenomenological approach derived from von Uexküll and Merleau-Ponty provides a provisional answer to the question of why solitary confinement functions as torture. Bodies in solitary confinement are removed from the sustaining relationships of their lifeworld, their felt connection points with beacons of meaning making. If, as Merleau-Ponty writes, "Our own body is in the world as the heart is in the organism,"[32] then solitary confinement "deprives the prisoner of the bodily presence of others, forcing her to rely on the isolated resources of her own subjectivity, with the (perhaps surprising) effect of eroding or undermining that subjectivity."[33] The constitutive relationality of bodies in their lifeworlds—what Guenther, following Merleau-Ponty, calls our interanimality—compels us to find beacons lancing out from the darkness. This compulsion is the kind of being we are—an ontophenomenology that maps why bodies feel the way they do—and why solitary confinement, the elimination of our affective oxygen, functions as torture.

EN CAVALE

The metaphors of *Papillon*—cavale, butterfly—speak to an ontophenomenology of bodies that supersedes the self-lawed, autonomous model of self by reaffirming animality. Bodies are not inert physical objects that choose to enjoy, feel, or experience. They are constituted inside a current of affects pulling them into networks of affectively mediated relationships. Isolation cuts the prisoner off from the matrix of desires that define the shape of a living world. To cut the tendrils of that shape is to make a bloody incision, even in the absence of a physical wound. This is what it means to be a body: to live inside economies of sovereign, recalcitrant compulsions extending into the world, binding with objects and pulling bodies behind them. Animality is compulsory affectivity, to be en cavale, horsey, butterflyesque. Bodies are desire in motion. Animals are moved by subtly rich and urgently necessary land-scapes of emotion.

Frans de Waal has called humans "obligatorily gregarious," writing that "origin stories that neglect this deep connection by presenting humans as loners who grudgingly came together are ignorant of primate evolution."[34] This is Guenther's approach as well, focusing on the ways that imprisoned bodies, even when they have access to "everything that an individual human being needs in order to survive," as well as "extras" such as TV or even CCTV teleconferencing with visitors, experience the excruciating pain of deprivation.[35] But I would go further and suggest that we are obligatorily affective: that animal bodies are, in every moment, seeking, desiring, and flowing in anticipation of all kinds of things in their worlds. This is why the solitary confinement regime Papillon describes includes not only solitude, but darkness, silence, and boarded-up windows. It is not only other bodies that our bodies need, but the array of materialities—colors, shapes, images, sounds, voices, motion, change—living and nonliving, that make up the affective beacons of animal lifeworlds. Affect theory, in concert with Guenther's critical phenomenology, corrects the presupposition that we are angels, that we can dictate to our bodies how to feel about our world, or lack thereof. It shifts the focus from religion as an ensemble of well-thought-out rationales to the animal religion of endless chase, being en cavale: our fragility, our compulsion, and our need.

Cruel Optimism

AFFECTIVE APPROACHES: VITAL MATERIALITY
AND SOLITARY CONFINEMENT

Merleau-Ponty writes that phenomenology is a philosophical practice for "relearn[ing] to *feel our body*."[36] Compulsion is important to the phenomenological tradition represented by von Uexküll, Merleau-Ponty, and Guenther, but the critique of behaviorism offered by critical phenomenology also dovetails with affect theory. Silvan Tomkins has his own concerns with behaviorism, which he criticizes for treating emotion "as though it were a means to the end of guaranteeing learned behavior." With his characteristically odd mixture of upper-middle-class aloofness and casual canniness, Tomkins goes on to dismiss this as "a craft union's view of the matter, and a particularly American view of it. Everyman is and always has been more interested in just the opposite question—*what must he do to guarantee that his life will be exciting and enjoyable?*"[37] In other words, where behaviorism sees affect as a means to an end, Tomkins insists that "*affect is an end in itself,* with or without instrumental behavior."[38] Eve Kosofsky Sedgwick glosses this by explaining that an affect "can be *autotelic,*" a self-enclosed telos. Affects are their own imperatives, blithely inscribing their own paths through fields of power and pulling our bodies behind them.[39] Compulsion is not about the future utility of an affect. Affect itself is the pulsing lifeblood of the Umwelt, the electricity that makes beacons call out to us.

How would affect theory offer a response to the question of why solitary confinement is a form of torture? It is worth starting with affect in the Deleuzian/Spinozist sense. Spinoza's approach, later absorbed into the Deleuzian model of affect, is an ontological project that reconceives all material bodies as existing on a single plane of substance—a "plane of immanence," in Deleuze's term, alive with transformation, always tremulous with affect. Jane Bennett, who calls Spinoza her "touchstone," reframes affect in terms of what she calls *vital materiality.* For Bennett, "organic *and* inorganic bodies, natural and cultural objects . . . *all* are affective." Affect in this Spinozist frame means "the capacity of *any body* for activity and responsiveness."[40] Body—for Spinoza and Bennett—means any material thing, any figment of the plane of immanence. Bennett is interested in the way that objects seem to evoke an affectively lively world of their own, which she plugs into Spinoza's word *conatus,* the "trending tendency to persist" found among all bodies.[41] Rather than trying to press human bodies down to the level of matter, Bennett's project is fundamentally one of bringing matter up to the level of vitality, of assigning every material object, every body, the aspirational striving of conatus, a share in the swishing play of affects.

The notion of matter as vital offers another way of thinking solitary confinement's effect on bodies. Confinement is a constriction, a binding of bodies that would seem to crush the growth, motion, and transformation that is the essence of Spinoza's picture of affective life—a suppression of becoming, a suffocation of vital materiality. But to say that all bodies are affective in the same way is not adequate to the question of why solitary confinement functions as torture. Suggesting that Papillon suffers in the same way as, for instance, the cot in his cell, is a nonstarter. More than just a compulsory affectivity that marshals the entire plane of immanence into a rippling tide of shifting affect, this book is interested in com-pulsory affectivity, a refocusing on biological bodies, things that have a pulse.

Phenomenological affect theory raises the analytic level of affect from the ontological to the biological. This shift enables a focus on feeling bodies, rather than the emphasis on the play of substances on the plane of immanence among Deleuzians.[42] From the perspective of phenomenological affect, the Spinozistic tendency to refer to all material things as bodies is misleading. Bodies—animals with particular onto-phenomenological configurations—are a special artifact of evolution, and the technical term that distinguishes them not only from other living organisms but from nonliving organisms is worth preserving as a central category of inquiry. This is the risk of forgetting phenomenological affects, even as ontological studies of affect open up profoundly important questions in ecology, politics, and science and technology studies. Papillon's anguish in his cage is only intelligible when we take this phenomenological viewpoint, a perspective that is perched at a different register than Spinoza's ontological affects.

On the other hand, there is a sense in which Bennett's insistence on the vitality of nonliving affects is productive for thinking the animality of bodies. It suggests the ways that embodied affects are not only intransigent, but recalcitrant: the ways that affects kick back. Material affects passing through the body take on their own modes of agency, overthrowing the fiction of the sovereign self. Bennett describes a simple example of this, eating potato chips and finding her body continuing to eat them even after she tells herself to stop. "To eat chips," she concludes, "is to enter into an assemblage in which the I is not the most decisive operator."[43] Compulsory affects, rather than angelic consciousness, maneuver bodies within fields of power. Phenomenological accounts of affect that merge this recognition of the recalcitrance of affect with a sense of how it feels to be nonsovereign are vital to understanding the way bodies are articulated by compulsions to systems of power. This is illustrated in the solitary confinement thought experiment as well as in Lauren Berlant's concept of cruel optimism.

BAD ROMANCE: CRUEL OPTIMISM
AND NONSOVEREIGN BODIES
Swann's love had reached the stage at which the boldest of physicians or (in the case of certain affections) of surgeons ask themselves whether to

deprive a patient of his vice or to rid him of his malady is still reasonable or indeed possible.—**Proust,** *Remembrance of Things Past*

Ordinary affects highlight the question of the intimate impacts of forces in circulation. They're not exactly "personal" but they sure can pull the subject into places it didn't exactly "intend" to go.—**Kathleen Stewart,** *Ordinary Affects*

The same animal affectivity that is used against prisoners in state torture is part of a broader category of instances in which the fiction of the autonomous subject is disrupted by compulsion—what the affect theorist Lauren Berlant calls *cruel optimisms.* Berlant defines optimism as the structure of attachment.[44] Like Sedgwick, Berlant stresses the flexibility of these attachments, but also points out that although optimism suggests a particular feeling state, attachments "do not all *feel* optimistic"—attachment can feel like dread, rage, or shame.[45] What Berlant means by *optimism* is what I term the compulsion of affect. Berlant, like Guenther, Merleau-Ponty, and Papillon locked in his cell, know that the felt lines between bodies and worlds are thick, living, pulsing veins, not a grid of wires supervised by a self with its finger on the switch.

Berlant describes the shape of optimistic attachment as "knotty tethering to objects, scenes, and modes of life."[46] *Tethering* suggests the tensed relationship—a relationship with spring in the system—of affects as pulling on bodies even when the self is looking away. The knottiness of the tethering is its historically derived complexity, the way that it is produced by overlapping intransigent forms that bunch it up, leaving it queerly patterned by circularity, confusion, and convergence. Those tethers may be shaped by language, but they cannot be reduced to language. They are how animals are guided through landscapes of power—the living parameters determining where bodies go.

In her book *Ordinary Affects,* the anthropologist Kathleen Stewart offers a series of illustrations of how these multivalent attachments move bodies. Ordinary affects, Stewart suggests, *can* be pleasure in "a clever or funny image, or in being able to see right through things, or in holing up to watch your favorite bad TV show, or in spinning classes at the gym, or singing along to loud music in the car."[47] But ordinary affects can also entice bodies in less obvious ways, pulling us toward unexpected emotions—anger, contempt, jealousy, sadness, the lurid indulgence of tabloid melodrama. "We will follow any hint of energy, at least for a little while," she writes. "When something happens, we swarm toward it, gaze at it, sniff it, absorb its force, pore over its details, make fun of it, hide from it, spit it out, or develop a taste for it. We complain about the compulsion to participate. We deny its pull. We blame it on the suburbs and TV and ourselves. But we desire it, too, and the cure is usually another kind of swarming."[48] Stewart's likening of affects to "the drugs of all kinds" is no accident.[49] Ordinary affects are a set of uncanny addictions: they are com-pulsory, flowing through the veins of our everyday experience and linking us to regimes of power.[50] "Like a live wire," Stewart writes, "the subject channels what's going on around it. . . . The self moves to react, often pulling itself someplace it didn't exactly intend to go."[51]

This same compulsory formation of optimistic attachment is reflected in another concept in Stewart's essay "Worlding Refrains," the image of the bloom space. For Stewart, a bloom space is an affectively suffused lifeworld—a space where the transaction between bodies and worlds sparks. A bloom space is a magnetic core, a zone of enticement, "an allure and a threat that shows up in ordinary sensibilities of not knowing what compels, not being able to sit still, being exhausted, being left behind or being ahead of the curve, being in history, being in a predicament, being ready for something—anything—to happen, or orienting yourself to the sole goal of making sure that nothing (more) will happen."[52] Stewart lists her stepson's homelessness, her daughter's elementary school assemblies, and her mother's admission to an assisted living facility as examples of bloom spaces, patterns of interaction with systems of power that spin off affects.[53] A bloom space is a process—the ongoing engulfing of the body by affect—but it is also a magnetism, a recalcitrant compulsion of a body toward a scrap of incandescent color, a heavenly scent, an inexorable flowering of affect. Bloom spaces entomologize us: through them, we become insects, pulled toward the incessantly erotic, dizzyingly colorful, and incomparably necessary shapes of the world.

Bodies, for Berlant and Stewart, are fastened by affects to the skeins of power running through their lifeworlds. But this tethering is not reducible to a smoothly functioning rational economy in which things that are good for us always feel good. Optimism as a binding is not necessarily well thought out: it can be an unhappy or destructive affinity, what Berlant calls cruel optimism. Cruel optimism, she writes, is "the condition of maintaining an attachment to a significantly problematic object," an attachment that in some way stands in the way of itself, or produces the conditions of its own painful dissolution even as it demands the investment of desire.[54] Berlant writes that *"pleasure does not always feel good, and . . . understanding the binding of subjects to both their negation and incoherence is key to rewiring the ways we think about what binds people to harmful conventions of personhood."*[55] Bodies can be mapped in terms of this queer system of ever-present pushes and pulls. Compulsions propel us in multiple dimensions through this complex, living topography of power.

Cruel optimism, then, is a moment when the nonsovereignty of the self blazes through. It is a moment in which you don't know what you want, or in which you know exactly what you want and you don't want to want it. The form of cruel optimism appears when you ask yourself why you can't be the person you want to be, or when your thoughts and desires and the look on your face come out wrong. Or when you try to talk yourself out of something, but your words only echo in the room, leaving faint etchings on the surface of your body, which then does whatever the hell it wants. Bodies in their animality are bound to worlds and moved by power along dimensions that are hidden or out of reach of language. Cruel optimism is the incoherent but binding mess of our plural desires, attachments, tetherings to worlds in ways that exceed a fresh and orderly arrangement of affects as indicators of health or well-being.[56]

Cruel optimism is a crucial concept for understanding religion. It makes sense of the moments when religion resolutely exceeds what passes for rational self-interest. Affect theory—especially in the work of Berlant and Stewart—highlights how animal forces disrupt the abstract prerogative of the reasoning, calculating, talkative subject and attach bodies to complex structures of feeling that cut against not only external appraisals of the right things for bodies to do, places for them to go, ways for them to believe and feel, but the sovereign self's own assessment of its best course of action. Cruel optimism's picture of affects tethered to worlds helps to shed light on the moments when religion is not good for us, when religion is self-sacrifice or suicide, is reckless acquiescence or risky defiance, is bloodlust or martyrdom, when religion is William James's "sick religion" or the "astringent relish" of Job contemplating his doom.[57] The affective economies that move religion are not strictly conformable to the self's or others' rational calculations about how to produce survival, meaning, solidarity, compassion, or happiness. They are animal economies with their own bullying agency.

"It is not the human beings who have their passions," writes Peter Sloterdijk, "but rather it is the passions that have their human beings."[58] More than just bodies open to the world, animal religion maps passions moving through bodies into worlds. What do you want to do? Why are you doing that? When someone asks, we answer. But even in a vacuum of language, we still have an answer written in where our body goes, what it does, what it seeks out, what it doggedly chases. The animal language of movement compelled by affect is the language in which religion is written. The spoken language, an accidental technology of human bodies, comes late in the game, an adventitious augmentation of religion rather than a compulsion driving religion forward. Affect theory maps power by asking, Where do bodies go?, rather than What do bodies believe?, or What do bodies say they want?

Rather than asking if the chimpanzees Jane Goodall finds dancing in a waterfall are behaving intentionally to derive some benefit, or if J. Z. Smith's farmer plunging his hands into the earth is formulating a cosmology that divides the world into different plots of conceptual terrain, affect theory views the relationship between bodies and worlds in terms of the way that bodies are shot through with the affects evoked by the world, desires tethering us to movement in ways that reflect complex, living architectures of overlapping embodied histories, rather than angelic intentions—compulsions that only sometimes manifest as a desire to produce cosmologies, to speak and conceptualize. What gets called religion, like other forms of power, is a nexus point of animal optimisms, cruel and otherwise.

Queer Religious Ecologies

PROUST, AFFECT, AND MATERIAL RELIGION

This return to the opening images of *Religious Affects*—the chimpanzees dancing in the waterfall and the farmer dipping his hands into the earth—indicates another aspect of the relationship between compulsion and religion: the Proustian sensibility by which material objects in the world are invested with the power to make bodies move. Marcel Proust's *Remembrance of Things Past* is a sustained meditation on the interlacing of bodies, materiality, and affect. It offers a set of guidelines for exploring the compulsions that structure the ensemble of animal relationships making up religions—especially the material culture of religion.

Proust's work has become one of the touchstones of affect theory but has been especially useful for scholars writing on religion and affect, including Eve Sedgwick and Ann Cvetkovich.[59] The roots of this reading lie in Gilles Deleuze's early work, *Proust and Signs*, which reassembles Proust's imagining of bodies into a flexible system for understanding affects as compulsions. Proust's writing, for Deleuze, is animated by the same recalcitrance of affect that Berlant draws out in her discussion of cruel optimism: affectively magnetized images reverberate through bodies, superimposing themselves on the body's sensory awareness in a process Proust (like Papillon reliving projected worlds in his cell) calls the *magic lantern*.[60] As Sedgwick's former student Jonathan Flatley writes, Proust's phenomenology maps an understanding of compulsions as traversing bodies and objects, as passing through bodies along thick affective cables: "Powerful emotional experiences—quite different from more cognitively mediated ones—connect us with, even transport us *into* the *materiality* of the world around us."[61] Proust figures selves as animal rather than angelic—as having only diluted sovereignty over bodies. Rather than autonomous agents, we are drawn into systems of power by recalcitrant affects crashing through us.

This runny, unruly self is the locus of Deleuze's analysis of *Remembrance of Things Past*. For Deleuze, Proust's work is a meditation on the sign. But Proust's signs, in Deleuze's reading, are not registers of signification: the Proustian sign must be understood as "half sheathed in the object" and "extended in ourself by another half which we alone can recognize."[62] Capturing histories of experience, signs wrap objects and bodies together in surging economies of affect. Proust's characters, Deleuze shows, always pursue signs and the affects sticking to them.[63] Affect—compulsion, the live wire running through our bodies "beyond the reach of intellect"—draws the maps of their migrations.[64] Deleuze's reading of Proust anticipates the body-affect conjunctions described in *Cruel Optimism*—including cruel optimisms such as Swann's fanatically jealous "scouring love" for Odette.[65] The sign is the involuntary effect of an encounter with the world: when we meet an object in our environment, it does not stand separately from us; it penetrates us just as our bodies reach out to savor it. We are compelled to enter into this labyrinth of affects—even when we know, as Swann does, that we are dooming ourselves to pain. Bodies and objects grip and infect one another, binding each other in a felt network of power.

Sedgwick's reading of *Remembrance* in the titular essay of *The Weather in Proust* picks up on this sense of a heterogeneous affective terrain, tracking how Proust deploys what she calls a *religious ecology* of places, bodies, practices, and material objects saturated with religious feeling. She identifies the book's "propulsive textual world" as offering an "atmosphere in which every act and landscape brims with a proliferation of genii, demigods, Norns, and other such ontologically exceptional beings," the pantheon of "queer little gods."[66] The religious ecology in Proust is the network of affectively charged material elements and relationships that makes up the aesthetic complex of his writing.

Just as for Deleuze the distinctive quality of objects in Proust is their ability to draw bodies toward them, Sedgwick finds the locus of religiosity in Proust in the gravity of things, their magnetic pulls. Sedgwick spotlights the eminently Proustian theme of compulsion, his portrait of bodies plunging into worlds, knocked off balance by forces that pull them forward along the knotty tetherings of affect. Sedgwick points out that for Proust, the significance of the recurring figure of the genie is that it is "earthier" than the transcendentally oriented Neoplatonism that inflected the fin-de-siècle European spiritualism of his time.[67] This earthiness of spirit, the connection to things in the world, is crucial for understanding Proust's "vast and varied divinity-field, the unsystematized proliferation of ontologically intermediate beings loosely attached—at once inside and outside—to places, persons, families, substances, ideas, music, buildings, machines, emotions, and natural elements."[68] As Berlant writes, Sedgwick's project is to discern the specificities of how embodied histories attach to us by making us desire in unexpected or queer ways.[69] Rather than an overarching, inaccessible God, Sedgwick traces in Proust the production of ambient, materially anchored feelings, a queer affectscape that emerges out of a topography of interactions between bodies and worlds.

These desiring histories are made visible in Proust's work through two images: the "human barometer" and the mannikin. The barometer in Proust suggests the receptivity of bodies to atmospheric forces around them—to affective currents circulating within materially constituted fields. The barometer is a hypersensitive instrument that cannot be deactivated, a "subtle, invisible, and indivisibly systemic index of weather."[70]

Bodies as barometers are quivering antennas of affect. Understanding the body as barometer repudiates the fallacy of human self-sovereignty: it makes human bodies susceptible to the weather rather than the authors of their own destiny.

Moreover, Sedgwick suggests that for Proust, "*to be* a human barometer seems to involve *containing* a human barometer, the little mannikin inside."[71] Like the genies of Proust's divinity field (which are "especially prone to get entrapped in objects")[72] the mannikin is indicative of the sovereignty of affects over selves. But where Sedgwick and Proust propose a mannikin as the image of compulsion, I want to suggest, instead, animals. The mannikin is an inanimate object, but thinking affects as animal images their own agency, what Bennett calls their vitality, their role in bodies as opaque courses of desire, moving us along networks of power. The "animated barometer" proposed by Proust, this "buoyant internal homunculus," is in fact a herd of animals moving through us, the compulsions of affects.[73]

Proust's central theme is the power of the involuntary, the pulsing lines of force running through bodies connecting propulsive affective architectures to worlds. Sedgwick's affective reading of Proust frames bodies in terms of their animal susceptibility to the material geographies around them. And inasmuch as these geographies are configured as religious formations, they are constituted as divinity fields, the religious ecologies that direct bodies through a skein of compulsions.

This Proustian sense of religion is examined from a different direction in Ann Cvetkovich's *Depression: A Public Feeling*. Cvetkovich presents the autobiographical segment of this book, her "depression journals," as a strategy for taking depression down from the level of a medical diagnosis or a social critique to the "lived experience" of formations of power.[74] In switching to memoir, Cvetkovich seeks to account for how feeling bodies navigate overlapping political and religious frames, often invoking a Proustian sensibility in which memory (both personal and collective) and material objects ramify into powerful religious affects.

After graduating from Cornell and taking up a tenure-track job in Texas, Cvetkovich found herself isolated and disoriented, still reeling from the anxieties of her final year of graduate school and the job market. This led to a depressive state in which she experienced acute pressure from the demands of her career as well as her everyday routines. Cvetkovich worked her way through and out of this debilitated state by creating a set of material configurations and habits that she interprets, in the depression journals, using an explicitly religious vocabulary.

She describes how she began to gather mementos while in graduate school, constructing what she calls altars—bricolages of accumulated materials that in the aggregate took on religious meaning, or as she puts it, "render[ed] material my emotional states and my hopes and dreams."[75] She also accumulated religious objects, such as an inherited crucifix. The crucifix, she writes, became meaningful for her in spite of the fact that Cvetkovich—after being raised Catholic—had declared herself a "vehement atheist" as a teenager.[76] This disjuncture between her declared atheism and her religiosity suggests that the material properties of the object were sitting transversally to the linguistic framework of her religious identity. This Proustian religion, for Cvetkovich, emerges within a postsecular, material-affective syntax that exceeds the propositional matrix of belief/nonbelief.

Altar making became an important practice for Cvetkovich as she worked through her later depression, building collections of religious paraphernalia, personal photographs, mementos of places she had lived, and gifts from friends. "The impulse driving me to do this seemed inexplicable but not to be ignored," she writes of altar building, calling it an "instinctive gesture"—what I would recast as a compulsion—that linked her professional and personal histories to her emotional life.[77] As with Proust's narrator, objects embedded in the strata of Cvetkovich's childhood (Catholic, in her case) rose to the surface and produced affective ligatures connecting her to the world. Her embodied memories jutted into her ordinary life and constituted themselves as religious shapes.

After arriving in Texas, for instance, Cvetkovich found herself drawn to an image of the Virgen de Guadalupe painted by a friend. Cvetkovich describes the power of the image in terms of its affective, precognitive compulsion, its transfixing of her body: "The moment I saw the rough unstretched canvas on the wall at [John's] boyfriend Skip's apartment I was mesmerized, even though I had no knowledge of what the image meant."[78] Although Cvetkovich writes that she gradually arrived at an understanding of the political and religious significations attached to the Virgen, "she also functioned at a more intuitive level for me, as a sign of how it might be possible to find a place in the borderlands of Texas. Although I felt self-conscious about being yet another white girl appropriating other cultures—both Tejano and indigenous—I desperately needed the emotional solace the Virgen provided and I considered her appearance in my life to be a version of a miracle."[79] Like Proust, Cvetkovich's work documents the ability of material objects to provoke configurations of power that work through embodied affects, not reducible to discourse but no less embedded in embodied histories. Cvetkovich's altars are clusters of accumulated, embodied memories that evoke formations of healing affect—affects which, in spite of her atheism, she understands as religious.[80]

Habits, bodily practices, and ritual are also part of these affective complexes. Cvetkovich describes how queer communities develop memorial rituals that improvise new religious forms in response to loss, forms that bring together material elements, narratives, landscapes, and the presence of other bodies. Out of this, she develops a theory of ritual practice as habits that heal through the reconfiguration of ordinary affects. Habits, for Cvetkovich, are practices for the production of affects, both quotidian and profoundly necessary.[81] Ritual becomes a strategy for rewiring affective configurations and pulling bodies out of the circumstances of despair or helping them navigate communal mourning.[82] This impact is often felt on a level outside of the remit of sovereign consciousness: "Unbeknownst to me," Cvetkovich writes, "I was sometimes healing myself by just waiting and doing nothing, or through what seemed like ordinary or insignificant activities—going swimming, doing yoga, getting a cat, visiting a sick friend."[83] Being able to talk about how a ritual or other material connection is rewriting the body—to render it in language—is incidental to its effectiveness. Like Sedgwick's pedagogy of Buddhism, our bodies can be reshaped—even healed—even when we don't realize we're being taught.

SWANN-LIKE BODIES: POWER, HEALING, AND MATERIAL RELIGION

Is it not the person but color that walks, color as an animal like a Swann on the edge of language?—**Michael Taussig**, *What Color Is the Sacred?*

Proust's work also provides a link between affect theory and recent work in religious studies on religion as material culture. What has been called the new subfield of material religion (not to be confused with the materialist shift, though Vásquez cites this work as part of that paradigm) focuses on how material objects emerge as ingredients in religious practice that serve to give shape to formations of power. Crucially, this emphasis on religious objects is not reducible to a network of discursive regimes volubly insisting on the importance of certain objects, but emerges instead out of a dynamic interplay between language, sensing bodies, and things in the world.[84] Material religion, consistent with the materialist shift, rejects the notion that religion is primarily about textual imperatives or grids of belief, seeing it instead as the result of a more fundamental set of correspondences between bodies and worlds, "as deriving," S. Brent Plate writes, "from rudimentary human experiences, from lived, embodied practices" that can then be modified and retouched by language.[85]

For instance, in *What Color is the Sacred?*, anthropologist Michael Taussig suggests that Proust disrupts the myth of the body's autonomy by shading in the body's susceptibility to objects. Properties of material objects such as color, for Taussig, pull bodies toward them, rather than being autonomously selected by choosing agents. Insulated bodies could not suffer from solitary confinement because they are not tethered to affects. The Proustian body, on the other hand, is a body susceptible to affects, located in its animality, and riven by compulsions.[86] "What all that intricate scaffolding of metaphor and imagery is meant to achieve," Taussig writes, "is not the transmission of ideas so much as the creation of an atmosphere."[87] Affects, rather than ideas or concepts, are the currency of Proust's work. Proust's technique of cultivating *memoires involontaires* brings us into the field of preintellectual, sensuous connections.[88] For Proust, we are "Swann-like bodies," animals absorbed in the folds of affects: "the self becomes part of that which is seen, not a sovereign transcendent."[89]

Crucially, Taussig is also explicit that his understanding of the relationship between religion and affect is fixated on material objects. The titular question of his book, he says, comes from the French College of Sociology of the 1930s, specifically the "sacred sociology" of Michel Leiris. Leiris, he writes, "came at religion and magic from a totally unexpected direction. He quickened one's interest in what he thought of as sacred with snapshots of the dining-room stove, *La Radieuse*, with the warmth of its glowing coals; his father's nickel-plated Smith and Wesson revolver; the bathroom antics with his brother; the mysteries of his parents' bedroom; the coining of names; the sudden recognition that one has been mishearing and mispronouncing words; and so forth—in short, charged spaces, dangerous objects, and prohibited events, lifting you off from the world of ordinary reality."[90] Taussig images a Proustian world of material things that are saturated with affective energy, things that are always pulling bodies toward them. Proust, read through the lens of affect theory, becomes a curator of magnetic artifacts, setting up material objects as silent loci of religious power.

Other scholars of religion working on materiality have begun to make even more explicit the correlation between religious materiality and power. Thomas Tweed in his ethnographic research with Catholic Cuban immigrant communities documents how a particular material artifact—a replica of the miraculous statue of Our Lady of Charity found off the waters of Cuba in the early 1600s—became a focal point consolidating the political unity of the postrevolutionary diaspora in Florida. Tweed describes the statue being smuggled out of Cuba in 1961 and delivered to a Miami baseball stadium to be displayed in front of 25,000 cheering Cuban exiles. "When the Miami crowd finally could see their national patroness," he writes, "they wept and waved, shouted and sang."[91] Building on the Virgin's extraordinary appeal among the politically energized Cuban expatriates, the Catholic diocese called for a fund-raising campaign to enshrine her, with her new home, La Ermita de la Caridad, consecrated in 1973. She continues to serve as a rallying point for a Cuban diasporic political-religious movement to the present day.[92]

Tweed points out that the religious backdrop out of which the Cuban American Virgin emerged was complex: most Cubans were ambivalent in their relationship with the institutional Catholic Church from colonization to Castro's revolution. The dominant tendency among Cubans was to practice "domestic religion" centered on household icons, often with strong inflections of African Yoruba traditions (for instance, by viewing the Virgin as simultaneously Mary and the Orisha Oshun). "Almost nine out of ten (88.8%) of the Catholics" in prerevolutionary Cuba, Tweed writes, "reported that they had not attended mass in the previous year. Most striking of all, more than half (53.5%) said that they had never even *seen* a priest."[93] Domestic religion filled this gap. Tweed reports that "Cesar, a sixty-four-year-old man from a rural township who had rarely attended mass as a child, trembled with emotion as he told me that his strong devotion to Our Lady of Charity began in the home. Each night before bedtime, as his mother had instructed, he knelt to kiss the feet of the statue of the Virgin enshrined in their living room."[94] The intense devotion to icons flourished, producing a matrix of object-oriented religious affects that set the stage for the later reception of Our Lady of Charity in Miami.

As importantly, the experience of exile seems to have decidedly transformed the makeup of Cuban diasporic religious practice. Tweed notes that the Miami-based Cuban diaspora became substantially more religious than prerevolutionary Cubans.[95] In addition to the extraordinary popular success of Our Lady of Charity, even formerly unchurched Cubans often made offerings and prayers to the Virgin in advance of attempting the hazardous passage through the Straits of Florida.[96] Tweed argues that "Cubans could gather around [the Virgin as a] shared symbol because . . . Our Lady of Charity had been identified with the homeland."[97] The religious intensity of the Miami Cuban community correlated exactly with the dramatic production of new regimes of terrestrial power, and the Virgin amplified the solidarity of the exilic community coalescing in opposition to Castro's rule.

This is why La Ermita de la Caridad itself is a deeply politicized structure. The cornerstone of the foundation of the shrine is a hexagon, with soil and stone samples from each of Cuba's six provinces embedded in its six sides. Furthermore, these earthen samples were mixed with water taken from a raft that had transported fifteen refugees who died in the passage.[98] The entrance to the shrine features a painted Cuban flag and a bust of an early Cuban independence leader.[99] The 740-square-foot mural inside the shrine depicts several centuries of Cuban history through a collage of images of historical figures, all arrayed around the Virgin in the center.[100] Tweed describes how an event he attended at the shrine at the end of 1993 had the phrase Libre '94 spelled out in garlands of yellow flowers on the wall, "signal[ing] their hope that the island would be liberated in the coming year."[101] The site of the shrine was chosen specifically because of its vantage across the strait to Cuba.[102] When Tweed interviews the shrinegoers, they report little interest in existential questions of "ultimate concern" or other linguistically mediated modes of being religious: "none of the hundreds of pilgrims I interviewed at the Miami shrine talked about being-itself. No one told me they wondered why there was something instead of nothing. . . . Almost every day during the five years I did fieldwork at the shrine, however, devotees reminded me in one way or another—a teary story about the hurried journey to South Florida or a ritual expressing longing for an imagined past— that the displacement of transnational migration had disrupted their sense of time and place."[103] The physical space of the shrine and the material object of the Virgin's statue become a nexus quickening a religious-political convergence.

Moreover, this convergence is structured by an ensemble of affective compulsions. Tweed writes that "devotees weep, smile, kneel, sing, wave, hope, complain, thank, and petition" in front of the Virgin and respond with "strong emotions" to the mural that is her backdrop.[104] At the dedication ceremony for the shrine in 1973, "one woman who was 'overcome by emotion' bounded through a security line to the elevated platform where the mass was being performed. There she prayed before the shrine's central portal, with a statue of the patroness in one hand and the Cuban flag in the other."[105] The network formed between bodies, religion, objects, and power is activated by a driving system of compulsions. These compulsions jump the barricades of religion understood as a set of inert discursive propositions or even as a display case of disconnected bodies.

Finally, religion as a power source is not devised by a top-down discursive regime. Tweed highlights that the shrine as a formation of religious power is animated by a set of compulsions that move orthogonally to discourses. For instance, the Catholic clergy—especially the white American clergy who controlled the diocese during the early years of the diaspora—and their authorized texts conceptualize the shrine as a mechanism to " 'purify' Catholicism by removing the residue of Santeria."[106] But in addition to the many practitioners who frequent the shrine or dwell outside it whose devotion hybridizes Santeria and Catholicism,[107] the "mature, white, middle-class Cubans who visit the shrine in the greatest numbers offer prayers and make vows for a variety of reasons—especially for healing, childbirth, and family."[108] And "almost all Cuban American visitors to the shrine in Miami see it as a place to express diasporic nationalism, to make sense of themselves as a displaced people."[109] The physical object's operation as a power source exceeds its enfoldment in discursive apparatuses.

This is illustrated in one of Tweed's own encounters with Our Lady of Charity. As he stands in the shrine in 1993 before the Virgin and beneath the yellow Libre '94 garlands, he finds himself whispering a prayer, in Spanish, along with the roomful of Cuban devotees: "Virgen Santisima, salva a Cuba." "I wasn't sure why I did that," he would write a decade later, "and I'm still not."[110] In spite of everything that separates Tweed from his consultants—historically, culturally, personally, religiously, and in terms of his stated set of intellectual commitments or "beliefs"—the network of bodies, affects, and objects in the room compels his body to move. As material religion theorist David Morgan writes, "Gazes or visual fields, of which there are many, engage the human body as an interface with other bodies—bodies of other people, things, and images, and through them interface with social bodies, or the groups that individuals inhabit as an integral aspect of their identities."[111] The circuit of power in the shrine is not dictated by a set of intellectual commitments, but by an affective alchemy of bodies, objects, and histories.

But just as importantly, thinking religion and compulsion together indicates that the practices of healing that attach to material religion are themselves political. Healing in the context of a political or economic system is a way of concretizing agency precisely by relieving pressure on bodies and enabling them to rewire the power relations visited on their bodies. Cvetkovich's studies of Christian acedia and crafting as varieties of Foucauldian ascesis—technologies of the body—highlight the bridges linking the domains of power, knowledge, affect, and what she calls spiritual practices.[112] Cvetkovich's work shows how a cycle of affective, economic, and political intuitions forms substantive formations of power that are not reducible to linguistic or ideological determination.[113] This is also exactly how solitary confinement interfaces with power: by shattering bodies' affective ligatures with material forms and interanimal relationships, it attempts to break bodies' capacity for resistance to existing political formations. Healing is often a retrieval and rehabilitation of a ring of joyful affects through reencountering other bodies as well as material things in the world.

Affect theory enriches accounts of material religion by underlining the impenetrability of this recalcitrant need for material objects—a need that kicks within our bodies. This compulsion of bodies to ring their worlds with material forms is consonant with Plate's model of the body as half object. In *A History of Religion in 5½ Objects*, Plate argues that bodies are best understood as "half objects," as intransigently incomplete entities that are always needful of other material processes around them. "We crave interaction," Plate writes: "sensing half bodies *need objects to sense*."[114] Echoing this sensibility Morgan writes, "We need objects as much as they need us."[115] Animalizing material culture affirms that the desire for material things is a compulsion—a peculiarity of a particular animal embodied history.[116] Material objects are part of the ineluctable affective economies of embodiment, figments of circuits of need that are inevitably recirculated into bricolages of power.

Conclusion: Power and the Passive Case

In her journal, Cvetkovich writes of traveling to New York and visiting an Orthodox church in the Lower East Side. She talks about the experience of trying to take communion there, but being stopped by a woman who discovers that she is a Roman Catholic and refuses to let her stand in line. "As the mass continued," she writes, "*I found myself* quietly weeping, wrought up by the combination of ritual and rejection."[117] This *I found myself* is the passive case of affect. It suggests the ways that affects and affectively organized desires—including desires for affects conventionally understood as negative—surge through bodies and compose themselves in religious forms. The passive case fractures the agency of the speaking, thinking subject, mapping the channels beneath, outside of, and within animal bodies by which religion takes place. Religion in this model is a domain within the complex sphere of affective compulsions.

Post-structuralist critiques of subjectivity have successfully disrupted the walls of the foundational fantasy, the myth of angelic self-sovereignty. But by eliding the body in its animality, these analyses risk leaving us with an understanding of the body as functionally inert—an archive of discursive effects. They remain susceptible to the linguistic fallacy: the myth that where bodies go is fundamentally determined by language, either as a sedimentation of verbal instructions teaching us what to want or as a Kantian subject intoning, "This I desire." The farmer kneeling in the earth, by the lights of the linguistic fallacy, can't be savoring the contact between his skin and cold earth; he must be writing the world into separate cosmological forms. Thinking affects as compulsory reanimates bodies by lifting the veil on the animals charging through us: the colors, shapes, patterns, lights, textures, and all the named and unnamed affects of religious ecologies. Bodies, Kevin O'Neill writes, invoking Brian Massumi, "are not always docile. They yelp."[118] Affects in the passive case are active; they befall us by trampling over tremulous things like selves and subjects.

Affects in the passive case—compulsions—are not intentional, in the sense that they are not "for-something." They are a landing site rather than a launch site. When Cvetkovich links affects to a queer, nongenerative form of creativity—"creative thought that doesn't have an immediate outcome"—she indexes this sense of affect in the passive case, recalcitrant affects that stand up on their own, rather than integrating themselves into grids of rational outcomes sketched by a knowing author.[119] As Tomkins writes, affects are "'ends-in-themselves,' positive and negative."[120] Taussig describes the flowers on Proust's desk as circuits of uselessness, material exemplars of affective forces supererogatory to human will.[121] This is what Sedgwick calls the "camp" value of affect, but camp thought not "in terms of parody or even wit, but with more of an eye for its visceral, operatic power."[122] Campy affects—the mise-en-scène of material objects evoking operatic power—are autotelic, ends in themselves, circuits of force passing through bodies and returning to themselves in lucid bubbles of eroticism. Religious affects are, to return to the classical etymology of the term *religion*, "binding." Rather than the window dressing of cognition, behavior, and meaning, affects are their foundation and their substance. Affects are compulsory, directing where bodies go through complex systems of pushes and pulls. This is the queerness of Proust's queer little gods—the recalcitrant, yelping gods of animal religion.

But although material religion is a crucial part of this picture, these compulsions need not land in material objects. As Bruno Latour writes in *The Modern Cult of the Factish Gods*, white Europeans had their own range of fetishistic attachments—for instance, they made a fetish of accusing other cultures of having fetishes. They also presented an overarching fetish for "objectively" accumulated facts. Latour calls these hybrids of fixation and language *factishes*, and it is this lens that he uses to think through the workings of religious language. Religious language, for Latour, is not a technology for the transmission of information. Rather, it is a mode of speech designed to compel, to produce "a shift from distance to proximity."[123] Religious talk is a way of articulating bodies to systems of power mediated by affect: it addresses itself to the problem of where bodies go not by explaining things but by instrumenting its own regime of compulsions.

In this, religious speech is analogous to love talk—a technique for transforming bodies rather than informing them. Religious discourses either "*transport the spirit from which they talk*, and they can be said to be truthful, faithful, proven, experienced, self-verifiable, or they don't reproduce, don't perform, don't transport what they talk from and immediately, without any inertia, they begin to lie, to fall apart, to stop having any reference, any ground."[124] As with Deleuze's reading of Proust as uncovering "the truth of bodies," Latour insists that these statements have a "truth" value—but this value exists completely to the side of their propositional content. Rather, truth is a configuration of affect, a play in the folds of compulsion.

Understanding affects as compulsory rewrites the coordinates of the hermeneutics of suspicion: instead of presupposing that bodies are rational actors prosecuting an agenda that transparently reflects their interests (and can tell you if you ask them what they're up to), affect theory proposes that affects work through bodies to achieve their own ends—sometimes coextensive with ideological or economic regimes but often not. Affects may be nonintentional, but they are nonetheless intimately linked with power, precisely because the phenomenological is political. Affects pulsing through bodies produce political effects at right angles to regimes of discourse, reason, "consciousness," health, flourishing, or even happiness.[125] Rather than asking, What do affects do for us?, affect theory asks, What do we do for affects?

Affect theory, then, reverses the polarity of some of the key questions that have traditionally been explored by the humanities. Where the rhetorical approach asks, how are affects deployed by strategic actors seeking to advance ideological or economic ends? affect theory opens up the possibility that sometimes the correct question is actually the reverse: how are discourses, ideologies, material forms, and other elements of religion generated to produce affects? Ann Pellegrini contrasts theatrical haunted houses, which use fear to satisfy the audience's desire for a thrill—and evangelical Hell Houses—which she suggests use fear to transform political subjects.[126] But maybe the gulf between the two genres is narrower than we might expect: maybe the compulsory desire for fear is animating and driving the theater of the Hell House as much as it is lining people up around the block to buy tickets for a horror movie. Affects are not simply being deployed in the service of power: affects are pulses of power, choreographing bodies and leaving behind political effects.

FIVE

SAVAGES: IDEOLOGY, PRIMATOLOGY,
AND ISLAMOPHOBIA

At the beginning of the first sentence of the European tradition, in the first verse of the *Iliad*, the word "rage" occurs. It appears fatally and solemnly, like a plea, a plea that does not allow for any disagreement.—**Peter Sloterdijk,** *Rage and Time*

Ideologies happen. Power snaps into place. Structures grow entrenched. Identities take place. Ways of knowing become habitual at the drop of a hat. But it's ordinary affects that give things the quality of a *some*thing to inhabit and animate. Politics starts in the animated inhabitation of things, not way downstream in the various dreamboats and horror shows that get moving.
—**Kathleen Stewart,** *Ordinary Affects*

In the summer of 2012, anti-Muslim advocacy group Stop Islamization of America (SIOA) posted ads on the New York and Chicago subway systems with the following text:

> In any war between the civilized man and the savage, support the civilized man. Support Israel. Defeat Jihad.

The first sentence is a paraphrase of a remark by Ayn Rand—the hero of SIOA's founder, a blogger and activist named Pamela Geller—commenting on the 1973 Arab-Israeli war. Rand in her lectures frequently drew on an explicitly racialized vocabulary to designate various colonized groups—including Palestinian Arabs and Native Americans—as animalistic.[1] The latter part of the ad recapitulates the vision statement of SIOA: that America faces an existential threat in the form of rising "Islamization." Geller writes in her book of the same name that "Muslims are working in the United States now to make sure that Islam dominates by destroying our constitutional freedoms."[2] A range of civil rights organizations protested against the campaign, arguing that it implied a subhuman status on the part of Muslims, an animalization: the word *savage* derives from the Latin *silvaticus*, a "creature of the forest."

After the disputed June 2009 Iranian presidential election, some friends invited me to attend a solidarity demonstration in Syracuse, New York, near a weekend farmer's market. Although most shoppers driving by that afternoon only looked at us blankly, many others honked, waved, smiled, or even flashed our V-signs back at us, grinning. There were also a few middle fingers. One man yelled "Fuck Iran!" out his window as he cruised by. Another woman shook her head wildly as she scanned our signs, then chanted "USA! USA!" while giving us a vigorous thumbs-down. But the face that stays with me most vividly from that day appeared in the window of a black SUV that slowed down as it passed our bedraggled row, sweating and exhausted from hoisting our signs on the sun-soaked grass. A heavyset white man, maybe forty, leaned his head out the window and flexed his burly arm. He stared us down from behind his wraparound shades. "*Fuck you*," he said coolly, lifting his chin. "Fucking *niggers*."

My reaction, as he roared away, was to feel more bemused than threatened. It was absurd: we were a group of whites and Persians. There were no black folks among us.[3] American antiblack racism as an ideological device authorizes a set of conditions of economic exploitation that serve white bodies at the expense of nonwhites. But why would a white man call another white man an antiblack epithet? How could that be part of an ideology of antiblack racism? And how do local formations of anti-Muslim hatred—which were certainly part of what we were experiencing that day—interlock with the economic parameters of American racism, when Muslims in the United States are generally not—with some exceptions—a pool of exploited labor in the American economy? The strangest part of it all, even as I think back on it now, was that without being any less saturated with anger or condescension, the racist epithet seemed somehow playful—a happy improvisation—the spontaneous flourish of a body delighting in its toys.

Why does a white man call a group of whites and Iranians "niggers"? Why does a Jewish woman describe Muslims as "savages"? Why do bodies go there? In both images, there is a movement to assemble boundary lines, to mobilize armed borders between social groups. Jasbir Puar has suggested that racialization enfolds "specific social formations and processes that are not necessarily or only tied to what has been historically theorized as 'race.' "[4] Racialization is not just about race, then, but any attempt to disdain an outsider—national, religious, class—as a savage. Eve Sedgwick notes this process at work in Marcel Proust's characterization of Françoise in *Remembrance of Things Past*, whom she calls the "most hated" figure in the series, a racially and class-determined other.[5] Sedgwick reads Françoise in Kleinian terms, as a figure of "the bad mother." But I think there is a sense in which Proust serves us Françoise in the same way that every other image in his feast of a book is served: in her "awfulness," she is an object of desire, a racialized other whom the narrator delights in disdaining. This queer desire for the loathsome other in her loathsomeness is the common motif of all these cases, a determination to transfix alterity that goes over and above racism as an abstract language game or a skirmish in a class war—an operatic battlefield rather than a dry ideology.

Contemporary analyses of racism have effectively drawn out the mechanisms by which race functions as a conventionalized proxy for class to consolidate existing economic structures. Systemic racism—such as anti-black or anti-Latino racism in the United States—is a strategy for maintaining the economic dominance of a hegemonic group by diminishing access to capital and political power on the part of racial underclasses. Affect theory puts forward an approach that is complementary to these structural analyses: it indicates the possibility that bodies may also use insider/outsider distinctions to produce economies of affect within or alongside economies of dollar signs—what Sara Ahmed calls *economies of hate*. Racism, in these moments, is a by-product of a regime of affects that operate transversally to economic and linguistic determinations. Economies of hate are motivated by clusters of compulsions surging through bodies in ways that are not necessarily thoughtful, useful, or even tactical—but no less desirable, contagious, or addictive. This non-economic variety of racism is, I would argue, on full display in contemporary American Islamophobia.

Thinking racism affectively suggests that racialization is not simply a conceptual mistake, a set of beliefs about another group of bodies that happens to be wrong and which could be erased through the provision of correct facts. Supplementing existing structural, economic, and linguistic approaches, an analytics of affect suggests that racism can also be produced or accelerated by bodies trafficking in viscerally charged economies of hate. This dimension of racism, which Sharon Patricia Holland calls the "erotic life of racism," flourishes not because of ignorance or lack of information, but because of a set of compulsions that drive bodies to generate and police the boundaries of their social worlds. Economies of hate distribute the heady thrill that comes from walling people off. The superimposition of one out-group epithet onto another, totally different group, or the relentless insistence that a global population of over one billion can be reduced to a homogeneous, seething sea of extremism, shows how this process, far from corresponding to an organized catalog of linguistic propositions about race, is an affective procedure—a strategy by which bodies extract meaning from social life-worlds. This is the hedonicity of hate, the desire to cast scorn, the lush, self-absorbed pleasure in erasing another body's face.

Islamophobia passes itself off as the exercise of a neutral, angelic reason and attacks its targets as savage: "It's just common sense."[6] American whiteness, too, forged in the violent rupture that is America's black/white binary, composes itself as the locus of the rational human subject over and against the bestial. But the fundamental irony of racialization is that even though it always and everywhere tries to install itself on the upper story of a human/subhuman split, it is consummately animal, an intransigent, sovereign affective machine—a tight web of compulsions—surging through bodies to form political and religious configurations. Affect theory sees racialization as an affectively mediated temptation, but rather than producing private feelings, this phenomenological structure is itself political. This is racism not as ideology, but as primatology, a prelinguistic or paralinguistic component of animality. Ultimately, then, affect theory helps us to think whiteness, the American public sphere, and what gets called Judeo-Christian civilization through the lens of animality—at the same time as it calls attention to the political complexity of nonhuman animal societies.

But the American religious landscape has not only responded to twenty-first-century Islam with aggression: a wide range of American religious bodies and institutions have launched coordinated campaigns to build different species of intercommunity relations with global Islam—for instance, through the positive response of the U.S. interfaith community to the proposed Park51 community center in Manhattan. Even if we are all, always, susceptible to the temptation of race, we are also defined according to other compulsions, other places bodies go—concern, compassion, love—the risky boundaries of *us* that we lightly pass over. These compassionate processes are also driven by compulsions with their own capacities to shape animal religions. These practices for dissolving the *us–them* binary are also visceral affective registers that pull bodies into formations of power. These compulsions, too—both primatological and ideological—are mixed into the foundation of the terrain of globalized religion.

This chapter explores how the affective turn offers new tools for analyzing not only the religious racialization of Islamophobia, but religious formations that counter Islamophobic rage. To illustrate this model, this chapter looks at a set of theoretical resources from affect theory on the relationship between affect and racializing ideologies, crossing them with contemporary primatology to define an approach in which the affective haloes of racial difference—whether racist hostility or intergroup solidarity—are viewed as compulsions, as centers of gravity constituted within embodied histories that are not necessarily reducible to ideological functionalism. I flesh this out with a survey of the affectively charged mediascape surrounding one of the most significant moments in the history of post-9/11 American Islam, the Park51 controversy of 2010.

Affectspheres: Ideology, Politics, and the Erotic Life of Racism

There are games you can play.—**Kathleen Stewart**, *Ordinary Affects*

In her essay "The Desire for the Political," Lauren Berlant describes ideology as a "surrealistic affectsphere" that sustains existing and imagined systems of power.[7] Affects, for Berlant, saturate politics and ramify in complex ways into the churn of power relations between bodies, institutions, media apparatuses, and discourses. The relationship between affect and ideology is a major theme for affect theorists, including members of the Public Feelings Collective such as Berlant, Sara Ahmed, and Ann Cvetkovich;[8] Deleuzians such as William Connolly, John Protevi, Patricia Ticineto Clough, Nigel Thrift, and Jane Bennett;[9] and other scholars working on affect such as Jonathan Flatley, Arjun Appadurai, and Peter Sloterdijk.[10] Collectively, they pose what might be called an *animal politics* in which affect becomes a central analytic term for the study of political organisms and the production of social boundaries.[11] When Berlant writes that "affect theory is another phase in the history of ideology theory," she is contending that affect provides a new locus for studying the binding relationships between bodies and power—the way the phenomenological itself, within and beside language, is political.[12]

Approaches to affect and ideology can be subdivided into two guiding questions: What do affects do?, and What do bodies do for affects? The first question frames affects as instruments for the intensification of ideological architectures—including racialized or nationalistic ideologies. Ahmed writes extensively about the way that affects such as fear are used to manufacture the "surfaces" of individuals and collectives by attaching negative affects to other bodies and positive affects to a collective identified as "us." Fear "*does something.* . . . It reestablishes distance between bodies whose difference is read off the surface, as a reading that produces the surface."[13] Arjun Appadurai describes this in terms of a particular form of patriotism, what he calls *full attachment*, "that *surplus of affect* which exceeds civic commitment, attribution of legitimacy to a state."[14] He suggests that full attachment can be parlayed into nationalisms that shore up the institution of a state by mobilizing the commitments of bodies—the "willingness to kill—or to die—for the good of a plainly artificial collective form."[15] Appadurai's *Fear of Small Numbers* is an extended meditation on the pathways by which fear provides the structural supports for globalist, state, and nationalist ideologies.[16]

But contemporary affect theory also asks the reverse question of ideology in the political affectsphere: What do bodies do for affects? For Appadurai, the surplus of affect flowing out of full attachment is "more libidinal than procedural."[17] Conventional understandings of identitarian political regimes, he suggests, cannot account for the "unsolved puzzle" of how ideology motivates the surplus of affective investment on display in full attachment.[18] Ahmed, in her work on happiness, proposes a "perverse" approach to affect that does not view it as instrumental for ideology—at least not with anything like unswerving intentionality. This understanding "refuse[s] to see the ambivalence of affect as pointed: maybe the point is that there is no point that points to some future horizon. Feelings may be perverse because *they don't always have a point.*"[19] Like Silvan Tomkins's notion that affect "is an end in itself, with or without instrumental behavior"—what Eve Sedgwick names "autotelic" affects—this question asks after the ways that political affects are compulsory.[20]

When Elizabeth Grosz suggests that we replace the critical term *ideology* with "force, energy, affect," she has in mind exactly this queer template of compulsory affectivity, the notion that rather than starting with a cluster of ideological goals and mapping out an ensemble of affective routes to reach those goals, affects may be better understood as ends in themselves, as pathways of a delirious, multidimensional maze that spins off ideological effects as it is explored.[21] Ideologies—including racialized ideologies—are not only felt things, but desired things: places that bodies go. "Cognition," Berlant writes, "follows the affects."[22] Ideology thought as a compulsion that flows through our veins suggests that rather than being used to achieve specific material or political ends, ideologies under some circumstances may be self-motivating, surging out of bodies and leaving behind them a wake of political accidents.

This leads to the question, What do bodies do for affects? In *Rage and Time*, philosopher Peter Sloterdijk proposes that modern Western perspectives on affect have mistakenly marginalized what he calls *thymos*, a body's felt need to assert itself—in rage or in more mundane expressions of dignity. In psychoanalysis, for instance, rage is understood exclusively in terms of the frustration of eros.[23] In Christianity, thymos is a by-product of sin that must be eradicated from the body. Thymos in these frames is taken as a symptom of pathology, rather than as an intransigent embodied compulsion.[24] By contrast, in the Greek paradigm Sloterdijk extracts from Homer's *Iliad*, thymos is its own affective engine—a *genius*, an antenna of impulses—like the genies, the queer little gods Sedgwick finds populating Proust's affectively prolific universe.[25] Sloterdijk writes that these impulses become the raw material of religion.[26] Thymos is a vector of religious force, a recalcitrant affective current passing through bodies to coassemble with formations of power.[27]

Thymos also shapes the textures of political ideologies. Politics is a by-product of the dynamic of embodied affects, affects that are produced queerly—for their own ends—or what Sloterdijk calls "auto-affirmative forces."[28] These thymotic technologies infuse the mobilization of racialized borders, the churning battlefronts of rage. Sloterdijk describes thymotic bodies as producing an "inner-outer gradient" that electrifies the perimeter between *us* and *them*.[29] Sustained by this thymotic force, nationalisms become hypersaturated systems that pull bodies over and above one-dimensional rational economies of survival or material benefit—the origin of Appadurai's puzzling "full attachment." "Of course there is always 'something' for which the fighting takes place," Sloterdijk writes. "Mainly, however, the struggle serves the goal of revelation: it reveals the fighting energy as such."[30] Rage is autotelic, an end in itself that subsumes other embodied desires. There are other things that bodies want beyond those that can be identified by political economists. Thymos is one of these centers of gravity, a compulsion, and a constitutive component of the erotic life of ideology, including racialized ideology.

This interpretation is even more pointedly articulated in Sharon Patricia Holland's *The Erotic Life of Racism*, which proposes that racism can be understood not merely as an abstract ideology, but as an ensemble of embodied encounters playing out within the sphere of ordinary affects. Holland begins her book with an anecdote about a racist encounter outside a California supermarket, writing, although the "psychic violation of that moment in the parking lot haunts me still . . . it is the *intimacy* of that moment that arrests me."[31] This intimacy of racialization is her concern, a vantage point from which she draws out for inspection a highly localized, eminently embodied "psychic life of racism"—the microlevel sinews that shape and accelerate racism as a macrolevel ideology.

Holland proposes a conjunction between critical race theory and queer theory, refocusing on "the *feeling* that escapes or releases when bodies collide in pleasure and in pain."[32] The "primary work of racism," by these terms, is the production of affects through the frisson and friction of everyday encounters—an arresting intimacy that is desired by racist bodies. Racism is a technology for the production of affects, a place to which bodies migrate. Racism, Holland writes, can be explained "as the emotional lifeblood of race; it is the 'feeling' that articulates and keeps the flawed logic of race in its place. When assessment is on the line," she continues, "the 'races' take their seats at the American *feast of difference*."[33] Racialization is a feast, a festival, an erotic space from and through which flow the currents of power.[34] Holland calls the bodies at this feast "blood strangers," queerly kinned by the circuits of compulsion sparking to life between them. Racism is not just an abstract set of ideological propositions: it is a space where bodies grind against each other, feeling the friction of other bodies.

The first question about the relationship between affect and ideology—What do affects do?—is not wrong. Affects coassemble with ideological forms on every level: there would be no political sphere without the socializing affective twists of bodies. But to view humans as masters of their affectspheres, sitting in high towers and pulling levers to seduce or manipulate others with irrational feelings, is to replicate the faulty model of calculating, sovereign angelic subjects. This misses out on a second, deeper question, one that fractures human agency and calls attention to the animal forces sliding through us: What do we do for affects? Racism as an erotic ideology is a configuration of animal embodied reactions, not a purely linguistic construct or economic proxy. Racialized ideology is often about dissimulation to protect a set of material interests. But it is also a feast, a game you can play.

Erotic Ideologies: Primatology and Racialization

Following suit with affect theory's interest in opening conversations with life science approaches—from Massumi's laboratory experiments to Sedgwick's long-standing engagement with Tomkins to Jasbir Puar's use of neuroscience—*Religious Affects* argues that our understanding of the relationship between racialization and power can be improved by turning to contemporary primatology, especially the recent offshoot of primatology known as evolutionary ethics. In *Through a Window*, Jane Goodall describes troupes of chimpanzees gathering to go out on patrol at the borders of their territory. As the troupes reach the margins, they occasionally run into lone individuals from other groups, whom they often attack. What is most startling about Goodall's account is her description of the demeanor of the apes: rather than bitter or even "angry" as they track their quarry, the chimpanzees seem to relish the hunt and the ensuing combat. When finished, they literally dance: "For the next five minutes the Kasakela chimpanzees, in a state of excitement that bordered on frenzy, charged back and forth around the scene of conflict, dragging and hurling branches, throwing rocks, uttering the deep, low-pitched hooting calls that sound like roaring."[35] It is a disturbing, dark inversion of the waterfall dance, an embodied celebration of the destruction of bodies rather than of the grandeur of falling water.

More startling still, the chimpanzee companies seem to form "spontaneously"—without any explicit intermember communication—and pick their targets seemingly without any linguistic conferral. Goodall describes a scene in which a group of males on patrol encounters a lone female of a rival group: "When one male passed close by, she reached out to touch him with a typical submissive gesture at which he jerked away, stared at the arm she had touched, seized a handful of leaves, and vigorously rubbed at his defiled hairs."[36] The quasi-ritualistic purification of the body of another body's touch images the erotic life of racism sketched by Holland emerging prior to discourse. Chimpanzee bodies produce complex social markings that ramify into equally complex behavior patterns without language. Conflict zones in an underpopulated area are not reducible to economically derived competitions for resources. Rather, regimes of sociality and alterity are constituted by animal bodies in ways that exceed cost-benefit calculations. For Goodall, the capacity to draw boundaries between *us* and *them* forms somewhere far upstream of the words themselves—let alone economies of rational self-interest.[37]

Goodall's conclusion is that chimpanzee bodies are invested with a biological predilection for warfare. The opposition that followed Goodall's discoveries tracked the classic behaviorist presupposition that depth and complexity of behavior could only be learned.[38] Goodall solves the problem of chimpanzee warfare in a way that is unintelligible to the behaviorist framework, suggesting that the predisposition toward the production and militarization of group boundaries is an affective process. Analyzing the Four-Year War in Gombe from 1974 to 1977, in which a subgroup of chimpanzees of the Kasakela community beat five chimpanzees of the Kahama community so badly that they later died of their injuries, Goodall writes that "some male chimpanzees, particularly the younger ones, found intercommunity conflict absolutely thrilling."[39] Sociality and the establishment of a social perimeter, Goodall believes, form a complex created by compulsory affects.

These primatological cameos set the stage for affect theory's critique of the linguistic fallacy, illustrating that behavioral depth and complexity exist prior to, beyond, and beside language. The war correspondent Chris Hedges contends that human bodies, too, experience the production of militarized social boundaries as a compulsion. In *War Is a Force That Gives Us Meaning*, Hedges argues that social division is not an external imposition on our naturally peaceful social worlds, but a desire embedded deep within our bodies—a lust for exclusion and destruction. For Hedges, religious formations coassembling with racialized ideologies—such as the attacks on Bosnian Muslims and Croatian Catholics by Serbian Orthodox Christians with Byzantine crosses sewn onto their uniforms during the Yugoslavian Civil War—become technologies for the production of embodied affects. Like Holland's description of the erotic life of racism, Hedges suggests that the compulsion to divide and shore up the borders of groups of bodies delivers what he calls "meaning." The cause of a nation, a pack of bodies, reorients communities (from pre–Civil War Yugoslavia to mid-1980s Argentina to the United States after 9/11) toward a shared affective expression.[40] Bodies experience a "passionate yearning" for the glorious cause of *us* against *them*.[41] Language is layered on top of these deeper embodied compulsions, a technology for sculpting and distributing their intransigent forms into political configurations.

Hedges writes that "the eruption of conflict instantly reduces the headache and trivia of daily life. . . . The communal march against an enemy generates a warm, unfamiliar bond with our neighbors, our community, our nation, wiping out unsettling undercurrents of alienation and dislocation."[42] Just as Kathleen Stewart likened ordinary affects to "drugs of all kinds," the language of a "headache" being "cured" by war is deliberate, for one of Hedges's primary metaphors for war is the drug. In the U.S. war on terror, Hedges writes, both the American home team and the jihad movement "ingest the anodyne of war . . . the same narcotic."[43] On all sides, war is an addiction, a compulsion running in our veins. When peace returns after a conflict—even for those who suffered—dreariness and tedium come along with it. Even the victims find themselves "alone, no longer bound by that common sense of struggle, no longer given the opportunity to be noble, heroic, no longer sure what life was about or what it meant."[44] War is a cruel optimism, so enticing that even when it is toxic, we find ourselves longing for it. Even the journalist's body is implicated, finding that "it is hard to live outside war's grip. It takes a higher and higher dose to achieve any thrill. Finally, one ingests war only to remain numb."[45] War as a narcotic compels our bodies—victim, aggressor, and bystander alike—along a giddy spiral of addiction.

But the erotic life of racism, for all its compulsory power, does not dominate bodies. Hedges tells the story of a Serbian woman who took in two Muslims during the war—the children of a former Bosnian classmate. Her Serb neighbors spat on her, taunted her, and vandalized her home, but she persisted, later insisting to Hedges that bringing the children in was her only choice—a compulsion.[46] Hedges pairs her story with that of a Serbian Christian family in Bosnia who were ostracized by their Muslim neighbors. The violence of the war shattered the family, leaving the daughter-in-law widowed and with an infant daughter she was physically unable to nurse. After five days of feeding the slowly dying baby tea, there was a knock on the door. A neighborhood farmer wordlessly handed the mother a half liter of milk from his cow. She described what happened next to Hedges in an interview after the war: "He came the next morning, and the morning after that, and after that. Other families on the street began to insult him. They told him to give his milk to Muslims, to let the Chetnik children die. He never said a word. He refused our money. He came for 442 days, until my daughter-in-law and granddaughter left Goražde for Serbia."[47] Hedges went to track down the farmer, living in an unheated concrete room with several other men, selling apples on the streets. "When I told him I had seen the Soraks," Hedges writes, "his eyes brightened. 'And the baby?' he asked, 'How is she?'"[48] The affective responsivity of bodies to other bodies is not limited to the hedonicity of hate: there are also compulsions pulling bodies across bounding lines, a recalcitrant compassion.

Recalcitrant Compassion: Primatology and Moral Sentiments

Warlike behavior is created by affective compulsions, but counteracting and in parallel with these violent, thymotic affects are others that draw bodies together in very different kinds of relationships. These affective complexes also surge through bodies, pulling us to borderlines where we can encounter other bodies in relations of care, compassion, or moral concern. Some philosophical approaches view ethical relationships as predicated on transcendence,[49] as outside of the natural order of things—a view the feminist philosopher Mary Midgley dismisses as an "unassimilable pattern at odds with all else on this planet."[50] By contrast, contemporary primatological approaches see care as a bodily response to other bodies, an animal compulsion shared by many animal genera.

Theories of evolutionary ethics run back to Darwin, who, in *Descent of Man*, proposed what the primatologist Barbara King calls the "need for belongingness," or, in affective terms, a compulsory sociality that motivates animal bodies.[51] In his *Notebook M*, Darwin wrote that "any animal whatever endowed with well-marked social instincts would inevitably acquire a moral sense or conscience."[52] Midgley glosses this by writing that humans are "heirs to a long, complex tradition of group life, deep social affection and interdependence"—an embodied history, rooted in animality, that has produced the various, semistable forms of sociality.[53]

This is why the primatologist Frans de Waal has argued that conscience should not be seen as "some disembodied concept that can be understood only on the basis of culture and religion."[54] Like other aspects of our bodies, conscience is a compulsion with foundations in complex embodied histories extending back into deep time. This approach views evolution by natural selection as an associating—as well as an individualizing—force, producing bodies that are not only well adapted to their environmental niches but are predisposed to form connections of aid and attachment with other bodies.[55] As E. O. Wilson writes, the "constructs of moral reasoning . . . are the learning rules, the propensities to acquire or to assist certain emotions and kinds of knowledge."[56] Evolutionary ethicists are not only interested in erasing the notion that morality is transcendent of bodies; they also reject the related hypothesis that moral behavior is a result of a late-blooming cognitive or social technology like organized religion, philosophy, or self-awareness: "Instead of being a surface phenomenon in our expanded neocortex," de Waal writes, "moral decision-making apparently taps into millions of years of social evolution."[57] Evolutionary ethics sees moral behavior as rooted in a set of animal compulsions that are not reducible to language.

Just like sex and eating, social instincts plug into the circuitry of compulsory affectivity, producing what de Waal calls "bodies with moral sentiments."[58] De Waal recounts a story about a primate facility he was overseeing where the keepers decided to build a new play space for the chimpanzee colony captive there. After spending a few days locked in separate pens while construction was underway, the chimpanzees were released into a state-of-the-art playground, which they promptly ignored. Instead, "the first minutes following the release were all about social connections. Some chimps literally jumped into each other's arms, embracing and kissing. Within a minute, the adult males were giving intimidation displays, with all their hair on end, lest anyone might have forgotten who was boss."[59] The priority of the chimpanzees on their release is joyful contact with other bodies. Like prisoners in solitary confinement, their compulsory sociality has been starved.[60] This surging of affects between bodies (highlighted by social deprivation) is the currency of moral decision making. "We are hardwired to connect with those around us and to resonate with them, also emotionally," de Waal writes.[61] This hardwiring is the intransigent compulsion of affect, the sovereign tangle of living forces moving animal bodies into and through social worlds.

Prior to language, moral decision making—in humans and other animals—is produced from embodied regimes of affect. De Waal suggests that classical evolutionary theories of prosocial behavior—such as kin selection and mutual aid—are inadequate because they fail to explore motives, the actual impulses at the level of bodies that make ethical behavior possible. Kin selection and mutual aid are macrolevel explanations rather than causes that compel individual animals. It is true that sex serves reproduction, hunger sustenance, and breathing oxygenation, but bodies perform these actions long before they know those links. Motives are now; evolution is ancient history.[62] Bodies are moved by economies of compulsion, not abstract calculations of need.[63]

Bodies with moral sentiments, then, are not just human bodies. Nonhuman primates, especially, have their own repertoire of compassionate behaviors—even in the absence of language. De Waal describes, for instance, Kuni, a bonobo in England's Twycross Zoo, who rescued and tended to an injured starling that landed in her enclosure.[64] Binti Jua, a gorilla at Brookfield Zoo in Chicago, staged an even more dramatic rescue, picking up an injured three-year-old boy who had fallen from a viewing platform near her and carrying him to safety.[65] Examples such as these—drawn from the limited data set of observations we can make of animals living on the artificial border region between our worlds and theirs—are corroborated by laboratory experiments showing, for instance, that mammals such as rats and monkeys will rigidly refuse to press levers that will shock others within their line of sight, even if doing so provides them with food rewards.[66] The everyday patterns of chimpanzee societies are structured, de Waal argues, not by conflict and fear, but by a surging network of prosocial behaviors.[67] The same prosocial behaviors were also recorded by Goodall. Their moral repertoire included an ongoing landscape of comforting, child-minding, food-sharing, risk-taking to help others, and reconciliation. Goodall even observed chimpanzees extending care not only to their own kin, but to those they had previously been in conflict with. Goodall saw these ethical behaviors, too, as innately driven, the by-products of an embodied history leading to protoforms of nonlinguistic morality.[68] Chimpanzees "may not *know* the golden rule," de Waal writes, "but they surely seem to follow it."[69]

This quality of not-knowing is important for understanding the primatology of racialization.[70] De Waal points out that in prosocial behavior, "much occurs on a bodily level that we rarely think about."[71] Although our compulsory sociality is filtered through the particularities of human cognition and then redistributed again by language, it is made up of the same elementary forms as are found among other mammals. The different onto-phenomenological constitutions of species according to different embodied histories leaves animal species with a "heterogeneous multiplicity," in Derrida's phrasing, of flexible architectures of morality. Though the "high end" of morality—what de Waal identifies as "abstract moral rules that can be studied and debated like mathematics"—may be unique to humans, moral reasoning is built on simpler cognitive and affective foundations that are available to nonhuman animals.[72]

What gets called religion is both driven by these compulsions and constructed to drive them. De Waal argues that—contrary to the view that religion and our moral ideals are "introduced by wise men (founding fathers, revolutionaries, philosophers) after a lifetime of pondering right, wrong, and our place in the cosmos"—religion grows out of a pulsing network of embodied affects.[73] Rather than inventing demands ex nihilo, he states, "in stressing kindness, religions are enforcing what is already part of our humanity. . . . They are not turning human behavior around, only underlining pre-existing capacities."[74] Michael Gazzaniga suggests that religion most likely emerged not to foment morality, but to explore the moral impulses we found animating our bodies.[75] Religion as a composite of compulsions is made possible by existing, intransigent bodily technologies, but it also motivates, activates, and drives those technologies.

Hedges's subjects are following these primatological channels of their bodies when they build relationships with others at the borders of their communities. This goes not only for the violent, destructive compulsions of war, but the compassionate, caring compulsions of ethical relating and moral responsibility. Viewing these sets of tendencies as animal opens up an understanding of religious conflict in terms of a collision between embodied affective regimes, rather than a debate between rival worldviews, as Stephen Prothero suggests.[76] The anthropologist of American religion Kevin O'Neill uses affect theory to argue that "a focus on the production of affective space prompts an interest in the politics of felt difference: between whiteness and the racialized other; between the saved and the sinner; between life and death."[77] The remainder of this chapter will use this approach to map the affective compulsions driving the media ecology of contemporary American Islamophobia.

Park51: Songs of Love and Hate

On December 21, 2009, Daisy Khan appeared on the Fox News program *The O'Reilly Factor* for an interview with guest host Laura Ingraham. Khan was speaking about her plan to work with her husband, Imam Feisal Abdul Rauf, and a New York real estate developer to found an Islamic cultural center in downtown Manhattan, to be known as Park51. Daisy Khan told Ingraham that she "wanted to strike a blow against terrorism and extremist visions of Islam" by building a mosque near Ground Zero that symbolized peace, and Ingraham, as if probing for a point of conflict but unable to find one, responded, "I can't find many people who really have a problem with it." At the end of the interview, Ingraham said, "I like what you're trying to do and, Ms. Khan, we appreciate it."[78]

On August 10, 2010, Ingraham appeared on the same network's *Fox and Friends* morning show. This time, she blasted the Park51 project— which Fox had begun calling "the Ground Zero Mosque"—as a "slap in the face" to the United States, "which has been so welcoming to Muslims," and attacked Daisy Khan's husband as a "radical."[79] She was one of many talking heads on the network—including Sean Hannity, Bill O'Reilly, Glenn Beck, and Megyn Kelly—who devoted hours of broadcasting time to assailing the mosque project and the people behind it. Between the two interviews, Ingraham and her Fox News colleagues radically shifted their affective scripts surrounding Park51 from faintly condescending to seething hostility. What changed in those eight months? How did the Fox talking points veer so sharply—from embracing Park51 to describing the same project as "disturbing" and "insensitive"?

The sequence leading to this transformation started on December 19, 2009, when Pamela Geller—the blogger and activist whose SIOA subway ads we encountered at the beginning of this chapter—responded on her blog *Atlas Shrugs* to a *New York Times* article on Park51 published the previous week. In this post, "Giving Thanks," Geller is sharply critical of the tone of the *Times* piece, which she accuses of being soft on the issue of Muslim "jihad" in the United States. "I don't know what is more grotesque," she writes, "jihad or the NY Times preening of it. The New York Times yet again misrepresents, obfuscates, and confuses infidels and kaffirs about Islam."[80] She challenges the *Times*'s characterization of Imam Rauf's Sufism as a "mystical" version of Islam, insisting that it is no such thing, and that regardless it is a minority viewpoint within the Muslim world. She goes on to remind her readers that the Burlington Coat Factory at 51 Park Place, where the center was slated to be built, had a piece of landing gear from a destroyed airplane fall through its roof on September 11. This was the beginning of Geller's attempt to feel Ground Zero into existence, in O'Neill's vocabulary, as a sanctified location—a repository of material relics animating a global economy of hate.

The Park51 issue lay mostly dormant for the next five months, but when the developers presented their project to a Manhattan Community Board 1 subcommittee in early May, Geller started another volley of critical blog posts. Increasingly, her attacks drew the battle lines of the dialogue in terms of an epic religious conflict.[81] In a May 6 post, she wrote of Park51: "This best demonstrates the territorial nature of Islam. This is Islamic domination and expansionism. The location is no accident. Just as Al-Aqsa was built on top of the Temple in Jerusalem. And what about the Hagia Sophia, the ancient cathedral of the church of Constantinople, one of the great buildings of the world, the grandest church in Christendom at that time and for 1000 years thereafter—and now a mosque? The Aya Sofya mosque—they didn't change the name, just Islamified it."[82] This time, as a later *New York Times* timeline of events showed, the attacks ignited, and right-wing activists and politicians picked up the cause.[83] When demonstrators packed the hearing of a New York City Landmarks Preservation Commission meeting about Park51's request to demolish the Burlington Coat Factory on May 25, one of the protesters shouted, "You're building on a Christian cemetery!"[84] The affective electricity of a dyad of religiously defined spaces—a shrill divide between "Judeo-Christian civilization" and "Muslim invaders"—was now inextricable from the dialogue surrounding the site.

One thing can be said of Geller's work: no one could accuse her of a dry style. Her writing is an incendiary barrage of slurs, accusations, insults, and demonizations. In "Islamic Antisemitism 101," for instance, she writes of a recent appearance by Khan on ABC, "How dare Daisy Khan evoke the holocaust and the mass genocide of the Jews to smear those brave Americans who dare to stand up against Islamic supremacism and the tower of triumph under proposal for Ground Zero? . . . This is Goebbels style propaganda at its most base. It is revolting, and decent men recoil at her unmitigated gall and insensitivity. Shame on ABC for not giving 911 families and lovers of freedom an equal stage."[85] Underlining the priority of affect in her work, Geller calls her literary flourishes of hatred her "little darlings":[86] writing, for her, is a technology for the production of affects, a site to splash around in rage.

The textual dimension of her relish in the production of barbed lines around other bodies aside, this affective electricity is visible on Pamela Geller's face and body as she cavalierly showers her disdain on Muslims. On her video blogs—an important side feature of *Atlas Shrugs*—she crackles with energy, alive with hate and contempt.[87] More than just a written practice, Geller's project turns her very body into an affective vector. Absorbing these compulsions and rebroadcasting them, right-wing and mainstream blogs, news sites, and commentators began to expand the cloud of hate Geller was building around the planned community center.[88] Geller's work—the attachment of an affective halo of rage to Park51— altered the parameters of the American right-wing media machine, turning it into a relay system for a circuit of embodied anti-Muslim fury.

This economy of hate spread outward from the right-wing media apparatus to infect a broader set of public conversations. As the issue took off, Republican presidential candidate Newt Gingrich called Park51 a "deliberate insult," claiming that the name of the proposed Islamic chapel inside Park51, Cordoba House, was designed to symbolize the Islamic conquest of Spain.[89] Mark Williams, the leader of the right-wing Tea Party Express, claimed that Park51 "would be a monument for the worship of the terrorists' monkey god."[90] American Muslims were accused of practicing *taqiyyah*—the traditional practice, among Shi'ite Muslims, of concealing their religious identity in order to avoid persecution. American Islamophobes reinterpreted this concept to mean dissimulating behind a putative opposition to terrorism in order to infest the nation with terrorist sleeper cells. Any attempt to refute the charge of *taqiyyah* was interpreted by anti-Muslim activists as evidence of *taqiyyah*, creating, in effect, a perpetual accusation machine.[91] This climate of hate materialized as physical attacks and threats of violence. Incidents of vandalism increased at mosques, and Rauf and Khan received numerous death threats.[92] In a tragic climax, a Muslim cab driver, Ahmed Sharif, was asked by a customer, an intoxicated film student, if he was Muslim.

When Sharif answered yes, the student went silent, then shouted, "This is a checkpoint! Allahu akbar!" and slashed Sharif with a knife in the throat and upper body.[93]

In the anti-Park51 backlash led by Geller, religion became a site for the play and production of affects—an economy of hate. Embodied compulsions surged across an affective landscape constructed using the distribution system of global media networks. This queer, affective economy gave shape to a set of new political formations in which bodies were situated on a battlefield of zones of good and evil delimited by religion. Islamophobic racism at the grassroots level represented by Geller is not about ideological manipulation or cashing in—neither an economy of dollar signs nor of complex geopolitical agendas. It is an erotics of racialization, a playground where anti-Muslims can savor their hate. When Geller plugs her anger into the American right-wing media machine, a global affective network is activated, recalibrating the mediascape to produce a new suite of endlessly fascinating affects ringing American Muslim bodies. This is why Fox News changed its song: it had been called to the American feast of difference.

The culmination of this summer of anti-Muslim hate came with the announcement by Pastor Terry Jones of the Dove World Outreach Center in Gainesville, Florida, that he was declaring the ninth anniversary of the September 11, 2001, terror attacks to be International Burn a Koran Day. Dove, a small congregation with only a few dozen members, had long styled itself an opponent of Islam, describing its mission, in part, as "bring[ing people] to awareness [of] the dangers of Islam and that the Koran is leading people to hell."[94] The church had a long history of using inflammatory slogans and public proclamations, once sending some of its teenage members to school with T-shirts reading "Islam is of the devil."[95] Jones seems to have hatched the idea for International Burn a Koran Day in a Twitter message sent out to his followers. This led to a rapid burst of media attention, with Jones's own body and voice becoming increasingly prominent on mainstream news networks. Jones insisted in these interviews that Islam was a false religion leading people astray, and that burning Qur'ans was the best way to send the message that Islam was unwelcome in America.

When Terry Jones emerges as a national figure, his religious identity becomes the platform from which a new array of affective channels becomes possible: suddenly he is the man feared, the man revered, the man of the hour, whose decisions are solemnly discussed. For Jones, the impulse to put pressure on Muslims is about not just a crackling economy of hatred but an economy of dignity. Jones's posture, grave expression, and sonorous voice reflect his imagination of his body as imperious and unflappable. He is driven by the tautness of his own righteousness, composed by confluent streams of secretly enticing affects. As Hedges explains, this use of religion as a technology of violence and exclusion is not new. In Kosovo, he describes how religious institutions facilitated and amplified affective compulsions: "it was easier to get Serb and Muslim commanders to the table for talks than opposing clerics."[96] These religious bodies go where they go not for political or financial benefit. They are motivated by queer economies of dignity, a fascination with erecting their own status at the expense of other bodies. Religion, here, coassembles with the erotics of racialization, driving bodies at the affective level and producing political effects in its wake.

But religious affects do not only yield politics of exclusion. The affectively motivated temptation of race coassembled with religion in other ways during this same season, playing, at precisely the same time, an exactly contradictory role. On the same complex mediascape, religious borderlines also became sites for an entirely different organization of compulsions—an erotics that sought to fade borders and produce transgressive, sticky, queer points of contact. The American feast of difference serves more than one dish: the economy of hate is not the only possible affective political economy.

The most compelling exemplars of this alternative organization of religious affects are the designers of the Park51 project itself, Imam Rauf and Khan. Khan was the founder of the American Society for Muslim Advancement, an organization that describes itself as "dedicated to strengthening an authentic expression of Islam based on cultural and religious harmony through interfaith collaboration, youth and women's empowerment, and arts and cultural exchange."[97] Imam Rauf was a founder of the Cordoba Initiative, a project designed to recall a "period of time during which Islam played a monumental role in the enrichment of human civilization and knowledge . . . [when] Muslims, Jews, and Christians coexisted and created a prosperous center of intellectual, spiritual, cultural and commercial life in Cordoba, Spain."[98] Placed side by side with Geller's blog posts, the texts of these organizations express a qualitatively different affective weight. Rather than fanning the flames of intercommunity conflict, Park51 as a Cordoba Initiative undertaking was designed to play inside a different affective economy, using religion to form social connections across borders, to circulate the embodied compulsions de Waal calls "moral sentiments." As Daisy Khan explained at the time, Park51 was designed to be a monument to a compassionate vision of Islam that emphasized connection with other religious communities—a repudiation of the exclusivist, imperialist version of Islam propagated by the jihad movement.[99] Rather than driving along affective axes of violent triumphalism, this vision trafficked in a set of compulsions that turned religiously identified borders into zones of embodied connection.

Nor was the affective response to Park51 from non-Muslims confined to scorn and condescension. A variety of religious groups and individuals—many of them allies from Khan and Rauf's interfaith projects—were early supporters of Park51. As the anti-Muslim economy of hate took over the airwaves, these same interfaith allies stepped into the breach, circulating an entirely different affective regime. In a series of interviews with religious leaders in August 2010, *Time* magazine found near-universal support for Park51.[100] Some of these supporters, such as the president of Hartford Theological Seminary, explicitly linked their enthusiasm for Park51 to religious practice: "One serves one's faith by living up to the ideals of that faith," she told *Time*. "The ideals of Christianity, like the ideals of Islam and Judaism, are . . . ideals of constructing peaceful and productive relationships with neighbors."[101] For these religious leaders, the theological prerogatives for supporting Park51 followed a particular set of embodied compulsions leading to alternative political outcomes. Like the anti-Park51 demonstrators, religion for them was enmeshed with affects produced at borderlines—but affects designed to produce connection and compassion rather than exclusion.

The same religious strategy of circulating prosocial affects came out in the Quaker response to Park51. Shortly after the controversy erupted, the Friends Committee on National Legislation (FCNL) delivered four poster boards printed with the names of eight thousand Quakers affirming their support for American Muslims to the Cordoba Initiative. Jim Cason of FCNL and the Cordoba Initiative staff "spoke for some time about the Koran's teaching that the spark of God is in everyone," Cason wrote on the FCNL blog, pointing out that it "sounded remarkably similar to the Friends perspective that the Light of God is in every person."[102]

Their meeting, however, was not an abstract dialogue exchanging theological orthodoxies: it was also a site for the production of certain affects. Aylin Karamehmetoglu, an employee at Cordoba, told Cason, "When I first saw all of those names, it almost had me in tears."[103] The space on the borderlines is an affectively rich terrain, not just for compulsions orbiting rage and hatred, but for the powerful affective structures feeding into solidarity, justice, and compassion.

These compulsions can manifest in more complex political forms, as well. Precisely because the production of compassion and solidarity is so affectively thick, it is a valuable asset in attempts to play off one group against another. This is seen, for instance, in the apology offered by Mark Williams, the Tea Party Express leader mentioned above, to Hindus who were offended by his remark about Muslims' "monkey God": "Hanuman," Williams wrote, "is worshiped as a symbol of perseverance, strength and devotion. He is known as a destroyer of evil and to inspire and liberate. Those are hardly the traits of whatever the Hell (literally) it is that terrorists worship and worthy of my respect and admiration not ridicule."[104] In this, he attempted to invoke a top-down, multicultural sensibility that authorized some religious formations (Hinduism) while rejecting others (Islam)—activating a regime of solidarity on one border while intensifying the militarization of another. The same method is used by Geller in her frequent insistence that Israel's positive record on gay rights gives it moral superiority to act with impunity against its enemies.[105] What Puar calls homonationalism—justifying imperialist projects under the mantle of protecting gay rights—relies on this same double affective maneuver of deploying an embodied demand for compassion within a regime of violent exclusion.[106] In a brilliantly sarcastic blog post, V. V. Ganeshananthan, a blogger at *Sepia Mutiny*, rejected Williams's apology on the grounds that it was "offered in a spirit that is completely antithetical to the Hindu faith and the Hindu community in which I was raised, and because it demeans Islam, a religion that is important to so many of my friends and loved ones."[107] Here, too, the play of compulsions takes on a recursive structure: it simultaneously opens passages of solidarity with some bodies at the same time as it closes off others (though in a gesture of defense rather than attack). Systems of power emerge in the crosscurrents of these complex, interlocking economies of affect.

This same set of religious affects was also marshaled in response to Terry Jones. Evangelical leaders such as Jim Wallis reached out to Jones to try to talk him down from his scheme, persuading him to relent just hours before he had planned to build his bonfire.[108] Wallis wrote that interfaith relationships had been strengthened by the controversy, reflecting, "I saw similarly powerful, productive and reflective exchanges in churches all over the country after 9/11, when hundreds of people routinely turned out to hear a visiting Muslim scholar or imam speak to their congregation."[109] Wallis saw in the tragedy of 9/11 and in the slow-burning seethe of the summer of 2010 not just an obstacle to be neutralized, but a power source, an opportunity to deepen intercommunity relationships—to construct new affective points of contact—drawing bodies together at the borders between religious communities exactly where others would force them further apart. Wallis's body, in other words, became what Ahmed calls a "conversion point"—capturing an affective intensity but redirecting its force.

Religion, during the Park51 controversy, was multiple, enfolding a range of configurations of primatological—rather than angelic—systems of power. In each of these examples, we find another face of the wheeling matrix of affective religion. Religion can be an engine for the production of racialized difference, a set of felt social categories that then spawn intellectualized justifications for scorn. But religion need not be socially divisive: it also operates on our bodies to elicit other affects—equally addictive, but entailing a different set of political effects. The struggle for justice, the felt interrelation of love, the demand for compassion—all are compulsions within bodies that can be elicited, activated, and charged by what gets called religion. Religion is not doomed or destined to either of these affective regimes; it coassembles with the full range of animal compulsions to produce complex, contradictory landscapes.

Islamophobia does not buttress a system of economic exploitation in the same way that anti-black racism does. And although Pamela Geller may be making money while prosecuting her anti-Islam vendetta, I would argue that is far from her prime motivation for doing it. Nor are Geller or Terry Jones best understood as sophisticated ideological profiteers marshaling affective forms to engage in global-scale media manipulation. Their religions are eminently animal—blocks of forces surging through them, each a complex of compulsions. They are motivated by a complex of the hedonicity of hate and a sustaining economy of dignity. Like the network of clumsy, confused bodies out of which it emerges, religion is a regime of accidents. The logic of "authentic" religion—whether it presumes that religion is always social control, always violent, or always peaceful—is unworkable for complex formations of power. The English Defense League thugs who demonstrated with Geller against Park51 wrapped in the cross of St. George or the violent protests against Jones in Indonesia and Afghanistan with signs like "Burn a Qur'an—Burn in Hell"—these are no less part of religion than the mission of organizations like the American Society for Muslim Advancement or Cordoba to weave together communities, or the church next door to Dove in Gainesville that countered Burn a Koran Day with an interfaith Gathering for Peace, Understanding, and Hope. Nor are they any less animal. Though taking different portions at the feast of difference, all these orientations of the affective religious body are part of the surging global complex of religion.

Conclusion: Silvaticus, the Temptation of Race

Oh, my brothers living in the West, I know how you feel, when I used to live there, I felt depressed. The cure for the depression is jihad.
—Islamic State propaganda video

In *Black Skin, White Masks*, Frantz Fanon writes that his Antillean philosophy professor advised him, "Whenever you hear anyone abuse the Jews, pay attention, because he is talking about you."[110] Fanon saw that racism as an ideology is only loosely glued to a specific set of cognitively organized propositional beliefs about other bodies, that racism, at the end of the day, is always susceptible to playing the same game with a new set of toys. The linguistic fallacy presumes that racism is the byproduct of a gridlike discursive architecture, a set of beliefs about races producing a logically consistent matrix of behavioral outcomes. Affect theory opens up the parallel possibility that racialization can sometimes be understood as an affective machine—a particular menu preference when seated at the feast of difference. When radical Islamist fighters proclaim that "the cure for depression is jihad," they are mapping an onto-phenomenological property of human (and other animal) bodies: the way that aggression evokes affective compulsions that lure and nourish bodies, spinning off political effects in the process. Although the texts they point to are different, the jihadis and Pamela Geller are affectively isomorphic. The proper nouns they traffic in are functionally interchange-able, a collection of masks floating on the surface of a far deeper, far more intransigent economy of hate.

Racialization, the militarization of social borders, and its antithesis—altruism, traveling to the borders where others dwell in order to reach out to them in community—are onto-phenomenological shapes that tether us to other bodies in complex, contradictory ways. The compulsions to define in-groups and attack out-groups are affective technologies embed-ded in the bodies of many social animals—especially humans and other primates. But these compulsions are counteracted and complicated by their interactions with other affects that deplete or disrupt those same boundaries. Out of the complex affective tangle produced by these in-teracting forces, the full array of social formations of power emerges—from the triumphantly righteous global solidarity movement all the way over and down to the casual, secretly thrilling gesture of contempt. As Stewart writes, "Politics starts in the animated inhabitation of things, not way downstream in the various dreamboats and horror shows that get moving."[111] Our bodies are constituted by these wheeling matrices of connective force, by the set of embedded bodily technologies bestowed on us through a staggeringly complex twist of genetic legacies and envi-ronmental impressions.

Islamophobia presents itself as a patient, reasoned critique. But as the primatological perspective shows, the production of religious identities emerges out of an eminently animal affective matrix. The mobilization of social boundaries is part of the erotics of racism, a set of meaning-making technologies embedded in bodies that flow through us and co-alesce into religious forms. At the same time, the countermaneuvers that travel to borderlines and demilitarize them are also part of an animal heritage. Religious machines are built out of complex confluences of these compulsory affective technologies, circulating within a complex of other heterogeneous historical economies that shape on-the-ground embodied responses. Ideology, especially racialized ideology, is a tech-nology for the production of affects—a uniquely human technology, but no less animal for it. This is especially true when bodies—such as white Islamophobes—try to mask economies of hate with an angelic countenance. Sloterdijk reminds us that the European discursive tradition begins with a plea for rage, even as it tries to dissimulate its bloody, lop-sided economies of rage and economies of dignity beneath a heavenly order of abstract language games. Secular and religious bodies alike are all savages, creatures of the forest.

Thinking ideology as compulsion opens up a set of possibilities for thinking racialization as something other than a veil for financial or political interests. Racialization may, under some circumstances, be a queer economy—an autoeroticism that desires only its own exercise—which in turn translates into political formations such as justice or oppression. It keys us into an intuition that we often have about violently radical bodies: that there is a streak of self-indulgence at the heart of their politics, that for all their archly declared *reasons* for loathing blacks, Muslims, Jews, immigrants, trans* people, queers, or any other marginalized group, they are, somehow, fundamentally *at play*. And it explains why racialization seems to be more contagious through affects than through discourses. Affect theory maps the ways that racialization builds an economy of dignity on the backs of other bodies. This doesn't mean that conventional ideology critique is abandoned. Rather, it adds a new dimension to the framework of questions scholars use to consider the production of religion.

If theodicy is interested in why bad things happen to good people, affect theory is interested in why good people do bad things. This is why part of thinking about animal religion will always mean thinking about the temptation of race. There is something deeply Proustian about racism, except the field of delightful objects becomes a field of delightful bodies to spit on—like Proust's reviled Françoise. Racialization activates a skein of affects between our bodies—affects playing out on a plane far upstream of a set of language games. The imaginary of race—the virtual, felt, prelinguistic sense of *us* and *them*—is a power source buried in bodies, electrifying the ground above it. But for this same reason, racial difference also becomes a powerful site for the activation of justice, compassion, and solidarity—affective engines that repurpose the circuitry of race and create rival technologies of what Hedges calls "meaning." The critique of racism, the obliteration of lines, is also "erotic" in Holland's sense. The temptation of race is as much about being drawn to antiracism as it is about racism—sometimes to the point of addiction. The embodied enactment of race is a temptation no matter the angle of approach.

Bodies are not smooth systems, operating in a singular granulated economy that orients all of its prerogatives and values toward a single focal point, a single common currency. Rather, the body is a cluster of bodily technologies crammed together in a single, heterogeneous space, each with its own priorities. The body contains multitudes and contradicts itself blithely. It chooses many different plates at the feast of difference, many different erotic preferences in the way it interacts with other bodies. And just as there is no single, smooth essential character to human bodies, there is no essential violence or essential lovingness to religion. Religion is a hybrid system, a set of embodied practices for the production of affects, skimming the surface of this spinning, multitiered network of historical (evolutionary and local) accidents. This chapter diagrams one paired example of these opposed bodily technologies: embedded in our bodies are machines surging for the production of both exclusionary, violent affects and inclusive, compassionate affects. In both complexes, we find opportunities to exercise the affective haloes that swirl around us in the presence of different bodies. Religious affects—animal religion—unfurl from this constellation of intimacies.

SIX

ACCIDENT: ANIMALISM, EVOLUTION,

AND AFFECTIVE ECONOMIES

The 2006 book *Breaking the Spell* outlines the philosopher of science Daniel C. Dennett's most sustained meditation on the subject of religion. While making his case for atheism, Dennett plays an animal soundtrack that recurs throughout his work: the nighttime howling of packs of coyotes in the woods around his Maine cabin.[1] Coyotes as they travel sing to one another in long, shivering trills. Their songs—I hear them in the evergreen forests of northern Vancouver Island—are uncannily beautiful, eerie and gorgeous at once. For Dennett, the coyotes' songs are a case study in the philosophical legacy of Darwinism, specifically the principle of the "stinginess" of nature. In works such as *Darwin's Dangerous Idea, Kinds of Minds,* and *Breaking the Spell,* Dennett takes what he calls an adaptationist stance in the evolutionary analysis of behavior. This stance authorizes lines of interpretation that produce explanations for animal actions in terms of their overriding fitness. Natural selection produces stingy results—neat columns on the balance sheet of a rationalized economy of survival. Religions, for Dennett, are shown to be unprofitable by this reckoning of accounts.

Behaviors such as the coyotes' midnight howling, Dennett says, although they appear to diminish survival advantage, must have a parsimonious rational cause. "But, then," Dennett asks, "what explains the pack's characteristic howling? What good accrues to the coyote from that conspicuous expenditure of energy? Hardly a low profile. Doesn't it serve to scare away their supper and draw their presence to the attention of their own predators? Such costs would not be lightly recouped, one would think. These are good questions. Biologists are working on them, and even though they don't yet have definitive answers, they are surely right to seek them. *Any such pattern of conspicuous outlay demands an accounting.*"[2] Coyote song, in the adaptationist view, is a math problem. It must be accountable, arithmetically fitted to the ledger of credits and debits calculated as an organism seeks to flourish in its environment and successfully reproduce. *Cui bono?* Dennett asks. Who benefits? What profit in this? What is its reason?

This supervisory role for reason pervades *Breaking the Spell.* In a somewhat dated passage found in an early chapter,[3] Dennett reaffirms his confidence in reason to calculate planetary-scale effects:

> We know when eclipses will occur centuries in advance; we can predict the effects on the atmosphere of adjustments in how we generate electricity; we can anticipate in broad outline what will happen as our petroleum reserves dwindle in the next decades. . . . We have avoided economic collapses in recent years because our economic models have shown us impending problems. . . . It has become something of a tradition in recent years for the meteorologists on television to hype an oncoming hurricane or other storm, and then for the public to be underwhelmed by the actual storm. But sober evaluations show that many lives are saved, destruction is minimized.[4]

For Dennett, this is the same operation that needs to be applied to religion. Religion must be analyzed within the framework of a rationally ordered economy, a spreadsheet of quantified values. Because there are both "good" and "bad spells" (religions), "we need to have a clear account of the reasons that can be offered for and against the different visions of the participants."[5]

Dennett advances a tactic common in sociobiological or evolutionary psychological studies of religion: analyzing religious phenomena in terms of their conformity to a matrix of arithmetically arranged prospects and advantages for survival. As far back as the publication of E. O. Wilson's *Human Nature*, it was assumed that religion could be assessed according to these benefits. Wilson, for instance, advanced Michael Harner's proposal that Aztec sacrifice likely emerged out of a scarcity of protein in the precolonial Mexican diet, with ritually slaughtered human corpses making up the deficit.[6] Religion, in this view, was perfectly conformable to an account of the measurable flows of nutrients within a population.

A broad cluster of presuppositions is built into these approaches, but they can, taken together, be seen to indicate one overarching assumption: that religion and other facets of embodied animal life are easily enfolded into a grid of readily intelligible rational causes—a logic. The Greek word *logos* herds together a ring of interrelated meanings, including language, reason, and order. To make religion, animality, or embodiment logical is to place it in the bright square of human intelligibility, as something that can be read, measured, arranged, and understood according to a well-behaved gear-work of causal propositions.

Although some readers of affect theory have suggested that affect as an episteme is oriented toward an analytics of just such smoothly ordered, "homeostatic" economies (much like the rational circulation of capital under the pressure of Adam Smith's posited invisible hand[7]), I think that a more thorough reading of affect theory aligns it instead with an antithetical theme: rather than a rationally ordered system, affect suggests the complexity, clunkiness, inefficiency, and heterogeneity of bodies themselves; rather than a compact metaphysical circuit, affects are jagged, uneven, and fluid; rather than a linear system, affect points us in the direction of analyses of laterality; rather than a predictable hierarchy assembled under the sovereign sign of *logos*, affects coalesce to form regimes of accidents. Although affect theory's introduction of biological accounts and deprioritizing of structures of intentionality could be seen as opening doors to hard determinism, affect is better understood as sketching bodies that are much more complex, much fuzzier, and all around less predictable than determinist or adaptationist models can accommodate.

In this chapter, I want to argue that affect theory's thematization of accident—a project that is synthesized out of a convergent reading of deconstruction and contemporary evolutionary theory—has important ramifications for the study of religion and power. Specifically, affect theory gives us a vocabulary and an intellectual framework for thinking bodies as affective economies—economies driven by a complex matrix of compulsions that do not necessarily follow predictable watercourses of functional clarity. Bodies as nodes of power do not land in geometric patterns, but produce religious-political formations reflecting the priorities of an eccentric ensemble of affects. In chapter 7, I show that this understanding—what I follow Jacques Derrida in calling animalism— is particularly relevant for theorizing the chimpanzee waterfall dance: animalism reframes language itself as an evolutionary accident and provides resources for sweeping away metaphysics, imagining religion as a jumbled, animal dance.

Animalism: Metaphysics, Evolution, and Différance

Affect theorists such as John Protevi and Eve Sedgwick have proposed readings of Derrida as a thinker who, by indicating the intractable contingency of the linguistic, paved the way for Deleuzian, performative, and affective analyses that map embodied power relations outside of language.[8] These projects situate deconstruction before affect, as a sort of prolegomenon to affect theory that enables us to trace the extradiscursive operations of power by disrupting the sovereignty of language. Without disputing this reading, this chapter aims to build a bridge to a more comprehensive way to read Derrida through affect theory. This bridge aligns with a particular exposition of the theme of accident in post-Darwinian evolutionary theory—a theme that is congruent with Derrida's animalist critique of Western metaphysics. I discuss the work of affect theorists Elizabeth Grosz and Sara Ahmed to develop more deeply a sense of how Derrida's animalism—the deconstruction of what Derrida calls carno-phallogocentrism, in concert with evolutionary theory—converges with an attention to accident in affect theory that can be incorporated into new methods in the analysis of formations of religious power.

Derrida's overall project is a destabilization of the foundational assumptions of the Western tradition of metaphysics—the presupposition of the centrality of *logos* (whether that means rationality, language, or order) in organizing meaning. But Derrida in his famous 1997 Cerisy-la-Salle lectures gives the legacy of his work a peculiar twist: "I have," he states, "a particularly *animalist* perception and interpretation of what I do, think, write, live, but, in fact, of everything, of the whole of history, culture, and so-called human society, at every level, macro- or microscopic."[9] The rededication of the broad scope of his work to animalism explains the cascade of zoological readings Derrida sets up earlier in the lecture series, in an extraordinary five-page meditation, methodically recoding his entire oeuvre as a *zootobiography*, a philosophical history told with silkworms, apes, horses, hedgehogs, fish, squirrels, and birds.[10] The deconstruction of metaphysics is, for Derrida, a disruption of the perimeter of anthropocentric privilege that shifts from an analytic of destiny—often wrapped up with the transcendent prerogative of human language[11]—to one of accident, or what Derrida and Catherine Malabou call *destinerrance*. This transition to a thematics of accident is the animalist turn that provides a complex plane of interface for Derrida with both evolutionary biology and affect theory.

Metaphysics in the Western mode is a presupposition that the flows of nature (*physis*) are governed by a set of abstract and unchanging laws etched above and beside (meta-) the world. Derrida's project, in this sense, is an extension of Martin Heidegger's project in *Being and Time* of displacing Western philosophy's fixation on the presence of Being: rather than thinking Being as an entity to be tracked and discovered, Heidegger suggested that Being was the process of probing for, or questioning after, Being—that Being was not separate from the self, but was organically integrated with the process of being a self.[12] Rather than theoretical behavior—rational, distant reflection on the world, what Heidegger disdains as "just looking"—Being-in-the-World involves absorption of the self in the menagerie of things around it.[13] Rather than a metaphysics of Being, this concern for Being is embedded in one particular kind of creature: Dasein, the human being that asks after Being.

In *Of Grammatology*, Derrida devises a conceptual tool to even more radically wrench apart the machinery of metaphysics: the notion of the *grammè*. Also called the trace or différance, this is the granular element of meaning production that separates beings, concepts, and phenomena to make signification possible. Différance differentiates in such a way as to make possible the lines of the grid of comprehension. It is an archewriting that sets up the possibility of meaning.[14] Although the term *grammè* suggests a literary locus, what Derrida calls writing is actually much more fundamental than human language: it is the very possibility of ontological, phenomenological, and epistemological differentiation governing all codes and systems of difference.[15]

But différance, the trace, also destabilizes the very grids of meaning production that it sets up. Derrida's primary insight is that if a thing is constituted through its differentiation from other things, then it is, in its essence, infected by its surroundings. Rather than a pristine, sui generis meaning, the object ringed by différance is susceptible—contingent— to the world, absorbed and impressed by the matrix of forms shaping its perimeter—the traces of everything else from which it has been differentiated. Différance as an "element without simplicity" is the grit in the machine, the necessary condition, but also the destabilizing ingredient of meaning: "it inaugurates the destruction, not the demolition but the de-sedimentation, the de-construction, of all the significations that have their source in that of the *logos*."[16] Meaning is created, for Derrida, not through the emergence of pristine universal categories, but through the accidental play of différance, the viral cross-contamination among words and concepts through the very mechanism that defines them in opposition to one another. If we understand only that a concept—God, truth, reason, the human, *logos*—is what it is by virtue of its différance from what is around it, it is mangled by the network of collisions that ring it.

But although Derrida uses Heideggerian themes and techniques, the grammè also interrupts Heidegger's project at its core. For Heidegger— especially the later Heidegger—Dasein is categorically human, a being that uses language to exercise its prerogative to probe Being. "Language," Heidegger writes in "The Letter on Humanism," "is the house of Being. In its home man dwells. *Those who think and those who create with words are the guardians of this home*."[17] The animal, by contrast, as Heidegger will spell out in his 1929–1930 lectures on metaphysics, published as *The Fundamental Concepts of Metaphysics*, is "poor in world," a being with potential access to Being, but cut off at the pass by virtue of its lack of language. For Heidegger, the animal is, in its essence, closed to the opening of the entity, to the entity as such.[18]

But exactly where Heidegger sees an overlap between language, Being, and the ontological orientation of human Dasein, Derrida insists that the deconstructive approach must be reapplied even more radically, an approach John D. Caputo terms *radical hermeneutics*. Heidegger puts forward a bipartite ontological frame made up of two internally uniform fields: Things-That-Question-after-Being and Things-That-Do-Not. Derrida writes that the actual heterogeneity of things emerging out of the play of traces cannot be comfortably accommodated to this frame: bodies are jagged, bumpy, off-kilter, eclectic—not binary. The two categories—

Dasein (qua node of Being) and everything else—are incompatible with the zigzagging lines of différance transecting the world.

Derrida will make this point all the more strongly ten years later, in his Cerisy-la-Salle lectures on the topic of "the autobiographical animal." Whereas the term *animal* suggests a singular field on the other side of the human, animals are by no means reducible to a uniform field: "Beyond the edge of the *so-called* human," he writes, "beyond it but by no means on a single opposing side, rather than 'The Animal' or 'Animal Life' there is already a heterogeneous multiplicity of the living."[19] Heidegger's error lies in his attempt to flatten the world, to eliminate complexity, to reduce being to clean-cut, vertically arranged strata. As Derrida writes in *Of Grammatology*, the trace "must be thought before the entity."[20] Bodies in their complexity—their ongoing embodied histories—always crash over the levees of metaphysics.[21]

The image of the human as a pristine node for the recovery of Being through language overlooks the profound "heterogeneous multiplicity" of beings, the set of structuring gaps that manifests as the proliferation of biological difference through the play of traces. Language, under the multiform pressure of the grammè, crumples as a mechanism for locating human bodies in the space of a pure presence. Rather than radically departing from metaphysics, Heidegger has inadvertently lapsed into and reinscribed its fundamental presupposition: that there is a straight line between humans and Truth. This simplistic, rectangular frame— into which only two categories of entity can be inserted—exhibits Heidegger's failure to perceive the complexity of bodies constituted through the play of traces: "The Heideggerian discourse on the animal is violent and awkward, at times contradictory. . . . [Animals'] simple existence introduces a principle of disorder or of limitation into the conceptuality of *Being and Time*."[22] This is why, in embracing the awkwardness of embodiment, Derrida labels the repudiation of metaphysics "animalism."

This decoupling of language from what Derrida calls in "Eating Well" the carno-phallogocentric version of subjectivity—the language-using, animal-eating, male subject who masters the world—disrupts the differentiation of human from animal bodies on the register of language. Derrida writes that "if one re-inscribes language in a network of possibilities that do not merely encompass it but mark it irreducibly from the inside, everything changes. . . . These possibilities or necessities, without which there would be no language, *are themselves not only human.*"[23] Language, in Derrida's work, is not a site for the production of the understanding of Being. It is, instead, an accident, a by-product of the collision of traces, far downstream of the production of meanings.

The intrinsic instability of language, what Caputo calls the "thunderstorm of dissemination," relinks Derrida's project to accident—to coalescences of forces producing unpredictable effects.[24] This is why, in Derrida's collaboration with Catherine Malabou, *Counterpath*, the two draw out the theme of destinerrance in Derrida's work—the inescapability of "loss of control . . . deviation or skidding."[25] Against metaphysics, which demands a fantasy of "bring[ing] order to the race: knowing from whence one has left, whither one is going, writing after having spoken, seen, traversed, explored," they pose the "unforeseen catastrophe . . . an accident befalling an essence."[26] Rather than a grid of rationally arranged inevitabilities, a straight line between humans and truth, Malabou and Derrida's critique of metaphysics poses the possibility that what is could have been otherwise, that we only awkwardly stumbled into being.[27]

This notion, for Derrida and Malabou, is itself illustrated by the figure of an animal—the hedgehog that Derrida takes as the mascot of poetry. Rather than following Heidegger's romantic sense of poetry as the paved superhighway to Being, Derrida suggests that poetry is an exposure to the possibility of accident. For Derrida, the answer to the question, What is poetry? is *hedgehog*: "the poem is a 'traversal *outside* yourself,' a crossing of no return, a voyage toward the other . . . the animal thrown onto the road, absolute, solitary, rolled up in [a] ball, *next to (it)self*. And for that very reason, it may get itself run over."[28] Poetry is an unfurling of animality, a vulnerable unspooling of embodiment into the play of accidents, wandering in a spiral across the highway, always at risk of becoming roadkill.

Derrida's animalist perspective—a synthesis of heterogeneous zoontologies, the play of différance, and contingency—is anticipated even in *Of Grammatology* itself, where Derrida writes that genetics, cybernetics, and all forms of intelligence from the amoeba to human writing are inscribed within the interdynamic of traces.[29] The dissemination of genetic material, the emergence of organisms, animal behavior, language, "conscious subjectivity, its logos, and its theological attributes" are all part of the shifting, uneven field of accidents.[30] Evolution itself, the tumbling of phenotypes and genotypes through their environments, is a cacophonous ensemble of forces animated by the dance of différance. Metaphysics is the myth that humans are not animals, not bodies, not queer artifacts of evolution.

For Derrida, systems of meaning—including religion[31]—are produced not by the integrity or wholeness of rational determination but by a network of colliding traces. Rather than a regime of stable, enduring metaphysical truths, meaning, bodies, and even evolution itself are constituted through crashes. Being itself is a junkyard, a sedimented landscape of accidents. Animality, the heterogeneous multiplicity of bodies, is a disorganized archive of the ongoing play of differences in the creation of species. As critical animal studies scholars such as Cary Wolfe and Kari Weil have suggested, Derrida's animalism is for this reason a crucial instigator of posthumanism, a way of moving past humanism and the humanistic privileging of *logos*, language, and rationality as the only possible loci for producing meaning, complexity, depth, and systems of power—what I have called the linguistic fallacy.

But for Dennett, evolutionary economies are the ultimate form of the balance sheet regulated by grids of geometrically intersecting cui bono relationships. How can evolutionary biology, under Dennett's adaptationist regime, be thought outside of the rationalized economies governed by *logos* rather than accident? The answer to this question lies in moving beyond popular misconceptions of evolutionary biology promoted by Dennett and others to a more complicated perspective, what might be called postadaptationism. Contemporary evolutionary biology in this mode crosses comfortably with Derrida's notion of destinerrance, the force of accident, and the rejection of metaphysics.

Foolproof: Dennett versus Gould

Clearly I do not honor Darwin by hagiography.—**Stephen Jay Gould,**
The Structure of Evolutionary Theory

Darwin's theory of evolution by natural selection was first brought to the attention of the international scientific community in 1859 with the publication of *On the Origin of Species*, but the ideas underpinning that theory had been percolating in his private journals for several decades previously. As far back as 1838, Darwin wrote in his *Notebook M*: "Origin of man now proved.—Metaphysic must flourish.—He who understands baboon would do more towards metaphysics than Locke."[32]

This passage becomes the epigraph to the opening chapter of Dorothy L. Cheney and Robert M. Seyfarth's volume *Baboon Metaphysics*, in which they describe how Darwin realized that an account of human origins emerging out of an animal biological lineage must disrupt the metaphysical presuppositions—the postulates of a fixed human essence—that had guided the Platonic strand of Western philosophy for three thousand years. Darwin realized that only by considering human behavior set against the backdrop of its winding differentiation from other animal species—nonlinguistic species—could we come to advance philosophical understanding.[33] This is why American evolutionary biologist George Gaylord Simpson, writing one hundred years after *Origin*, brazenly insists that "all attempts to answer [the] question [What is human?] before 1859 are worthless and . . . we will be better off if we ignore them completely."[34] For Simpson and all other modern evolutionary biologists, metaphysical accounts that see humanity as angelic, turning away from the emergence of our bodies out of a sloppy trellis of animal forerunners half-submerged in the murk of deep time—a jerky, imperfect trajectory of transition and transformation—are doomed from the start.

But even though Darwinian evolution is the only game in town in evolutionary biology, the particular frame of interpretation of Darwinism brought forward remains a debate among scientists. This debate has implications for the conjoined projects of advancing an understanding of the links between animality, religion, and affect. This section lays out the contours of this conversation, showing that contemporary evolutionary theory, far from indicating a new *logos*—a balance sheet of adaptive survival advantages—is heavily invested in an analytics of accident that can be productively integrated with Derrida's critique of metaphysics and with affect theory.

Simpson's passage is the opening meditation of another landmark work of evolutionary biology, Richard Dawkins's *The Selfish Gene*. For Dawkins, too, Darwinism checkmates metaphysics, leading to a new set of ontological questions rooted in biology. But there is nonetheless a divergence in tone and emphasis between Dawkins and Simpson: where Simpson stresses biology as a field intrinsically oriented to biological organisms in their overwhelming, unmanageable complexity,[35] Dawkins's work unfurls into what feels like a remarkably uniform ontology, what he calls *gene selfishness*, in which the gene is understood to be the fundamental unit of selection, responding swiftly and efficiently to selection pressures to steadily improve its organismic host.[36]

Dawkins's gene selfishness model dives far beneath the level of populations and organisms to produce analyses on the level of elemental genetic material. In a sense, Dawkins's vision is similar to the granular ontology of Spinoza, a highly plastic economy of forces—a sandbox— that can be reconfigured efficiently and rationally in pursuit of higher degrees of adaptiveness. Selection pressure is formulated as an exquisitely corrosive shaping influence, a fluid that prunes away extraneous features of organisms until only a highly adaptive core set of properties remains. Selfishness streamlines organisms, driving them to become ever sharper in an endless race against ruthless competitors. Even when organisms appear to be being altruistic, Dawkins suggests, they are in fact being selfish: "At some subconscious level," he writes, "*something functionally equivalent to mathematical calculations is going on.*"[37] This is why the philosopher of science Kim Sterelny approvingly dubs Dawkins "a wholehearted son of the Enlightenment"—a believer in the fundamental rationality of things.[38] Gene selfishness and its cousin, sociobiology, Steven Rose suggests, build on the image of a genetic balance sheet—a monetarist metaphor that reduces the complex plane of the genescape to a single currency.[39]

This image of evolution by natural selection as a "universal acid" is developed by one of Dawkins's primary intellectual allies, Daniel C. Dennett, who in *Darwin's Dangerous Idea* more fully spells out the set of presuppositions that inform what he calls the adaptationist perspective.[40] For Dennett, the universal acid of Darwinian evolution is expressed not just through its shaping force, but through the destabilizing effect it has had on the ideological presuppositions of metaphysics, on the presupposition that life, the world, and the human—the living artifacts of complexity—must be the products of an intelligent, structuring mind. Dennett interprets Darwin's contribution to biology as a reframing of the process of speciation as one of gradual transformation according to the procedures of an algorithm, an essentially "mindless process" with "guaranteed results": "Whatever it is that an algorithm does," he writes, "it always does it, if it is executed without misstep. An algorithm is a *foolproof recipe.*"[41] Darwin upsets the traditional cosmic pyramid of metaphysics by showing that there can be order (organization) without design (telos).[42]

But even though there is no overarching intelligence constructing the spectacular living array of bodies, evolution is nonetheless understandable in terms of intelligence—as a process of what Dennett calls *genius,* even if it is itself lacking foresight, what Dawkins elsewhere refers to as the "blind watchmaker."[43] "Time and again," Dennett writes, "biologists baffled by some apparently futile or maladroit bit of bad design in nature have eventually come to see that they have underestimated the ingenuity, the sheer brilliance, the depth of insight to be discovered in one of Mother Nature's creations."[44] Francis Crick is quoted by Dennett in support of this point: "Evolution is cleverer than you are."[45] Evolution, for Dennett, Dawkins, and their allies, is intelligent, efficient, and rationalized, the by-product of a nonmetaphysical but no less compelling intelligence embedded in the micrological algorithms of natural selection.

Dennett draws parallels between evolution by natural selection and fields driven by human cognition such as artificial intelligence and engineering. Dennett's overarching point is that Darwinian theory, although it does not rely on a transcendent intelligence, nonetheless produces structures of intelligibility, rationally organized ontological matrices that can be illuminated from within by human reason. Evolution is best understood as the ongoing development of cost-effective solutions to problems—as an engineering problem on the table of a unified "Design Space."[46] Rather than a random coalescence of mutations zigzagging across the evolutionary landscape, natural selection rings these drifting currents with a rationalizing, sculpting force out of which are generated the variety of species.

For Dennett, then, the overriding methodological assumption brought out by Darwinian theory is the value of taking what he calls the *intentional stance*—of assuming that something was designed for a particular purpose. We must "treat the artifact under examination as a product of a process of *reasoned* design development, a series of *choices* among alternatives, in which the *decisions* reached were those *deemed best* by the designers. Thinking about the postulated functions of the parts is making assumptions about the *reasons* for their presence, and this often permits one to make giant leaps of inference that finesse one's ignorance of the underlying physics, or the lower-level design elements of the object."[47] If a found object is good at something, it was probably devised for that purpose—flowers, for instance, have their colors for a reason— to attract bees.[48] For Dawkins, too, the universe is one "in which everything has an explanation even if we still have a long way to go before we find it."[49] The world is constituted according to a series of lines of reason, a grid of rational organization according to an economy of survival values, functions, R&D costs and offsets. Evolution is precise, smart, even angelic in its viewpoint on the world.

This perspective is consistent with a certain Darwin—the Darwin who wrote that "natural selection is daily and hourly scrutinising, throughout the world, the slightest variations; rejecting those that are bad, preserving and adding up all that are good; silently and insensibly working, *whenever and wherever opportunity offers*, at the improvement of each organic being in relation to its organic and inorganic conditions of life."[50] But although this version of Darwinian theory is the prevalent understanding of evolutionary biology in popular discourse, it is not widely accepted among scientists.[51] Feminist philosophers of science such as Evelyn Fox Keller and Mary Midgley have pointed out that the sociobiological frame presupposes a particular model of subjectivity—an autonomous, reasoning Hobbesian subject—entirely determined by its location in a field of competition with other organisms. This leads to an imaging of evolutionary economies as strictly deductive, a zero-sum game structured by simple payoff matrices.[52]

But criticism of the adaptationist perspective also emerges within evolutionary biology itself. This is the approach advanced by the self-described pluralists of evolutionary theory, including Stephen Jay Gould, Elizabeth Vrba, Niles Eldredge, Steven Rose, and Richard Lewontin.[53] In 1979, just a few years after the release of *The Selfish Gene*, Gould and Lewontin published "The Spandrels of San Marco and the Panglossian Paradigm: A Critique of the Adaptationist Programme," in which they argued that adaptationism, the view that "natural selection is so powerful and the constraints upon it so few that direct production of adaptation through its operation becomes the primary cause of nearly all organic form, function, and behaviour," is, at best, a selective reading of Darwin.[54] In this perspective, any suboptimal functioning of an organism is explained away as a necessary mediation of other competing forms, a "contribution to the best possible design for the whole," as a calculated accommodation evening out a balance sheet.[55]

The Panglossian paradigm Gould and Lewontin describe is named for Dr. Pangloss of Voltaire's *Candide*, who incorrigibly insisted that we live in an ideal and benevolent world—and one that is radically intelligible to human minds. Venereal disease, for instance, is explained by Pangloss as "indispensable in this best of worlds. For if Columbus, when visiting the West Indies, had not caught this disease . . . we should have neither chocolate nor cochineal."[56] Pangloss—literally, the "talkative one"— argues that there is a reason for everything, that all things are intelligible according to a rational balance sheet, that we can use language to cast light on every tidy corner of the logical matrix of causal relationships around us.

The adaptationist programme, Gould and Lewontin suggest, follows the same lines, insisting on the radical intelligibility of evolutionary processes according to their adaptiveness or survival value in withstanding the acidic currents of natural selection. Gould and Lewontin counter that although natural selection is and remains a powerful force of evolutionary transformation, it is not the only source.[57] What Gould and Lewontin propose instead of doctrinaire adaptationism is a rich, pluralist approach, a perspective that enfolds multiple layers and dimensions of evolutionary transformation, subsisting not only at the highly granular level of genes but at the more cluttered level of bodies, populations, and relationships, putting "organisms, with all their *recalcitrant, yet intelligible, complexity*, back into evolutionary theory."[58] Rather than a singular Design Space within which moves are made by intelligent algorithms to engineer rational adaptations, organisms are a convergence of capricious, awkwardly interlocking fields.

Exploring these other axes of transformation is the project of Gould's career. In "Spandrels" and his work with Elizabeth Vrba on exaptation— organismic traits emerging in one context but repurposed for another[59]— Gould and his collaborators suggest that rather than thinking of evolution exclusively in terms of adaptive forms, engineering solutions devised to solve particular problems, we consider it a compilation of semi-inert structural features that produce their own dynamics of constraint and accident. The "spandrels" of Gould's work with Lewontin are architectural by-products or sequelae of a set of structural convergences— rounded domes held up by arches between columns placed together at right angles—that were then harnessed for new aesthetic purposes.[60] In *The Panda's Thumb*, Gould describes how the enlarged sesamoid "thumb" of giant pandas came to be used by these herbivorous carnivores to strip bamboo, which became the staple of their diet. Rather than an ingeniously devised solution, the thumb—which may have emerged as the result of a single genetic mutation—is "a contraption," one that "wins no prize in an engineer's derby."[61] It is a remnant, a feature of an organism that may have emerged for no reason whatsoever—or was conserved because it was adaptive in some earlier context that has now shifted—but was eventually incorporated into a new embodied routine. Structural inertia and the accidents of genetic mutation are part of the repertoire of evolutionary change, operating orthogonally to the economizing pressures of natural selection.

Crucial to understanding the pluralist model is a consideration of Gould's home field of paleontology. Rather than beginning as a zoologist studying animals' functional relationships with their environments (as Dawkins did) or as a philosopher studying engineering and artificial intelligence (as Dennett did), Gould's primary data set is the fossil record. This has two ramifications. First, Gould picks up on the problem identified by Darwin, as far back as 1859, that there are very few clear examples of "transitional species" in the fossil record, suggesting that the smooth, linear operation of force—gradual adaptation through evolution by natural selection—is not historically substantiated. Rather than a fast-acting corrosive, selection pressure seems to work in fits and starts, alternating long periods of stasis with short bursts of widespread species extinction or explosive speciation. The terrain of evolution is erratic.

Second, Gould's paleontological background orients his focus to the effects of geology—to the deep penetration of landscape into the matrices of evolution. The cycles of stasis and widespread speciation he documents are, he suggests, often the result of catastrophic change in the geography of organisms—glaciers, floods, earthquakes, impacts from extraterrestrial objects, or the recursive modification effected by organisms themselves, such as the oxygenization of the atmosphere by plankton. Landscapes, Gould reminds us, are dynamic, active systems of force, crisscrossed by currents of vibration. They are the shifting parameters through which evolution unfolds.

This means that there is no such thing as a transcendent or global register of fitness or improvement in the field of natural selection, only local modification and adaptation to existing conditions. These fluctuating landscapes are not a rationally organized, univocal Design Space, but a set of geological accidents. "The sequence of local environments in any one place should be effectively random through geological time—the seas come in and the seas go out, the weather gets colder, then hotter, etc.," Gould points out. "If organisms are tracking local environments by natural selection, then their *evolutionary history should be effectively random as well*."[62] Landscapes drag genomes behind them in a rambunctious, uneven series of stochastic processes, drawing and then scribbling over the definition of *fitness* through a kaleidoscope of shifting ecosystems.

Landscapes, then, are rogue agents, actively impressing themselves into the embodied histories of organisms. In Karen Barad's term, they are *intra-active*—material forces as upstart actants rather than inert background features. Or they are invested with what Jane Bennett calls vital materiality, nonpersonal agents that nonetheless take an active role in conditioning fields of possibility. Natural selection as a process of conserving adaptive accidents is itself historically bounded, which means that the relationship between a genome and its environment is always a changing thing—a slow dance of material forces, including genetic material. What is adaptive in one era may be neutral or maladaptive in another 100,000 years, then adaptive again a millennium later. Or the histrionics of landscape can happen in an instant, as Gould frequently reminds us, with a meteorite strike or an earthquake.

Organisms do not respond to these pressures in real time: there is play in the system, a lag time in the reorganization of features, as well as the intransigence of existing structures, what Gould calls the *Bauplanë* of bodies. "Even if fishes hone their adaptations to peaks of aquatic perfection," Gould writes, "they will all die if the ponds dry up. But grubby old Buster the Lungfish, former laughing stock of the piscine priesthood, may pull through. . . . Buster and his kin may prevail because a feature evolved long ago for a different use has fortuitously permitted survival during a sudden and unpredictable change in rules."[63] Rather than a rationally streamlined system, evolution produces an explosion of lotteries, lotteries in which the winners and losers may not be notified of their victory or their death sentence until eons later. Rather than sleek, polished, high-functioning machines, bodies are messy, heterogeneous, and archaic, scrap heaps advertising contraptions of old, broken, fortuitous parts. Evolution leaves remnants, remainders, fixtures jutting out at odd angles. "You cannot demonstrate evolution with perfection," Gould points out, "because perfection *need not have a history*."[64] Evolution as the production of embodied histories is an awkward sedimentation of accidents.

The result of this collage of forces is a biosphere determined in its particulars by more than just the planing effects of reason. Gould in his review of *Darwin's Dangerous Idea* accuses "ultra-Darwinists" like Dennett of the "conviction that natural selection regulates everything of any importance in evolution, and that adaptation emerges as a universal result."[65] Instead of sanctifying Darwin, Gould in his final magnum opus, *The Structure of Evolutionary Theory*, proposes the elimination of the lingering vestiges of nineteenth-century metaphysics in Darwin's thought, such as "a privileged locus of causality, a single direction of causal flow, and a smooth continuity in resulting effects."[66] Although natural selection is a force that can be seen to exert a rationalizing force on organisms, it is only one part of the broader, more hallucinatory picture of evolution, which includes the retrieval of strange shapes from the past for new and unexpected functions or disruptions, the ongoing aleatory interruptions of rogue landscapes, and convergent effects taking shape out of the interactions between evolved physiological forms, producing novel emergent properties. Not evolution as acid, trimming away extraneous forms and leaving behind safe, predictable clockwork functions, Gould presents us with evolution on acid—a decidedly more hair-raising experience.

It is this understanding of biological systems as driven by multiple trajectories of influence that informs biochemist Steven Rose's rejection of determinism in his monograph *Lifelines*. Rose allies himself with Gould in criticizing the ultra-Darwinist approach that insists on the rational predictability of genomic behavior. For Rose, the signal feature of genomes is not their movement along predictable grids, but their susceptibility to the ensemble of environmental cues around them. What Rose calls lifelines are the individualized histories of organisms as they pass through a succession of ontogenetic embryological and developmental stages. "It is in the nature of living systems to be radically indeterminate," Rose writes, "to continually construct their—our—own futures, albeit in circumstances not of our own choosing."[67] Rather than a homeostatic system, then, that tends toward well-insulated equilibrium, Rose suggests that organisms are better understood as homeodynamic, as absorbing fields of influence around them as they transition between different mobile configurations.

The notion of lifelines defeats the emphasis on linear movement— on the orderly unfurling of *logos*—and replaces it with an unspooling, a reeling-around in concert and collision with the play of forces enfolding living systems. "Life as we now know it," Rose suggests, "results from the combinations of chance and necessity that comprise evolutionary processes."[68] Rather than an orderly unfolding, evolutionary biology is fundamentally a "theory of higgledy-piggledy," an opening up of organisms to différance and the reeling play of accidents.[69] Ultra-Darwinists, with their resolute fascination with reason, erase the dynamics of awkwardness at the heart of Darwinism.[70]

Although evolutionary biology is popularly mistaken as a way of rationally explaining bodies, the pluralist approach to Darwinism is better understood as a form of animalism—a way of upsetting the metaphysical presupposition that a *logos*, a fundamentally intelligible form of rationality, permeates our bodies and worlds. In conjunction with natural selection, the lashing forces of selection pressure bearing down on bodies, the slow-motion collision between different economies, come to look much more like a skein of accidents—destinerrance, an inescapable contingency. Ultra-Darwinists who emphasize the overweening rationality of the products of evolution paradoxically give comfort to those who see man as an angel by reenfolding us within the circle of sovereign *logos*.

What might be called postadaptationist evolutionary biology, then, is a species of deconstructive animalism, a set of intellectual procedures for destabilizing carno-phallogocentric metaphysics.[71] It tracks the influence of rogue landscapes on bodies, the susceptibility of bodies to matrices of force that crisscross us, the waste, the redundancy, the stumbling foolishness of animality. If there is a logic to evolution, it is a geo-logic, an ordering by the succession of cataclysms and catastrophes that reverberate across the earth. Or it is what Elizabeth A. Wilson calls a bio-logic, tightly binding intransigent, colliding forms into emerging bodies understood as nonidentical fields of difference. Rather than a metaphysics—an unyielding regime of truths that stands outside of the play of traces—evolution and deconstruction as animalisms converge to recover the regime of accidents, the mangle of collisions that are animal bodies and animal systems of meaning making. As Wilson writes, "perhaps all biology wanders."[72]

Magnificent Makeshifts: Affect Theory on Accident

Modern evolutionary theory portrays man as an adapted organism, fearfully and wonderfully made, but also imperfectly adapted because he is a patchwork thrown together, bit by bit, without a plan, remodeled opportunistically as occasions permitted. The conjoint operation of blind mutation, genetic recombination and natural selection contrived that magnificent makeshift, the human being.—**Silvan Tomkins**, *Affect Imagery Consciousness*

Derrida is read by Protevi and Sedgwick in different ways as a precursor to affect theory. They are correct that Derrida's work is not sufficient for a map of the relationships between affects and power, but *Religious Affects* suggests that the theme of accident in animalism—whether Darwinian or Derridean—is a major analytic concern for affect theory and for religious studies. This is demonstrated in the work of Elizabeth Grosz and Sara Ahmed, affect theorists who develop analyses of the links between bodies and power attentive to the nonlinearity of affects. Grosz focuses on Darwin's notion of sexual selection, pointing out that sexual selection creates an economy of affects that intersects orthogonally with economies of survival. Ahmed details how affects fragment the expectation that bodies are pulled in straight lines by systems of power. Affective economies are queer economies that are driven by the uneven circulation of pleasures and desires rather than a disembodied *logos*.

Darwin in *The Descent of Man* develops a description of a mechanism of evolution that he mentions only briefly in *Origin*: sexual selection. Where natural selection advances an organism's fitness in relationship to its landscape, sexual selection advances its fitness in relationship to other bodies within its species, providing an advantage that has nothing to do with survival, only with reproduction. This is exhibited, Darwin writes by way of example, when "we behold two males fighting for the possession of the female, or several male birds displaying their gorgeous plumage, and performing strange antics before an assembled body of females."[73] Like coyote song, these traits correlate negatively to survival value, depleting resources or preventing natural camouflage that would protect against predators. For Darwin, sexual selection is a major contributing factor to macro- and microevolution that works laterally or at cross-purposes with "survival of the fittest."[74]

Feminist philosopher of science and Deleuzian affect theorist Elizabeth Grosz has done more to draw out the implications of Darwin's work for theoretical work in the humanities than almost any other contemporary scholar. In *Time Travels*, she points out the close resonance between Darwin's project and Derrida's, noting that, in accord with

Derrida, "Darwin's work offers a subtle and complex critique of essentialism and teleology."[75] In her more recent works, Grosz has gone further to develop the links between sexual selection and affect theory. Where natural selection creates a *cui bono* balance sheet of costs and benefits to fitness, Darwinian sexual selection, Grosz points out, is "*in excess* of mere survival."[76] Instead of streamlining survival prospects, sexual selection increases erotic appeal. Erotic affinity is about "pleasure, taste, sensation," while natural selection is about "survival, fitness, gain." The currency of desire indicates an animal lifeway "over and above" the total war plot-and-purge cycles of the selfish genes of ultra-Darwinian mythology.[77]

Sexual selection, then, tracks the digressions of excess, nonreason, and accident. Supplanting earlier models of homeostatic functioning that focus on the production of predictable, closed, efficiently operating systems, sexual selection is "a fundamentally dynamic, awkward, mal-adaptation that enables the production of the frivolous, the unnecessary, the pleasing, the sensory for their own sake."[78] This zone of erotic accident in the field of sexual selection is also, for Grosz, the site of affect. Art, science, and philosophy are the lateral effects of the production of "sensations, affects, intensities" emerging out of the cyclone of accidents.[79] Rather than a teleological orientation toward the production of rationally devised states of equilibrium, affects in this view are lines of flight, a matrix of play "where intensities proliferate, where forces are expressed *for their own sake*, where sensation lives and experiments, where the future is affectively and perceptually anticipated."[80] Affects invert the metaphysical emphasis on the human's rational sovereignty over its body, retracing us as nests of animal becoming, finding pleasure in spinning out of control. Affective economies are directed by compulsions—by autotelic forces that derail the abacus of rational self-interest. Derrida and Darwin, Grosz shows, both dissolve logocentric narratives of destiny, replacing them with the disturbed lines of destinerrance.

Like Gould and Lewontin's spandrels, affect "coincides with and harnesses evolutionary accomplishments into avenues of expression that no longer have anything to do with survival."[81] In this way, affect is an animalism: animalism roots art, which Grosz understands as a machine for producing affects, "not in the creativity of mankind but rather in a superfluousness of nature, in the capacity of the earth to render the sensory superabundant in the bird's courtship song and dance, or in the field of lilies swaying in the breeze under a blue sky. It roots art in the natural and in the animal, in the most primitive and sexualized of evolutionary residues in man's animal heritage."[82] Emerging out of the accidental networks of animal embodied histories, the zones of collision and digression, affect crystalizes chaos, overturning *logos* by creating its own economies of sensation. Sexual selection loops affect through and outside of the geometry of cost-benefit calculation. Like Derrida's hedgehog, it crawls across the highway, exposing itself to the risk of uncertainty in the pursuit of sensation. Like Darwinian evolutionary theory, it operates in a hypercomplex matrix of interlocking economies tumbling and twisted by the random flows of landscape and genetic mutation.

Language, too, is part of this wheeling, scrap-heap economy. For Darwin, language is not originarily a mechanism that developed to improve fitness. Rather, language is an outgrowth of a sexually selected trait—the capacity to sing or bellow to evoke erotic desire in other bodies—shared by other animal species, especially birds and other mammals. "We must suppose," Darwin writes in *Descent*, "that the rhythms and cadences of oratory are derived from previously developed musical powers. We can thus understand how it is that music, dancing, song, and poetry are such very ancient arts. We may go even further than this, and ... believe that musical sounds afforded one of the bases for the development of language."[83] Grosz points out that for Darwin, language "is not the uniquely human accomplishment that post-Enlightenment thought has assumed," but, instead, "already a tendency, residing within the voice and in other organs capable of resonating sound, to articulate, to express, to vibrate, and thus in some way to affect bodies."[84] Language is an outgrowth, a benign tumor on the genescape, swelling out at an odd angle from unexpected origins. In keeping with Gould's understanding of the recursive relationship between evolution and contingency, language may have come to assume the status of a near necessity within human communities—a spandrel whose day has come. But its origins lie in a dance of accidents swirling through affects, not *logos*,[85] and this has implications for the way we conceptualize the role of language in the humanities. As Grosz writes, setting language against the backdrop of animality opens up new ways of studying language—not as a rational production, but as a form of song, an expression set against an animalist backdrop.[86] Language need not be a pristine path to Being; it can be a queer compulsion sticking out from our bodies.

Grosz's consideration of deconstruction and evolution together can be seen, for instance, in James Harrod's argument for chimpanzee religion related to death rituals. Harrod's extensive review of the ethological literature on chimpanzees comes up with several instances of chimpanzees responding to death in what he identifies as ritualized patterns. One of these responses incorporates the "charging display" used in chimpanzee hierarchy maintenance, a performance of aggression that is designed to intimidate or accrue status. When chimpanzees are responding to death, they perform their charging display, but with no visible target. "In everyday situations," Harrod writes, "the charging display aggressively asserts dominance, but in the context of the death ritual there is no target for this aggression, not even a non-directed target aimed at anyone who might be in the vicinity. Thus the ritualization appears to decontextualize the aggression display and deploy it in a non-everyday manner."[87] This "decontextualization" illustrates how behaviors produced by Darwinian processes can be rearranged in the creation of religious formations that are better analyzed as functions of awkwardness rather than fitness—in terms of accident rather than *logos*.

Grosz's focus on the powerful role of sexuality in warping the grids of calculative behavior also merges with Ann Pellegrini's analysis of the effects of evangelical Christian Hell Houses in the United States. Pellegrini writes that Hell Houses use the affect-distributing technologies of theater to scare audiences away from sin—demonizing homosexuality, abortion, and vices by strongly associating them with the fear of damnation.[88] But Pellegrini contends that Hell Houses cannot be viewed as perfectly replicating regimes of behavioral control. Many of the sexual scenes in the Hell House Outreach Kit produced by New Destiny Christian Center in Denver are carefully scripted—even limited—with an acknowledgment on the part of Hell House organizers that sexual scenes are "especially volatile for both actors—and the audience."[89] In a documentary about Hell Houses, a producer nixes the idea of a same-sex love scene because the actors will be "together too much" as it is: "the concern here is that the intense intimacy of rehearsal will lead to other kinds of intimacies, in which life too much imitates art."[90] The erotic cannot be so easily confined inside an imagined economy of survival.

Moreover, audience reactions to the plays may extend at obtuse angles to the intended effects: "The complex, unpredictable interactions among performer, performed, and audience," Pellegrini points out, "are among the reasons theater's emotional reach cannot be so easily micromanaged. The audience member who knows she is seeing a married couple just playing at being gay men but 'really' kissing may find herself alongside another spectator who sees two men exchanging vows and a kiss and then witnesses one stretched in grief over his dying lover's body, a final embrace as his beloved passes from life. The emotional power of this scene exceeds, or potentially exceeds, theological straitjacketing."[91] In forming systems of power, affects easily crash through the barricades of discursive apparatuses. There is, Pellegrini writes, "such a thing as theater that succeeds too well."[92]

This does not mean that sexual selection is a zone of untrammeled randomness. Sexual selection is itself an economy, a system with a set of rules and procedures.[93] But the parameters of that system resemble what Sara Ahmed calls an *affective economy* more than a rationalized economy. They are oriented around what Darwin calls "so fluctuating an element as taste," responsive to the rapidly shifting landscape of embodied affective preferences rather than the glacial and continental flows of the ecological landscape. Moreover, Darwin points out that the affective locus of sexual selection deflects teleological analysis by serving as its own terminus point.[94] The currency of embodied sensations animating affective economies is not subject to an analytics of *logos* that pins itself to a calculation of the rational functioning of bodies. Affects are autotelic compulsions running their own agendas within bodies. Evolutionary biology viewed through this lens becomes the ultimate queering of sexuality, language, art, and religion—the transformation of reproduction from a metaphysical heterosexual order etched across the cosmos into a series of accidents—a constellation of kinks.

Ahmed goes into further detail on the functioning of affective economies, both in her 2004 essay of that title and in her later work, *The Promise of Happiness*. For Ahmed, economies oriented around affect employ the same fluid, nonlinear set of patterns of motion articulated by Grosz in her examination of sexual selection. What Ahmed proposes is a "theory of passion not as the drive to accumulate (whether it be value, power, or meaning), but as that which is accumulated over time."[95] As in chapter 4, the passive case is important here: emotion is something that happens,[96] an effect of compulsions rather than an a priori product of intentional, angelic subjects. Affect, she writes, "does not reside in an object or sign, but is an effect of the circulation between objects and signs."[97] Affect is the material currency of these economies, a kaleidoscope of constitutive forces, rather than a fixed net of objects.

The channels of circulation in this economy resemble the nonlinear counterpaths described by Derrida and Grosz—subject to transformation and accident rather than gridlike precision. Affects do not proceed along straight, clear-cut paths from objects to subjects, but rather circulate within and between bodies and worlds, intersecting at multiple levels and reshaping objects as they swerve. Ahmed describes the motion of affect as a "rippling effect," moving "sideways . . . as well as backward" or as a "sliding," involving "movements or associations whereby 'feelings' take us across different levels of signification, not all of which can be admitted in the present."[98] Affective economies are expansive, off-balance economies, operating in registers of complexity that often exceed human intelligence.

In Ahmed's presentation, as currents of intransigent force circulating in a matrix of processes, affects need to be understood according to their "stickiness" rather than their liquidity. Affect moves into the interstices between things and binds them.[99] This binding force enables affects to interface with and reconfigure systems of power. "In such affective economies," she writes, "emotions *do things*, and they align individuals with communities—or bodily space with social space—through the very intensity of their attachments."[100] Fear, for instance, is not simply about militarizing existing borders: in its binding force, it is the ongoing constitution of those borders.[101] Affective economies are the wobbling but durable infrastructure of power.

For all the emphasis on uncertainty and excess in "Affective Economies," the thematics of accident in Ahmed's picture of affect emerge even more strongly in her later work. Ahmed begins *The Promise of Happiness* with a critique of what she calls the new science of happiness. Predicated on the presupposition of the self's logic—its clarity, its fundamental intelligibility to itself—the science of happiness "relies on a very specific model of subjectivity, where one knows how one feels, and where the distinction between good and bad feeling is secure, forming the basis of subjective as well as social well-being."[102] Ahmed rejects this transparency of the self to itself, and in so doing imports the animalist deconstruction of metaphysics into affect theory.

Ahmed's critique of the "happiness industry" focuses on the confidence that some psychologists and pop self-help authors express in happiness as the terminus of a "path," as that which "lies ahead of us, at least if we do the right thing."[103] Ahmed shows that whereas happiness now is taken to be a programmed response or a default state—an equilibrium—the etymology of the term actually points to a very different theme, one "relat[ing] precisely to the question of contingency: it is from the Middle English word *hap* suggesting chance. The word *happy* originally meant having 'good "hap" or fortune,' to be lucky or fortunate."[104] Hap is not what you do, but what happens to you, what you're left with when you walk away from a collision. Using this semantic lever, Ahmed pries apart the associational bonds between *happiness* and *promise*. She shows that the logocentric orientation of promise eliminates the contingency of happiness, replacing it with a rigid, prescriptive program that yields oppressive political effects—silencing dissenting voices who have fallen off the grid of What Is Supposed to Happen. "The promise of happiness," she writes, "takes this form: if you have this or have that, or if you do this or do that, then happiness is what follows."[105] The science of happiness tries to hawk a straight line in the curved space of an affective economy.

For Ahmed, the life cycle of affects must be staged inside a field of contingency—the collisions with the world that disrupt predictable trajectories. This, for instance, is the heart of her critique of Teresa Brennan's version of transmission of affect. While recognizing the way that one "feels the room" on entering a new space, Ahmed suggests that the sliding motions of affect produce unpredictable results against this field: "to be affected by another does not mean that an affect simply passes or 'leaps' from one body to another. The affect becomes an object *only given the contingency of how we are affected*. We might be affected differently by what gets passed around."[106] She describes, for instance, the classroom as a hypercomplex space for the transmission of affect, an encounter "full of angles."[107] Like the multilateral landscapes that transform genomes through an avalanche of rogue incursions or global power-media complexes, spaces thick with bodies provide an overflow of affective points of contact. Bodies are nontransparent territory—thick nests rather than spacious grids—a fortiori when they roam in packs.

These fluctuating, hybrid systems are driven by a matrix of forces that exceeds the capacity of human *logos* to anticipate: they are conditioned by a set of unpredictable collisions, the multiform pressure of accident. The transmission of affect is queerly formed, in Ahmed's phrasing—a process of perversion, studded with "conversion points" that throw curves into the straight lines of sight between bodies.[108] The effect of this, for Ahmed, is that happiness must be understood as contingent, as destinerrant rather than inevitable. Affect is not subsumable under the constrictions of controlled *logos*, but emerges out of hypercomplex systems mediated by hap. "Happiness," she writes, "means living with the contingency of this world, even when we aim to make happiness necessary."[109]

The queerness of the formations of power built by affective economies are on display in, for instance, *Jesus Camp*, where politics is devised not merely by the promise of happiness, but by other affective configurations including rage, shame, and grief. In the prayer meeting shown early in the film at the Kids on Fire School of Ministry camp, a shy blond boy (figure 3.1) generates a network of attention and affective solidarity not by making promises, but by displaying his shame. The audience, in their desire to consume shame, coalesces as a social organism through this theatrical (neither insincere nor spontaneous) performance. The same effect is achieved by the singer wailing in the background of the children's prayers: the drama of grief amplifies the sense of collective proximity in the room. We see it most conspicuously when Tory Binger takes the microphone, tears streaming down her face, and leads the group in prayer (figure 3.3). Tory, barely able to speak through her sobs, raises her hand, and the other bodies in the room repeat her gesture. The thickness of the sociality of the space—its resoluteness as a venue of political power—is accelerated by sadness, rather than happiness. Happiness per se is not the currency of power in affective economies: they are constituted by a more diverse and effective ensemble of nonlinguistic forces.

Ahmed ends her book by returning to Derrida's evocation of the event, the unpredictable "to-come" from *Politics of Friendship*. "We might remind ourselves," she writes, "that the 'perhaps' shares its 'hap' with 'happiness.' The happy future is the future of the perhaps."[110] Reading Ahmed in conjunction with Grosz—drawing on the insights of both phenomenological and Deleuzian affect theory—highlights the potential offered by an animalist analytics of affect. This convergence point between deconstruction, postadaptationist evolutionary biology, and affect theory suggests that rather than treating deconstruction merely as a prolegomenon to an affective turn, we view it—as an animalism—as an integral conversation partner with affective analytics of power.

Conclusion

Dennett, the philosopher of engineering, listens to the coyotes howling in the towering trees of the dark Maine forest. *Cui bono?*, he asks. Who benefits from this? What is its profit? He attaches a footnote to their song:

> Current thinking is that the various coyote calls serve different purposes. The bloodcurdling "group yip-howl" is most plausibly "important in announcing territorial occupancy and preventing visual contact between groups of coyotes" (Lehner, 1978a, p. 144; see also Lehner, 1978b). If you can *avoid* an actual battle over territory by engaging in impressive saber-rattling, this may be the thrifty way of preserving energy and health for another day's hunting. On this hypothesis, the signal's impressive volume is a hard-to-fake sign of its veracity, a common phenomenon in animal communication. (See Hauser, 1996, chapter 6, for an excellent discussion of the theoretical and experimental investigations of the evolution of honest signaling.) It also suggests some interesting experiments to be conducted in using high-quality playbacks of recorded coyote howls to regulate population densities. Would the coyotes catch on? How long would it take?[111]

Can the howling of the coyotes be calculated? Perhaps. But what if it is an accident? Or a set of laterally assembled lines of force that is exponentially more complicated than the *cui bono* question could grasp? What if rather than an attempt to get ahead in a rational economy, coyote song is a by-product of an affective economy? What if it is erotic, in Grosz's sense—a recalcitrant flourish of artistic excess? What if, rather than a *cui bono*, it is a bonus, a windfall, an accident of landscape? What if, rather than a steady striving in a sharply organized meritocracy, it is, perhaps, a glitch, an inassimilable remainder emerging out of a shapeshifting accidentocracy? What if they didn't do it to survive, reproduce, or get ahead, but because they felt like it?

This is the question that the affective approach allows religious studies to ask. In affective economies, there doesn't have to be a "reason." Affects sit closer to the engines of power than reasons, circulating their own compulsions that easily and often overwhelm rational, logocentric determination—the linguistic explanations that arrive after the fact of a body moving into place. Dennett argues that evolutionary algorithms are foolproof. But our bodies, animal bodies, are foolish: redundant, errant, desiring. They echo the accidents of landscape out of which they emerged. Affect itself is an explanatory terminus, the junction between bodies and systems of power: Why are you doing that?

This doesn't mean that the adaptationist question posed by Dennett should not be asked, as Gould himself acknowledges.[112] It is an important line of analysis not only for biology, but for religious studies, framing crucial questions of desire, expediency, and social and political control, as well as the floating explanatory frames that we invoke to make sense of our bodies' actions to ourselves after the fact. (How did we get here?) But the affective approach illustrates how difficult and how necessary it is to think pluralistically, to expect bodies to come as hybrid systems devised by the competing interference patterns of rational organization and chance, predictability and chaos, clarity and opacity. Affect theory brings these geological contours to the surface, creating space for nonrational structures of meaning insolubly fused with the satisfying, soothing, and constructive chains of causality and explanation. Animalism maps hybrid systems, where rational organization and stochastic processes interlace.

This is why Lewontin and Gould have no patience for the attempt to force complex behavioral systems—like the practice of Aztec ritual sacrifice and cannibalism—into a simplex, balance-sheet analysis. "We strongly suspect," they write, "that Aztec cannibalism was an 'adaptation' much like evangelists and rivers in spandrels, or ornamented bosses in ceiling spaces: a secondary epiphenomenon representing a fruitful use of available parts, not a cause of the entire system. To put it crudely: a system developed for other reasons generated an increasing number of fresh bodies; use might as well be made of them. Why invert the whole system in such a curious fashion and view an entire culture as the epiphenomenon of an unusual way to beef up the meat supply[?]"[113] Out of an already complex system—a mash-up formed by the intersecting lines of ancient embodied histories with the local, the social, the ecological, the felt reality of an animal world—a complex behavioral pattern emerges. To take this endpoint and read it backward as the rational, organizing principle of all these complex components is to presuppose the transparency of that system to human cognition. It presupposes that there is a reason, that a rational mechanism composed entirely out of crystalline computations must be discernible to the human mind. But as Gould and Lewontin point out, "cultural practices can be orthogenetic and drive towards extinction in ways that [classical] Darwinian processes, based on genetic selection, cannot. . . . It would not have been the first time that a human culture did itself in."[114] How did we get here?

This perspective on the study of religion is not new, of course. Dennett himself uses it in *Breaking the Spell*, suggesting that religion may have exaptive or parasitic functions that work tangentially or contrary to an organism's survival value.[115] But many studies of religion—even some oriented around affect, such as Antonio Damasio's *Looking for Spinoza*— rely on some version of a homeostatic account, in which religion helps bodies or social systems achieve equilibrium. For Spinoza and contemporary neurobiologists, Damasio writes, "organisms strive to achieve a 'greater perfection' of function, which Spinoza equates with joy. All of these endeavors and tendencies are engaged unconsciously."[116] Religion is a set of strategies for achieving this homeostatic equilibrium:[117] "an intense experience of harmony . . . the sense that the organism is functioning with the greatest possible perfection."[118]

This relentless optimism of a certain Spinozistic approach must be left behind in light of the correlation of affect and accident. Damasio, following Spinoza, suggests that affects are the ultimate indicator of our embodied flourishing, that we can reliably follow what feels good or avoid what feels bad to settle our homeostatic drives.[119] Using affects to understand bodies is urgently necessary, but, as Ahmed shows, bodies are too complex to be so easily rendered transparent, whether by reason or by affective response. Religion is an extraordinarily powerful distribution network through the global nervous system of affect. But this distribution network should not be presupposed to cleanly align with any single snapshot of health and flourishing. The compulsions of affect produce too many collisions for anyone to walk away unscathed. We must allow for the possibility that affect does not register the well-being of bodies, but a fluctuating set of awkward compulsions. Damasio's presupposition that religion is always good for you is not compatible with an affective analytics.

Inserting accident into religious studies fractures not only optimistic anthropocentrism but various forms of functionalism and adaptationism, including the hawkeyed cynicism that can only see in religion a strategically deployed set of technologies of social control—the social-rhetorical model that views religion as a balance sheet of masked economic and political interests. There is, across the humanities, a subtle bias toward thinking power as inveterately rational—an assumption that power is smart. This is often a version of the linguistic fallacy that tries to map power according to a grid of aligned propositional statements. Sedgwick calls this *paranoid reading*: "whatever account it may give of its own motivation, paranoia is characterized by placing, in practice, an extraordinary stress on the efficacy of knowledge per se—knowledge in the form of exposure."[120] Allowing accident into our assessment of the relationships between bodies and systems of power makes it easier to propose that sometimes power may not be out to get you, that the things bodies do with religion may be about healing, joy, or nurturing— no matter what the starting point may have been. Where the paranoid critical landscape is uniform—marching in lockstep—queer critique is open to accident.[121] Precisely by inviting biology into the conversation, affect theory insists on the fuzzy queerness of bodies.

Animalism does not deny the possibility that features of religious systems may have functional weight, may hold on to a repertoire of ideological instruments. But it deflects the assumption that they must have a place in a rationalized economy: bodies just aren't that smart. Nor does it mean that religion as a set of semistable parameters built on a shifting network of accidents cannot be better understood or its functional relationships better mapped. The analytics of affect stops well short of the approach taken in Catherine Malabou's solo work on accident, which sees it as an "absolute existential improvisation" disconnected from the intransigent features of bodies.[122] Rather, animalism calls on us to consider religion as an affective economy in its complexity, as a hybrid system driven by erotic accident in conjunction with rationalized lines of force. A nonangelic economy is not so much a systematic, logical arrangement of interlocking pieces as a slamming-together, a chart of accidents. The animalist approach sees religion as a site of collisions, a junkyard, what Silvan Tomkins calls a "magnificent makeshift," never assuming that beliefs, practices, or emotions will assemble into a coherent whole.[123] Religious affects are not random, but they are accidental. The claim that religion always needs to be oriented to gaining material benefits (the social-rhetorical analysis discussed in chapter 1) is as flimsy as the argument that evolution is always driven by adaptation. Animal bodies—and animal religions—are simply much queerer than that.

SEVEN

A THEORY OF THE WATERFALL DANCE:
ON ACCIDENT, LANGUAGE,
AND ANIMAL RELIGION

The world—whose litany of praise and sorrow was the subject of her singing—was also the world she watched inside her mind beyond her blindness. Bright with light and thick with shadows, it was the world of green and yellow life that she had seen from the day of her birth. It was filled with dusty yards and high green fields and other fields that were mown and yellow. It was white, overhead, and all the places in the wood were silver and blue and brown. It was teeming with life—all of it vital—all of it in motion— all of it crying to her: Wasn't it wonderful here!—**Timothy Findley,** narrating the death song of Mottyl, the blind cat, in his novel *Not Wanted on the Voyage*, 332–333

In its *being* subjectivity undoes *essence* by substituting itself for another. Qua one-for-another, it is absorbed in signification, in saying or the verb form of the infinite. Signification precedes essence. . . . It is the glory of transcedence. [*sic*]—**Levinas,** *Otherwise Than Being*

Nothing risks becoming more poisonous than an autobiography. —**Derrida,** The Animal That Therefore I Am

On Accident [*sic*]

Jane Goodall writes that the chimpanzee waterfall dance, though disconnected from linguistically mediated belief, can be understood as an animal religion. Both the affective and the animal turns help to clarify this classification by clarifying links between bodies and systems of power outside the register of language. This chapter aims to pull together the conceptual resources of affect theory to provide a comprehensive understanding of the waterfall dance, an approach that casts light not only on why chimpanzee bodies might dance at the foot of a waterfall (in a ritual that, were we to see it in humans, would certainly be labeled as "religion"), but how human religion can itself be understood as a prelinguistic dance. The affective/animalist approach fleshes out the materialist phenomenology of religion, diagramming religion as a complex, embodied response to a world, trafficking in non-linguistic forms of power, invoking complex evolutionary histories, and fundamentally not reducible to a functionalist or adaptationist economy. This is as true for religion entangled with language as it is for non-linguistic religion. Religion, like other forms of power, moves bodies by creating affective ligatures between bodies and their worlds.

For many philosophers of religion, religion without language is a contradiction in terms. In *Otherwise Than Being*, the Jewish philosopher Emmanuel Levinas writes that language is the contact plane between human bodies and transcendence. For Levinas, language activates access to the divine through our ethical encounters with other humans. When a speaking face, a locus of infinite signification, encounters another face, a religio-ethical call ignites in the space between their bodies. This, Levinas writes, is "the glory of transcedence [*sic*]."[1] The ethical moment is the moment of "prophecy."[2] The transcendence that erupts between bodies is activated by the recognition of an infinite gulf between your language world and mine.

For Levinas, this register of transcendence activated by language lifts humans beyond the realm of the animal. In *Totality and Infinity*, Levinas writes that only the "absolutely foreign" relation of another's language can generate the transcendent relation, and that "it is only man who could be absolutely foreign to [us]."[3] Animal bodies, by virtue of their lack of a signifying "face," cannot be part of this ethical interaction that transcends its own essence. For Levinas, the animal condition is the Darwinian condition, a state of being radically in thrall to biological need. This is why Levinas insists in a 1986 interview that "in relation to the animal, the human is a new phenomenon":[4] the Darwinian economy of rational self-interest is overturned by language-using human beings who alone can tread across the void between bodies.[5] As Peter Atterton points out, Levinas rejects Darwinism not because it privileges instinct over reason, but because it reduces bodies to reasoning machines. For Levinas, "it is man's capacity to break with reason by putting the needs of the Other first that constitutes his human essence" and divides him from the animal world.[6]

As we have seen in chapter 6, this is a mistaken reading of Darwin, who was as concerned with the mobilization of ethical relationships and with accident-driven economies of affect as he was with rational self-interest. This attention to accident even extended to his understanding of language: Darwin viewed language as an analogue (and an outgrowth) of evolution, starting with his discussion of the distribution of languages and dialects as a template for the distribution of species and phyla in *Origin of Species* and continuing with his extensive discussion of language as an evolved trait combining natural selection and sexual selection in *The Descent of Man*.[7] Stephen Jay Gould also uses linguistics to explain evolutionary processes, showing, for instance, that evolutionary genealogies, like languages, conserve outdated or inutile forms, or take circuitous routes branching off from the same origin point.[8] For Darwinians, language, like genetic material—rather than being a tightly structured circuit of self-replication—is a fluctuating field roiled by destinerrance, troubled by intersecting, broken waveforms of accident.

In chapter 6, we saw how Elizabeth Grosz, among others, developed this Darwinian understanding into a way of thinking language, bodies, and religion as slippery affective economies. Levinas traffics, instead, in the consummate form of metaphysics: the presupposition that there is something about human bodies that makes us nodes of divine truth. As vessels of the overarching purpose of the cosmos, we can be absolved of animality, destined to glory rather than destinerrant. For Levinas, as with his teacher, Martin Heidegger,[9] the royal road of this transfiguration is language. And Levinas goes further than Heidegger in placing this species-local prioritization of language within an explicitly religious frame, making it the vessel of the call of the holy Other through the register of signification emerging in the human face.

Derrida argues that Levinas's transcendence-prone, speaking human subject is an iteration of a long line of knowing beings posited by philosophers from Descartes to Kant to Heidegger. This series of autobiographical tropes writes the human as the metaphysical locus of the highest form of meaning—and writes off the animal.[10] Levinas refuses the face of the animal even though, as Derrida points out, the animal should be exactly that "wholly other" who for Levinas calls us to an ethical relation.[11] More bluntly, Matthew Calarco writes that "Levinas's efforts to draw a sharp break between human beings and animals on [ethics/religion] is not just bad biology—it is also bad philosophy, inasmuch as it reinforces uncritically the metaphysical anthropocentrism of the Western philosophical tradition."[12] Even refashioned as a radical departure from metaphysics, as Heidegger and Levinas pretend, their work is a reaffirmation of an unexamined species localism that takes human bodies as angels.[13]

This is why the glitch in the last word of Levinas's passage from *Otherwise Than Being*, cited above, is telling: a typographical error, a [sic], photobombs Levinas's earnest attempt to persuade us that human language is a harbinger of transcendence. This tiny mistake gives us a way out of anthropocentric metaphysics, offering a toehold for reconnecting with a Darwinian, animalist understanding of language and embodiment. What if instead of what philosopher Søren Kierkegaard called a "sickness unto death"—a need for divine meaning that orients human subjects to "the glory of transcedence" [sic]—we reframed embodiment as a *sic*-ness, a thus-ness without endpoint—as a record of a crash? The [sic] is the marker of the passive case of affects—a faded sign marking the site of an accident—disrupting the transcendent why of Heidegger's questioning Dasein, the passage to otherwise-than-being in Levinas, and the *cui bono* move of the adaptationist. [Sic]-ness nullifies teleological interpretation, reorienting bodies to bodies and the shapeshifting affective economies of embodied life. Accident points us to embodiment as a play of collisions, animalizing language—and animalizing theory—by suggesting that bodies are better understood as dances of colliding forces rather than bridges to ascension.

In a 1985 interview, Levinas confesses, "I always say—but privately—that in humanity the only serious things are the Greeks and the Bible; everything else is dancing."[14] For Levinas, only the book matters, and religion only emerges from philosophical traditions routed through the language of transcendence. This is where not only non-Western and non-European religious traditions, but also Goodall's chimpanzees dancing in the waterfall, the heavy rain, or at the edges of wildfires are left behind. For carno-phallogocentric philosophers who make language central to their accounts of religion, animal religion cannot exist because it lacks the angelic transmission of language. It looks too much like an accident, not enough like *logos*.

An animalist approach to the elemental dances refocuses us not on the semantic content of religious experience—the network of signs we tattoo on its skin—but on the way a collision between a body and a world becomes a ligature for the circulation of affects. Affective economies produce formations of power that then get called religious—in humans no less than in other animals. Rather than a discursive apparatus, affect theory understands religion as a dance: a homeodynamic correspondence between a body and a thickly textured world propelled by the fluid currency of affect.

This chapter develops an understanding of animal religion as a dance– a play between bodies and worlds. To formulate a theory of the waterfall dance, it works through a series of moments in feminist affect theory that have pushed religion away from the domain of *logos* and toward an understanding of religion—literally and figuratively—as dance. This dance is not a pure, chaotic flux, but a mobile interaction among intransigent components of bodies. Religion as dance is a bricolage of available elements, not a field of formless static noise.

Theorizing the waterfall dance also requires invoking contemporary evolutionary perspectives on the relationships between natural landscapes and bodies. This leads to the biophilia hypothesis of Edward O. Wilson, which posits that bodies experience particular affective resonances when confronted with different facets of nature—compulsions that are then absorbed into religious matrices. Read queerly, the biophilia hypothesis in conjunction with affect theory suggests that the waterfall dance emerges out of the interplay of our intransigent emotional drivers colliding with a set of forms in the environment. Animal religion is best understood as just such an interaction, the play of articulated embodied histories in an accidental dance with the world.

Dance and Affective Economies

The affect theorist whose work most directly engages with dance is the philosopher-dancer Erin Manning. For Manning, dance is a model for affect as a set of bodily movements that emerge and manifest prior to language. Her primary interest is ontogenesis: the moving raw material of becoming, in Gilles Deleuze's sense. She writes in *Relationscapes* that bodies can feel movement before it happens. In dance, she suggests, "this is felt as the virtual momentum of a movement's taking form before we actually move."[15] Affects, for Manning, are the prelinguistic impulses to motion circulating within bodies, what she calls "pulsions"—jets of force linking bodies to relay systems of power in the world.

In this view, rather than of the common-sense understanding of bodies as contained within themselves, dancing bodies are stuck to the world around them by webs of pulsing affective lines. When bodies encounter this web they merge with it to form a living, organic dance—a body-world as assemblage.[16] Like the sliding affective economies described by Sara Ahmed, Manning's sense of dance as an assemblage between bodies and worlds translates into a complex set of relationships that often follow twisted lines. The teleologies of affects are, like dance itself, improvisational, leading to unpredictable outcomes.[17] Dance does not slot into straightforward functionalisms or teleologies.

At the same time, Manning's model of dance imports a Deleuzian sense of affect—emphasizing the micrological forces transfiguring bodies in their relationships with worlds rather than the phenomenological plane of how the world feels. Like Brian Massumi, she follows the line of the Spinozist-Deleuzian definition of affect (singular) as the raw material of becoming or ontogenesis. She identifies bodies as "pure plastic rhythm" produced by the passage of images, relationships, and affects.[18] Although Massumi focuses more on the granular production of bodies and Manning focuses on relationships, both emphasize the plasticity of bodies—the sandbox rather than the collection of semistable forms that accumulate with embodied histories. Although Manning writes of the importance of "folds" and "spaces" that form the rhythm of refrains, her emphasis is on pure becoming.[19]

As with Deleuze, this understanding of affect in Manning and Massumi comes across in the form of a fascination with a poetics of novelty. For Manning, this novelty comes out of the pure plasticity of the "body-becoming."[20] Thinking affect as the raw material for ontogenesis creates an infinitely expansive horizon for newness. But this emphasis on novelty is only partially helpful for mapping animal religion. Although Manning's framing of dance in terms of pulsions resonates with an understanding of animal religion as affective,[21] my argument is that animal religion also needs an account of the intransigent histories of bodies—the way bodies arrive with a set of semistable structures of feeling already in place.[22]

Deleuzian affect can tell only part of the story of animal religion, then, because animal religion is not simply about becoming. Deleuze, in leaving the intransigence of bio-logic behind—in his emphasis on antistructure over structure, white noise over images—allows animal bodies to recede out of focus. From the perspective of biology, bodies are already long since structured—structures with history, queer structures, structures arriving in many shapes and sizes in the zigzags of phylogenesis—but intransigent, semistable structures, nonetheless. Deleuzian affect, taken on its own, obscures the thick, messy, chunky textures of bodies beneath a pure liquid dance of becoming.

This is why Donna Haraway has criticized Deleuze and Félix Guattari's poetics of novelty in *When Species Meet*, arguing that their meditation on becoming-animal as radical ontogenesis in *A Thousand Plateaus* lapses into a sort of romantic self-indulgence that replicates a "philosophy of the sublime."[23] This masked idealism creeps in, for instance, in Deleuze and Guattari's rejection of the "old woman" with pets in favor of the horizon of newness of "becoming-wolf." Haraway points out that in this antimundane framework, "the old, female, small, dog- and cat-loving . . . must be vomited out by those who will become-animal."[24] Deleuze and Guattari, she argues, offer a romanticization divorced from the lived dynamic between familiarity and novelty, comfort and excitement, joy and thrill, structure and antistructure.

Haraway, too, is interested in the theme of dance, which she uses in her *Companion Species Manifesto* to explore the complex relationships that emerge between animal bodies. But for Haraway, this dance is not primarily about plasticity, let alone pure plasticity. What Haraway calls the dance of relating is fixated not on the production of the new, but on what she calls *situated histories*.[25] Instead of becoming, Haraway's model of dance focuses on finding zones of cohesion and bringing them into relation. The dance of relating, for Haraway, is not a pure production of novelty, but a retrieval of existing embodied histories. These histories are intransigent: love in the context of companion species is attentiveness to the conditions for the evolutionarily composed possibilities of their flourishing—not an explosion of newness.[26] The dance of relating, for Haraway, is not a horizon of ontogenesis, but the swirling coalescence of tangible, onto-phenomenological shapes. Our dances are not with liquid becoming—affect—but with the semistable formations within organismic life emerging out of the refrains of embodied histories—affects.[27]

This sense of dance—as an accretion of forms tied together by the ligatures of affect—is further explored by Elizabeth Grosz. As we saw in chapter 6, Grosz points out that where biologists such as Herbert Spencer viewed music as a by-product of language that became "adaptive"—profitable for the organism—Darwin speculated that music was correlated to sexual selection, to an economy that had nothing to do with survival and everything to do with eroticism, pleasure, and affect.[28] This is the Darwinian motif of accident: for Darwin, bodies are not reducible to survival machines, but are heterogeneous assemblages of parts with their own competing priorities, not necessarily univocally oriented toward "survival." Grosz concurs that music is best understood as "resonances affect[ing] living bodies, not for any higher purpose but for pleasure alone"—rather than in terms of a balance sheet of costs and benefits for survival.[29] Music is animalist: an affective economy arranged by accident rather than function.

Like Manning, Grosz is invested in a Deleuzian vocabulary of becoming—one set in motion by a thematics of music and dance. But Grosz departs from the sandbox of affect by reaffirming a set of embodied, phenomenological particularities—semistable affects emerging from the static. Art, for Grosz, is not the pure expression of an internal state of becoming. It builds on networks of evolutionary-historical components within bodies—reticulated soft technologies—to devise new modes of expression. "Art," Grosz argues, "hijacks survival impulses and transforms them through the vagaries and intensifications posed by sexuality [as an engine of evolution], deranging them into a new order, a new practice."[30] In the process, these impulses are derailed from any correlation they may have had with survival. The dynamic of intransigent forces within bodies produces a mangle, an accidental complex of affective engines that leaves functional calculations on the side of the road. Art "coincides with and harnesses evolutionary accomplishments into avenues of expression that no longer have anything to do with survival."[31] Bodies produce shifting affective matrices through the living collage of their evolutionary histories. This is why art is best understood as a dance: a rhythmic gathering together, to the music of accident, of the different pulsing parts of the body.[32]

As with Manning, Grosz is interested in the creation of spaces within which bodies dance. She suggests that architecture—the "most primordial and animal of all the arts"—begins with a floor, a platform on which bodies begin to move in concert with things in the world to produce new sensations.[33] As important as the floor is an assemblage of furniture within the architecture of the dance space. The furniture provides a set of raw materials with which the body begins to form a dynamic set of relationships.[34] Architecture—understood as a space within which bodies dance—is fundamentally a zone for the convergence of forces. This bricolage "of interlocking frames" is an unmooring from the natural into the play of affects.[35] For Grosz, a dance is contingent on a set of collisions between rogue landscapes and bodies.

This image of intransigent forms affixed to bodies by a mobile wheel of affects is echoed in Kathleen Stewart's image of the bloom space. For Stewart, a bloom space is a territory that propels bodies into contact with systems of power. But although the bloom space is driven by affects, its power comes from its structure as a refrain, a "scratching on the surface of rhythms, sensory habits, gathering materialities, intervals, and durations."[36] The music of a bloom space does not emerge out of a "pure plastic rhythm" (in Manning's terminology) but out of a set of chunky, thick textures—textures that are then played by surging bodies as regimes of affect. In each case, a bloom space forms out of a dynamic relationship between an ensemble of shapes in the world. "The body," Stewart writes, "has to learn to play itself like a musical instrument in this world's compositions."[37] Affective economies emerge out of the thick, thrumming ligatures between bodies and material elements in their worlds.

Proustian Birds: The Lifeworld as Lek

Rather than being an indicator of an anthropocentric sublime, however, for Grosz, art as a bricolage of affects reiterates the animality of our bodies. Grosz writes that "all art begins with the animal, for it is the animal, and not machines, minds, or subjects, that carves territories and bodies simultaneously."[38] A bloom space, a body linked to material objects and animated by a web of affects, is produced by an animal in a furnished space. This is why Grosz, like Merleau-Ponty and Lisa Guenther in chapter 4, turns to Jakob von Uexküll's ethological approach. For von Uexküll, an animal is a site of a contrapuntal dynamic between the components of its body and its lifeworld.[39] As discussed in chapter 4, von Uexküll hypothesized that bodies are driven by a set of beacons that make up their worlds—from the simple cluster of brilliant compulsions of the tick to the more complex constellation of fascinations of the astronomer. "As the spider spins its threads," von Uexküll writes, "every subject spins his relations to certain characters of the things around him, and weaves them into a firm web which carries his existence."[40] An animal body, for von Uexküll, is a melodic improvisation in response to things in its world.[41]

Von Uexküll's ethological method has been developed, in recent decades, by cognitive ethologists who merge lifeworld theory with new research in animal cognition. The cognitive ethologist Marc Bekoff's work on play among canids is a particularly helpful touchstone for thinking of the relationships between animal bodies and worlds as dances. Play, Bekoff notes, precedes by eons what we recognize in humans as language, but even in the absence of language, play exhibits deep structural complexity. Bekoff's research demonstrated that animals often initiate play by bowing, signifying their intentions and desires to other bodies around them.[42] During the game, animals follow a set of procedures to maintain a particular "play mood." Larger or stronger animals will play less aggressively or vigorously with juveniles or smaller creatures, for instance, by carefully modulating jaw pressure—play bites. Dominant animals will sometimes reverse roles with subordinates, performing actions that do not actually correlate to their status in the group's hierarchy.[43] Bekoff describes situations where animals step outside of the repertoire of acceptable play actions but then "attempt to negotiate with their partner(s) so that play will continue."[44] This cycling of embodied forms produces an "imaginary situation" between playing animals without the need for linguistic direction.[45]

Moreover, this imaginary situation, Bekoff writes, is thoroughly affective, a contagious whirlpool of joy and happiness. Many animals are "play addicts" and in controlled laboratory settings will pursue a chance for play even at risk or cost to themselves.[46] Although animal play has been associated with increased cognitive, social, and bodily fitness and flexibility,[47] Bekoff argues that play is best understood as that which appears to be purposeless.[48] Play, Bekoff argues, may evoke certain benefits, but bodies do not engage in play in the service of a higher end: it is an accidental behavior, a [*sic*]-ness prior to language or cognition. Play is an affective economy composed out of a repertoire of compulsions that do not necessarily fit into rational cost-benefit calculations.

Just as importantly, though, play is not random, a pure exercise in chaos, or an explosion of radical becoming. "As animals play," Bekoff points out, "it's not unusual to see known mating behaviors intermixed in highly variable kaleidoscopic sequences along with actions that are used during fighting, looking for prey, and avoiding becoming someone else's dinner."[49] Play is a process in which other gestures and forms—from predation, evasion, and mating—are resituated and recombined to generate new affective concoctions.[50] Animal play cites the intransigent forms of bodies and worlds, bringing them together in an improvisational creative process. Like art or dance, play is a prelinguistic, animal mode of relationship with worlds, sunk deep into biologically organized bodies.

As an example of the animal as artist marshaling the affective forms of the world through dance, Grosz and Deleuze and Guattari introduce us to the bowerbird.[51] Bowerbirds are a group of perching birds (passerines) found throughout New Guinea and Australasia and known for a distinctive courtship behavior: males of the species construct special studios—leks—within which they gather colorful objects such as shells, leaves, petals, and pebbles to attract females. They then perform a rhythmic dance for their prospective mates against the backdrop of their treasure chamber—the feather in the cap of their erotic appeal.

As Grosz points out, bowerbird dancers encapsulate the relationship between all animal bodies and worlds. Their stylized dances embody the rhythmic flow of forms surging through bodies, resonating with the pulsing waves of affect. It is "the bird as event"—the body as node of sensation—in Deleuze and Guattari's phrasing.[52] But where Deleuze and Guattari see the bowerbird as a site of pure affective becoming, Grosz emphasizes the way that bowerbirds pull together a range of intransigent forms: like all bodies, bowerbirds are collectors—gathering material things that are not useful, but compulsory. As collectors, bowerbirds are artists, rearranging, recombining, and reconfiguring the resources available to them into bricolages. And as dancers, bowerbirds draw from the matrix of thick material forces flowing through them and giving shape to their desires to fashion queer affective economies. A bowerbird lek is what von Uexküll or Merleau-Ponty would call a lifeworld—a body embedded in a set of relationships with its environment. The bowerbird is the bird of Proust, a shrine maker, making visible the dance of affects that glues together the elements of a material religious ecology.

Rhythmic Bodily Movement: Dancing and Religion

The animal dance also serves as a template for understanding religion. In her 2002 presidential address to the American Academy of Religion, Vasudha Narayanan argued for a decolonization of method in religious studies, a shift beyond the traditional European foci of text, language, and belief.[53] In a call that presaged her colleague Manuel Vásquez's later description of the materialist shift in religious studies, she pressed for a passage beyond what *Religious Affects* terms the "linguistic fallacy" toward a confrontation with other formations of religion—architecture, healing, astronomy, ecology, and dance—charting paths beyond our "text-dominated academy and society where we privilege the word."[54] For Narayanan, contra Levinas, it is among dancing—rather than bookish—bodies where we find religion taking place.

The feminist philosopher, dancer, and theorist of religion Kimerer L. LaMothe offers a set of theoretical resources for tracing the deep intertwining of religion, affect, and dance. Crucially, her hybrid framework is attentive both to motion and to intransigent embodied histories. LaMothe writes that dance is found in almost all religious traditions and cultures but was neglected in the early years of the discipline of religious studies because it was viewed as an invalid art form that could not adequately express faith—religion was understood as a compendium of words and concepts aimed at transcendence.[55] For LaMothe, not only must we attend to dance within religious studies, religion itself is best understood as a dance—a dynamic interplay between bodies and worlds compelled by affects.

But LaMothe also rejects the notion that dance is merely a mode of representation—a religious art form consisting of symbols arranged to signify theological propositions.[56] LaMothe dismisses approaches, such as that of Clifford Geertz, which return us to the implicit presupposition that religion is always cosmological—a form of writing.[57] Because religion, for LaMothe, is more than linguistic, it cannot always be translated into signification. Religion must be reconceived "as a kind of dance—as rhythmic bodily movement enacting a logic of bodily becoming *and* a cultural spiral of discovery and response."[58] Where understanding dance as a system of representation returns us to the linguistic fallacy that sees language as the only possible medium of power, conceptualizing dance as an interplay of bodily becoming and intransigent histories places it within the domain of affect. Religion as dance captures the thick strata of embodied experience touched by, but not reducible to, language.[59]

This template of religion as a dance does not forbid the introduction of conceptual, cognitive, or textual analysis. It only points out that these forms of religious experience and expression will be, at most, one facet of a more complicated network of influences, "a defiantly dialectical relation between reason and experience—a dynamic, bi-directional, generative connection whose movement produces meaning of different kinds, both conceptual and kinesthetic."[60] Cognition is an element of animal bodies, but not the ground of religion or any other formation of power. The conceptual order of signification is only a set of shapes within the human repertoire, one facet of the polyhedral dance of religion. Nietzsche writes that "consciousness is the last and latest development of the organic, and consequently also the most unfinished and least powerful of these developments."[61] LaMothe's project rephrases this intuition, allowing cognitive-linguistic components a role, but framing them as only part of a broader ensemble of embodied processes making up religion.

Following Nietzsche, LaMothe sees dance as an affectively mediated expression of embodiment. But like Grosz's bower birds, LaMothe's dancers—Ruth St. Denis, Isadora Duncan, Martha Graham—while rejecting technical bravado in favor of spontaneous, fluid, and natural motions, were fundamentally invested in dance as a bricolage of preexisting shapes. These philosopher-dancers "turned their attention to basic forms of human movement—walking, skipping, jumping, breathing— and designed practices for discovering and releasing a human's capacity to make new movements."[62] LaMothe emphasizes that motion and dancing tap into our experiences of a particular time and place, a particular network of people, memories, experiences, affects: "As we move, we also *bring into being the network of relationships* with persons, places, and powers of the universe that support us in making those movements and becoming the (dancing) persons we have the potential to be. Any dancing represents and makes real *the vast matrix of living tissue that enables it.*"[63] All dancers, then, seek "to learn from resources available to them how to create dances for their own time and place."[64] Bodies are not pure and do not participate in a pure logic of becoming: they orchestrate mobile, spinning webs of influences to dance religious meaning into existence.

For Narayanan, too, dance is a mobile archive of forms—a repertoire of embodied knowledges, gestures, affects, postures, expressions, and narratives—that is not only found onstage, but seeps into the ordinary.[65] These ordinary dance forms integrate bodies into religiously cast systems of power, for instance, in the living tradition of Indian dance taught in the United States to immigrant girls: "The dance classes 'Hinduize' the young immigrant daughter," Narayanan writes, "making her physically and mentally part of the narrative structures. The body becomes a vehicle to salvation, but it is also a site of transgression, pleasure, pain, and the senses. It is a site of resistance, where agencies of power, prestige, the past, the present, and the demanding cultures of the many 'others' clash."[66] Dance coalesces as a torrent of forms that connect bodies to religious histories, practices, and affective technologies. These ligaments form a historically mediated set of power relations, simultaneously etching and reformulating women's bodily relationships with historical traditions and global migrations.

For LaMothe and Narayanan, it is within this mobile network, at the site of the hyperconcentrated nodes of affect that are bodies, that we find religion. Religions, LaMothe writes, are "the patterns of bodily movement—patterns of sensation and response—that humans create and become as they exercise their potential to bring into being the network of relationships that will support them in becoming who they are."[67] The "rhythms of bodily becoming" that make us up enable us to connect to a "larger creativity" interfacing with the organic forms of lived religion.[68] As Sebastian Schüler writes, "it is the embodiment of ritual practice, emotions, movement, dynamic bodily interactions, and social representations that shape the way we perceive the world and act in it."[69]

Can animals dance? LaMothe seems to suggest that dance is about the affirmation of particularly human modes of being.[70] But her work leaves open the possibility that there can be other dances with other meanings corresponding to other types of bodies. Religion, LaMothe insists, "is not what a person believes, nor what he has or does per se. Religion rather exists *in the moment of its performances as a kind of doing that embodies a person in relation to a sense of the world.*"[71] This religion as dance of relating is animal religion: a compulsory, affective web fusing bodies to worlds. As a dance, religion is a cycling of semistable bodily forms—what LaMothe calls the "terms and conditions" of embodiment—that draws out a range of affects. And these terms and conditions that make up dance emerge differently for different bodies. As Narayanan writes, "There are infinite vernaculars in the world."[72] These vernaculars jump the species barrier, allowing for a heterogeneous multiplicity of religious formations linked to different animal bodies.

This sense of religion is best understood not as faith or belief—though these terms are elements in the specifically human embodied engagement with the world and so part of the human religious dance—but as an affective, radically embodied encounter with the world, our histories, our relationships, and the semistable forms of our bodies. Dance is more than corporeal knowledge or a uniquely inefficient replica of human language used to transmit cosmologies. Dance, for Narayanan, correlates bodies and spaces, producing affective economies that constitute religious worlds: "The dancer dances her worship in the temple, creates the temple within her body, and dances the temple in her performance."[73] Like bowerbirds dancing in their leks, bodies in the world play with the array of forms presented to them to produce streams of affect. The [*sic*]-ness of religious bodies manifests in this collision between animals and our vivid landscapes.

Like Moths to a Porch Light: The Biophilia Hypothesis and Religion

To pose religion as an embodied dance is not to fully answer the question of why the chimpanzees in the Kakombe valley danced at the base of the waterfall. What is it in the onto-phenomenology of primate bodies that makes these particular affective transactions with the world possible? The affective turn contributes to a materialist phenomenology by understanding animal religion as emerging from evolutionary histories. These evolutionary histories—mediated by affect—can guide the ways bodies respond to features of the natural world, what E. O. Wilson has called biophilia.

The cognitive anthropologist Stewart Guthrie argues for the use of a specific set of tools from the evolutionary and cognitive science of religion to account for the chimpanzee waterfall dance. Guthrie begins by rejecting the presupposition that religion is exclusively human, preferring to see it instead as rooted in "a biological matrix shared by other animals."[74] Specifically, this biological matrix includes an adaptive cognitive tendency to interpret "ambiguous environments" in an overcautious way: in scanning for "hidden agents" who might pose a threat in our environment, we are predisposed to err on the side of caution.[75] Developing the cognitive scientist Justin Barrett's notion of "hyperactive agent detection devices," Guthrie writes that religion "is an aspect of a still broader animal tendency to see the world as animate."[76] What Guthrie calls animal animism is the by-product of a cognitive bias built into the brains of any number of animal bodies, including birds, coyotes, caribou, and primates.[77]

For Guthrie, the chimpanzee waterfall dance represents the playing out of an evolved relationship between organisms and landscapes. In this case, the dancing chimpanzees perceive the waterfall as alive—in the same way human bodies perceive a symbol, space, icon, idol, or text to have holy power—and respond to it as if it were a threat. They resolve a perceptual uncertainty in their environment—a noisy, moving waterfall, a rogue landscape that grabs their attention—by erring on the side of caution and interpreting it as an agent to which they must perform a display as they would an unknown, potentially hostile body.[78] Reflecting what Nathaniel Barrett would call an "interactive" or "selectionist" cognitive approach, this interpretation sees the dance as an interaction between an organism's cognitive drivers and its landscape, a correlation between corresponding structural properties and limitations.[79] Only by accident is the dance between a body and its lek, in this instance, an actual dance.

This dance is also an awkward economy, a set of relationships that exceeds functionalist or adaptationist analysis. Guthrie writes that religion may have functions, but its emergence is better explained as "a byproduct of something else: a perceptual and cognitive strategy."[80] Religion, like other "accidental products of [an] evolutionary process," may serve a set of functional ends,[81] but in its emergence it is, in N. Barrett's words, "radically non-functionalist." Religion as a cognitive device emerges out of an interplay between bodies and multilayered adaptive landscapes that, by its sheer complexity, exceeds the adaptationist framework.[82] An affective economy is a multidimensional system of desires, forces, compulsions, and constraints within which bodies dance. Flattening that economy to a single plane of cost-benefit analysis is only seldom a workable method. The chimpanzee dance is, in this view, a by-product of adaptive mechanisms, but not adaptive in itself.

At the same time, N. Barrett points out that cognition and the traffic in concepts represent only a small fraction of the landscape of our mental world.[83] As Ilkka Pyysiäinen has suggested in his critique of Guthrie, strictly cognitive, belief-oriented, computational models miss the importance of emotionality in religion.[84] Barbara J. King in *Evolving God* writes that "while something can be learned from [cognitive accounts of religion], they are sterile to the degree that they fail to grasp the significance of what matters most: people deeply and emotionally engaged with others of their kind, and eventually with the sacred."[85] This matches Goodall's intuition, as well, that the chimpanzee reaction to the waterfall is mediated by an emotion, that the dance is not simply a clicking cognitive appraisal of a situation, but a dance of awe.[86]

An approach from evolutionary biology, Edward O. Wilson's biophilia hypothesis, helps draw this link between environments and nonfunctionalist affective economies. The biophilia hypothesis suggests that bodies have what Wilson describes as an "innate tendency to focus on life and lifelike processes."[87] Animal bodies contain built-in modules that compel us toward living organisms and other elements of living biomes: "We learn to distinguish life from the inanimate," Wilson writes, "and move toward it like moths to a porch light."[88] Biophilia is part of the onto-phenomenological makeup of our bodies: a semistable (shapeable, but also not radically flexible) compulsion toward living things.

Wilson proposes that biophilia is not a single mechanism, but "a complex of learning rules that can be teased apart and analyzed individually."[89] Like the suite of cognitive modules proposed as the basis for religion by cognitive scientists of religion,[90] Wilson suggests that organisms have been equipped, by selection pressures, with an array of impulses toward life and the things that encourage or endanger life. Natural landscapes, water, sunshine, and living things, for most organisms, are necessary for their own survival and flourishing. As Roger S. Ulrich explains, "both the *rewards* and the *dangers* associated with natural settings during human evolution have been sufficiently critical to favor individuals who readily learned, and then over time remembered, various adaptive responses . . . to certain natural stimuli and configurations."[91] These responses, Ulrich suggests, can be both biophilic, life-seeking, and biophobic, life-avoiding, according to how they have been sculpted by evolutionary histories. But either way, bodies emerged in a biocentric world—a landscape where the elements of life became beacons of attraction—evolving a set of priorities that persist in our bodies today.[92] Dorion Sagan and Lynn Margulis write that rather than a monolithic biophilia, we understand it in terms of Ivan E. Wallin's notion of prototaxis—"the generalized tendency of cells and organisms to react to each other in distinct ways."[93] Both biophilia and biophobia are "aspects of global prototaxis," a set of coordinates that interact to shape the contours of where bodies go. These coordinates become complex folds in the living network of power.[94]

Although Wilson's chosen term focuses on life—the *bios*—biophilia encompasses landscapes in addition to living organisms. Wilson discusses a particular configuration of landscape—what he calls the "savanna gestalt"—the "intermediate terrain" that human bodies are driven to re-create in their environments.[95] Wilson proposes that there is "a deep genetic memory of mankind's optimal environment," an ancestral landscape still etched in our affective topography.[96] Even nonliving features of the landscape matter. Certain natural spaces have a compulsory power over bodies, and a landscape that veers too far from this template becomes "a department of hell," in which "people would find their sanity at risk."[97] Like the body in solitary confinement, a body that has been severed from these channels of affective meaning risks derangement. The pressure of isolation and deprivation dangerously narrows an animal body's affective economy, leaving it vulnerable to collapse.

This phenomenological orientation clues us in to the fact that biophilic impulses driving bodies are eminently affective. Although Wilson's 1984 definition of biophilia uses a vocabulary of "mental processes," by the time of the 1993 volume on his work, his language had shifted to emphasize an "innately emotional affiliation of human beings to other living organisms."[98] Wilson frames biophilia as a set of "learning rules" circumscribed by feelings playing out along a range of emotional spectra, "from attraction to aversion, from awe to indifference, from peacefulness to fear-driven anxiety."[99] One of the most effective proponents of the biophilia hypothesis, ecologist Stephen R. Kellert, describes biophilia in terms of an array of affective qualities, including the "naturalistic" sense of "awe," the "negativistic" experience of fear, and the "aesthetic" experience of "feelings of tranquility, peace of mind, and a related sense of psychological well-being and self-confidence."[100] Queer theorist and literary critic Dianne Chisholm explores biophilia in terms of what she calls the "ecological future of queer desire":[101] a set of nonstraight fascinations that connect bodies to worlds. The affective responses prompted by biophilia tether bodies to landscapes.

Wilson argues that it is these affective ligaments that lead to the imbrication of biophilia with religion. Images of gardens, animals, and forests all have powerful resonances in religious iconography.[102] Wilson describes a "spiral trajectory" of evolutionary-religious transformation, during which our bodies' biophilic impulses—shaped by eons of rogue landscapes embedding themselves in our bodies—become the raw material of religious formations.[103] Judith H. Heerwagen and Gordon H. Orians write that there is an intransigent repertoire of "things and places that bring us pleasure" that are enfolded into narratives and material religious practices focusing on animals, landscapes, weather patterns, and vegetation.[104] "Once a tendency exists," Frans de Waal writes, "it is permitted to soar free from its origin."[105] For Chisholm, this allows nature writers such as Ellen Meloy to "see beyond the set schemata of natural selection to whatever queer couplings enable life to thrive in the desert's volatile landscape."[106] Biophilic religion is not in itself adaptive, but, like art for Grosz, it harnesses onto-phenomenological features of bodies that may have at one time been selected by Darwinian processes.[107]

Wilson's prime example of this postadaptationist perspective is the serpent. He writes that evolutionary time has taught bodies to feel intense emotions toward snakes: "The mind is primed to react emotionally to the sight of snakes," he argues, "not just to fear them but to be aroused and absorbed by them, to make stories about them."[108] Wilson describes his own fascination with snakes as a child growing up in northern Florida and Alabama, where a rich repertoire of legends surrounded the animals. They became "creatures of startling power."[109] He attributes this affective power—a deep, collective fixation on the bodies of snakes—to semistable properties of mammalian brains: for all organisms in the mammalian lineage, "snakes mattered," and the biophobic response—heightened affective arousal when confronting the image of serpents—fostered survival, in a classic Darwinian adaptation.[110]

But the biophobic response also soars free from its origins. The affective potency of the image of the snake is reflected in the "awe and veneration of the serpent" in the religious traditions of the world, surveyed by Wilson in *Biophilia*.[111] As Wilson explains, the mind "has to create symbols and fantasies from something." Following the watercourses of affect, bodies incline "toward the most powerful preexistent images . . . including that of the serpent."[112] Snakes appear in dreams, not because of a deferral of their meaning onto sexuality, as Freud suggested, but because they have their own intrinsic "meaning." The non-signifying, compulsory power of the snake evokes a queer affective resonance within our bodies that is not reducible to its aversive response.[113] The fear of snakes is inherited, and we weave that fear into cultural forms, harnessing its power into our own affective bricolage: the snake's "sinuous form, and its power and mystery are the natural ingredients of myth and religion."[114] The more sinuous, the better. So with other biophilic and biophobic aspects of our embodied evolutionary legacy: they are the raw material of religious forms, but material that we stumble upon by accident, the echoes of ancient landscapes reverberating through our bodies.

The natural environment dictated the emergence of the set of affectively accelerated priorities characterizing the bodies we have now. "Snakes *mattered*," Wilson writes,

> the smell of water, the hum of a bee, the directional bend of a plant stalk *mattered*. The naturalist's trance was adaptive: the glimpse of one small animal hidden in the grass could make the difference between eating and going hungry in the evening. And *a sweet sense of horror*, the shivery fascination with monsters and creeping forms that so delights us today even in the sterile hearts of the cities, could see you through to the next morning. Organisms are the natural stuff of metaphor and ritual. Although the evidence is far from all in, the brain appears to have kept its old capacities, its channeled quickness. We stay alert and alone in the vanished forests of the world.[115]

Dennett's reflection that the coyotes in the woods near him "mattered" to him suggests the same affectively construed vocabulary of meaning making. Affective compulsions linking bodies to insistent landscapes are the legacy of our embodied histories, but the survival economies that once shaped them have been replaced by awkward economies— sliding, queer economies of affect.

Nor is biophilia limited to humans. Wilson spends several pages discussing biophobic responses to snakes in wild and laboratory monkeys,[116] pointing out that responsivity to snakes must be a naturally selected trait for other animal species. Darwin also notes the primate response to snakes, linking it to universal animal affects of wonder and curiosity.[117] Wilson contends that human biophilic mechanisms extend backward in our evolutionary chronology to a span of time before the human species itself existed, and that a set of biophilic tendencies almost identical to our own is exhibited even among contemporary chimpanzees.[118] Other species have their own intransigent biophilic and biophobic configurations. Biophilia as a set of compulsions surges through many—maybe all—animal bodies.

This is why Wilson, like Grosz, is interested in Proustian birds. He describes in detail—cataloging the particulars of color, shape, and movement—the male birds of paradise (another passerine bird in Papua New Guinea) dancing in their leks in the Huon forest to attract females.[119] This distinct dance, Wilson says, is the product of a long, spiraling chain of events in natural selection, a dynamic interplay between embodied affects, cognitive priorities, physiological structures, shapes, muscle groups, colors, textures, hormones, landscapes—all driven by "millions of generations of natural selection . . . an architecture culminating an ancient history."[120] The body is not just dancing, the body *is* a dance, a reiteration and recombination of moving intransigent components, a bricolage of bodily forms tethered to living landscapes.

Wilson suggests that humans, as the "poetic species," use symbols to amplify biophilic sensations.[121] Other products of human language work along the same lines: science, he writes, is a synthesis of linguistic forms, an elegant recapitulation of the mind's preexisting cognitive structures through a bricolage of new information, new priorities, new elements, new shapes—all animated by the polychromatic electricity of affect.[122] LaMothe, too, points out that the linguistic devices used by scholars are shot through with training regimens that instill sensitivities to specific affects: "The theory and method we choose," she writes, "is one whose use gives us pleasure."[123] Language is not invisible to affect, which enfolds cognition even at the most fundamental levels. It is part of the human dance to talk, to think, to question, to play within the chain of accidents that is language.

This is why Wilson suggests that each species generates its own "spirit" or moral architecture. "Civilized termites," he proposes, by way of example, "would support cannibalism of the sick and injured, eschew personal reproduction, and make a sacrament of the exchange and consumption of feces." He goes on, "The termite spirit, in short, would have been immensely different from the human spirit—horrifying to us, in fact."[124] The feminist philosopher of religion Grace Jantzen (who, like Grosz, takes Irigaray's philosophy of embodied difference as a starting point) writes that the religious traditions proposed by different bodies in different times and places reflect precisely these different sets of embodied priorities. "The attributes valorized as divine" by humans, she writes, "are those humans consider to be the best of themselves, which they partly have and partly long to achieve or become."[125] The human animal religion emerges out of a projection of our own onto-phenomenological set of priorities, just as Irigaray in "Divine Women" will write that religion is only possible in anticipation of a particular "horizon" specific to the kind of bodies we are.[126]

The diversity of animal bodies—the "heterogeneous multiplicity" of onto-phenomenological constitutions—leads to an array of dances, an array of religions. The human spirit includes the effluvia of language—such as scientific, cosmological, and philosophical questioning—as well as the postadaptive affective haloes of our suite of biophilic and biophobic impulses, as well as the pressing power of other bodies, as well as however many other—finitely many ($n > 2$)—heterogeneous shapes, patterns, forms, images, and textures.[127] These forces in our bodies are alive, moving around in the lek of the world, interacting with one another in a profound, messy dance—in conjunction with all the other sedimented accidents of our individual embodied histories. They are the infinite vernaculars of the heterogeneous multiplicity of bodies.

It is this embodied vernacular animating the chimpanzees in the rogue landscape of the waterfall that helps us make sense of their dance of awe. A biophilic fascination with the natural, life-giving world—an ensemble of affective triggers designed by a distinct evolutionary history—surges in their bodies. Their bodies respond with movement, recapitulating, reinforcing, and transforming these affective impulses. Their dance just happens to be a dance, a mobile interaction between bodies and leks, just as it is other dances between human bodies and leks that produce our variegated religious forms. Animal religion as an affective economy cannot be reduced to language: it emerges out of an embodied, affective response to the things of power in the world, a dance of emotions, sensations, bodies, compulsions, and memories interspersed with an onto-phenomenological repertoire. This is religion as [*sic*]-ness: it just so happens that the kinds of bodies we are and the kinds of bodies they are dance the way they do.

At the same time, an analytics of the chimpanzee waterfall dance need not be divorced from an analytics of power. Although the linguistic fallacy encourages us to overlook the possibility of animal politics, primatologists have documented how primate societies are constituted by complex, mobile power relations enfolding political economy, embodied relationships, and local histories.[128] Goodall notes that for chimpanzees, "displaying" is a performative symbol of leadership—as with the ritual tree shaking and rock throwing that alpha males will perform in front of their groups in the morning before they set out for the day's travel.[129] Just as human political-religious complexes are shaped by assemblages of images, bodily displays, and material objects, it seems likely that chimpanzee formations of power are conditioned by the affective interplay between socialized chimpanzee bodies and chimpanzee religion.

The chimpanzees' religious reaction to the waterfall is external to any determination by language. It emerges, instead, out of a complex dynamic of articulated embodied histories dancing between bodies and their worlds. A chimpanzee in the lek of a waterfall is enfolded in a complex, rhythmic affective experience; the materialist phenomenology of that experience has its own shape, its own depth, and its own compulsion, coalescing into a formation that we would call religion in chimpanzees just as we would in humans. But the question of why the reaction to these affects is translated into an actual dance remains open. We may not get to have an answer. It may be, as Guthrie suggests, a "raiding of the repertoire" of threat responses that is reconstituted in religious form. But this is a tendency that has soared free of its origins, in de Waal's terms. What matters for the analytics of power is not the initial adaptive context, but the later affective, embodied redistribution within a new lek. The affective economy that spins out embodied reactions is not a determination, but a play space that produces unexpected, accidental results. Evolutionary histories—heterogeneous embodied trajectories that come into focus with the tools of biology—set the parameters of affective economies; but the [*sic*]-ness of affect dissolves the bonds of determinism, pointing to religion as "over and above" rigid functional economies.

Conclusion: At Play in the Lek of the World

I have *discovered* for myself that the old humanity and animality, yea, the collective primeval age, and the past of all sentient being, continues to meditate, love, hate, and reason in me. . . . Among all these dreamers, I also, the "thinker," dance my dance.—**Nietzsche,** *The Joyful Wisdom*

The body surges. Out of necessity, or for the love of movement.
—**Kathleen Stewart,** *Ordinary Affects*

This chapter is about thinking embodied life beyond adaptationism, phenomenological depth beyond language, and religion beyond the human empire. This approach to what Manuel Vásquez calls materialist phenomenology pulls together insights from phenomenological and Deleuzian understandings of affect, mapping the intransigent dynamics between vital materiality and feeling bodies. Viewing religion as dance has three advantages for the project of materialist phenomenology. First, it thematizes the bands of religion outside of language, as interfacing with a deep, moving architecture of embodied forms. Second, it understands religion as a sort of mobile bricolage, a set of compulsions embedded in relationships between bodies and worlds. Third, it traces religion as a thing that transpires in queer, affective economies— complex religious ecologies of sliding formations of power rather than teleologically oriented, two-dimensional balance sheets that see only cost/benefit, adaptive/nonadaptive, money, domination, and control.

Language, from the animalist viewpoint, is on accident [*sic*]. Where *by accident* is syntactically correct, *on accident* reflects a common mutation, a deformation caused by the swirling of language's macrogranular elements within a field of complexly formed desires, limitations, and structural constraints. David Foster Wallace's essay "Tense Present"—a book review of six dictionaries—notes that it is impossible to decisively assess whether a change in a linguistic expression is "natural" or a "corruption."[130] Many changes, Wallace argues, are improvisations driven by an aesthetic feel. He zooms in on the solecism "Where's it at?," pointing out that "the apparent redundancy of 'Where's it at?' is offset by its metrical logic. What the *at* really does is license the contraction of *is* after the interrogative adverb. You can't say 'Where's it?' So the choice is between 'Where is it?' and 'Where's it at?,' and the latter, a strong anapest, is prettier and trips off the tongue better than 'Where is it?,' whose meter is either a clunky monosyllabic-foot + trochee or it's nothing at all."[131] *On accident* enjoys a similar rhythmical advantage—a timely improvisational dance within language as a musical field. The evolution of language unfolds in part under the pressure of an economy of selection that operates according to lateral flows analogous to sexual selection rather than the linear schema of natural selection. Language, in other words, is affectively suffused, an affective economy, a play of compulsions skidding laterally through bodies that happen to speak. Discourse itself, as Nietzsche saw, is a dance; or rather, language is a gesture within the human dance, an aspect of our embodied life that becomes one plane of the broader affective economy of religion.

Dance as a rhythmic marshaling of forms—whether phonemes, genes, or gestures—helps us diagram the emergence of bodies in the long, granulated picture of evolutionary time, the turbulent coalescence of animality. The ancient records of these evolutionary flows—a fascination with life and the foundations of life, such as running water itself—are still built into bodies: powerful, living engines driven by affects. These semistable forms converge in animal bodies and produce dances, and sometimes, completely by accident, a real dance—bodies responding with rhythm, moving muscles, and surging emotion to the grandeur of a towering waterfall. This can be chimpanzees or humans as easily as it can be passerines hopping madly in their leks as the pounding waterfall of shapes, colors, neurochemicals, rhythms, and the presence of other bodies overwhelms them. This dance happens to be a dance.

But also, far more often, but no less accidental, religion is an invisible dance, bodies surging, in Kathleen Stewart's phrasing, through bloom spaces, the polytextured landscapes of the ordinary. Religion, like other forms of power, draws on the unseen galaxies of affects, thoughts, images, encounters, "every time a history, a memory, sensations, scars, ways of perceiving—in sum of reading the book of the world with one's body"—that ferment and recombine on bodily surfaces, the endlessly folded sheets of skin that are bodies, producing the luminescent beacons of religion.[132] The animalist approach, by focusing on the organization of power outside of *logos*, interrupts carno-phallogocentrism by separating bodies from the necessity of language for thought, cognition, sensation, and movement. It extinguishes the vestigial Euro-Enlightenment axiom that language is necessary for depth—and certainly necessary for what gets called religion.

A lek is a space marked by a set of forms—a waterfall, a forest, a church filled with bodies. When a body enters the lek, the beacons start to dance, luring the body into a swirl of compulsions mediated by affects. Religion emerges out of this swirl—as we see in the final soliloquy of Mottyl the house cat, the protagonist of queer Canadian novelist Timothy Findley's retelling of the Genesis flood story, *Not Wanted on the Voyage*. Mottyl, the mottled creature, as she sings her death song, evokes a vibrating affective economy, a dance of memories, emotions, places, images, colors, and other bodies—from every direction the wordless, lancing beacons of the world:

> The singing was gutteral [*sic*] and rich and the song had a pattern to it, and many notes. Bip and Ringer had never heard such singing before, though they recognized at once the meaning of it, since almost every animal has a song it sings at death—and some would have said they were songs addressed *to* death.
>
> The content of Mottyl's song was only known to her. Her children, her Crowe and her *whispers* had all died before her. And now, the world would die. Her song described that world—the world into which Mottyl had been born and in which she had lived. It also described all her kittens and all their various births over time and all their colours and their markings. It described Mottyl's mother and Mottyl's own birth and Mrs Noyes and the porch where they had sat on summer evenings. It described the rocking chair, its size, its smell, its age and the noise it made. It described the place where Mottyl had lain through most of her evenings, in the shadow of the trumpet vine, and it described the smells that surrounded her there—the smell of dust—the smell of gin and the smell of flowers and herbs. It told of all the mice she had killed and eaten. It told of milk she had drunk—and broth and water. It told of the wood and the place where the catnip grew up high above the chamomile and it told of broken fence rails and whole ones—places to avoid and ways of entry to and from the wood. It told of Crowe. It told of Whistler. It told of the Vixen and the Porcupine. It told of Japeth's wolves at the gate. It told of demons,

dragons and other dangers and it told of the greatest danger of all: it told of Doctor Noyes.

The world—whose litany of praise and sorrow was the subject of her singing—was also the world she watched inside her mind beyond her blindness. Bright with light and thick with shadows, it was the world of green and yellow life that she had seen from the day of her birth. It was filled with dusty yards and high green fields and other fields that were mown and yellow. It was white, overhead, and all the places in the wood were silver and blue and brown. It was teeming with life—all of it vital—all of it in motion—all of it crying to her:
Wasn't it wonderful here!
    Goodbye. Goodbye.[133]

Mottyl's nemesis, Dr. Noyes, Noah, who steals Mottyl's kittens to be used in his experiments, never to be seen again, the ontotheologue who colludes with the dying Yaweh to destroy the world that has escaped his grasp, is the Man of Reason, the embodiment of carno-phallogocentrism.[134] He dreams of a planet beyond bodies, a domain ruled by *logos*, a Bookworld. In this Bookworld, women, children, animals, the transgender Lucy/Lucifer, and the stowaway Mottyl—are exiled, imprisoned, or tossed into the rainy gutter for their failure to master the logic of a rigged language game. Religion for Noah and Yaweh is an empire of books, a place that pretends to be above affect and animality. It is the religion of the angels who consign everything that is not in Bookworld to the gutter, dismissing it all as "merely dancing."[135] This starry-eyed religion of transcendence—like Levinas picking up the affectively rich language games of the Judeo-Christian tradition and joyfully whirling around with them—is an affective economy—an organic by-product of the human spirit, in Wilson's term, a toxic but inevitable dance between our human passion for reason, our delight in language, and our lust to divide *us* from *them* and build our shining economies of dignity on the broken backs of other bodies.

There is a lingering sense that religion makes us human by severing our animality. This is a religious autobiography, and its results are just as poisonous as Derrida warned us they would be. What if we follow Derrida in writing zootobiographies instead of autobiographies? What if religion makes us animal, is our animality, our destinerrance to our bodies? For Levinas, this is impossible: the dancing chimpanzees are out-side of the sphere of what matters. They are an accident, a nonsignifying typo in the script of the world, a don't-care.[136] The only thing that matters for Levinas and his anti-Darwinian heavenly host are the people of the book—the architects of language, concept, and text, the antianimalists. Only the *logos* that lifts human bodies to the world beyond matters. Everything else, Levinas insists, is dancing.

To which the affect theorist, attuned to the ways that power, religion, and language itself are animal forces moving through bodies, playing us to their music, can only demur: My Lord, I am on the side of dancing.

UNDER THE ROSE

It is interesting to contemplate a tangled bank, clothed with many plants of many kinds, with birds singing on the bushes, with various insects flitting about, and with worms crawling through the damp earth, and to reflect that these elaborately constructed forms, so different from each other, and dependent upon each other in so complex a manner, have all been produced by laws acting around us. . . . There is grandeur in this view of life, with its several powers.—**Darwin,** *On the Origin of Species*

Power is a thing of the senses. It lives as a capacity, or a yearning, or a festering resentment. It can be sensualized in night rages.
—**Kathleen Stewart,** *Ordinary Affects*

The animal that I am (following), does it speak? . . . Language is like the rest—it is not enough to speak of it. From the moment of this first question, one should be able to sniff the trace of the fact that this animal seems to speak French here, and is no less asinine for it.—**Derrida,** The Animal That Therefore I Am

Although this book begins with the religious practices of a few specific animals, my aim is not to produce a static catalog of forms of animal religion. Instead, by placing religious studies into conversation with affect theory, it seeks to intercept and rewrite the parameters of the membrane of what gets called religion. In trying to understand religion, in deciding what gets called religion, expanding the field of possible religious bodies to include nonhuman animals helps us better understand not only other animals but the terms and conditions of our own human religions.

Like other objects of study such as language, morality, and society, whatever religion is, it bears a family resemblance to behavioral forms that we find among nonhuman animals. Affect theory traces these resemblances by moving past the linguistic fallacy—the presupposition, still dominant in some corners of the humanities, that language is the only model for power—and the only way to draw maps of where bodies go. Rather, affect theory shows that power is a thing of the senses, a feature of our embodied, affective, animal lives, of which discourse is only one domain.[1] Affect theory shows us bodies that register and transmit power through a wide spectrum of shifting channels, a subtle, sub-rosa matrix of interactions that happens between bodies and worlds. These are the things that happen unspoken, under the rose.

Following suit with Manuel Vásquez's call for a materialist phenomenology—an approach to religion "as it is lived by human beings, not by angels"—*Religious Affects* is a way of feeling out religion.[2] It draws on resources from affect theory to begin mapping the ligaments that bind bodies to worlds, concluding that the phenomenological dimension of experience is itself political: it gives power its shape. Religious studies has a distinct role to play in the exploration of affect because the intellectual tradition it inherits has developed a rich body of concepts and strategies for thinking through the way bodies are tethered to worlds, objects, and other bodies prior to language. Religions, like other formations of power, are reservoirs of compulsory links to the world. A religion is a lek—a network of beacons calling out to our animal bodies.

The primatologist Frans de Waal writes, "No human institution, not even our celebrated morality," should be presupposed, a priori, to be beyond the capacity of other creatures, such as primates: "there must at some level be continuity."[3] Could the same be said of religion? We think of animals as one-dimensional machines entirely devoid of history, experience, or phenomenological depth. Richard Dawkins, in his critique of de Waal, churlishly insists that animals "are there to survive and reproduce."[4] This is the same error we find in Daniel C. Dennett— the mulish refusal to see how bodies might dance to the side of economies of function, might create affective economies of queer desires, compulsions, and fascinations that are at variance with calculable regimens of survival. But the chimpanzees dancing at the base of the waterfall compel us to ask: is there more depth to animal lives—more strata of feeling—than we know? Maybe there is an "over and above" that exceeds the flat biofunctionalist economy we attribute to them (and to us). Not a transcendence—an angelic ascent—but expansive affective horizons not reducible to language, to belief, or to "thinking through a situation."

George Levine in *Darwin Loves You* redescribes the famous scientist as attendant not, as his critics and many of his contemporary interpreters suggest, to the world as a rational clockwork mechanism, but to the extraordinary, wormlike processes, in the earth, under the rose, by which the thrashing currents of landscape and genescape intertwine and unfurl. This attention to the minutely extraordinary—far more extraordinary than a creator with a magic wand—came along with what Levine identified as a consummately Darwinian passion: wonder. Rather than writing another ode to the wonder of discovery, however, I will only point out here that embedded in this move is one of the overarching themes of affect theory: drawing the little devices of language—including scientific knowledge production—into the wide domain of embodied affect, effectively animalizing them. When Hélène Cixous writes, "I write on all fours in the dark. . . . I write below earth-level,"[5] she is invoking this intuition: that language itself is a strange, animalistic thing that some apes do, a wormlike process rather than an angelic choir.

Even though the reading of affect theory proposed here has returned often to the techniques that affect theory deploys to subvert the classical liberal model of subjectivity, affect theory is more than another poststructuralist takedown of Enlightenment liberalism. It creates a new vocabulary for materialist phenomenology, replanting the study of bodies away from the landfill of all anthropocentrisms—humanism, liberalism, and even Heideggerian and Levinasian critiques of humanism that end up reconstituting, as Derrida shows, the same angelic metaphysical organism. Thinking of bodies as affective animals rather than as angelic subjects expands the available dimensions to track where bodies go. Affect theory gives us a set of tools to begin mapping the channels by which bodies are pulled by power after subjectivity.

The Affective Turn and Religious Studies

The affective turn pushes a new understanding of bodies as driven primarily by mobile matrices of feeling, rather than bits and bytes of information. What Teresa Brennan calls the foundational fantasy of personal autonomy—the homunculoid subject ensconced in a bodysuit, craftily pulling the levers, making decisions, deriving information about the world and then efficiently processing it into a response, as if in a fishbowl—is mistaken.[6] Bodies are always surging into the world, worming their way forward, pulling their accumulated residues behind them, rather than living in solitary confinement, soberly choosing, from time to time, to step out and dance. Animal religion, in a Proustian mood, flows across this ground of pulsing, involuntary relationships.

Affect theory, then, pursues the materialist shift, following Vásquez's call to move beyond the "suffocating textualism" of classical Protestant-inflected religious studies.[7] According to affect theory, even belief is not (just) about belief. Beliefs are themselves affectively driven, motivated, sustained, and manipulated by their roots in landscapes of feeling. We are bodies who laugh and cheer when we recite our beliefs—especially the beliefs that mark our identities, hence the particular concern in this book with how it feels to believe as an *us*. When we add religion to this prism, it becomes clear that the reduction of religion to belief, ideology, or a discursive illusion obscures the multitude of subterranean ways that religion flows through our bodies. Affect theory sees the passion for belief that is unique to the human bodily experience of religion as one facet of the broader matrix of animal religions—a bodily technology persisting in certain human bodies interfacing with our particular religious animality. Discourse is just one of many intransigent shapes grafted into the worldwide creature of animal religion.

Affect theory thematizes what Derrida calls the heterogeneous multiplicity of animal bodies, interlocking affective economies emerging out of the bricolage of embodied histories. Bodies seem unified—envelopes of skin, selves, minds, more or less cohesive and coherent economies of actions—but they are made up of many animals. Different pieces accumulated over the history of evolution form expansive, onto-phenomenological apparatuses: limbs, organs, articulations, kinds of minds, a color wheel of emotional textures. Different bodily economies pursue their own priorities and prerogatives wielding their own technologies for achieving those priorities. Relationships, shapes, colors, faces, textures, ecstasies, touches, sex, horror, frustrations, boredom, landscapes, the cycles of sleep and waking, flavors, temperatures, images, global mediascapes—a thick forest of influences—create the pulsing animal lek. As the feminist evolutionary biologist Sarah Blaffer Hrdy writes, "We are not ready-made out of somebody's rib. We are composites of many different legacies, put together from leftovers in an evolutionary process that has been going on for billions of years. Even the endorphins that made my labor pains tolerable came from molecules that humans still share with earthworms."[8] The history of bodies is an archive of accumulated transformations forming intransigent affective textures, but also linked by lateral, queer affinities.[9]

The affective approach takes affects to be the material out of which religion is formed. Bodies are pushed toward affects, driven to pursue and savor the world. Religions build on a body's available repertoire of affective bodily technologies, bending them, deterritorializing them, and reconstituting them in new configurations with other technologies fixed in the same orbit. It's an ongoing process, the emergence of a cyclonic affective economy. Received religion is only part of the story of animal religion—a dog-eared and scribbled-over manual that bodies adapt, with varying degrees of precision, to add to their own religious experiential worlds. Bodies combine and recombine these discursive elements with their own soft bodily technologies to form new animal religions.

Derrida in *The Animal That Therefore I Am* says that the question confronting contemporary philosophy is, Can the animal speak? And his response is, "This animal before you is speaking French, and is no less asinine for it."[10] We could just as well ask, Do animals have religion?, and answer by pointing to ourselves. Animal religion means examining the practices of human religious lifeways using the same tools that we use to analyze religious lifeways of other bodies. But where, as feminist and antiracist scholars have long pointed out, women, nonwhite, non-Christian, and non-Euro-American bodies are well accustomed to being recorded in the imperial ledger of Bookworld as animal, placing nonhuman animal religion and human animal religion side by side opens a new field of comparisons. It highlights the animality of whiteness, the animality of the Enlightenment, the animality of liberal citizenship, the animality of Protestant Christianity (the animality of our books), the animality of secularism, the animality of masculinity. The animalist approach reorients all these bodies to the earth from which they came, partnering them in queer dances with impulsive, roguish landscapes.

Affect theory, by reframing bodies as complex economies of forces, proposes that we ask questions about religion as something that affects bodies first and foremost. This means reorienting theory to an analytics of throughness that explores the matrix of compulsions linking bodies to leks. Hubert Duprat asks, "Is the caddis worm's precious case the work of the insect or the work of the artist?" and then immediately runs off the rails with a consummately animalist response: "This is not the right question."[11] The animalist approach sidelines questions of intention, color-staining the wormlike processes flowing through bodies, rather than the intact agents resolutely moving through their worlds. The forces of globalization pass through us, depositing different shapes—new tensions, new compulsions—as they rewire the intransigent coordinates they find pulsing there.

But for all the range of implications of affect theory for human religion, animal religion is more than just a turn of phrase. Animal religion means animals have religion—human animals as well as the multitudes teeming outside the gates. If religion is a massing of affects, a core response of bodies in the world prior to ideas, words, thoughts, then it is open to nonlinguistic bodies. Animal religion overturns the sentence of solitary confinement imposed on human bodies by our own anthropocentric presuppositions, returning us to other bodies on and in the earth.

What Gets Called Religion?

There has not always been, therefore, nor is there always and everywhere, nor will there always and everywhere ("with humans" or elsewhere) be *something*, a thing that is *one and identifiable*, identical with itself, which, whether religious or irreligious, all agree to call "religion."—**Derrida,** "Faith and Knowledge"

Animal religion lands to the side of debates about what gets called religion by proposing a postessentialist framework. It follows Ann Taves in a wariness toward a fixation on defining religion a priori—but also an uncertainty that the term can be abandoned, instead accepting religion as a "temporarily constituted set" established for purposes of comparison of "*things* that may or may not be considered religious" rather than "religious things."[12] Affect theory contributes to Taves's call for "a cognitively and/or affectively based typology of experiences often deemed religious."[13] Materialist phenomenology, by situating animal bodies within the field of things that get called religious, helps us understand the sub-rosa currents of what in humans gets called religion—as well as our embodied affinities with other species.

Affect theory opens up new strategies of attunement to the intransigent textures and permutations of lived religion. Kimerer LaMothe points out that one of the hazards of humanistic scholarship is the way it presses us to model everything after the tool of our trade—language—exclusively emphasizing training "from the neck up," in Michelle Mary Lelwica's phrase.[14] Affect theory merges with LaMothe's call to begin studying religion with bodies, using our embodied practices, habits, and sensitivities to understand religious worlds. This also means recognizing the limits of the literary medium of scholarship—words on the page—for capturing the embodied indexes of affect, including postures, muscle tension, tones of voice, facial expressions, gestures, speeds, and all our other subtle affective cues. (How many times, while writing our books about religious bodies, do we wish we could just embed a clip?) These indexes are, I would contend, vitally important for understanding religion—especially the imbrication of bodies with systems of power—perhaps more so than words on the page. Power as a thing of the senses feels before it thinks. It surges at the micro- and macroscales a thousand times over—the hurricane of *memoires involontaires*—before anyone remembers to pick up a book.

We fail to see nonhuman animal religion because we only search for religion in places where we already know we will find it. Religion, too, as Derrida suggested, may be a heterogeneous multiplicity. Animal religion calls us to look at the movements of animals differently, to hear their calls differently, to watch their interactions with their worlds and with other bodies differently. It means opening the possibility that there is a phenomenological, affective depth to these gestures that is also found in us—a register of value that unfolds without the paraphernalia of language. At the same time, animal religion means looking at our own gestures—our practices, languages, habits, traditions—differently. This means erasing the myth that we are angels. It means recognizing our radical indebtedness to wormlike processes, to the system of forces that drives bodies far upstream of the things that are subsumed under the aegis of logos, and far upstream of us.

Affect theory adds to the repertoire of questions in the field of religious studies, mapping lived religion's continuities with other fields of power linking bodies to worlds. Why do some dances get called religion and not others? The animal religion approach doesn't answer this question. But it does provide a new set of tools for answering it, proposing a suite of typological parameters drawing on affects rather than beliefs. If, as I have argued, affects need to be understood as more fundamental in articulating bodies to power than propositional beliefs, affect is a productive starting point for asking why some things get called religion rather than others.

The Same Abattoirs: The Animal Exploitation Industry and Interspecies Community

Heaven goes by favor. If it went by merit, you would stay out and your dog would go in.—Mark Twain

One of the refrains of this book—"what gets called religion"—indicates a way that the theoretical work of animal religion seeps into an actual politics of bodies, where the naming of something as religious parlays into systems of power. There is a presupposition that animal bodies have no depth—that they exist only to feed and reproduce—that an animal paradise would be nothing but a nutrient cycle. But as Mark Twain writes, this is heaven run on favor rather than merit.[15] A human world that ignores zones of depth and complexity behind animal eyes makes possible the extraordinary violence of the North American factory farm system—a massive, brutal, ruthless animal exploitation machine. Derrida argues against calling this a genocide because

> the annihilation of certain species is indeed in process, but it is occurring through the organization and exploitation of an artificial, infernal, virtually interminable survival, in conditions that previous generations would have judged monstrous, outside of every presumed norm of a life proper to animals that are thus exterminated by means of their continued existence or even their overpopulation. As if, for example, instead of throwing a people

into ovens and gas chambers (let's say Nazi) doctors and geneticists had decided to organize the overproduction and overgeneration of Jews, gypsies, and homosexuals by means of artificial insemination, so that, being continually more numerous and better fed, they could be destined in always increasing numbers for the same hell, that of the imposition of genetic experimentation, or extermination by gas or by fire. In the same abattoirs.[16]

The thousands of miles of cages, the concrete walls concealing the violence of industrial-scale abuse, neglect, and confinement, the conjoined exploitation of livestock and economically disempowered agricultural workers who absorb the sedimentation of violent acts in their own bodies—these are symptoms of an ambient sense that animal bodies are one-dimensional, a sense that is advanced to the bloodiest extremes by late capitalism.

But as Donna Haraway points out in her critique of Derrida's work, without discounting the importance of allowing ourselves to feel horror at mass-produced violence, there is a danger in overemphasizing the capacity of animal bodies to suffer without offering an image of animal bodies finding meaning in their worlds. "How much more promise," she asks, "is in the questions, Can animals play? Or work? And even, can I learn to play with *this* cat? Can I, the philosopher, respond to an invitation or recognize one when it is offered? What if work and play, and not just pity, open up when the possibility of mutual response, without names, is taken seriously as an everyday practice available to philosophy and to science? What if a usable word for this is *joy*?"[17] Animal religion is a way of expanding this promise, diagramming not merely the possibility of liberation from suffering, but the hopes of animal bodies. If what gets called religion in humans is an index of value, complexity, and meaning, tracing the contours of the wordless religions of animal bodies opens a window onto their own living phenomenological landscapes—their affective economies of joy, wonder, and desire, some of which must be called religious.

Identifying these onto-phenomenological structures enables us to begin new dances between our bodies and other animal bodies—dances of compassion, play, dignity, and joy. Thinking about animal religion (animal rituals, animal communities, animal paradises) enables new ways of relating with animals—new formations of interspecies community—

allowing us to, as Haraway says, "become coherent enough in an incoherent world to engage in a joint dance of being that breeds respect and response in the flesh, in the run, on the course."[18] In a postsecular context in which religion is always not only an open question but a horizon of respect—a way of recognizing the intransigent phenomenological needs and hopes of another body—attributing religion to others becomes a way of allowing dignity and joy to flourish and expand beyond the confines of a single species.

Power without Authority: Animal Religion and Postsecularism

Naturalistic takes on religion from science and philosophy—and the study of religion—are hardly new and have often been used to confirm a narrative of inevitable secularization. But the affective approach is distinct from a garden-variety secularism. In the introduction to *Secularisms*, Janet R. Jakobsen and Ann Pellegrini chart a series of features of the secularization narrative: rationalization, Enlightenment, social-structural differentiation (religious and secular, for instance), freedom, privatization, universalism, and modernization/progress. Saba Mahmood shows that what gets called secularism presupposes a particular set of practices and dispositions—what she calls "affective commitments"—that constitute the perimeter of "the religious" according to Euro-Enlightenment intellectual coordinates.[19] This volume is postsecular inasmuch as affect theory complicates each of these facets of secularization—and calls attention to the way what gets called secular is itself affectively constituted. Affect theory makes it possible to ask Jakobsen and Pellegrini's question—"What does secularism 'feel' like?"—to map the way language, confession, knowledge, reason, theology, belief, and disbelief are wrapped up in affective economies.[20]

Fundamentally, affect theory underlines that the embodied dimension of religion, the zoo of religious affects—including embodied beliefs—is not false or falsifiable. Secularization narratives start with a firm stance vis-à-vis the proposition "God Is." That framework is too limited to understand religion, because it sees religion only as a mistake, a miscalculation. Secularism is still inscribed within the carnophallogocentric machine: it sees religion as no more than a set of words describing the world. Sensed by affect theory, religions are powerful animals, sheathed in bodies and carrying them on their backs into the lek of the world. Affect theory exceeds the critical horizons of secularism because it understands that power does not need to be true, does not need to be right, does not need to get an A. Religion understood as an affective economy is a thing of power not subordinate to the decision tree of *true* or *false*. Affects are in the passive case, a [*sic*]-ness, a kicking, recalcitrant regime that fuses bodies to power.

Animal religion is a way of overloading the secularization narrative— by unleashing the beasts of affect, the intensities that are the drivers not only of religion, but of what gets called "rationality" itself. As Durkheim saw, the claims to literal truth about religion are always beside the point: what matters are the masses of bodies migrating to religion, migrating since long before there were words, statements, sentences, or books. Religion is prior to truth both historically and phylogenetically. Instead, religion is a place that bodies go, a flame to which bodies are drawn like moths. This is why the upper-class British Christian men in Oxford laugh and cheer when Benjamin Disraeli tells them they are angels: affective economies of religious desire will always pull bodies into particular orbits of knowledge, even as they are crosscut by other compulsions, other queer economies, including ostensibly secular commitments like science, nation, liberty, and reason itself. Animal religion interfaces with bodies, subtly playing the systems of affects embedded within them in exquisite harmony or heart-stopping dissonance or any range of possibilities in between. Religion is a creature of power—even if this is power without authority.

Is it possible that religion is just a by-product of a particular confluence of cognitive technologies, as some cognitive scientists claim? By some accident, perhaps. But the affective mechanisms that drive those cognitive technologies will always be seeping through the walls of that machine. To believe something is not merely to write it down and file it away. Beliefs are not, according to animal religion, systems of punch cards in a clunking computer. They are tissues of passion, identity, desire, fear, hope, force, arrogance, bliss, and meaning, sewn and grafted together— skillfully or clumsily. The reduction of this multihued affective economy to an ensemble of statements of fact is a fallacy practiced by theists and atheists alike—often speaking in the same Protestant Christian patois. Affect theory enables new ways of thinking postsecularism by moving past the imperative to think religion as a set of linguistic propositions that need straightening out.[21] Secularization is a hypothesis of which animal religion has no need.

The overarching question animal religion addresses, then, is this: Does religion emerge early or late in the history of bodies? Is religion a technology so complex and intricate that only human language, human concepts, human reason could have crafted it? This is the implicit assumption of Smith's description of religion as "the relentlessly human activity of thinking through a situation." It is the lens that pushes him to propose that the farmer plunging his hands into the earth does so to conceptually divide the world into two. It reduces desire to writing, sensation to cosmology, and movement to signification. None of this is compatible with an affective approach. Dennett suggests that there was a time in human prehistory before religions existed: religion arrived late. A case could be made for that, one that draws on the text-centered Protestant episteme that Dennett and Smith swim in. I think, though, that a stronger case—one that harnesses more of the multiplex understandings of religion that have emerged in the wake of the materialist shift—would see religion as early. It would suggest that the religious explanations we scrawl in the field of language are layered on top of a far earlier set of wormlike processes—a deep history of moments when bodies plunged into the earth.

Affect theory situates religion in the ordinary. Religion, Kathleen Stewart writes, is "one of the many little *some*things worth noting in the direct composition of the ordinary."[22] Religion is a bloom space—something that grows out of the earth. An animalist approach sees religion as a byproduct of bodies. Do all bodies have religion? Are all animals religious? Those questions are open. Maybe we'll need to say, as de Waal does of morality, that animals "occupy many floors of the tower" of religion.[23] But maybe religion isn't a tower at all; maybe it's a jungle, a meadow, a coral reef made up of twisting polyps, a field of standing stones, improbable articulations of the earth—so like our bodies in that way.

There's an enduring risk in religious studies and in humanistic work generally that we get sucked into Bookworld, that we think the only way to understand our bodies and the only way to understand religion is by flipping pages. Affect theory, following the materialist shift, tries to think of religion as dance, as a surging of multileveled, deeply stratified bodies into the world that is not reducible to language: "The music and the meaning are absolutely indissociable," Cixous writes, before asking "Why do we love music that is without words?"[24] The world, in this view, is not an inert mechanism that waits for us to push its buttons or decode its symbols. It arcs through us as we surge into it. Rather than a linguistic machine or a conceptual puzzle, the world is a dance floor, a lek, that is met by bodies in motion.

Affect makes our understanding of systems of power waver. It shows how power is roiled by bodies, bodies sometimes acting according to predictable calculations of financial or political interest, but as or more often according to the operation of subtler, more textured, but far more resolute affective economies of rage, dignity, joy, compassion, desire, or fascination. Affects wordlessly crawl through our bodies on the way to the world, producing systems of power as they do—some of which get called religious. Affect theory's exploration of religion, as with all examinations of the ligaments between bodies and power, starts with these animal bodies under the rose.

Introduction

1. Goodall with Berman, *Reason for Hope*, 188–189.
2. Goodall, "Primate Spirituality," 1304.
3. On rain, de Waal, *Bonobo and the Atheist*. On winds, Bekoff, *Minding Animals*. On wildfires, Pruetz and LaDuke, "Brief Communication." See also the proposal that chimpanzees have ritual responses to earthquakes and pythons in Harrod, "Case for Chimpanzee Religion," 32.
4. De Waal, *Bonobo and the Atheist*, 199.
5. See Bekoff, *Emotional Lives of Animals*; Bekoff, *Minding Animals*; Goffman, "Miracle Dolphin"; Masson, *Pig Who Sang*; Moss, *Amboseli Elephants*; Moss, *Elephant Memories*; Schaller, *Year of the Gorilla*; Smuts, "Encounters with Animal Minds"; White, "Dolphin's Gaze." See Schaefer, "Do Animals Have Religion?" for an overview of these accounts.
6. Disraeli, *Church Policy*.
7. As Donna Haraway famously wrote in her "A Cyborg Manifesto," "by the late twentieth century in United States scientific culture, the boundary between human and animal is thoroughly breached. The last beachheads of uniqueness have been polluted if not turned into amusement parks—language, tool use, social behaviour, mental events, nothing really convincingly settles the separation of human and animal." Haraway, *Simians, Cyborgs and Women*, 151.
8. Goodall with Berman, *Reason for Hope*, 189, emphasis added.
9. Goodall, "Dance of Awe," 653–654.
10. Goodall with Berman, *Reason for Hope*, 189.
11. Goodall with Berman, *Reason for Hope*, 72. See also Goodall, "Primate Spirituality," 1304; Patton, "He Who Sits," 426.
12. Browne, *Charles Darwin*, 251–252.

13. See Darwin, *Descent of Man*; Teilhard de Chardin, *Phenomenon of Man*; Maringer, *Gods of Prehistoric Man*; Eliade, *History of Religious Ideas*; Burkert, *Creation of the Sacred*; Wilson, *Biophilia*. Some of these works are listed in Harrod, "Trans-species Definition of Religion," and I would like to extend my gratitude to him for calling my attention to them. See Patton, "He Who Sits"; Guthrie, "Animal Animism"; King, *Evolving God*; Tiger and McGuire, *God's Brain*; Harrod, "Trans-species Definition of Religion"; and Harrod, "Case for Chimpanzee Religion." A number of scholars have also examined this question through the prism of various religious traditions. See, for instance, Aftandilian, "Toward a Native American Theology of Animals," on Creek and Cherokee traditions; Harris, "Vast, Unsupervised Recycling Plant," on Buddhism; Nelson, "Cows, Elephants, Dogs," on Hinduism; Foltz, "This She-Camel of God," on Islam; Hobgood-Oster, "Holy Dogs and Asses"; Jenkins, *Ecologies of Grace*; Miller, "Adam, Eve, and the Elephants," on Christianity; and Bhogal, "Animal Sublime," on Sikhism. See Schaefer, "Do Animals Have Religion?" for an overview of this work. Bhogal's work is particularly interesting as an exemplary case not discussed in my "Do Animals Have Religion?" exploring the theological implications of animality for Sikh mysticism. Bhogal points to Rilke's poetic reversal, in the Eighth Duino Elegy, of the spiritual priority of the human over the animal, and correlates it with the Sikh mystical poetry of Bhagat Kabīr and Pūran Singh. In all of these writers, the animal becomes a figure of sublime religious life and strength "not sought in thinking alone" (867–868). Bhogal appends his retrieval of the figure of the animal for Sikh mysticism to a postcolonial project designed to override the Enlightenment hermeneutics that have historically been applied to Sikhism, emphasizing the abandonment of the animal in the transcendence of the body (857–859). Here, the postcolonial, affective, and species critiques converge. Affect theory is interested in this same interdisciplinary encounter.

This question has also received some attention at conferences, such as in Mortensen, "The Problem"; Brand, "What Gets to Count as Religious Behavior?"; and a variety of papers at the 2011 Animals as Religious Subjects conference in Hawarden, Wales, hosted by Chester University, later published as Deane-Drummond, Clough, and Artinian-Kaiser, *Animals as Religious Subjects*. At the 2010 annual meeting of the American Academy of Religion in Atlanta, where Frans de Waal was invited to address a large joint session of the Animals and Religion Group and the Cognitive Science of Religion Group, the question of whether or not chimpanzees have religion came out in the respondents' dialogue.

14. The exception is a monograph written in the 1940s by the French philosopher Georges Bataille, *Theory of Religion*. Bataille advances the notion that animal bodies are not only religious, but are in fact the highest form of religious creature. For Bataille, the condition of animality is "pure immediacy," a state of radical intimacy with the world. To be animal is to be in permanent proximity to the divine. Human bodies, by contrast, are out of joint, mediating our experience of the world through the thick pollution of concepts (29).

Bataille has no ethological data to support his case: neither the dancing chimpanzees nor any other narrative accounts of actual animal bodies are incorporated into his study. Although Bataille reverses the traditional valence of human and animal, his work retains an abstract view of animal bodies as the homogeneous other to rational, civilized man—neighbors of "the primitive" and the female. Bataille's religious animals are poetic figments, not complex bodies. This book, by contrast, is interested in exploring how the complex of culture, race, and gender that Bataille pushes off from—the white, European, human male—is itself determined by an animalist affective history.

15. Smith, "Map Is Not Territory," 291.

16. See, in addition to Smith's critique of the uses of the category of religion for colonization, Wasserstrom, *Religion after Religion*.

17. Smith, "Map Is Not Territory," 307.

18. Sharf, "Experience," 111.

19. Smith, "Map Is Not Territory," 298.

20. Smith presages this through, for instance, his essays "The Influence of Symbols upon Social Change" in *Map Is Not Territory*, and "Here, There, and Anywhere" in *Relating Religion*. See chapter 1 of this volume for further discussion.

21. Smith, *Relating Religion*, 32. Aaron Gross in *The Question of the Animal in Religion* argues for a more comprehensive dialogue between Smith's work and the theoretical question of animal religion. He points out, for instance, that Smith's attention to the way that racialized cosmologies of social division invoke a vocabulary of animality indexes his sympathy with the broader project of critical animal studies, especially an intersectional approach that analyzes how affect-distributing discursive technologies simultaneously enable violence against nonhuman and minoritarian communities—what critical animal theorist Cary Wolfe in *Animal Rites* has called the "ready-made symbolic economy" of animality (8).

22. Foucault, *History of Sexuality*, 82.

23. This critique ultimately led Asad to a position that looks like an affective account: "One does not have to subscribe to a full-blown Freudianism," he writes, "to see that instinctive reaction, the docile body, and the unconscious work, in their different ways, more pervasively and continuously than consciousness does" (15). The work of Asad and his successors is especially concerned with a subfield that has been expressly linked to affect—a reframing of ethics as the cultivation of dispositions. See, for instance, the writings of two of Asad's students, Saba Mahmood (*Politics of Piety* and "Religious Reason and Secular Affect") and Charles Hirschkind (*Ethical Soundscape*).

24. And see the longer bibliography developed in Vásquez, *More Than Belief*, 3–4.

25. Vásquez, *More Than Belief*, 5.

26. John Corrigan is the most prominent exponent of this method, arguing in his own work and through two edited volumes of the last decade that the study of religion must attune itself to the emotional realities of its practitioners if it is to grasp the complex textures of lived religion. See *Business of the Heart, Emotion and Religion, Religion and Emotion*, and *Oxford Handbook of Religion*

and Emotion. Corrigan points out that although a range of approaches from religious studies have made emotion central, only recently have research tools for the programmatic study of emotion come into focus ("Introduction: The Study of Religion and Emotion," 7). "Emotion," he writes, "no longer can be set aside as an unknown, as a hopelessly complex area of human life unsusceptible to analysis" (11). Instead, emotion must be made central to the study of religion. To fail to do so "is to strip religion of one of its central components, and in so doing to render it motionless, inert, and monotonous" (12). Affect theory develops this notion of inertia by thematizing the link between affect and power. A number of other contemporary scholars have begun to explore religious studies through the prism of emotion, sometimes dipping into affect theory but without programmatically spelling out the overlap between those fields. See, for instance, Burrus, *Saving Shame*; Fuller, *Wonder*; Fuller, *Spirituality in the Flesh*; Hollywood, *Sensible Ecstasy*; Jakobsen and Pellegrini, *Love the Sin*; Jantzen, *Becoming Divine*; Lundberg, "Enjoying God's Death"; Marion, *Erotic Phenomenon*; Thandeka, *Learning to Be White*; Thandeka, *Embodied Self*; and Wilson, *Emotions and Spirituality*. Several articles also directly address links between affect theory and religious studies, including McAlister, "What Is Your Heart For?"; O'Neill, "Beyond Broken"; Pellegrini, "Movement."

27. Stewart, *Ordinary Affects*, 84.

28. Smith, "Map Is Not Territory," 308.

29. Heterosexual bodies do not belong on this list. When it comes time to defend heteronormative civilization, the forces of religious conservatism suddenly become pious Darwinians, fiercely intent on preserving "the natural order." *Religious Affects* incorporates contemporary, postadaptationist evolutionary biology, designed to smoothly strip apart the integrity of "the natural," bringing sexuality, among other features of embodied life, into a technological understanding that functionally grafts the natural and the cultural together. Sexuality in the animalist frame is an extension of what Grosz has called the open system of the Darwinian model of evolution, not a static determinism. This also means reconsidering some of Grosz's own views about the fixity of gender at the end of *Becoming Undone*. See Schaefer, "Let's Be Queer about Darwin."

30. Kant, *Religion within the Boundaries*, 63.

31. Gross, "Question of the Animal," 163.

32. See also Edward Slingerland's critique of the divide between *Naturwissenschaften* and *Geisteswissenschaften* as it is enforced by what he calls the "High Humanities" in *What Science Offers the Humanities*, 3.

33. For instance, the 2008 *Oxford Handbook of Religion and Emotion* does not refer to most contemporary affect theorists and gives only glancing mention of Sedgwick and Tomkins.

34. See Ahmed, "Affective Economies," "Collective Feelings," *Cultural Politics of Emotion*; Brennan, *Transmission of Affect*, chapter 5; Connolly, *Why I Am Not a Secularist, Neuropolitics, Pluralism, Capitalism and Christianity*; Cvetkovich, *Depression*, part II, chapter 1; Sedgwick, *Touching Feeling*, chapter 5, and *Weather in Proust*, chapters 1–2.

35. Catherine Malabou in *What Should We Do with Our Brain?* uses this language to reflect her Hegelian reading of contemporary neuroscience. She draws a distinction between "flexibility" and "plasticity"—a term commonly used in neuroscience to refer to the brain's ability to be reconfigured through experience. She identifies flexibility as a symptom of post-Fordist capitalism in which workers are required to conform their bodies and lives to an exploitative system of production. Plasticity, by contrast, entails not only the capacity to absorb change, but the capacity to produce events, to explode—as in plastique, plastic explosives—and reassert subjectivity against the pressures of economics (12). I find in this distinction a subtle reaffirmation of an anthropocentric metaphysics of autonomy that is unproductive for thinking affect or animality. Cf. Schaefer, "Se Plastiquer."
36. Gould and Lewontin, "Spandrels of San Marco," 584.
37. Many affect theorists are interested in queering the very idea of "positive" and "negative" emotions, suggesting that we see affective economies as producing outcomes that pop psychological accounts of "happiness" can't account for. See, for instance, Sedgwick, *Touching Feeling*, especially chapters 1 and 3, as a starting point; see also Ngai, *Ugly Feelings*; Ahmed, *Promise of Happiness*.
38. De Waal, *Our Inner Ape*, 230.
39. Derrida, *The Animal That Therefore I Am*, 47.
40. Weil, *Thinking Animals*, 12.
41. Grosz, *Becoming Undone*, 13.

1. Religion, Language, and Affect

1. Prothero, *God Is Not One*, 337, emphasis added.
2. Prothero describes this frame as an "admittedly simplistic" approach (*God Is Not One*, 15), and as a heuristic for arranging the "doctrinal" differences between religions in introductory courses it is certainly successful. In my own Introduction to World Religions class, I teach Prothero's book in tension with anthropological accounts that complicate his text-centered picture. On the risks of consolidating popular and student expectations about religion as a set of beliefs, see Schaefer, "On Dictionaryism."
3. Smith, *Relating Religion*, 207.
4. Smith, *Map Is Not Territory*, 131.
5. Hence his analysis of the wave of colonization after contact between Europe and the Americas as, "for all its frightful human costs . . . primarily a linguistic event" (Smith, *Relating Religion*, 274). Power follows in the wake of language.
6. McCutcheon, *Discipline of Religion*, xv.
7. Aaron Gross points out in *The Question of the Animal and Religion* that Smith's work is not reducible to the social-rhetorical method, and that many other features of his work are excellent starting points for a discussion of animal religion. In that *Religious Affects* focuses on affect theory, I have chosen here to focus on a portion Smith's project to consider the status of language as a methodological anchor in religious studies, but I recognize that other strands

of Smith's work would lead to other outcomes, including many that resonate with affect theory. For a fuller discussion, see the preface of this volume.

8. Berlant, *Cruel Optimism*, 53.

9. Pellegrini, " 'Signaling through the Flames,' " 917.

10. Sedgwick, *Touching Feeling*, 147.

11. Tweed, *Crossing and Dwelling*, 15.

12. Vásquez, *More Than Belief*, 12.

13. Vásquez, *More Than Belief*, 147.

14. Vásquez, *More Than Belief*, 59.

15. Cvetkovich also points out that the "affective turn" is something of a misnomer, since affective approaches have been current in feminist and queer theory for decades. Cvetkovich, *Depression*, 3–4.

16. Barad, "Posthumanist Performativity," 120. She also supplies the epigraph to Vásquez's *More Than Belief*.

17. Berlant, *Cruel Optimism*, 53.

18. Latour, "How to Talk about the Body?" See also Blackmann and Venn, "Affect."

19. For other, more detailed genealogies of affect theory, see especially Sedgwick, *Touching Feeling*, introduction; Ahmed, *Promise of Happiness*, introduction; Blackmann and Venn, "Affect"; Cvetkovich, *Depression*, introduction; Puar, *Terrorist Assemblages*, conclusion.

20. This puts *Religious Affects* on a different track for thinking the possibility of animal religion than that of the most prominent treatment of this question to date, Kimberley C. Patton's " 'He Who Sits in the Heavens Laughs': Recovering Animal Theology in the Abrahamic Traditions." Even though, as I argue in "Do Animals Have Religion?," Patton's work is vital for posing two of the central problems for a study of animal religion—affect and embodied difference—Patton suggests that one of the primary undertakings necessary for studying animal religion is resolving the problem of animal subjectivity (421). The affect approach sidesteps this problem by turning away from the priority of consciousness for religion. Rather than asking whether or not animals have free will, affect theory reframes what gets called "free will" in humans as a system of forces—compulsions connecting bodies to worlds—and so regrounds human bodies within an animal lineage.

21. Nietzsche, *Gay Science*, 74.

22. Massumi's essay was republished in 2002 in *Parables for the Virtual*. Gregg and Seigworth also turn back to these two 1995 texts for their genealogy of the Deleuzian and "psychobiological" versions of affect theory, identifying them as "the watershed moment for the most recent resurgence of interest and intrigue regarding affect." Gregg and Seigworth, "Inventory of Shimmers," 5.

23. See note 15 above.

24. Spinoza, *Ethics*, 69 [II/138].

25. Deleuze, *Spinoza*, 124.

26. Spinoza, *Ethics*, 101ff. [II/187].

27. Massumi's use of neuroscientific research has been sharply criticized in articles by Ruth Leys and Constantina Papoulias and Felicity Callard. I evaluate these criticisms in chapter 2.

28. Massumi, *Parables for the Virtual*, 23.

29. Massumi, *Parables for the Virtual*, 24.

30. Massumi, *Parables for the Virtual*, 27.

31. Massumi, *Parables for the Virtual*, 29.

32. Shouse, "Feeling, Emotion, Affect."

33. Manning, *Always More than One*, 6.

34. Shouse, "Feeling, Emotion, Affect."

35. Massumi, *Parables for the Virtual*, 35.

36. Massumi, *Parables for the Virtual*, 40.

37. Massumi, *Parables for the Virtual*, 38.

38. Connolly, *Capitalism and Christianity*, viii.

39. Connolly, *Capitalism and Christianity*, 40.

40. O'Neill, "Beyond Broken," 1094.

41. O'Neill, "Beyond Broken," 1102.

42. O'Neill, "Beyond Broken," 1095, emphasis in original.

43. O'Neill, "Beyond Broken," 1101.

44. Tomkins, *Exploring Affect*, 28.

45. See, for instance, Ann Pellegrini's analysis of evangelical Christian Hell Houses in "'Signaling through the Flames'" as theatrical performances designed (but sometimes failing) to traffic particular affects between scenes, actors, and audience members, or Eve Sedgwick's affective analysis of drag in the introduction to *Touching Feeling*.

46. Tomkins, *Exploring Affect*, 44.

47. Tomkins, *Exploring Affect*.

48. Tomkins based a number of his ideas on his experiences as a middle-class academic parent afforded the luxury of spending significant amounts of time fathering his infant son and observing his developmental milestones. *Religious Affects* wonders aloud how the history of Western thought would look if the embodied practices and experiences of parenting were installed at an earlier stage as a central topic. Tomkins, *Affect Imagery Consciousness*, xxxvii.

49. Nathanson, "Prologue," xi.

50. Tomkins, *Shame and Its Sisters*, 37.

51. Tomkins, *Shame and Its Sisters*, 44.

52. Tomkins, *Shame and Its Sisters*, 57.

53. Sedgwick, *Touching Feeling*, chapter 1. See also the discussion of shame in chapter 3, this volume.

54. Sedgwick, *Touching Feeling*, 19.

55. Sedgwick, *Touching Feeling*, 17.

56. Sedgwick, *Touching Feeling*, 111.

57. Sedgwick, *Touching Feeling*, 114.

58. Ahmed, *Promise of Happiness*, 13.

59. Ahmed, "Collective Feelings," 39, n. 4.

60. Deleuze and Foucault were hostile to what they saw as phenomenology's enthrallment to the philosophy of the subject. Affect theory attempts to devise a phenomenology that builds on the Deleuzian and Foucauldian sensitivity to bodies as convergence points of historical forces. See Foucault, "Theatrum Philosophicum," 170–171.

61. Cvetkovich, *Depression*, 4.

62. Mazzarella, "Affect," 301.

63. Cvetkovich, *Depression*, 4; Chen, *Animacies*, 11–12.

64. See chapters 4 and 7, this volume, respectively.

65. Pellegrini, "Movement," 73.

66. Tweed, *Crossing and Dwelling*, 54.

67. Tweed, *Crossing and Dwelling*, 72.

68. Pellegrini, " 'Signaling through the Flames,' " 917.

69. This project is analogous, but not homologous, with James Harrod's work in essays such as "A Trans-species Definition of Religion" and "The Case for Chimpanzee Religion." Where Harrod focuses on how theories of religion from twentieth-century religious studies can be brought into conversation with ethological literature to diagram a remarkable array of instances of chimpanzee religion, this book draws on theoretical concerns from affect theory, science and technology studies, and evolutionary theory to consider the implications of animal religion for the analytics of power.

70. Sedgwick, *Weather in Proust*.

71. Foucault, *Discipline and Punish*, 27.

72. Haraway, *Companion Species Manifesto*, 15–16.

2. Intransigence

1. Klassen, "Ritual," 144.

2. Sophie Connell ("Feminism and Evolutionary Psychology") has a helpful survey of botched attempts to use sociobiology, roughly synonymous with the more recent term *evolutionary psychology*, on the axis of gender. The limitations of sociobiology are further explored in chapter 6, while chapter 7 constructively absorbs some of E. O. Wilson's other work into the conversation around affect theory and religion.

3. See, for instance, Bruno Latour's "Why Has Critique Run Out of Steam?," Edward Slingerland's *What Science Offers the Humanities* (especially chapter 2), and Thomas Tweed's *Crossing and Dwelling* (especially chapter 3).

4. Klassen, "Ritual," 144.

5. Tweed, *Crossing and Dwelling*, 54.

6. Vásquez, *More Than Belief*, 84.

7. An early version of the material in Massumi's *What Animals Teach Us about Politics*. Unfortunately, that book was released too close to the print date of *Religious Affects* to be included in my discussion here. My reading of Massumi should be taken with a grain of salt in light of my not having access to this text and his most recent thoughts on the relationship between affect, biology, and power.

8. Spinoza, *Ethics*, 1 [II/46].

9. Massumi, *Parables for the Virtual*, 15.

10. Massumi, *Parables for the Virtual*, 8.

11. Massumi, *Parables for the Virtual*, 217.

12. Hardt, "Foreword," x.

13. Massumi uses ontogenesis as a metaphysical counterpoint to ontology, not in the biological sense of the formation of the organism through embryonic and postpartum growth.

14. Massumi, *Parables for the Virtual*, 28.

15. Massumi, *Parables for the Virtual*, 36.

16. Massumi, *Parables for the Virtual*, 217.

17. Clough, "Introduction," 14.

18. Interestingly, although Massumi is interested in building intellectual relationships with the life sciences and brain-mind sciences, a substantial portion of his metaphorics and theoretical resources come out of math and quantum physics. *Parables for the Virtual*, 8, 13, 37.

19. Somewhat confusingly, Papoulias and Callard use Sedgwick, Frank, and Tomkins as a framing device for their piece before launching a substantial attack on the Deleuzian branch of affect theory expressed in the work of Massumi, William Connolly, and Mark Hansen. The conflation of these two different branches is an error also perpetuated by Ruth Leys, discussed below, and is, as I argue in this chapter, a mistake that obscures how the tensions within affect theory can be maneuvered into productive conversation.

20. Papoulias and Callard, "Biology's Gift," 35.

21. Papoulias and Callard, "Biology's Gift," 41, emphasis added.

22. Papoulias and Callard, "Biology's Gift," 36.

23. Panksepp, *Affective Neuroscience*, 37.

24. Panksepp, *Affective Neuroscience*.

25. They indict Connolly, Brennan, and Massumi's use of terms such as "reveals," "confirm," and "verified" (37). Interestingly, Ruth Leys's critique of affect uses the same overconfident vocabulary, marshaling a different coalition of psychologists to try to overturn the pet science of various affect theorists and buttressing that coalition with red-flag phrases like "recent research has shown" and "the consensus among this group of well-informed scientists." Leys, "Turn to Affect," 440.

26. Leys points out, rightly, that imagining affect as antithetical to form ends up re-creating an ontological dualism between structure and antistructure. But she expands this attack to include Sedgwick and Tomkins, whom she sees as secretly allied with their Deleuzian counterparts. There are a number of insurmountably serious problems with the way Leys diagrams this connection, including imputing a gap between affect and the order of meaning to Sedgwick and Tomkins, even though Tomkins's insistence that the title of *Affect Imagery Consciousness* be printed without commas—because they form a seamless system—would seem to be a prima facie rebuke to that claim. Ultimately, Leys's mistake lies in failing to differentiate Deleuzian and phenomenological

affect theory. See also Jonathan Flatley's critique of Leys in "How a Revolutionary Counter-mood Is Made" and Connolly's in "Complexity of Intention."

27. Spinoza himself, of course, had a more nuanced view, allowing a discussion of recognizable emotions to become a pivotal fold of his survey of affect in part III of the *Ethics*. It may be fair to say that Spinoza is not a Spinozist, or at least not a Deleuzian.

28. Sedgwick, *Touching Feeling*, 109, emphasis in original.

29. Sedgwick, *Touching Feeling*, 93.

30. Sedgwick, *Touching Feeling*. As Donna Haraway wrote of attempts to define femininity through biological registers, "ordination has been generally bad for the health of females" (*Primate Visions*, 279). Sedgwick and Frank write that they "have no interest whatsoever in minimizing the continuing history of racist, sexist, homophobic, or otherwise abusive biologisms, or the urgency of the exposures of them, that have made the gravamen of so many contemporary projects of critique" (*Touching Feeling*, 108). Navigating a space for politically progressive academic work that has neither a drastic allergy to evolutionary theory nor an enthrallment to sociobiological explanation is part of the project of affect theory, especially in the context of the study of religion. Almost completely unknown to most scholars in the humanities, this agenda has also been a major part of what the neurobiologist Steven Rose has called the "radical science movement," a commitment to debasing hierarchies of sex, sexuality, race, and class (and, I would add, species) by interrupting the marshaling of science for the propagation of conservative ideology. Gould's *Mismeasure of Man* serves as an example. See also Grosz, *Time Travels*; Schaefer, "Tight Genes"; Schaefer, "Let's Be Queer about Darwin."

31. See Panksepp, *Affective Neuroscience*, chapter 1.

32. Sedgwick, *Touching Feeling*, 108.

33. Sedgwick, *Touching Feeling*, 114.

34. Slingerland, *What Science Offers the Humanities*, 15, emphasis in original.

35. But see Spivak, *Critique of Postcolonial Reason*, for a catalog of the failings of the Enlightenment to live up to its own universalizing values.

36. "Angelic subject" refers to Disraeli's "ape or an angel" question. Of course, angelic subjectivity is its own distinctive subfield in medieval theology. It is interesting, in this context, that Disraeli articulates a proposition—that humans are angels—that would have been utterly bizarre to medievals. The argument could be made that Disraeli's ostensibly Christian religious model of subjectivity is itself an artifact of modernity that insisted on the binary detachment of human reason from the animal world.

37. Sedgwick, *Touching Feeling*, 101.

38. Sedgwick, *Touching Feeling*, 111. Sedgwick and Frank also take Tomkins to task for sometimes leading to an unproductive emphasis on "density of neural firing" that flattens affect into the digital model he claimed to want to move away from (104–105).

39. Probyn, "A-ffect," emphasis added.

40. Probyn, "A-ffect."

41. Sedgwick, *Touching Feeling*, 114.

42. This does not mean that Sedgwick's project is exclusively oriented toward the production of a definitive list of affects. Although she has a special interest in Tomkins for composing new tools for the analytics of shame, she is also happy to tether her inquiries to the phenomenology of paranoia and healing (chapter 4), recognition (chapter 5), desire (*Weather in Proust*), or depression ("Teaching/Depression"). The cataloging of distinct emotions may have been of special interest to Tomkins, but affect theory need not be confined to that paradigm, what Sianne Ngai has called the exploration of a swarming "bestiary of affects." Ngai, *Ugly Feelings*, 7.

43. Darwin is himself agnostic on the biology of emotional experience. In this way, he presages the complexity of the debates on affect throughout the twentieth century.

44. See Cain, "Introduction," xxii; Tomkins, *Affect Imagery Consciousness*, xxxvii. See chapter 1, this volume, n. 48, on the relationship between parenting and the study of affect.

45. Cain, "Introduction," xxx.

46. Nathanson, "Prologue," xii.

47. Tomkins, *Affect Imagery Consciousness*, 15.

48. Tomkins, *Affect Imagery Consciousness*, 12.

49. Tomkins, *Affect Imagery Consciousness*, 14.

50. See chapter 6 for further discussion of this collision of embodied emotional compulsions.

51. Gould, *Structure of Evolutionary Theory*, 10.

52. For Tomkins, all animals rise to this threshold of complexity by virtue of their capacity for mobility: in ranging across a variety of informational contexts, the heterogeneous textures of what Tomkins calls "consciousness" were a necessity for navigating multilayered sensory worlds. Tomkins, *Affect Imagery Consciousness*, 7.

53. Sedgwick, *Touching Feeling*, 19; cf. Spinoza, *Ethics*, 78 [II/151].

54. Sedgwick, *Touching Feeling*, 99.

55. Sedgwick, *Touching Feeling*, 100.

56. Tomkins, *Shame and Its Sisters*, 151.

57. Sedgwick, *Touching Feeling*, 105–106. Sedgwick and Frank also point to Tomkins's syntactical similarity with Proust here, discussed further in chapter 4.

58. Wilson, *Psychosomatic*, 4.

59. Wilson, "Organic Empathy," 390.

60. Wilson, *Psychosomatic*, 64.

61. Tomkins, *Shame and Its Sisters*, 142.

62. Tweed, *Crossing and Dwelling*, 70.

63. Tweed, *Crossing and Dwelling*, 70.

64. Haraway, *Companion Species Manifesto*.

65. Barrett, "Toward an Alternative Evolutionary Theory of Religion," 585.

66. Vásquez, *More Than Belief*, introduction, chapter 6.

67. Alaimo and Hekman, "Introduction," 1.

68. Alaimo and Hekman, "Introduction," 4.

69. Alaimo and Hekman, "Introduction," 9.

70. Barad, "Posthumanist Performativity," 147. See also Susan Hekman's reading of the work of Linda Martín Alcoff in "Constructing the Ballast."

71. Sedgwick, *Touching Feeling*, 17; Berlant, *Cruel Optimism*, 8.

72. Ahmed, "Collective Feelings," 39 n. 4. See also introduction, this volume.

73. For Wills (in *Dorsality*), our understanding of human bodies must take "a technological turn." But Wills opens up the definition of technology to include any articulation ("bending") of limbs. Tendons, muscles, nerves, and cells—any part of a body that moves or is moved—becomes technological.

74. Pettman, *Love and Other Technologies*, xvi.

75. Darwin, *Expression of the Emotions*, 285.

76. Panksepp, *Affective Neuroscience*, 47.

77. Panksepp, *Affective Neuroscience*, 206.

78. Panksepp, *Affective Neuroscience*, 215.

79. Tomkins, *Shame and Its Sisters*, 57.

80. Ahmed has a debatable take on Darwin and the biology of fear in her early book *The Cultural Politics of Emotion*. Ahmed attributes to Darwin a "dumb view" of emotions, a coarse functionalism that understands emotion only in terms of survival. This is based on a contorted reading of *The Expression of the Emotions in Man and Animals*, in which she seems to think that Darwin saw humans as superseding emotion as we passed beyond our animal nature (3). This is, I would argue, precisely the opposite of Darwin's intent with this text. As Joe Cain writes, Darwin's tactic is, in fact, to "find human-like qualities in animals to show that humans are not exceptional and to make animals seem less brutish" ("Introduction," xx). Darwin's biographer, Janet Browne, writes that "the expressions that pass over human faces were, to him, a daily, living proof of animal ancestry" (*Charles Darwin*, 369). Darwin uses *The Expression* as an appendix to *The Origin of Species* and *The Descent of Man* (of which it was originally a part)—as a new archive designed to illuminate the commonalities between human and animal bodies.

This possible misreading on Ahmed's part leads up to her claim that our fears—of bears, for example—are culturally constructed: "We have an image of the bear as an animal *to be feared*, as an image that is shaped by cultural histories and memories. . . . This contact is shaped by past histories of contact, unavailable in the present, which allow the bear to be apprehended as fearsome" (*Cultural Politics of Emotion*, 7). My sense is that this is wrong: placing a roaring bear in front of a child would not necessitate the aggregate memory of grown-ups speaking in hushed tones about the danger of bears for the child to experience terror. But I would suggest that Ahmed's overstatement can be corrected by citing Haraway's insistence that histories are not just "cultural," but are actually expansive, heterogeneous naturecultures that enfold both phylogenetic and ontogenetic scales. Ahmed is correct, then, that fear of bears is "shaped by past histories of contact"—but this must be understood in an evolutionary time scale, as an embodied history forming a set of onto-phenomenological parameters in our bodies now, as well as a local memory of past encounters with bears.

81. Ahmed, "Affective Economies," 128.
82. Ahmed, "Affective Economies," 40.
83. Ahmed, "Affective Economies," 47.
84. Ahmed, "Affective Economies," 126.
85. Whitehouse, "Terror," 270.
86. Whitehouse, "Terror," 259.
87. Whitehouse, "Terror," 268.
88. Whitehouse, "Terror," 269.
89. Darwin, *Expression of the Emotions*, 83, 201–202.
90. Otto, *Idea of the Holy*, 42.
91. Sedgwick, *Touching Feeling*, 155.
92. Sedgwick, *Touching Feeling*, 156.
93. Sedgwick, *Touching Feeling*, 165.
94. Sedgwick, *Touching Feeling*.
95. Sedgwick, *Touching Feeling*, 176.
96. Slingerland, *What Science Offers the Humanities*, 111.
97. Morgan, *The Embodied Eye*, xiii.
98. Sedgwick, "Dialogue on Love," 616.
99. Sedgwick, *Touching Feeling*, 178.
100. Cvetkovich, *Depression*, introduction. See also chapter 4, this volume.
101. Cvetkovich, *Depression*, 174–175.
102. Cvetkovich, *Depression*, 179. Cf. Sedgwick's interpretation of karma as an echo of Melanie Klein's exploration of micrological chains of causality running along projective identification in "Teaching/Depression."
103. Derrida, *The Animal That Therefore I Am*, 31.
104. Sedgwick, *Epistemology of the Closet*, 22.
105. Durkheim, *Elementary Forms of Religious Life*, 417.
106. Klassen, "Ritual," 157.
107. This is not to say that speciation produces cookie-cutter bodies. Bodies within species are always individually variegated, and species should not be mistaken as a template of total uniformity of onto-phenomenological architecture. See the discussion of Elizabeth Grosz in chapter 6 on the role of contingency in evolution and Schaefer, "Let's Be Queer about Darwin."

3. Teaching Religion, Emotion, and Global Cinema

1. Sedgwick, *Touching Feeling*, 153.
2. Sedgwick, *Touching Feeling*, 167, emphasis in original.
3. Sedgwick, *Touching Feeling*, 164.
4. For Derrida, expanding on Lévi-Strauss's earlier formulation of the processes of myth in "Structure, Sign and Play in the Discourse of the Human Sciences," bricolage is also the figure of language as an accidental composition of available parts. See chapter 5 for further discussion of accident as a motif linking deconstruction, language, and evolution.

5. Besson and Duprat, "Wonderful Caddis Worm."

6. Besson and Duprat, "Wonderful Caddis Worm."

7. Besson and Duprat, "Wonderful Caddis Worm."

8. Besson and Duprat, "Wonderful Caddis Worm." See also the discussion of bowerbirds in chapter 7.

9. Steve Baker in *The Postmodern Animal* suggests that this is an instance of the artist rendering animals entirely in terms of human meaning, that "these creatures have been brought into meaning by the artist, and appear to be exhibited principally as the living display of that meaning" (82). The pedagogical perspective would seem to challenge this assertion, showing how different bodies reaching into one another's worlds through their available technologies can produce conjoined syzygies of meaning, two affective-aesthetic-technological worlds knitting together.

10. Though what is local telescopes as technology transforms the range of sensation of individual bodies.

11. Vásquez, *More Than Belief*, 1–2.

12. Vásquez, *More Than Belief*, 292.

13. Aravamudan, *Guru English*, 5.

14. Aravamudan, *Guru English*, 25.

15. Aravamudan, *Guru English*, 6.

16. Aravamudan, *Guru English*, 9.

17. We also concluded that it would be wrong to overemphasize the motif of Guru English as liquid if this were taken to mean only passivity. Whereas discourse-oriented scholars such as J. Z. Smith and Stephen Prothero, we noted, only offered ways of thinking religion as a function of historically constituted discourses, a network of linguistic sand castles, Guru English as a theolinguistics is a current of intransigent force with its own capacity to intervene in and interrupt fields of power. Guru English effects a high-impact inversion of postcolonial power networks, deploying a suite of formidable cultural agents that go to work rewriting the scripts of European imperialism: the "historical empires were only preparatory ditch-diggers for Indian spiritual currents to flow through" (Aravamudan, *Guru English*, 56). The liquidity of Guru English is not irresolution, but a versatile, force-projecting technology for reshaping networks of power (16).

18. Aravamudan, *Guru English*, 21.

19. Aravamudan, *Guru English*, 31, emphasis added.

20. Aravamudan, *Guru English*, 10. Cf. Elizabeth de Michelis's *A History of Modern Yoga* as an example of this process, an illustration of how elements of Indian religion were distributed through global networks and reconstituted in new forms to create what the West now knows as yoga.

21. Aravamudan, *Guru English*, 7.

22. O'Neill, "Beyond Broken."

23. In addition to Sedgwick's chapter and "Teaching Depression," Megan Watkins has published extensively on the relationship between affect and education. Anthropologists of religion working in the Asadian vein such as Saba

Mahmood (*Politics of Piety*) and Charles Hirschkind (*Ethical Soundscape*) also focus on the pedagogies of embodied instruction that underpin the techniques adopted by the Islamic resurgence in Egypt. Cf. Berlant's notion of intuition as "dynamic sensual data-gathering through which affect takes shape in forms whose job it is to make reliable sense of life" as another pedagogical motif. Berlant, *Cruel Optimism*, 52.

24. Brennan, *Transmission of Affect*, 1.

25. Brennan, *Transmission of Affect*, 70. Brennan's particular thematic focus is scent: she wants to underline how olfaction maps the actual physical contact and communication between bodies without touching. Imagistic transmission doesn't suggest the reconfiguration of the body as strongly as the trope of olfactory invasion does (11).

26. Brennan, *Transmission of Affect*, 71.

27. In the final chapter of *Transmission of Affect*, Brennan poses a range of speculations about the nature of the affects that have been largely ignored by later writers. These speculations seem to hover around a picture of the self as constituted by an innate sense for the production of its own equilibrium, an intuition that is distorted by the interference of "the affects" working in collusion with "the ego's imaginary anxieties" (155). This framework is incompatible with the understanding of affect in *Religious Affects*. In particular, in spite of her attempts to distance herself from what she calls "Neo-Darwinism," Brennan seems to have lapsed into an uncritical sense of evolution as producing smoothly sculpted homeostatic systems. Instead, I think it is better to think of bodies as uneven compendia of forces, affective arteries driving not only our self-destructive or egoistic impulses but also healing, associating, and nourishing impulses.

28. Brennan is not oblivious to how TOA involves mutation (see *Transmission of Affect*, 9, 73), but her predominant emphasis is on entrainment as TOA through replication.

29. Ahmed, *Promise of Happiness*, 40, emphasis added.

30. Ahmed, *Promise of Happiness*, 41.

31. Ahmed, *Promise of Happiness*, 44.

32. Ahmed, *Promise of Happiness*, 22. Ahmed's project of mapping the drama of contingency is a synthesis of Brennan's TOA with the theme of accident. Transmission cannot be relied on to unfold through predictable hydraulic processes; it is subject to chance, what Ahmed calls the *hap* (41). The word *contingency* has a double sense, meaning that which touches, *con-tingent*, and accidentality, a touching by chance. Here I want to focus on the drama of contingency as an image of globalization, a living portrait of how bodies touch and are touched in transformative and transforming ways through an unfolding matrix of relationships. See chapter 5 for further exploration of the thematics of accident in Ahmed's work.

33. Ahmed, *Cultural Politics of Emotion*, 6.

34. Ahmed, *Cultural Politics of Emotion*, 14.

35. Ahmed, *Promise of Happiness*, 23.

36. Ahmed, *Promise of Happiness*, 35.

37. Ahmed, *Promise of Happiness*, 24.

38. Ahmed, *Promise of Happiness*, 27.

39. Ahmed, "Affective Economies," 121.

40. Ahmed, *Promise of Happiness*, 39.

41. Hamner, *Imaging Religion in Film*, xii. Even though Hamner fashions her framework out of Deleuze's work on cinema (which emphasizes the ability of film to shape political subjectivity outside the register of language), she is interested primarily in tracking the progress of two intransigent affective religious forms—what she calls "transcendence" and "nostalgia"—as they are manufactured and distributed by film (20–29).

42. Harris, "Film Shows Youths Training."

43. Fischer, Jesus Camp, "Rachael, Age 15."

44. Harris, "Film Shows Youths Training."

45. Fischer, Jesus Camp, "All the Way across the World."

46. Fischer, Jesus Camp, "FAQ."

47. Fischer, Jesus Camp, "Ongoing Intrigue."

48. McAlister, "What Is Your Heart For?," 871.

49. Ewing and Grady, *Jesus Camp*.

50. Ewing and Grady, *Jesus Camp*.

51. Melani McAlister, in "What Is Your Heart For?," has argued that a felt proximity to certain locations in the world where Christians are persecuted—a globalized "heart"—is also part of the affective assemblage of white U.S. evangelicalism.

52. Ewing and Grady, *Jesus Camp*.

53. Ewing and Grady, *Jesus Camp*.

54. Ewing and Grady, *Jesus Camp*.

55. McAlister, "What Is Your Heart For?," 870.

56. Ewing and Grady, *Jesus Camp*.

57. Ewing and Grady, *Jesus Camp*.

58. Ewing and Grady, *Jesus Camp*.

59. Ewing and Grady, *Jesus Camp*.

60. Otto, *Idea of the Holy*, 43.

61. Pellegrini, " 'Signaling through the Flames,' " 915.

62. Ewing and Grady, *Jesus Camp*.

63. Pellegrini, "Movement," 72.

64. Ewing and Grady, *Jesus Camp*.

65. Brennan, *Transmission of Affect*, 51.

66. See Tomkins, *Shame and Its Sisters*, 134–135, for a description of the aspect of shame exactly matching this image.

67. Ewing and Grady, *Jesus Camp*.

68. Sedgwick, *Touching Feeling*, 36.

69. This youth is also prominently featured in Becky Fischer's photo essay attached to her blog, for instance, wearing an ersatz Plains Indian eagle feather headdress as part of a prayer for "Native American children who are being rav-

aged by suicides" (Fischer, "Photos You Never Saw"). This highly visible role in a later ritual practice indicates to me that the boy is invested in the flows of power of the space rather than standing outside them.

70. Sedgwick, *Touching Feeling*, 64–65.

71. Massumi, *Parables for the Virtual*, 24.

72. Fischer notes that when Lou Engle is preaching on the final night of the camp, he singles Levi out from the crowd to prophesy his future. Ewing and Grady are fortunate that the subject of their earlier documentary footage is given such a prominent role at the camp itself—they seem to have made the right choice in following him around. Do they choose him because of the way that O'Brien's embodied charisma elicits religious affects in the bodies of adults around him?

73. Ewing and Grady, *Jesus Camp*.

74. Engle's body itself registers a global confluence of religious gestures, for instance, bobbing rhythmically in prayer, physiologically citing the image of Haredim at the Western Wall. Later, we see Levi O'Brien picking up this same pattern of motion from his mentor on their trip to Washington.

75. Ewing and Grady, *Jesus Camp*.

76. Ewing and Grady, *Jesus Camp*.

77. Ewing and Grady, *Jesus Camp*.

78. Ewing and Grady, *Jesus Camp*.

79. Ewing and Grady, *Jesus Camp*.

80. Fischer, Jesus Camp, "Levi O'Brien, Age 19."

81. This formulation was particularly well articulated by one of the seminar participants, Lauren Hawkins, who put it to brilliant effect in our discussion of *Children of Men* in the final weeks of the course. She proposed that the film be viewed not only in terms of a record of a particular pattern of racial subjectivity, but as a pedagogy, as designed to make us view race in a new way. I am making the same argument, mutatis mutandis, about *Jesus Camp* in this section, but indexing the postsecular American political-religious landscape rather than race.

82. At least one of my students mentioned to me—privately—that she identified with the world of KFSM; this student's voice was obstructed by the rapid emergence of a rigid regime of affective identification within the conversational landscape of the seminar that aligned itself with a presumed secular liberal audience. Highlighting the limits of the professorial body in the pedagogical space, I attempted to keep the regime of interpretation emerging out of the discussion open, and failed as the momentum of the conversation hardened. An intransigent set of affective boundary lines crystallized quickly in the dialogue, foreclosing certain lines of discussion with an implicit threat of shame.

83. Ewing and Grady, *Jesus Camp*.

84. He seldom smiles, but his neutral expression is soft rather than grave. He draws up his eyebrows in the middle of his forehead. He often gently shakes his head from side to side, suggesting weariness or uncertainty, not unlike the blond boy discussed above.

85. Ewing and Grady, *Jesus Camp*.

86. Ewing and Grady, *Jesus Camp*.

87. See also the discussion of the term *warfare*, above.

88. Fischer is comfortable with the language of indoctrination, stating, "As I understood, your question to me is, 'Do you feel it's right for the fundamentalists to indoctrinate their children with their own beliefs?' I guess fundamentally, yes I do. Because every other religion is indoctrinating their kids. Hellooooo? I would like to see more churches indoctrinating." Ewing and Grady, *Jesus Camp*.

89. Ewing and Grady, *Jesus Camp*.

90. Fischer, Jesus Camp, "FAQ."

91. Even when Papantonio tries to erect this wall, he needs to use an affective technology, a sense of shame: "This entanglement of politics with religion," he pleads, "what kind of lesson is that for our children?"

92. Connolly, *Capitalism and Christianity*, x. See also Connolly, *Why I Am Not a Secularist*; Mahmood, "Religious Reason."

93. Fischer, Jesus Camp, "FAQ."

94. At the same time, affective compositions are not sand castles. The sedimented affective meanings that attach to images, words, and bodies within the register of embodied histories are not all created equal. It may be that brainwashing is best understood as a particularly invasive form of affective pedagogy. This opens up a difficult set of questions on how to quantify affects that have not been addressed in affect theory.

95. Berlant, *Cruel Optimism*, 238.

96. Pellegrini, "'Signaling through the Flames,'" 931.

97. Vásquez, *More Than Belief*, 323.

98. Pellegrini, "Movement," 71.

99. Lingis, *Dangerous Emotions*, 18.

100. Lingis, *Dangerous Emotions*, 56.

4. Compulsion

1. Waterboarding, a technique favored by torturers employed by the Bush administration during its war on terror, accomplishes the same effect. Waterboarding triggers an innate physiological response in the victimized body, an evolutionarily constructed mechanism that throws the body into a terrified panic, what Jaak Panksepp calls the *suffocation alarm* (*Affective Neuroscience*, 166). Like solitary confinement, it looks harmless, but the way it contorts our embodied affects is excruciating. Proponents of waterboarding who were on the front lines of the use of the practice, of course, knew exactly what its effects were.

2. Derrida, *Of Grammatology*, 20. For the links between the critique of autoaffection and animality, see Derrida, "Eating Well."

3. This question itself has direct implications for religious studies in the way that it opens up an understanding of how bodily practices that compel solitude or isolation trigger religious effects. The power of isolation to throw the body

into states of extreme affect makes it a useful technology for the production and activation of emotional potentials embedded within the body that are then coded as religious or "mystical." See, for instance, the discussion of Pamela Klassen's meditation exercises at the beginning of chapter 2.

4. Berlant, *Cruel Optimism*, 53.
5. Smith, *Prison*, 92.
6. Smith, *Prison*, 82.
7. Beaumont and Tocqueville, *Report on the Penitentiary System*, 41, in Smith, *Prison*, 82.
8. De Waal, *Our Inner Ape*, 6.
9. Charrière's narrative is believed to be a composite drawing on his own experiences as a prisoner and the stories of others. His descriptions are consistent with other accounts of solitary confinement, but are especially useful for this discussion because of the way he uses the imagery of animality to explore that experience.
10. Charrière, *Papillon*, 233.
11. Charrière, *Papillon*, 15.
12. Charrière, *Papillon*, 233.
13. Charrière, *Papillon*, 246.
14. Charrière, *Papillon*, 230.
15. Charrière, *Papillon*, 20.
16. Guenther, *Solitary Confinement*, xi.
17. See also the discussion of *essential* in chapter 2.
18. Guenther, *Solitary Confinement*, xiii, emphasis added.
19. Discussed in chapter 2 of this volume.
20. G. Berkson in 1973, as described in de Waal (1997), 226, fn. 12. See also LeDoux, *Synaptic Self*, 74–79.
21. As de Waal writes, the behaviorist school "wreaked more havoc than any other" (*Age of Empathy*, 12). Cf. Panksepp, *Affective Neuroscience*, 22–23, for a description of some of the crucial achievements of behaviorist research (for instance, in managing certain addictions) in the context of an account of its intellectual decline. See also Cheney and Seyfarth, *Baboon Metaphysics*, chapter 1.
22. Smith, *Prison*, 97. Panksepp and de Waal point out that one of the death knells of this framework was the research of René Spitz in Romanian orphanages in the 1940s. Spitz determined that even when a baby's "physical" needs for food, water, and controlled interiors were met, many would die prematurely without human contact (Panksepp, *Affective Neuroscience*, 262; see also de Waal, *Age of Empathy*, 14). Teresa Brennan also picks up on this same research in explicating her claim that bodies are vitally dependent on the affects of other bodies. Brennan, *Transmission of Affect*, 34. See also Breland and Breland's seminal 1961 article "The Misbehavior of Organisms," which highlights how intransigent behaviors upset regimes of behaviorist conditioning.
23. See, for instance, Heidegger, *Fundamental Concepts of Metaphysics*, as well as the discussion of Maurice Merleau-Ponty, below.

24. Von Uexküll, "Stroll through the Worlds," 6.

25. Von Uexküll, "Stroll through the Worlds," 11.

26. Von Uexküll, "Stroll through the Worlds," 49.

27. Von Uexküll, "Stroll through the Worlds," 14.

28. Guenther, *Solitary Confinement*, 120.

29. Guenther, *Solitary Confinement*, 107.

30. Guenther, *Solitary Confinement*, 119, emphasis added.

31. Guenther, *Solitary Confinement*.

32. Merleau-Ponty, *Phenomenology of Perception*, 235.

33. Guenther, *Solitary Confinement*, xii.

34. De Waal, *Our Inner Ape*, 219.

35. Guenther, *Solitary Confinement*, xiii.

36. Merleau-Ponty, *Phenomenology of Perception*, 239.

37. Tomkins, *Exploring Affect*, 51, emphasis added.

38. Tomkins, *Exploring Affect*, emphasis added.

39. Sedgwick, *Touching Feeling*, 19.

40. Bennett, *Vibrant Matter*, xii, emphasis added.

41. Bennett, *Vibrant Matter*, 2.

42. Though this is not Spinoza's exclusive emphasis. Spinoza's *Ethics* has distinct ontological (parts I–II) and phenomenological (part III—the catalog of affects, presaging Sedgwick and Frank's finitely many $n > 2$) segments that are not necessarily in full communion with each other.

43. Bennett, *Vibrant Matter*, 40.

44. Berlant, *Cruel Optimism*, 23.

45. Berlant, *Cruel Optimism*, 24.

46. Berlant, *Cruel Optimism*, 51–52.

47. Stewart, *Ordinary Affects*, 94–95.

48. Stewart, *Ordinary Affects*, 70.

49. Stewart, *Ordinary Affects*, 94.

50. The notion of ordinary affects seems to correspond closely to Catherine Bell's concept, elaborated in *Ritual Theory, Ritual Practice*, of redemptive hegemony. "Although awkward," she writes, "the term 'redemptive hegemony' denotes the way in which reality is experienced as a natural weave of constraint and possibility, the fabric of day-to-day dispositions and decisions experienced as a field for strategic action" (84). In analyzing ritual, Bell had hit on an insight later discerned by affect theory: the need to consider economies of gestures not exclusively in terms of discourses, but as a practical orientation embedded in bodies. Like the question posed by affect theorists—where do bodies go?—Bell's notion of redemptive hegemony "addresses the question of why people do something or anything, but in a form that attempts to avoid the reductionism of most self-interest theory" (83).

51. Stewart, *Ordinary Affects*, 79.

52. Stewart, "Worlding Refrains," 340.

53. Stewart, "Worlding Refrains," 353.

54. Berlant, *Cruel Optimism*, 24.

55. Berlant, *Cruel Optimism*, 159, emphasis added.

56. In this sense, affect theory updates a phenomenological motif developed by Martin Heidegger in *Being and Time*, the notion of "thrownness," or *Dasein's* inescapable "concern" with the world. Our thrownness is revealed by the fact that we are always immersed in a "mood," or *Stimmung* (Heidegger, *Being and Time*, 173; and see also Flatley, *Affective Mapping*). Manuel Vásquez also makes use of Heidegger's notion of thrownness to define religion as practices of being in the world (*More Than Belief*, 71). Vásquez, like Guenther, turns to Merleau-Ponty to increase the depth of this insight by fusing it with a robust account of embodiment. My suggestion here is to move through and beyond Merleau-Ponty's recentering on bodies in their complex particularity to an affective account. Merleau-Ponty is an invaluable resource, but remains embedded in an epistemological register of how things seem or are perceived rather than how things feel.

57. James, *Varieties of Religious Experience*, 76.

58. Sloterdijk, *Rage and Time*, 9.

59. For instance, Sedgwick and Adam Frank note the parallelism in the "postmodern syntax" of Silvan Tomkins's and Proust's branching "or-" lists of motivations. Each is a syntactical device suggesting a shifting catalog—the matrix made up of finitely many ($n > 2$) possibilities—that is central to affect theory's flexible typologies of the lines of power connecting bodies and worlds (Sedgwick, *Touching Feeling*, 106). Sianne Ngai, in her discussion of disgust in *Ugly Feelings*, develops affect theory's displacement of the binary distribution of emotions into good and bad by documenting how, from the work of Proust to the films of John Waters, "desire and disgust [have been] dialectically conjoined" (332–333). Proust's literary world has been taken up as a register of how affects drive bodies off the grids of rational self-interest or Epicurean configurations of happiness, joy, and pleasure.

60. Deleuze, *Proust and Signs*.

61. Flatley, *Affective Mapping*, 18.

62. Deleuze, *Proust and Signs*, 26.

63. Deleuze, *Proust and Signs*, 27.

64. Proust, *Remembrance of Things Past*, 48.

65. Berlant, *Cruel Optimism*, 25. See also Proust, *Remembrance of Things Past*, 253.

66. First quotation, Sedgwick, *Epistemology of the Closet*, 252; others, Sedgwick, *Weather in Proust*, 6, 43.

67. Sedgwick, *Weather in Proust*, 18.

68. Sedgwick, *Weather in Proust*, 15.

69. Berlant, *Cruel Optimism*, 123.

70. Sedgwick, *Weather in Proust*, 9.

71. Sedgwick, *Weather in Proust*, 13.

72. Sedgwick, *Weather in Proust*, 19.

73. Sedgwick, *Weather in Proust*, 9. Sedgwick also points out that this barometric interactivity between bodies and worlds is not always defined in terms of pleasure. Like Deleuze, she takes us to the thematics of jealousy in Proust, the

"excruciating erotic situation" of the narrator. If "every woman is a goddess and most men too," the Proustian frame for understanding religion pins bodies to situations of cruel optimism where their attachment is as painfully toxic as it is insoluble. Proust's genies are not necessarily happy in their bondage to the affective currents of the weather of the world (10–15).

74. Cvetkovich, *Depression*, 12.

75. Cvetkovich, *Depression*, 54.

76. Cvetkovich, *Depression*, 52.

77. Cvetkovich, *Depression*, 54.

78. Cvetkovich, *Depression*, 52.

79. Cvetkovich, *Depression*.

80. This affective angling toward religion is not only a matter of material things, though. So, too, are concepts. In several instances, Cvetkovich describes how, after an initial moment of affective impact with an object or ritual, she began to layer on conceptual significations. These significations are themselves part of the bricolage of emotionally charged forms that she builds into her altars. Cvetkovich, *Depression*, 55.

81. Cvetkovich, *Depression*, 80.

82. Proust is also interested in the healing force of habit, which he describes as arriving, he says, to "take me in her arms and carry me all the way up to my bed like a little child." Proust, *Remembrance of Things Past*, 125.

83. Cvetkovich, *Depression*, 82.

84. Meyer et al., "Introduction."

85. Plate, *History of Religion*, 15.

86. Taussig, *What Color Is the Sacred?*, 36. Taussig asserts that color, heat, and religion share a common denominator that runs through animal bodies—"some quite other medium," in Taussig's phrase—what he will flippantly go on to call "polymorphous magical substance." This substance is the medium of experience itself, what Deleuze has in mind when he writes of the fluid propulsive force of signs on bodies, and what I am calling compulsion. "It affects the senses, not just sight," Taussig writes. "It moves. It has depth and motion just as a stream has depth and motion, and it connects such that it changes whatever it comes into contact with" (40).

87. Taussig, *What Color Is the Sacred?*, 189.

88. Taussig, *What Color Is the Sacred?*, 188.

89. Taussig, *What Color Is the Sacred?*, 14.

90. Taussig, *What Color Is the Sacred?*, 32.

91. Tweed, *Our Lady of the Exile*, 16.

92. Tweed, *Our Lady of the Exile*, chapter 1.

93. Tweed, *Our Lady of the Exile*, 17–18.

94. Tweed, *Our Lady of the Exile*, 18.

95. Though Tweed (*Our Lady of the Exile*, 30–32) notes this shift is a by-product of a cluster of demographic and political factors.

96. Tweed, *Our Lady of the Exile*, 33.

97. Tweed, *Our Lady of the Exile*, 32.

98. Tweed, *Our Lady of the Exile*, 102.

99. Tweed, *Our Lady of the Exile*, 4.

100. Tweed, *Our Lady of the Exile*, 107.

101. Tweed, *Crossing and Dwelling*, 168.

102. Tweed, *Our Lady of the Exile*, 101.

103. Tweed, *Crossing and Dwelling*, 86.

104. Tweed, *Our Lady of the Exile*, 104, 108.

105. Tweed, *Our Lady of the Exile*, 100.

106. Tweed, *Our Lady of the Exile*, 12.

107. Tweed, *Our Lady of the Exile*, chapter 2.

108. Tweed, *Our Lady of the Exile*, 12.

109. Tweed, *Our Lady of the Exile*, 10.

110. Tweed, *Crossing and Dwelling*, 181.

111. Morgan, *Embodied Eye*, xvii.

112. Cvetkovich, *Depression*, part II.

113. Cvetkovich, *Depression*, 202. See also Cvetkovich, *Archive of Feelings*.

114. Plate, *History of Religion*, 10, emphasis added.

115. Morgan, *Embodied Eye*, 53.

116. Moreover, phenomenological affect theory suggests that we think of the desire for material objects not as a univocal field of sensation, but according to mixed affective textures: shame, fear, pleasure, lust, anger. See Howes, "Sensation."

117. Cvetkovich, *Depression*, 53.

118. O'Neill, "Beyond Broken," 1102.

119. Cvetkovich, *Depression*, 22.

120. Tomkins, *Affect Imagery Consciousness*, 12.

121. Taussig, *What Color Is the Sacred?*, 180.

122. Sedgwick, *Weather in Proust*, 66.

123. Latour, *On the Modern Cult*, 103.

124. Latour, *On the Modern Cult*, 101, emphasis added.

125. For the same reason, this approach deflects neo-Spinozist approaches that see affects as clear reflections of the body's register of health—and religion as accretions of healthy practices. Damasio, *Looking for Spinoza*. See further discussion in chapter 6, this volume.

126. Pellegrini, " 'Signaling through the Flames,' " 917.

5. Savages

1. Rand's original comment referencing the Arab-Israeli conflict identified the Arabs as "savages" (Rand, *Ayn Rand Answers*, 96). In the same year, Rand gave a graduation address at West Point in which she stated that Native Americans have no claim to land in the Americas because their only use of the land is to "just keep everybody out so that [they] will live practically like an animal, or a few caves above it. Any white person who brings the element of civilization has the right to take over this continent" (Rand, "Philosophy"). A racialized sense of the savage and of animality are closely conjoined concepts in Rand's vocabulary.

2. Geller, *Stop the Islamization of America*.

3. The U.S. Census still lists Iranians as white. The geonym *Iran* means Land of the Aryans.

4. Puar, *Terrorist Assemblages*, xii.

5. Sedgwick, *Weather in Proust*, 24.

6. Geller, "Why There Shouldn't Be a Mosque."

7. Berlant, *Cruel Optimism*, 263.

8. See, in addition to works discussed in the previous chapters, Staiger, Cvetkovich, and Reynolds, *Political Emotions*; Berlant, *Compassion*; Berlant, *Female Complaint*.

9. See, in addition to works discussed in the previous chapters, Bennett, *Enchantment of Modern Life*; Clough and Halley, *Affective Turn*; Glezos, *Politics of Speed*; Protevi, *Political Physics*; Protevi, *Political Affect*; Thrift, "Intensities of Feeling"; Thrift, *Non-representational Theory*.

10. See, in addition to works discussed in the previous chapters, Appadurai, *Fear of Small Numbers*; Appadurai, "Grounds of the Nation-State"; Flatley, "How a Revolutionary Counter-mood"; Sloterdijk, *Rage and Time*. See also Marcus, Neuman, and MacKuen, *Affective Intelligence*, for a cluster of approaches to affect from political science perspectives.

11. Brian Massumi has now published a work on the relationship between animality, politics, and affect, *What Animals Teach Us about Politics*. Unfortunately, this volume was released too close to the print date of *Religious Affects* to be included in my discussion here.

12. Berlant, *Cruel Optimism*, 53.

13. Ahmed, "Affective Economies," 126.

14. Appadurai, "Grounds of the Nation-State," 130.

15. Appadurai, "Grounds of the Nation-State," 129.

16. Directly addressing the link between affect and race, José Esteban Muñoz has argued that different racialized subcultures can be understood according to their distinctive sets of affective performances ("Feeling Brown," 68). Adding to this insight, I would suggest that the relationship between racialization and affect is even more complex: not only does affect constitute the landscape of different racialized communities, race authorizes different configurations of affect for different bodies. Anti-Muslim rage is a permitted structure of feeling for white bodies, while rage on the part of nonwhites is stringently policed and controlled. Whiteness in the United States might, by these lights, be considered in part as the prerogative to exercise a wider range of affects with impunity—for instance, to exercise a self-indulgent economy of hate and not be labeled as a terrorist by state and media apparatuses.

17. Appadurai, "Grounds of the Nation-State," 131.

18. Appadurai, "Grounds of the Nation-State," 131.

19. Ahmed, *Promise of Happiness*, 177, emphasis added.

20. Tomkins, *Exploring Affect*, 51; Sedgwick, *Touching Feeling*, 19.

21. Grosz, *Time Travels*, 171.

22. Berlant, *Cruel Optimism*, 145.

23. Sloterdijk means *eros* in the psychoanalytic sense. Sharon Patricia Holland's word "erotic"—discussed further below—is more resolutely queer, referring to a pleasure between bodies that is not reducible to sexual desire.

24. Sloterdijk, *Rage and Time*, 17.

25. Sloterdijk, *Rage and Time*, 11.

26. Sloterdijk, *Rage and Time*, 8.

27. Sloterdijk points out that for the ancients, heroism through the intransigence of thymos meant human defiance of *physis* (*Rage and Time*, 4). *Religious Affects*, by contrast, sees affects as entirely absorbed by the slipstream of *physis*— as the currents of our embodied animality rather than in any way resisting them.

28. Sloterdijk, *Rage and Time*, 20.

29. Sloterdijk, *Rage and Time*, 21–22.

30. Sloterdijk, *Rage and Time*, 9.

31. Holland, *The Erotic Life of Racism*, 2–3, emphasis added.

32. Holland, *The Erotic Life of Racism*, 6.

33. Holland, *The Erotic Life of Racism*, emphasis added.

34. Holland suggests that she is supplementing Randalle Halle's notion that queer desire is a way of overturning established power relations. "My project," she writes, "comes from the other end of that question; rather than see desire as the force that 'conflict[s] with the present order,' I enlist the erotic as a possible harbinger *of the established order*" (Holland, *Erotic Life of Racism*, 9). The temptation of race is a queer desire that is consummately invested in maintaining existing power relations, as much as it can be marshaled to transform power.

35. Goodall, *Through a Window*, 99.

36. Goodall with Berman, *Reason for Hope*, 112.

37. Goodall, *Through a Window*, 209–210. See also de Waal, *Chimpanzee Politics*. Cf. Donna Haraway's critique of de Waal's early work in *Primate Visions*, 147–148.

38. Goodall with Berman, *Reason for Hope*, 120.

39. Goodall with Berman, *Reason for Hope*, 128. See also Goodall, *Through a Window*, 103–109.

40. This is not to say that war is only a single compulsion. Rather, it is better understood as a composite of convergent currents of force: the thrill of violence, the heady air we find ourselves in when we climb outside of the structured conventions of mundane life, the enchantment of camaraderie—whether small-scale esprit de corps or large-scale nationalism and xenophobia (writing people off, body by body)—and the delirium of battle all connect and overlap to make war possible. War is an epitechnology, a by-product of a convergent network of subsystems that all play a part in sculpting war as an observable, social-level phenomenon. The same may be true of compassion.

41. Hedges, *War Is a Force*, 45.

42. Hedges, *War Is a Force*, 9.

43. Hedges, *War Is a Force*, 5.

44. Hedges, *War Is a Force*, 7.

45. Hedges, *War Is a Force*, 162.

46. Hedges, *War Is a Force*, 49.

47. Hedges, *War Is a Force*, 52.

48. Hedges, *War Is a Force*, 53.

49. Such as that of Emmanuel Levinas, discussed further in chapter 6.

50. Midgley, *Ethical Primate*, 6.

51. King, *Evolving God*, 5; Darwin, *Descent of Man*, 71.

52. In Levine, *Darwin Loves You*, 97.

53. Midgley, *Ethical Primate*, 119.

54. De Waal, *Good Natured*, 217.

55. De Waal, *Good Natured*, 5.

56. Wilson, "Biophilia and the Conservation Ethic," 38.

57. De Waal, *Our Inner Ape*, 32.

58. De Waal, *Our Inner Ape*, 170.

59. De Waal, *Age of Empathy*, 15.

60. De Waal goes on to describe how the chimpanzees of the colony continued to spend much of their playtime at the old playground on rickety old equipment. The Proustian backdrop—attachment to familiar objects—is also part of this picture of compulsory affectivity.

61. De Waal, *Our Inner Ape*, 176.

62. Eldredge, *Why We Do It*, 227.

63. De Waal, *Our Inner Ape*, 171.

64. De Waal, *Our Inner Ape*, 2.

65. De Waal, *Our Inner Ape*, 25.

66. De Waal, *Our Inner Ape*, 178.

67. De Waal, *Good Natured*, 194.

68. Goodall, *Through a Window*, 210–214.

69. De Waal, *Our Inner Ape*, 186, emphasis added.

70. Humans often behave ethically in not-knowing ways, as shown by the host of early experiments with human infants demonstrating predispositions toward compassion and fairness prior to the onset of language. See Bloom, *Just Babies*.

71. De Waal, *Age of Empathy*, 9.

72. De Waal, *Good Natured*, 10.

73. De Waal, *Our Inner Ape*, 210.

74. De Waal, *Our Inner Ape*, 173.

75. Gazzaniga, *Ethical Brain*, xix.

76. See introduction, this volume.

77. O'Neill, "Beyond Broken," 1104.

78. Ingraham, *O'Reilly Factor*.

79. *Fox and Friends*, 2010.

80. Geller, *Atlas Shrugs*, "Giving Thanks."

81. Raised in a more or less secular, high-holy-days Jewish family on Long Island, Geller becomes politicized after 9/11, reading a variety of anti-Islamic authors to try to understand the jihad movement. She frequently appeals in her

writings to the "Judeo-Christian ethic" on which America was founded, and writes that she considers the United States "a Christian nation," adding, "and I am Jewish." I see in Geller's writings a certain attempt to leverage her minority status to embed herself within a majority system at the expense of another minority group. My argument, however, is that Geller is not doing this to secure personal protection, but for the thrill of a private crusade against Islam. Geller, *Atlas Shrugs*, "President Hussein."

82. Geller, *Atlas Shrugs*, "Mosque at Ground Zero."

83. Barnard and Feuer, "Outraged and Outrageous." Park51 became an issue in the 2010 New York gubernatorial race, but Republican candidates running for Congress as far away as North Carolina, Ohio, and West Virginia used the issue in their campaign commercials.

84. Barnard and Feuer, "Outraged and Outrageous."

85. Geller, *Atlas Shrugs*, "Islamic Antisemitism 101."

86. Barnard and Feuer, "Outraged and Outrageous."

87. Geller, *Atlas Shrugs*, "Official Rally Videos."

88. Barnard and Feuer, "Outraged and Outrageous."

89. A claim refuted by Carl Pyrdum in "Professor Newt's History Lesson."

90. Hutchison, "Tea Party Leader."

91. For instance, Peter Gadiel leveled this accusation against Daisy Khan on Christiane Amanpour's special town hall session of *This Week*, "Holy War: Should Americans Fear Islam?" On the same program, the Reverend Franklin Graham accused Muslims of trying to infiltrate American life: "They want to build as many mosques and cultural centers as they possibly can so they can convert as many Americans as they can to Islam." Amanpour, "Holy War." See also Slajda, "At TN Mosque Hearing."

92. Responsible for Equality and Liberty, "NYC."

93. Eligon, "Hate Crime Charges." Enright had worked as a documentary filmmaker embedded with a Marine unit in Afghanistan. In 2013, Enright pled guilty to the charges against him and apologized to Sharif—who had been too disturbed by the experience to return to work—and his family. Enright said that he had descended into alcoholism after a traumatic experience in Afghanistan. Vulnerable, traumatized bodies seem to be particularly susceptible to economies of hate, which facilitate the transfer of their own experience of violation from their body to other bodies. Considering the political effects of economies of hate requires special attention to the disproportionate impact of these economies on already-vulnerable bodies.

94. Gerhart and Londoño, "Pastor Terry Jones's Koran-Burning Threat."

95. Gerhart and Londoño, "Pastor Terry Jones's Koran-Burning Threat."

96. Hedges, *War Is a Force*, 46.

97. American Society for Muslim Advancement, http://www.asmasociety.org /home/index.html.

98. Page since removed. Quoted in Faith in Public Life, "Park51—Responding to Attacks." http://www.faithinpubliclife.org/blog/park51_-_responding_to _attack/.

99. Khan and Niebuhr, "Why We Should Build."
100. Only the Rev. Franklin Graham explicitly condemned the project. Dias, "Many Religious Leaders."
101. Dias, "Many Religious Leaders."
102. Cason, "Delivering the We Stand with American Muslims Petitions."
103. Cason, "Delivering the We Stand with American Muslims Petitions."
104. Ganeshananthan, "Tea Party Official Apologizes." Hanuman is a deity in the form of a monkey who plays a major role in, for instance, the Indian epic poem the *Ramayana*.
105. Geller, *Atlas Shrugs*, "Netanyahu Checkmates Obama."
106. Puar, *Terrorist Assemblages*.
107. Ganeshananthan, "Tea Party Official Apologizes."
108. Jones stopped short of an apology but promised to refrain from future Qur'an-burning endeavors, a promise he would break in April 2011.
109. Wallis, "Jim Wallis on the Story."
110. Fanon, *Black Skin, White Masks*, 12.
111. Stewart, *Ordinary Affects*, 15–16.

6. Accident

1. See not only Dennett, *Breaking the Spell*, 57; but Dennett, *Consciousness Explained*, 452, where he affirms that he enjoys and appreciates the presence of coyotes and other wild animals near his property. This affective relationship with other animal bodies is discussed in further detail in chapter 7.
2. Dennett, *Breaking the Spell*, 57, emphasis added.
3. Since it was published in 2006, one must conclude that *Breaking the Spell* was in press before Hurricane Katrina hit the southern U.S. Gulf Coast on August 29, 2005.
4. Dennett, *Breaking the Spell*, 38.
5. Dennett, *Breaking the Spell*, 14.
6. Harner, "Ecological Basis."
7. Dierdra Reber's "Headless Capitalism: Affect as Free-Market Episteme" is heavily dependent on making Antonio Damasio's popular neuroscientific account of affect the be-all and end-all of affect theory. I discuss Damasio's proposals for understanding religion and affect together below; Reber's argument that affect is homeostatic falls apart once Damasio has been repositioned. Reber does not demonstrate that Sedgwick, Tomkins, or any other affect theorists she cites by name are sufficiently invested in the notion of homeostasis for her argument to stand on its own.
8. Sedgwick, *Touching Feeling*, 5–8; Protevi, *Political Physics*, introduction.
9. Derrida, *The Animal That Therefore I Am*, 92, emphasis added. His Cerisy-la-Salle lectures were published in English in 2008 as *The Animal That Therefore I Am*.
10. Derrida, *The Animal That Therefore I Am*, 34–38.
11. See, for instance, the discussion of the work of Levinas in chapter 7.
12. Heidegger, *Being and Time*, 259–261.
13. Heidegger, *Being and Time*, 99.

14. Derrida, *Of Grammatology*, 60.
15. Derrida, *Of Grammatology*, 10.
16. Derrida, *Of Grammatology*, 9.
17. Heidegger, "Letter on Humanism," 217, emphasis added.
18. Heidegger, *Fundamental Concepts of Metaphysics*, 240.
19. Derrida, *The Animal That Therefore I Am*, 31.
20. Derrida, *Of Grammatology*, 47.
21. This is not to abandon entirely the word *essence*, which as shown in chapter 1 can be productively rehabilitated using evolutionary biology and affect theory—conceptually reframing bodies as mixtures of slow-moving and fast-moving embodied histories. As John Protevi argues in *Political Physics*, Derrida's work "performs the labour necessary to shake free of millennia of philosophical idealism, thus moving us from the pretensions of the cultural stratum to the point where a Deleuzean investigation of the material forces of all strata can begin" (2).
22. Derrida, "Eating Well," 277.
23. Derrida, "Eating Well," 285.
24. Caputo, *Radical Hermeneutics*, 154.
25. Malabou and Derrida, *Counterpath*, 1.
26. Malabou and Derrida, *Counterpath*, 189, 6.
27. As Quentin Meillassoux writes in *After Finitude*, the minimal claim of metaphysics is "that such and such an entity must absolutely be" (32).
28. Malabou and Derrida, *Counterpath*, 262.
29. Derrida, *Of Grammatology*, 84.
30. Derrida, *Of Grammatology*.
31. In "Faith and Knowledge: The Two Sources of Religion at the Limits of Reason Alone," Derrida shows how the category of religion is itself constituted by the play of traces running across it, including from all that which is considered to be "not-religious"—the automatic, the technological, or the profane. Rather than being "unscathed" or "immune"—religion is open to the accidents of différance. See also Schaefer, "Blessed, Precious Mistakes."
32. Darwin, *Notebook M*.
33. Cheney and Seyfarth, *Baboon Metaphysics*, 4.
34. Simpson, *Biology and Man*, 80.
35. See Simpson, *Biology and Man*, chapter 1, and further discussion below.
36. Dawkins, *Selfish Gene*, 12.
37. Dawkins, *Selfish Gene*, 104, emphasis added.
38. Sterelny, *Dawkins vs. Gould*, 13.
39. Rose, *Lifelines*, 53.
40. Dennett confirms that he began thinking about evolution in tandem with his standing philosophical interests in philosophy of mind and artificial intelligence a year after this article was published, when he first read *Selfish Gene* in 1980. Dennett, *Darwin's Dangerous Idea*, 143. Stephen Jay Gould, in "Darwinian Fundamentalism," acerbically refers to Dennett as Dawkins's publicist or, variously, his "lapdog."

41. Dennett, *Darwin's Dangerous Idea*, 51, emphasis added.
42. Dennett, *Darwin's Dangerous Idea*, 64.
43. Dawkins, *Blind Watchmaker*.
44. Dennett, *Darwin's Dangerous Idea*, 74.
45. Dennett, *Darwin's Dangerous Idea*. Crick calls this "Orgel's Second Rule" in honor of its author, the biologist Leslie Orgel.
46. Dennett, *Darwin's Dangerous Idea*, 135.
47. Dennett, *Darwin's Dangerous Idea*, 230.
48. Dennett, *Darwin's Dangerous Idea*, 233.
49. Dawkins, *Unweaving the Rainbow*, xi.
50. Darwin, *On the Origin of Species*, 67.
51. Steven Rose writes that "among practising biologists—those who spend a significant part of every working day thinking about and designing experiments, persuading some research body to fund them and then actually carrying them out in the laboratory—there is an audible grumbling about why 'we' should give the claims of either Dawkins or Dennett serious consideration. These are, after all, people who either no longer do science or never did it; they are not part of 'our' discourse of careful experimentation and allied theoretical claim" (*Lifelines*, x). But Rose goes on to point out that "Dawkins, Dennett and their camp-followers, as best-selling authors in the public understanding of science lists, frame the public debate. We can see their influence on the writers and readers of Sunday newspapers, and on politicians and novelists alike. Culturally, they are too important for practising biologists to ignore them" (x).
52. Keller, "Language and Ideology," 92. See also Midgley, *Solitary Self*.
53. Vrba and Eldredge are the dedicatees of Gould's *Structure of Evolutionary Theory*. He calls their trio the Three Musketeers.
54. Gould and Lewontin, "Spandrels of San Marco," 584–585.
55. Gould and Lewontin, "Spandrels of San Marco," 581.
56. In Gould and Lewontin, "Spandrels of San Marco," 585.
57. This, too, is a Darwinian position, and they quote from the final—1872—edition of *Origin:* "As my conclusions have lately been much misrepresented, and it has been stated that I attribute the modification of species exclusively to natural selection, I may be permitted to remark that in the first edition of this work, and subsequently, I placed in a most conspicuous position—namely at the close of the Introduction—the following words: 'I am convinced that natural selection has been the main but not the exclusive means of modification.' This has been of no avail. Great is the power of steady misrepresentation." Darwin, *On the Origin of Species*, xxxvii. See also Gould and Lewontin, "Spandrels of San Marco," 588; Gould, "Darwinian Fundamentalism."
58. Gould and Lewontin, "Spandrels of San Marco," 597, emphasis added.
59. Gould and Vrba, "Exaptation." Gould writes in 1993, "When I read 'Spandrels' today, my strongest criticism lies in the textual confusion still present because we did not then have a term like 'exaptation.'" Gould, "Fulfilling the Spandrels," 332.

60. Actually, Gould mislabels this feature. They are pendentives, as Dennett points out (with thinly disguised glee) in his critique of Gould in *Darwin's Dangerous Idea*.

61. Gould, *Panda's Thumb*, 24.

62. Gould, *Full House*, 140, emphasis added.

63. Gould, *Wonderful Life*, 48.

64. Gould, *Panda's Thumb*, 28, emphasis added.

65. Gould, "Darwinian Fundamentalism." Dennett's response to Gould's work is outlined in two chapters of *Darwin's Dangerous Idea*. He accepts the need to reject "lazy" adaptationism, which finds a neat explanation for something but refuses to test it, producing a proliferation of "Just So Stories" (245). But Dennett still seems to want to insist that intelligence takes precedence over accident; that evolution is driven more by serendipity—by accident polished by rationality—and that adaptationism therefore remains the best approach to take to understanding bodies. He suggests that adaptationism must always be the epistemological starting point of biological inquiry, setting us up to ask the series of questions that will either recover the reason behind a particular evolutionary modification or the constraints that determine it—which for Dennett are much the same thing (257).

   Dennett does recognize certain nonadaptive formations within the biosphere; he pegs them with the engineering jargon of the "don't-care," an irrelevant feature that has no design impact: "'Why are all the doors in this village hinged on the left?' would be a classic adaptationist question, to which the answer would be 'No reason. Just historical accident.' So is that a good architectural example of a spandrel? Perhaps, but, as the example of the autumn leaves in the preceding chapter showed, it is never a mistake to *ask* the adaptationist's 'why' question, even when the true answer is that there is no reason" (276). One gets the sense that Gould is correct in his assessment that Dennett "only gets excited when he can observe adaptive design, the legitimate algorithmic domain" (Gould, "Darwinian Fundamentalism"). Highlighting the interplay between rationality and affect, Dennett only sees the unfolding of reason in evolution because that is all he is interested in; when organismic features drop off the side of this frame, they become affectively blank for Dennett—he doesn't care anymore. The beacon of interest is deactivated.

   There is also a sense in which Dennett and Gould simply aren't that far apart in their actual perspectives: both would happily acknowledge that natural selection is the primary shaping force of evolution, and only in the particulars of the relative power of other identifiable forces do they differ. (Dennett thinks that the rationalizing force of natural selection is more pervasive, but at least pays lip service to the fact that it is not all-pervasive.) In this light, the sourness between them is all the more mystifying. This is especially the case in Dennett's criticisms of Gould. The fury in Dennett's chapters on Gould is confusing, particularly given how much it warps the otherwise smooth unfolding of Dennett's argument in the preceding chapters, careening off into surreal ad hominem attacks (Dennett, *Darwin's Dangerous Idea*, 300, 309).

There is a strong reading to be made here that this debate is a case study in the affective politics of science, the felt sense of intellectual territorialism, and particularly the affective mobilizations that take place in defense of the mythological sovereignty of reason.

66. Gould, *Structure of Evolutionary Theory*, 31.

67. Rose, *Lifelines*, 7.

68. Rose, *Lifelines*, 15.

69. Rose, *Lifelines*, 186.

70. Rose, *Lifelines*, 231.

71. In an edited volume on "The Spandrels of San Marco" written by a range of humanities scholars, Debra Journet ("Deconstructing 'The Spandrels of San Marco'") suggests that Gould and Lewontin offer a deconstruction of the adaptationist position but fail to see how their own scientific narrative could also be deconstructed. She then goes on to deconstruct her own essay, concluding that deconstruction is ultimately useless for the production of science. Writing in the early 1990s, her project did not have the benefit of the longer range of Derrida's development of his interest in deconstruction and animality; I think in this she misses some of the deeper resonances between deconstruction and evolutionary theory.

In his own contribution to the volume, Gould himself disavows any knowledge of the relationship between his work and deconstruction, writing, "I'll be damned if I have ever been able to penetrate this movement, although twenty people have tried to explain it to me. If I ever comprehend Derrida, who knows—I might even be ready for *Finnegan's Wake*." Gould, "Fulfilling the Spandrels," 327.

72. Wilson, *Psychosomatic*, 13.

73. Darwin, *Descent of Man*, 211.

74. Contrast this with the near invisibility of sexual selection in Dennett's work: the term appears only once in the five hundred pages of *Darwin's Dangerous Idea*.

75. Grosz, *Time Travels*, 17.

76. Grosz, *Chaos, Territory, Art*, 7, emphasis added.

77. Grosz, *Chaos, Territory, Art*, 33.

78. Grosz, *Chaos, Territory, Art*, 7.

79. Grosz, *Chaos, Territory, Art*, 1.

80. Grosz, *Chaos, Territory, Art*, 78, emphasis added.

81. Grosz, *Chaos, Territory, Art*, 11.

82. Grosz, *Chaos, Territory, Art*, 10.

83. Darwin, *The Descent of Man*, 572.

84. Grosz, *Becoming Undone*, 19.

85. Gould writes that reading and writing may now be essential to our survival, but "no one could argue that natural selection acted to enlarge our brains for this purpose—for *Homo sapiens* evolved brains of modern size and design tens of thousands of years before anyone thought about reading or writing." Gould, *Full House*, 196.

86. Grosz, *Becoming Undone*, 21.

87. Harrod, "Case for Chimpanzee Religion," 22.

88. Pellegrini, "'Signaling through the Flames,'" 915.

89. Pellegrini, "'Signaling through the Flames,'" 922.

90. Pellegrini, "'Signaling through the Flames.'"

91. Pellegrini, "'Signaling through the Flames,'" 923.

92. Pellegrini, "'Signaling through the Flames,'" 922.

93. When affective economies interface with local selection pressures, the ensuing collision of complex systems produces effects that resemble even more a stochastic matrix that is beyond the scope of easy prediction. As Niles Eldredge argues, from a different vantage, in *Why We Do It*, organisms in terms of what they do are much more than just a gene-centric caricature of reproduction machines. Rather, organisms are a set of interlocking economies of behavior and desire, creating complex systems with parameters that exceed logocentric determination: "no 'purpose' to life is manifest in this description: organisms are just there, processing energy and occasionally making babies." Eldredge, *Why We Do It*, 36.

94. Darwin, *The Descent of Man*, 569.

95. Ahmed, "Affective Economies," 120.

96. For Ahmed, *affect* and *emotion* are interchangeable terms. See discussion in chapter 1, this volume, and Ahmed, "Collective Feelings," 39 n. 4.

97. Ahmed, "Affective Economies," 120.

98. Ahmed, "Affective Economies."

99. Ahmed, "Affective Economies," 119.

100. Ahmed, "Affective Economies."

101. Ahmed, "Affective Economies," 128.

102. Ahmed, *The Promise of Happiness*, 6.

103. Ahmed, *The Promise of Happiness*, 29.

104. Ahmed, *The Promise of Happiness*, 22.

105. Ahmed, *The Promise of Happiness*, 29.

106. Ahmed, *The Promise of Happiness*, 39.

107. Ahmed, *The Promise of Happiness*, 41.

108. Ahmed, *The Promise of Happiness*, 44.

109. Ahmed, *The Promise of Happiness*, 31.

110. Ahmed, *The Promise of Happiness*, 198.

111. Dennett, *Breaking the Spell*, 393 n. 2.

112. Gould terms his approach *pluralist* rather than *antiadaptationist*. His argument—and Darwin's—was not that adaptation never exists, only that we should avoid the temptation to make it the only analytic axis we bring to bear to a question of animal behavior. Gould and Lewontin, "Spandrels of San Marco," 589.

113. Gould and Lewontin, "Spandrels of San Marco," 584.

114. Gould and Lewontin, "Spandrels of San Marco."

115. This nod to the internal complexity of religion, however, severely complicates Dennett's overall adaptationist framework.

116. Damasio, *Looking for Spinoza*, 13.

117. Damasio also wants to replace the term *homeostatic* with *homeodynamic*, but his inflection is subtly different from that of Steven Rose: for Damasio, "The word homeodynamics is even more appropriate than homeostasis because it suggests the process of seeking an adjustment rather than a fixed point of balance" (*Looking for Spinoza*, 302 n. 5). Even though Damasio sees bodies as being always in motion, they nonetheless are invariably oriented toward a fixed state of holistic integration.

118. Damasio, *Looking for Spinoza*, 284.

119. Damasio, *Looking for Spinoza*, 89.

120. Sedgwick, *Touching Feeling*, 138.

121. Sedgwick, *Touching Feeling*, 147.

122. Malabou, *Ontology of the Accident*, 2.

123. Tomkins, *Affect Imagery Consciousness*, 14. This is not to say that Tomkins is thoroughgoing in his Darwinism. Reading Tomkins, one is struck (as Sedgwick and Frank were) by his intellectual entanglement with the emerging field of artificial intelligence, often starting with the cybernetic viewpoint, which asks, How could we build a machine like us? Sedgwick and Frank consider this an interesting and fruitful perspective, bringing to the study of affect the insights of cybernetic theory in terms of complex systems (Sedgwick, *Touching Feeling*, 105). But the evolutionary question is different, asking instead, how did bodies like ours actually come together over time? Rather than seeing us as a complete picture and finding ways to replicate us, it looks at us as an accumulation of bodily technologies, sedimented over vast spans of time. Tomkins's work, unfurling in uneven clumps over several decades, is tempered by an omnivorous approach to theoretical source material, merrily hybridizing Darwinian, cybernetic, psychoanalytic, and psychological resources. An affectless automaton, he suggests, that was only a neutral information-processing machine would never be humanlike: it "must be motivated" (Tomkins, *Shame and Its Sisters*, 41). Other theorists who take a more rigidly cybernetic approach are unable to trace the shapes of affect in bodies. This is the case with Dennett.

7. A Theory of the Waterfall Dance

1. Levinas, *Otherwise Than Being*, 13.

2. Levinas, *Otherwise Than Being*, 149.

3. Levinas, *Totality and Infinity*, 73.

4. Levinas, "Name of a Dog," 50. Levinas's confidence in his response to the question, in this interview, of whether or not animals have a face, is wobbly: he confesses, "I cannot say at what moment you have the right to be called 'face.' The human face is completely different and only afterwards do we discover the face of an animal. I don't know if a snake has a face. I can't answer that question. A more specific analysis is needed" (49). Commentators such as Llewelyn (*Middle Voice*), Atterton ("Ethical Cynicism"), Calarco ("Faced by Animals"), Gross ("Question of the Creature" and *Question of the Animal*

and Religion), and Derrida (*Animal That Therefore I Am*) have made much out of this waffling, reading it in conjunction with Levinas's description of a dog who visited him and his fellow prisoners of war in a Nazi concentration camp in World War II—whom Levinas and his confederates named Bobby, "the last Kantian in Nazi Germany" (*Difficult Freedom*, 153). As all of these authors point out, with varying degrees of insistence, Levinas's philosophy is deeply troubled by the ethical insistence of animal bodies. Ultimately, Levinas will lapse into a metaphysics of human exceptionalism, insisting, although "I do not know at what moment the human appears . . . what I want to emphasize is that the human breaks with pure being, which is always a persistence in being. This is my principal thesis" ("Name of a Dog," 50). As Atterton underlines, even when he wavers in his anthropocentrism, Levinas wants to reserve the domain of the religious for humans alone: "we are still a long way from the 'epiphany' of the human face described so rhapsodically in *Totality and Infinity*" ("Ethical Cynicism," 58). Much as with Derrida's analysis of Heidegger (see chapter 6), the figure of the animal leads the covert metaphysics of Levinas's project out of the shadows.

5. For Levinas, the "Other" of the you—your neighbor—is the locus of absolute ethical responsibility. But Levinas himself was inconsistent in the application of this principle. In a notorious interview shortly after the massacres of Palestinian refugees by Lebanese Phalangist militiamen supported by the Israeli Defense Forces at Sabra and Shatila in 1982, he asserted that the Palestinians resisting the Israeli occupation of Gaza and the West Bank were not neighbors because they had attacked "your other neighbor," at which point "the other [could] become an enemy" (in Caro, "Levinas and the Palestinians," 673–674). I would suggest that this inconsistency is the result of the concealed metaphysical foundation of Levinas's philosophy: as feminist critics such as Beauvoir (*Second Sex*), Irigaray ("Questions to Emmanuel Levinas"), and Sonia Sikka ("Delightful Other") have pointed out, precisely by overlooking the particularity of difference—the resources of reflection that allow us to analyze our multitextured affective responses to other bodies—and calling us to an abstract ethical relation based on transcendence, Levinas eliminates the possibility of an ethics that is keyed to the introspective practices required to construct complex political-ethical relationships in the highly affectively charged currents of global politics.

6. Atterton, "Ethical Cynicism," 60.

7. Darwin, *On the Origin of Species*, 405; Darwin, *Descent of Man*, chapter 2. See further discussion in chapter 5, this volume.

8. Gould, *Panda's Thumb*, 27–30.

9. For an overview of Derrida's critique of Heidegger's crypto-metaphysics, see chapter 6.

10. Derrida, *Animal That Therefore I Am*, 90. This perspective echoes through contemporary religious studies. Elliot Wolfson, for instance—the winner of an American Academy of Religion book award for *A Dream Interpreted within a Dream* in the Constructive-Reflective Studies category—insists on using

language as a barrier to separate human/religious bodies from nonhuman/ nonreligious bodies. For Wolfson's subjects—kabbalistic mystics—"the most important feature of human imagination is language, for the images through which we braid the strands of reality in our lived bodily experience are linguistic in nature" (Wolfson, *Language, Eros, Being*, 10). Embodied experience—the multiparous texture of affect—is subsumed by a single, superordinate feature of embodied life: language. The human faculty of language is taken to be the overriding, determinative feature of human existence—and to specially set human bodies apart from other creatures of the world (Wolfson, "Dreams and the Specter").

Moreover, through language—even a language understood as receding into an infinite play of signifiers—human bodies are able to collect the traces of the divine. Wolfson builds this link between language and Being by turning to Heidegger, whom he reads as a thinker with a distinctly kabbalistic resonance: even though the meaning of words themselves is subject to the play of accidents, the absorption in that field of play is, following Heidegger, the point of access between human bodies and Being. Language is a tissue of veils, but is also "the veil through which the veil must be unveiled," and so "the unveiling itself is a form of veiling that will be veiled in the unveiling" (*Language, Eros, Being*, 10). "The special task of the thinker," Wolfson writes, "shared inimitably by the poet, is related to the propensity of language, and particularly to the act of saying, to name the opening that must remain open if it is the opening that is (un)named, the 'originary retrieval' . . . of the 'first beginning'" (*Language, Eros, Being*, 13). The truth extracted from language is the play of signifiers itself, hence Heidegger's refrain: "the being of language; the language of being" (*Language, Eros, Being*, 16). For this reason, as with Heidegger, Wolfson suggests that "poesy is privileged as the paradigmatic art, for it is thought to manifest what is disclosed most fully in uncovering the showing of the saying" (*Language, Eros, Being*, 16). The aesthetics of language provide human bodies—and human bodies alone—with a pathway to the house of Being. This is a shimmering metaphysics, but a metaphysics all the same.

11. Derrida, *Animal That Therefore I Am*, 107.

12. Calarco, "Faced by Animals," 119.

13. The counterargument is that for Levinas and Heidegger, transcendence is always in a state of withdrawal, and so is not a thing to which even humans can have access. Levinas is better understood, along these lines, as theocentric rather than anthropocentric. I have never been persuaded that this is anything more than a reinscription of a fundamentally metaphysical presupposition that refashions our bodies as "chasers" rather than "havers." This is Derrida's critique of the *Dammerung* in Heidegger (the oscillation of the spirit in and out of evil, like the cycling of day and night). For Heidegger, the animal cannot lapse into evil. Only the human "is that being who can overturn the elements which compose his essence, overturn the ontological fit [*die Seynsfuge*] of his Dasein and disjoin it [*ins Ungefüge*]" (in Derrida, *Of Spirit*, 103). For Heidegger, as Derrida writes, "This deportation is a gift," an exclusive

property of the human (Derrida, *Of Spirit*, 104). Although the role of species is complex, it is human bodies alone that are given the prerogative to orbit, to move along a track, to chase spirit or transcendence. As Atterton points out, although Levinas claims to be beyond ontotheology, his work is susceptible to a Nietzschean critique that would immediately point to his absorption in the eminently Judeo-Christian tradition of "anti-natural morality." Atterton, "Ethical Cynicism," 61.

14. Levinas, "Intention, Ereignis, und der Andere." This translation is Robert Bernasconi's, found in his "What Are Prophets For?"
15. Manning, *Relationscapes*, 6, emphasis added.
16. Manning, *Always More Than One*, 2.
17. Manning, *Relationscapes*, 6.
18. Manning, *Relationscapes*, 124.
19. Manning, *Relationscapes*, 21.
20. Manning, *Relationscapes*.
21. See also her reflections on the culture of play that emerges between Dawn Prince and the bonobo Kanzi as a quasireligious relational space. Manning, *Always More Than One*, "Coda."
22. See discussion of intransigence and ontogenesis in chapter 2.
23. Haraway, *When Species Meet*, 28.
24. Haraway, *When Species Meet*, 30.
25. Haraway, *When Species Meet*, 25.
26. Haraway, *Companion Species Manifesto*, 81.
27. Haraway, *Companion Species Manifesto*, 50.
28. Grosz, *Chaos, Territory, Art*, 31. See also Darwin, *Descent of Man*, 248–250.
29. Grosz, *Chaos, Territory, Art*, 33.
30. Grosz, *Chaos, Territory, Art*, 11.
31. Grosz, *Chaos, Territory, Art*.
32. Grosz, *Chaos, Territory, Art*, 29.
33. Grosz, *Chaos, Territory, Art*, 13, 15.
34. Grosz, *Chaos, Territory, Art*.
35. Grosz, *Chaos, Territory, Art*, 13.
36. Stewart, "Worlding Refrains," 339.
37. Stewart, "Worlding Refrains," 341.
38. Grosz, *Chaos, Territory, Art*, 35.
39. Grosz, *Chaos, Territory, Art*, 40.
40. Von Uexküll, "Stroll through the Worlds," 14.
41. Grosz, *Chaos, Territory, Art*, 42.
42. Bekoff, *Emotional Lives of Animals*, 96.
43. Bekoff, *Emotional Lives of Animals*, 99.
44. Bekoff, "Playing with Play," 177.
45. Bekoff, "Playing with Play," 165.
46. Bekoff, *Emotional Lives of Animals*, 95. Resuming the theme of addiction developed in chapter 3, Bekoff cites Panksepp as pointing out that play engages the same addicting brain endorphin systems that are stimulated by, for

example, opiates. Bekoff, *Emotional Lives of Animals*, 95; cf. Panksepp, *Affective Neuroscience*, chapter 15.

47. Bekoff, *Emotional Lives of Animals*, 100.
48. Bekoff, "Playing with Play," 167.
49. Bekoff, *Emotional Lives of Animals*, 94.
50. Bekoff, *Minding Animals*, 124. See also Bekoff, "Wild Justice."
51. Grosz, *Chaos, Territory, Art*, 12.
52. Deleuze and Guattari, *What Is Philosophy?*, 21.
53. Published the following year as "Embodied Cosmologies: Sights of Piety, Sites of Power."
54. Narayanan, "Embodied Cosmologies," 499.
55. LaMothe, *Between Dancing and Writing*, 2.
56. LaMothe, *Between Dancing and Writing*, 5.
57. LaMothe, *Between Dancing and Writing*, 104.
58. LaMothe, *Between Dancing and Writing*, 242, emphasis added.
59. LaMothe, *Between Dancing and Writing*, 245.
60. LaMothe, *Between Dancing and Writing*, 243.
61. Nietzsche, *Gay Science*, 30.
62. LaMothe, "What Bodies Know," 582.
63. LaMothe, "What Bodies Know," 583–584, emphasis added.
64. LaMothe, "What Bodies Know," 582.
65. Narayanan, "Embodied Cosmologies," 499.
66. Narayanan, "Embodied Cosmologies," 504.
67. LaMothe, "What Bodies Know," 592.
68. LaMothe, "What Bodies Know," 584.
69. Schüler, "Synchronized Ritual Behavior," 82.
70. LaMothe, "What Bodies Know," 583.
71. LaMothe, *Between Dancing and Writing*, 248.
72. Narayanan, "Embodied Cosmologies," 517.
73. Narayanan, "Embodied Cosmologies," 508.
74. Guthrie, "Animal Animism," 38.
75. Guthrie, "Animal Animism."
76. Barrett, "Exploring the Natural Foundations," 92; Guthrie, "Why Gods?," 95.
77. Guthrie, "Why Gods?," 103. This list is not exhaustive: Guthrie was cataloguing studies he had found as of the writing of his piece, over a decade ago, that determined the existence of a hyperactive agent detection device in these species.
78. Guthrie, "Animal Animism," 44.
79. Barrett, "Toward an Alternative Evolutionary Theory," 599.
80. Guthrie, "Animal Animism," 39.
81. Guthrie, "Animal Animism," 39.
82. Barrett, "Toward an Alternative Evolutionary Theory," 603.
83. Barrett, "Toward an Alternative Evolutionary Theory," 604.
84. Pyysiäinen, "Cognition, Emotion, and Religious Experience," 71.
85. King, *Evolving God*, 8.

86. Quite by accident, Daniel C. Dennett puts us on the same track. He writes of his farmhouse in Maine, "I love the fact that there are bears and coyotes living in my woods. . . . *It matters to me* that there are wild creatures, descendants of wild creatures, living so close to me" (Dennett, *Consciousness Explained*, 452, emphasis added). Dennett seems to be using the language of compulsion explored in chapter 4: the importance of the animals near his home is not about their utility or about a coolly assessed preference for the presence of other living organisms, but about an affective compulsion drawn between our bodies and theirs. Why do these living features of the landscape matter to our bodies?

87. Wilson, *Biophilia*, 1.

88. Wilson, *Biophilia*, 1.

89. Wilson, "Biophilia and the Conservation Ethic," 31.

90. In addition to Guthrie, see monographs such as Boyer, *Religion Explained*; Atran, *In Gods We Trust*; Wilson, *Darwin's Cathedral*; Barrett, *Why Would Anyone Believe in God?*; and anthologies such as Andresen, *Religion in Mind*; Pyysiäinen and Anttonen, *Current Approaches in the Cognitive Science of Religion*; and Slone, *Religion and Cognition*.

91. Ulrich, "Biophilia, Biophobia, and Natural Landscapes," 75.

92. Wilson, "Biophilia and the Conservation Ethic," 32. See also Heerwagen and Orians, "Humans, Habitats, and Aesthetics."

93. Sagan and Margulis, "God, Gaia, and Biophilia," 347.

94. Sagan and Margulis, "God, Gaia, and Biophilia."

95. Wilson, *Biophilia*, 111.

96. Wilson, *Biophilia*, 112.

97. Wilson, *Biophilia*, 115.

98. Wilson, "Biophilia and the Conservation Ethic," 31.

99. Wilson, "Biophilia and the Conservation Ethic."

100. Kellert, "Biological Basis," 50.

101. Chisholm, "Biophilia, Creative Involution, and the Ecological Future," 377.

102. Wilson, *Biophilia*, 1. See also Kellert, "Biophilia," 187.

103. Wilson, "Biophilia and the Conservation Ethic," 33.

104. Heerwagen and Orians, "Humans, Habitats, and Aesthetics," 164.

105. De Waal, *Our Inner Ape*, 171.

106. Chisholm, "Biophilia, Creative Involution, and the Ecological Future," 360.

107. In Stephen R. Kellert's entry "Biophilia" in the *Encyclopedia of Religion and Nature*, this accidental quality of biophilia is played down in favor of a language of flourishing that is not compatible with the orientation to accident built into the framework of affective economies. This seems to be Kellert's interpretation more than Wilson's; Wilson is more interested in hooking biophilia as an affective economy up to a new conservation ethic, repurposing our embodied fascination with organic environments for new religio-ethical ends. Chisholm takes this a step further in her queer reading of Ellen Meloy, who found in biophilia "an erotic-ethical affiliation between human and non-human life in experimental symbioses whose ecological benefits are sensed

and desired, if not fully cognizable." Chisholm, "Biophilia, Creative Involution, and the Ecological Future," 360.

108. Wilson, *Biophilia*, 86.

109. Wilson, *Biophilia*, 89.

110. Wilson, *Biophilia*, 93.

111. Wilson, *Biophilia*, 85–86, 98–100.

112. Wilson, *Biophilia*, 98.

113. Wilson, *Biophilia*.

114. Wilson, *Biophilia*, 97.

115. Wilson, *Biophilia*, 101.

116. Wilson, *Biophilia*, 91–95.

117. Darwin, *Descent of Man*, 42.

118. Wilson, "Biophilia and the Conservation Ethic," 32.

119. Wilson, *Biophilia*, 53.

120. Wilson, *Biophilia*.

121. Wilson, *Biophilia*, 74.

122. Wilson, *Biophilia*, 54.

123. LaMothe, "What Bodies Know," 589.

124. Wilson, "Biophilia and the Conservation Ethic," 38. See also Darwin, *Descent of Man*, 99.

125. Jantzen, *Becoming Divine*, 90.

126. Irigaray, "Divine Women," 62. Irigaray is making an argument for a deeply entrenched embodied gender difference that I would like to sidestep here, if at all possible. What is worth taking away is the possibility that biological differences produced by different articulated embodied histories produce different sets of parameters for religious dances, different bodies in different leks.

127. James Harrod refers to these as the suite of "recombinatory and permutable formulaic behaviors" deployed in decontextualized venues in the production of chimpanzee religion ("Case for Chimpanzee Religion," 33). Harrod's framework also notes that these pairings—such as silence and then the charging display—tend to bring together behaviors with opposite affective valences (33). An exploration of the way the oscillation between affective polarities produces new affective forms that are distinctive to chimpanzee ritual would be a valuable component of a more detailed discussion of primate religion.

128. See de Waal, *Chimpanzee Politics*; as well as Goodall, *Through a Window*; and Cheney and Seyfarth, *Baboon Metaphysics*, for starting points into this literature.

129. Goodall, *Through a Window*, 51.

130. Wallace, "Tense Present," 43.

131. Wallace, "Tense Present," 51.

132. Cixous and Calle-Gruber, *Rootprints*, 55.

133. Findley, *Not Wanted on the Voyage*, 332–333.

134. See Genevieve Lloyd's *Man of Reason* for an explication of this term. Lloyd shows, through a tour of the Western philosophical tradition, that rationality "has been conceived as transcendence of the feminine; and the 'feminine' itself

has been partly constituted by its occurrence within this structure" (Lloyd, *Man of Reason*, 104).

135. This is a simplification of Levinas's position, because Levinas himself is fascinated by passion and the things outside of reason. But no matter how these terms are arranged, for Levinas these things steer humans into the register of the transcendent and away from animality, which aligns him, with only minimal discomfort, with Noah Noyes.

136. See chapter 6 n. 65 on Dennett's use of the "don't-care."

Conclusion

1. Stewart, *Ordinary Affects*, 84.
2. Vásquez, *More Than Belief*, 5.
3. De Waal, *Good Natured*, 1.
4. Dawkins, *Unweaving the Rainbow*, 211.
5. Cixous and Calle-Gruber, *Rootprints*, 45.
6. This does not mean jettisoning important concepts like freedom and intention, but it does mean reconceiving them. Freedom—in the ordinary and in the macroregisters of politics—can only be understood in the wake of a phenomenological account that enfolds the necessity of other bodies—the necessity of many things, including, for some, religions.
7. Vásquez, *More Than Belief*, 12.
8. Hrdy, *Mother Nature*, xv.
9. Haraway, *The Companion Species Manifesto*, 9.
10. Derrida, *The Animal That Therefore I Am*, 32.
11. Besson and Duprat, "Wonderful Caddis Worm."
12. Taves, *Religious Experience Reconsidered*, 123.
13. Taves, *Religious Experience Reconsidered*, 163.
14. Lelwica, "Embodying Learning," 125.
15. In McVay, "Siamese Connexion," 8.
16. Derrida, *The Animal That Therefore I Am*, 26.
17. Haraway, *When Species Meet*, 22.
18. Haraway, *The Companion Species Manifesto*, 62.
19. Mahmood, "Religious Reason," 861.
20. Jakobsen and Pellegrini, "Introduction," 22.
21. As I argue in "Embodied Disbelief."
22. Stewart, *Ordinary Affects*, 48.
23. De Waal, *Good Natured*, 212.
24. Cixous and Calle-Gruber, *Rootprints*, 46.

Aftandilian, David. "Toward a Native American Theology of Animals: Creek and Cherokee Perspectives." *CrossCurrents* 61 (2011): 191–207. doi: 10.1111/j.1939-3881.2011.00175.x.

Ahmed, Sara. "Affective Economies." *Social Text* 79, vol. 22, no. 2 (summer 2004): 117–139.

———. "Collective Feelings; or, The Impressions Left by Others." *Theory, Culture and Society* 21, no. 2 (2004): 25–42.

———. *The Cultural Politics of Emotion*. New York: Routledge, 2004.

———. *The Promise of Happiness*. Durham, NC: Duke University Press, 2010.

Alaimo, Stacy, and Susan Hekman. "Introduction: Emerging Models of Materiality in Feminist Theory." In *Material Feminisms*, edited by Stacy Alaimo and Susan Hekman, 1–19. Bloomington: Indiana University Press, 2008.

Amanpour, Christiane. "Holy War: Should Americans Fear Islam?" *This Week*, ABC, October 3, 2010.

Andresen, Jensine, ed. *Religion in Mind: Cognitive Perspectives on Religious Belief, Ritual, and Experience*. Cambridge: Cambridge University Press, 2001.

Appadurai, Arjun. *Fear of Small Numbers: An Essay on the Geography of Anger*. Durham, NC: Duke University Press, 2006.

———. "The Grounds of the Nation-State: Identity, Violence, and Territory." In *Nationalism and Internationalism in the Post–Cold War Era*, edited by Kjell Goldmann, Ulf Hannerz, and Charles Westin, 129–142. New York: Routledge, 2000.

Aravamudan, Srinivas. *Guru English: South Asian Religion in a Cosmopolitan Language*. Princeton, NJ: Princeton University Press, 2005.

Asad, Talal. *Genealogies of Religion: Discipline and Reasons of Power in Christianity and Islam*. Baltimore, MD: Johns Hopkins University Press, 1993.

Atran, Scott. *In Gods We Trust: The Evolutionary Landscape of Religion*. Oxford: Oxford University Press, 2002.

Atterton, Peter. "Ethical Cynicism." In *Animal Philosophy: Ethics and Identity*, edited by Peter Atterton and Matthew Calarco, 51–61. New York: Continuum, 2004.

Baker, Steve. *The Postmodern Animal*. London: Reaktion, 2000.

Barad, Karen. "Posthumanist Performativity: Toward an Understanding of How Matter Comes to Matter." In *Material Feminisms*, edited by Stacy Alaimo and Susan Hekman, 120–154. Bloomington: Indiana University Press, 2008.

Barnard, Anne, and Alan Feuer. "Outraged, and Outrageous." *New York Times*, October 8, 2010.

Barrett, Justin. "Exploring the Natural Foundations of Religion." In *Religion and Cognition: A Reader*, edited by D. Jason Slone, 86–98. New York: Equinox, 2006.

———. *Why Would Anyone Believe in God?* Walnut Creek, CA: Altamira Press, 2004.

Barrett, Nathaniel F. "Toward an Alternative Evolutionary Theory of Religion: Looking Past Computational Evolutionary Psychology to a Wider Field of Possibilities." *Journal of the American Academy of Religion* 78, no. 3 (September 2010): 583–621.

Bataille, Georges. *Theory of Religion*. Translated by Robert Hurley. New York: Zone, 1992.

Beaumont, Gustave de, and Alexis de Tocqueville. *Report on the Penitentiary System in the United States, and Its Application in France*. Philadelphia: Carey, 1833.

Beauvoir, Simone de. *The Second Sex (Le Deuxième Sexe)*. Paris: Éditions Gallimard, 1949.

Bekoff, Marc. *The Emotional Lives of Animals: A Leading Scientist Explores Animal Joy, Sorrow, and Empathy—and Why They Matter*. Novato, CA: New World Library, 2007.

———. *Minding Animals: Awareness, Emotions, and Heart*. New York: Oxford University Press, 2003.

———. "Playing with Play." In *The Evolution of Mind*, edited by Denise Dellarosa Cummins and Colin Allen, 162–182. New York: Oxford University Press, 1998.

———. "Wild Justice, Social Cognition, Fairness, and Morality: A Deep Appreciation for the Subjective Lives of Animals." In *A Communion of Subjects*, edited by Paul Waldau and Kimberley Patton, 461–486. New York: Columbia University Press, 2006.

Bell, Catherine. *Ritual Theory, Ritual Practice*. New York: Oxford University Press, 1992.

Bennett, Jane. *The Enchantment of Modern Life: Attachments, Crossings, and Ethics*. Princeton, NJ: Princeton University Press, 2001.

———. *Vibrant Matter: A Political Ecology of Things*. Durham, NC: Duke University Press, 2010.

Berlant, Lauren. *Compassion: The Culture and Politics of an Emotion*. New York: Routledge, 2004.

———. *Cruel Optimism*. Durham, NC: Duke University Press, 2011.

———. *The Female Complaint: The Unfinished Business of Sentimentality in American Culture*. Durham, NC: Duke University Press, 2008.

Bernasconi, Robert. "What Are Prophets For? Negotiating the Teratological Hypocrisy of Judeo-Hellenic Europe." *Revista Portuguesa de Filosofia* 62 (2006): 441–455.

Besson, Christian, and Hubert Duprat. "The Wonderful Caddis Worm: Sculptural Work in Collaboration with Trichoptera." Translated by Simon Pleasance. *Leonardo On-line* 31, no. 3 (June–July 1998). http://www.leonardo.info/isast/articles /duprat/duprat.html.

Bhogal, Balbinder Singh. "The Animal Sublime: Rethinking the Sikh Mystical Body." *Journal of the American Academy of Religion* 80, no. 4 (December 2012): 856–908.

Blackmann, Lisa, and Couze Venn. "Affect." *Body and Society* 16, no. 1 (2010): 7–28.

Bloom, Paul. *Just Babies: The Origins of Good and Evil.* New York: Crown, 2013.

Boyer, Pascal. *Religion Explained: The Evolutionary Origins of Religious Thought.* New York: Basic Books, 2001.

Brand, Ryan. "What Gets to Count as Religious Behavior? Merleau-Ponty, Atran, and Instinct." Paper presented to the Animals and Religion Group at the American Academy of Religion in Chicago, Illinois, November 17, 2012.

Breland, Keller, and Marian Breland. "The Misbehavior of Organisms." *American Psychologist* 16 (1961): 681–684.

Brennan, Teresa. *The Transmission of Affect.* Ithaca, NY: Cornell University Press, 2004.

Browne, Janet. *Charles Darwin: The Power of Place.* New York: Knopf, 2002.

Burkert, Walter. *Creation of the Sacred: Tracks of Biology in Early Religions.* Cambridge, MA: Harvard University Press, 1996.

Burrus, Virginia. *Saving Shame: Martyrs, Saints, and Other Abject Subjects.* Philadelphia: University of Pennsylvania Press, 2007.

Cain, Joe. Introduction to *The Expression of the Emotions in Man and Animals,* by Charles Darwin, xi–xxxiv. Edited by Joe Cain and Sharon Messenger. New York: Penguin, 2009.

Calarco, Matthew. "Faced by Animals." In *Radicalizing Levinas,* edited by Peter Atterton and Matthew Calarco, 113–133. Albany: State University of New York Press, 2010.

Caputo, John D. *Radical Hermeneutics: Repetition, Deconstruction, and the Hermeneutic Project.* Bloomington: Indiana University Press, 1987.

Caro, Jason. "Levinas and the Palestinians." *Philosophy and Social Criticism* 35, no. 6 (2009): 671–684.

Cason, Jim. "Delivering the We Stand with American Muslims Petitions." 2C: *The FCNL Staff Blog,* October 13, 2010. http://fcnl.wordpress.com/2010/10/13 /delivering-the-we-stand-with-american-muslims-petitions.

Charrière, Henri. *Papillon.* Translated by June P. Wilson and Walter B. Michaels. Richmond Hill, ON: Simon and Schuster of Canada, 1970.

Chen, Mel Y. *Animacies: Biopolitics, Racial Mattering, and Queer Affect.* Durham, NC: Duke University Press, 2012.

Cheney, Dorothy L., and Robert M. Seyfarth. *Baboon Metaphysics: The Evolution of a Social Mind.* Chicago: University of Chicago Press, 2007.

Chisholm, Dianne. "Biophilia, Creative Involution, and the Ecological Future of Queer Desire." In *Queer Ecologies: Sex, Nature, Politics, Desire,* edited by Catriona Mortimer-Sandilands and Bruce Erickson, 359–381. Bloomington: Indiana University Press, 2010.

Cixous, Hélène, and Mireille Calle-Gruber. *Rootprints: Memory and Life Writing.* Translated by Eric Prenowitz. New York: Routledge, 1997.

Clough, Patricia Ticineto, and Jean Halley, eds. *The Affective Turn: Theorizing the Social.* Durham: Duke University Press, 2007.

———. "Introduction." In *The Affective Turn: Theorizing the Social,* edited by Patricia Ticineto Clough and Jean Halley, 1–33. Durham, NC: Duke University Press, 2007.

Connell, Sophia Elliott. "Feminism and Evolutionary Psychology." Paper presented at the Fourth European Feminist Research Conference, Bologna, Italy, September 28–October 1, 2000. www.women.it/quarta/workshops/re-figuring3/selliot.htm.

Connolly, William E. *Capitalism and Christianity, American Style.* Durham, NC: Duke University Press, 2008.

———. "The Complexity of Intention." *Critical Inquiry* 37, no. 4 (summer 2011): 791–798.

———. *Neuropolitics: Thinking, Culture, Speed.* Minneapolis: University of Minnesota Press, 2002.

———. *Pluralism.* Durham, NC: Duke University Press, 2005.

———. *Why I Am Not a Secularist.* Minneapolis: University of Minnesota Press, 1999.

Corrigan, John. *Business of the Heart: Religion and Emotion in the Nineteenth Century.* Berkeley: University of California Press, 2002.

———, ed. *Emotion and Religion: A Critical Assessment and Annotated Bibliography.* Westport, CT: Greenwood, 2000.

———. "Introduction: Emotions Research and the Academic Study of Religion." In *Religion and Emotion: Approaches and Interpretations,* edited by John Corrigan, 3–31. New York: Oxford University Press, 2004.

———. "Introduction: The Study of Religion and Emotion." In *The Oxford Handbook of Religion and Emotion,* edited by John Corrigan, 3–13. Oxford: Oxford University Press, 2008.

———, ed. *The Oxford Handbook of Religion and Emotion.* New York: Oxford University Press, 2008.

———, ed. *Religion and Emotion: Approaches and Interpretations.* New York: Oxford University Press, 2004.

Cuarón, Alfonso. *Children of Men.* Film. Universal Pictures, Strike Entertainment, Hit and Run Productions, 2006.

Cvetkovich, Ann. *An Archive of Feelings: Trauma, Sexuality, and Lesbian Public Cultures.* Durham, NC: Duke University Press, 2003.

———. *Depression: A Public Feeling.* Durham, NC: Duke University Press, 2012.

———. *Mixed Feelings: Feminism, Mass Culture, and Victorian Sensationalism.* New Brunswick, NJ: Rutgers University Press, 1992.

Damasio, Antonio. *Looking for Spinoza: Joy, Sorrow, and the Feeling Brain*. New York: Mariner, 2003.

Darwin, Charles. *The Descent of Man*. New York: D. Appleton, 1872.

———. *The Expression of the Emotions in Man and Animals*. 1890. Edited by Joe Cain and Sharon Messenger. London: Penguin, 2009.

———. *Notebook M*. Darwin Online. http://darwin-online.org.uk/content /frameset?viewtype=side&itemID=CUL-DAR125.-&pageseq=1.

———. *On the Origin of Species*. 1859. New York: Washington Square, 1965.

Dawkins, Richard. *The Blind Watchmaker*. New York: Norton, 1996.

———. *The God Delusion*. New York: Mariner, 2008.

———. *The Selfish Gene*. New York: Oxford University Press, 1976.

———. *Unweaving the Rainbow: Science, Delusion and the Appetite for Wonder*. Boston: Houghton Mifflin, 1998.

Deane-Drummond, Celia, David Clough, and Rebecca Artinian-Kaiser, eds. *Animals as Religious Subjects: Transdisciplinary Perspectives*. London: Bloomsbury T&T Clark, 2013.

Deleuze, Gilles. *Bergsonism*. Translated by Hugh Tomlinson and Barbara Habberjam. New York: Zone, 1988.

———. *Difference and Repetition*. Translated by Paul Patton. New York: Columbia University Press, 1995.

———. *Proust and Signs*. Translated by Richard Howard. New York: George Braziller, 1972.

———. *Spinoza: Practical Philosophy*. Translated by Robert Hurley. San Francisco: City Lights Books, 1988.

Deleuze, Gilles, and Félix Guattari. *A Thousand Plateaus: Capitalism and Schizophrenia*. Translated by Brian Massumi. Minneapolis: University of Minnesota Press, 1987.

———. *What Is Philosophy?* Translated by Hugh Tomlinson and Graham Burchell. New York: Columbia University Press, 1994.

de Michelis, Elizabeth. *A History of Modern Yoga*. New York: Continuum, 2005.

Dennett, Daniel C. *Breaking the Spell: Religion as a Natural Phenomenon*. New York: Viking, 2006.

———. *Consciousness Explained*. Boston: Little, Brown, 1991.

———. *Darwin's Dangerous Idea: Evolution and the Meanings of Life*. New York: Simon and Schuster, 1995.

———. *Kinds of Minds: Toward an Understanding of Consciousness*. New York: Basic Books, 1996.

Derrida, Jacques. *The Animal That Therefore I Am*. Edited by Marie-Louis Mallet. Translated by David Wills. New York: Fordham University Press, 2008.

———. "Eating Well." In *Points . . .* , by Jacques Derrida. Edited by Elisabeth Weber, 255–287. Stanford, CA: Stanford University Press, 1995.

———. "Faith and Knowledge: The Two Sources of 'Religion' at the Limits of Reason Alone." In *Acts of Religion*, by Jacques Derrida. Edited by Gil Anidjar, 42–101. New York: Routledge, 2002.

———. *Of Grammatology*. Chicago: University of Chicago Press, 1974.

———. *Of Spirit: Heidegger and the Question*. Translated by Geoffrey Bennington and Rachel Bowlby. Chicago: University of Chicago Press, 1989.

———. *The Politics of Friendship*. Translated by George Collins. New York: Verso, 2006.

———. "Structure, Sign, and Play in the Discourse of the Human Sciences." In *Writing and Difference*, by Jacques Derrida. Translated by Alan Bass, 278–294. London: Routledge, 1978.

de Waal, Frans. *The Age of Empathy: Nature's Lessons for a Kinder Society*. New York: Three Rivers, 2009.

———. *The Bonobo and the Atheist*. New York: Norton, 2013.

———. *Chimpanzee Politics: Power and Sex among Apes*. 25th anniversary edition. Baltimore, MD: Johns Hopkins University Press, 2007.

———. *Good Natured: The Origins of Right and Wrong in Humans and Other Animals*. Cambridge, MA: Harvard University Press, 1997.

———. *Our Inner Ape: A Leading Primatologist Explains Why We Are Who We Are*. New York: Riverhead, 2005.

Dias, Elizabeth. "Many Religious Leaders (Except for Franklin Graham) Support Mosque." *Time*, August 18, 2010.

Disraeli, B. *Church Policy: A Speech Delivered by the Right Hon. B. Disraeli, M.P. at a meeting of the Oxford Diocesan Society for the Augmentation of Small Living in the Sheldonian Theatre, Oxford, November 25th, 1863*. London: Gilbert and Rivington, 1864.

Durkheim, Emile. *The Elementary Forms of Religious Life*. Translated by Karen E. Fields. New York: Free Press, 1995.

Eldredge, Niles. *Why We Do It: Rethinking Sex and the Selfish Gene*. New York: Norton, 2005.

Eliade, Mircea. *A History of Religious Ideas, Vol. 1*. Translated by Willard R. Trask. Chicago: University of Chicago Press, 1978.

———. *Patterns in Comparative Religion*. Translated by Rosemary Sheed. Lincoln: University of Nebraska Press, 1996.

———. *The Sacred and the Profane: The Nature of Religion*. Translated by Willard R. Trask. San Diego: Harcourt, 1959.

Eligon, John. "Hate Crime Charges in Stabbing of a Cabdriver." *New York Times*, August 30, 2010.

Ewing, Heidi, and Rachel Grady. *Jesus Camp*. Film. A&E IndieFilms, Loki Films, 2006.

Fanon, Frantz. *Black Skin, White Masks*. Translated by Charles Lam Markmann. New York: Grove, 1967.

Findley, Timothy. *Not Wanted on the Voyage*. Toronto: Penguin Books Canada, 1984.

Fischer, Becky. Jesus Camp: My Story. http://jesuscampmystory.com/.

———. "Photos You Never Saw." Jesus Camp: My Story. http://jesuscampmystory.com/photos-you-never-saw/.

Fitzgerald, Timothy. *The Ideology of Religious Studies*. New York: Oxford University Press, 1999.

Flatley, Jonathan. *Affective Mapping: Melancholia and the Politics of Modernism.* Cambridge, MA: Harvard University Press, 2008.

———. "How a Revolutionary Counter-mood Is Made." *New Literary History* 43 (2012): 503–525.

Foltz, David. " 'This She-Camel of God Is a Sign to You': Dimensions of Animals in Islamic Tradition and Muslim Culture." In *A Communion of Subjects*, edited by Paul Waldau and Kimberley Patton, 149–159. New York: Columbia University Press, 2006.

Foucault, Michel. *Discipline and Punish: The Birth of the Prison.* Translated by Alan Sheridan. New York: Vintage, 1977.

———. *The History of Sexuality: An Introduction, Volume 1.* Translated by Robert Hurley. New York: Vintage, 1990.

———. *The Order of Things.* New York: Vintage, 1973.

———. "The Subject and Power." In *Michel Foucault: Beyond Structuralism and Hermeneutics.* Edited by Hubert L. Dreyfus and Paul Rabinow, 208–226. Chicago: University of Chicago Press, 1982.

———. "Theatrum Philosophicum." In *Language, Counter-Memory, Practice: Selected Essays and Interviews.* Ithaca, NY: Cornell University Press, 1980.

Fox and Friends. FOX, August 10, 2010. Gretchen Carlson, Steve Doocy, Laura Ingraham, Brian Kilmeade.

Fuller, Robert C. *Spirituality in the Flesh: Bodily Sources of Religious Experience.* New York: Oxford University Press, 2008.

———. *Wonder: From Emotion to Spirituality.* Chapel Hill: University of North Carolina Press, 2006.

Ganeshananthan, V. V. "Tea Party Official Apologizes to Hindus after Insulting Muslim 'Monkey God'; Local Hindu Says, Take Your Apology and Shove It." *Sepia Mutiny*, May 20, 2010. http://sepiamutiny.com/blog/2010/05/20/tea _party_offic/.

Gazzaniga, Michael S. *The Ethical Brain.* New York: Dana, 2005.

Geller, Pamela. "Giving Thanks." *Atlas Shrugs.* http://pamelageller.com/2009/12 /giving-thanks.html/

———. "Islamic Antisemitism 101: The Daisy Khan Con." *Atlas Shrugs.* http:// pamelageller.com/2010/08/islamic-antisemitism-101-the-daisy-khan-con .html/

———. "Mosque at Ground Zero: Adding Insult to Agony." *Atlas Shrugs.* http:// pamelageller.com/2009/12/mosque-at-ground-zero-adding-insult-to-agony .html/

———. "Official Rally Videos: The 911 FDI/SIOA Rally of Remembrance." *Atlas Shrugs.* http://pamelageller.com/2010/09/video-the-911-fdisioa-rally-of -remembrance-against-ground-zero-mosque.html/

———. "President Hussein: 'We Are Not a Christian Nation.' " *Atlas Shrugs.* http://pamelageller.com/2009/04/president-hussein-we-are-not-a-christian -nation.html/

———. *Stop the Islamization of America.* Washington, DC: WND Books, 2011.

———. "Why There Shouldn't Be a Mosque at Ground Zero." *Human Events.* http://humanevents.com/2010/09/04/why-there-shouldnt-be-a-mosque-at -ground-zero/

Gerhart, Ann, and Ernesto Londoño. "Pastor Terry Jones's Koran-Burning Threat Started with a Tweet." *Washington Post,* September 10, 2010.

Glezos, Simon. *The Politics of Speed: Capitalism, the State and War in an Accelerating World.* New York: Routledge, 2013.

Goffman, Oz. "Miracle Dolphin." In *Between Species: Celebrating the Dolphin-Human Bond,* edited by Toni Frohoff and Brenda Petersen, 162–167. San Francisco: Sierra Club Books, 2003.

Goodall, Jane. "The Dance of Awe." In *A Communion of Subjects,* edited by Paul Waldau and Kimberley Patton, 651–656. New York: Columbia University Press, 2006.

———. "Primate Spirituality." In *The Encyclopedia of Religion and Nature,* edited by Bron Taylor, 1303–1306. New York: Continuum, 2005.

———. *Through a Window: My Thirty Years with the Chimpanzees of Gombe.* Boston: Houghton Mifflin, 1990.

Goodall, Jane, with Philip Berman. *Reason for Hope: A Spiritual Journey.* New York: Soko, 1999.

Gould, Stephen Jay. "Darwinian Fundamentalism." *New York Review of Books,* June 12, 1997.

———. "Fulfilling the Spandrels of World and Mind." In *Understanding Scientific Prose,* edited by Jack Selzer, 310–336. Madison: University of Wisconsin Press, 1993.

———. *Full House: The Spread of Excellence from Plato to Darwin.* New York: Harmony, 1996.

———. *The Mismeasure of Man.* New York: Norton, 1981.

———. *The Panda's Thumb: More Reflections in Natural History.* New York: Norton, 1980.

———. *The Structure of Evolutionary Theory.* Cambridge, MA: Belknap, 2002.

———. *Wonderful Life: The Burgess Shale and the Nature of History.* New York: Norton, 1989.

Gould, Stephen Jay, and R. C. Lewontin. "The Spandrels of San Marco and the Panglossian Paradigm: A Critique of the Adaptationist Programme." *Proceedings of the Royal Society of London* B 205 (1979): 581–598.

Gould, Stephen Jay, and Elisabeth S. Vrba. "Exaptation: A Missing Term in the Science of Form." *Paleobiology* 8, no. 1 (winter 1982): 4–15.

Gregg, Melissa, and Gregory J. Seigworth, eds. *The Affect Theory Reader.* Durham, NC: Duke University Press, 2010.

Gregg, Melissa, and Gregory J. Seigworth. "An Inventory of Shimmers." In *The Affect Theory Reader,* edited by Melissa Gregg and Gregory J. Seigworth, 1–25. Durham, NC: Duke University Press, 2010.

Gross, Aaron. "The Question of the Animal and Religion: Dietary Practices, Subjectivity, and Ethics in Jewish Traditions." PhD diss., University of California, Santa Barbara, 2010.

————. *The Question of the Animal and Religion: Theoretical Stakes, Practical Implications*. New York: Columbia University Press, 2014.

————. "The Question of the Creature: Animals, Theology and Levinas' Dog." In *Creaturely Theology: On God, Humans and Other Animals*, edited by Celia Deane-Drummond and David Clough, 121–137. London: SCM Press, 2009.

Grosz, Elizabeth. *Becoming Undone: Darwinian Reflections on Life, Politics, and Art*. Durham, NC: Duke University Press, 2011.

————. *Chaos, Territory, Art: Deleuze and the Framing of the Earth*. New York: Columbia University Press, 2008.

————. *Time Travels: Feminism, Nature, Power*. Durham, NC: Duke University Press, 2005.

Guenther, Lisa. *Solitary Confinement: Social Death and Its Afterlives*. Minneapolis: University of Minnesota Press, 2013.

Guthrie, Stewart. "Animal Animism: Evolutionary Roots of Religious Cognition." In *Current Approaches in the Cognitive Science of Religion*, edited by Ilkka Pyysiäinen and Veikko Anttonen, 38–67. New York: Continuum, 2002.

————. "Why Gods? A Cognitive Theory." In *Religion in Mind: Cognitive Perspectives on Religious Belief, Ritual, and Experience*, edited by Jensine Andresen, 94–111. Cambridge: Cambridge University Press, 2001.

Hamner, M. Gail. *Imaging Religion in Film: The Politics of Religious Nostalgia*. New York: Palgrave Macmillan, 2011.

Haraway, Donna J. *The Companion Species Manifesto: Dogs, People, and Significant Otherness*. Chicago: Prickly Paradigm, 2003.

————. *Primate Visions: Gender, Race, and Nature in the World of Modern Science*. New York: Routledge, 1990.

————. *Simians, Cyborgs, and Women*. New York: Routledge, 1991.

————. *When Species Meet*. Minneapolis: University of Minnesota Press, 2008.

Hardt, Michael. "Foreword: What Affects Are Good For." In *The Affective Turn: Theorizing the Social*, edited by Patricia Ticineto Clough and Jean Halley, ix–xiii. Durham: Duke University Press, 2007.

Harner, Michael. "The Ecological Basis for Aztec Sacrifice." *American Ethnologist* 4, no. 1 (1977): 117–135.

Harris, Dan. "Film Shows Youths Training to Fight for Jesus." ABC News, September 17, 2006. http://abcnews.go.com/WNT/story?id=2455343.

Harris, Ian. "'A Vast Unsupervised Recycling Plant': Animals and the Buddhist Cosmos." In *A Communion of Subjects*, edited by Paul Waldau and Kimberley Patton, 207–217. New York: Columbia University Press, 2006.

Harrod, James B. "The Case for Chimpanzee Religion." *Journal for the Study of Religion, Nature, and Culture* 8, no. 1 (2014): 8–45.

————. "A Trans-species Definition of Religion." *Journal for the Study of Religion, Nature, and Culture* 5, no. 3 (2011): 327–353.

Hedges, Chris. *War Is a Force That Gives Us Meaning*. New York: Anchor, 2003.

Heerwagen, Judith H., and Gordon H. Orians. "Humans, Habitats, and Aesthetics." In *The Biophilia Hypothesis*, edited by Stephen R. Kellert and Edward O. Wilson, 138–172. Washington: Shearwater/Island Press, 1993.

Heidegger, Martin. *Being and Time*. New York: Harper Perennial Modern Classics, 1962.

———. *The Fundamental Concepts of Metaphysics*. Translated by William McNeill and Nicholas Walker. Indianapolis: Indiana University Press, 1983.

———. "The Letter on Humanism." Translated by Frank A. Capuzzi and J. Glenn Gray. In *Basic Writings*, edited by David Farrell Krell, 213–266. New York: HarperCollins, 1993.

Hekman, Susan. "Constructing the Ballast: An Ontology for Feminism." In *Material Feminisms*, edited by Stacy Alaimo and Susan Hekman, 85–119. Bloomington: Indiana University Press, 2008.

Hirschkind, Charles. *The Ethical Soundscape: Cassette Sermons and Islamic Counterpublics*. New York: Columbia University Press, 2006.

Hobgood-Oster, Laura. "Holy Dogs and Asses: Stories Told through Animal Saints." In *What Are the Animals to Us? Approaches from Science, Religion, and Folklore, Literature, and Art*, edited by David Aftandilian, 189–203. Chattanooga: University of Tennessee Press, 2007.

Holland, Sharon Patricia. *The Erotic Life of Racism*. Durham, NC: Duke University Press, 2012.

Hollywood, Amy. *Sensible Ecstasy: Mysticism, Sexual Difference, and the Demands of History*. Chicago: University of Chicago Press, 2002.

Howes, David. "Sensation." *Material Religion* 7, no. 1 (2011): 92–99.

Hrdy, Sarah Blaffer. *Mother Nature: A History of Mothers, Infants, and Natural Selection*. New York: Pantheon, 1999.

Hulse, Carl. "G.O.P. Seizes on Mosque Issue Ahead of Elections." *New York Times*, August 16, 2010.

Hutchison, Bill. "Tea Party Leader Says Muslims Worship a 'Monkey God,' Blasts Ground Zero Mosque." *New York Daily News*, May 19, 2010.

Ingraham, Laura, guest host. *The O'Reilly Factor*. FOX, December 21, 2009.

Irigaray, Luce. "Divine Women." In *Sexes and Genealogies*, translated by Gillian C. Gill, 55–72. New York: Columbia University Press, 1993.

———. "Questions to Emmanuel Levinas: On the Divinity of Love." In *Re-Reading Levinas*, edited by Robert Bernasconi and Simon Critchley, 109–118. Bloomington: Indiana University Press, 1991.

Jakobsen, Janet R., and Ann Pellegrini. "Introduction: Times Like These." In *Secularisms*, edited by Janet R. Jakobsen and Ann Pellegrini, 1–35. Durham: Duke University Press, 2008.

———. *Love the Sin: Sexual Regulation and the Limits of Religious Tolerance*. New York: New York University Press, 2003.

James, William. *The Varieties of Religious Experience: A Study in Human Nature*. New York: Collier, 1961.

Jantzen, Grace. *Becoming Divine: Towards a Feminist Philosophy of Religion*. Bloomington: Indiana University Press, 1999.

Jenkins, Willis J. *Ecologies of Grace: Environmental Ethics and Christian Theology.* New York: Oxford University Press, 2008.

Journet, Debra. "Deconstructing 'The Spandrels of San Marco.'" In *Understanding Scientific Prose,* edited by Jack Selzer, 232–255. Madison: University of Wisconsin Press, 1993.

Kant, Immanuel. *Religion within the Boundaries of Mere Reason and Other Writings.* Edited and translated by Allen Wood and George di Giovanni. Cambridge: Cambridge University Press, 1998.

Keller, Evelyn Fox. "Language and Ideology in Evolutionary Theory: Reading Cultural Norms into Natural Law." In *The Boundaries of Humanity: Humans, Animals, Machines,* edited by James J. Sheehan and Morton Sosna, 85–102. Berkeley: University of California Press, 1991.

Kellert, Stephen R. "The Biological Basis for Human Values of Nature." In *The Biophilia Hypothesis,* edited by Stephen R. Kellert and Edward O. Wilson, 42–69. Washington, DC: Shearwater/Island Press, 1993.

———. "Biophilia." In *The Encyclopedia of Religion and Nature,* 183–188. New York: Continuum, 2005.

Khan, Daisy, and Gustav Niebuhr. "Why We Should Build Cordoba House at Park51," Syracuse University, Syracuse, NY, October 6, 2010.

Kierkegaard, Søren. *The Sickness unto Death.* Princeton, NJ: Princeton University Press, 1980.

Kim, Ki-duk. *Spring, Summer, Fall, Winter . . . and Spring.* Film. Korea Pictures, LJ Film, Pandora Filmproduktion, 2003.

King, Barbara J. *Evolving God: A Provocative View on the Origins of Religion.* New York: Doubleday, 2007.

Klassen, Pamela E. "Ritual." In *The Oxford Handbook of Religion and Emotion,* edited by John Corrigan, 143–161. New York: Oxford University Press, 2008.

LaMothe, Kimerer. *Between Dancing and Writing: The Practice of Religious Studies.* New York: Fordham University Press, 2004.

———. "What Bodies Know about Religion and the Study of It." *Journal of the American Academy of Religion* 76, no. 3 (September 2008): 573–601.

Latour, Bruno. "How to Talk about the Body? The Normative Dimension of Science Studies." *Body and Society* 10, no. 2–3 (2004): 205–230.

———. *On the Modern Cult of the Factish Gods.* Durham, NC: Duke University Press, 2010.

———. "Why Has Critique Run Out of Steam? From Matters of Fact to Matters of Concern." *Critical Inquiry* 30, no. 2 (winter 2004): 225–248.

LeDoux, Joseph E. *Synaptic Self: How Our Brains Become Who We Are.* New York: Viking, 2002.

Lelwica, Michelle Mary. "Embodying Learning: Post-Cartesian Pedagogy and the Academic Study of Religion." *Teaching Theology and Religion* 12, no. 2 (April 2009): 123–136.

Levinas, Emmanuel. *Difficult Freedom: Essays on Judaism.* Translated by Séan Hand. Baltimore, MD: Johns Hopkins University Press, 1990.

————. "Intention, Ereignis, und der Andere: Gespräch zwischen Emmanuel Levinas und Christoph von Wolzogen am 20 Dezember 1985 in Paris." In *Humanismus der anderen Menschen*, 140. Hamburg: Felix Meiner, 1985.

————. "The Name of a Dog, or Natural Rights." In *Animal Philosophy: Ethics and Identity*, edited by Peter Atterton and Matthew Calarco, 46–50. New York: Continuum, 2004.

————. *Otherwise Than Being, or Beyond Essence*. Translated by Alphonso Lingis. Pittsburgh: Duquesne University Press, 1998.

————. *Totality and Infinity: An Essay on Exteriority*. Translated by Alphonso Lingis. Pittsburgh: Duquesne University Press, 1969.

Levine, George. *Darwin Loves You: Natural Selection and the Reenchantment of the World*. Princeton, NJ: Princeton University Press, 2006.

Leys, Ruth. "The Turn to Affect: A Critique." *Critical Inquiry* 37, no. 3 (spring 2011): 434–472.

Lingis, Alphonso. *Dangerous Emotions*. Berkeley: University of California Press, 2000.

Llewelyn, John. *The Middle Voice of Ecological Conscience: A Chiasmic Reading of Responsibility in the Neighborhood of Levinas, Heidegger and Others*. New York: St. Martin's Press, 1991.

Lloyd, Genevieve. *The Man of Reason: "Male" and "Female" in Western Philosophy*, 2nd ed. Minneapolis: University of Minnesota Press, 1993.

Lopez, Donald. *Curators of the Buddha: The Study of Buddhism under Colonialism*. Chicago: University of Chicago Press, 1995.

Lundberg, Chris. "Enjoying God's Death: 'The Passion of the Christ' and the Practices of an Evangelical Public." *Quarterly Journal of Speech* 95, no. 4 (2009): 387–411.

Mackey, Robert. "The Case for ISIS, Made in a British Accent." *New York Times*, June 20, 2014. http://www.nytimes.com/2014/06/21/world/middleeast/the -case-for-isis-made-in-a-british-accent.html.

Mahmood, Saba. *Politics of Piety: The Islamic Revival and the Feminist Subject*. Princeton, NJ: Princeton University Press, 2005.

————. "Religious Reason and Secular Affect: An Incommensurable Divide?" *Critical Inquiry* 35 (summer 2009): 836–862.

Malabou, Catherine. *Ontology of the Accident: An Essay on Destructive Plasticity*. Translated by Carolyn Shread. Cambridge, MA: Polity, 2012.

————. *What Should We Do with Our Brain?* Translated by Sebastian Rand. New York: Fordham University Press, 2008.

Malabou, Catherine, and Jacques Derrida. *Counterpath*. Translated by David Wills. Stanford, CA: Stanford University Press, 2004.

Manning, Erin. *Always More Than One: Individuation's Dance*. Durham, NC: Duke University Press, 2013.

————. *Relationscapes: Movement, Art, Philosophy*. Cambridge, MA: MIT Press, 2009.

Marcus, George E., W. Russell Neuman, and Michael MacKuen, eds. *Affective Intelligence and Political Judgment*. Chicago: University of Chicago Press, 2000.

Maringer, Johannes. *The Gods of Prehistoric Man*. New York: Knopf, 1960.

Marion, Jean-Luc. *The Erotic Phenomenon*. Chicago: University of Chicago Press, 2007.

Masson, Jeffrey Moussaieff. *The Emperor's Embrace: The Evolution of Fatherhood*. New York: Atria, 2001.

———. *The Pig Who Sang to the Moon: The Emotional World of Farm Animals*. New York: Ballantine, 2004.

———. *When Elephants Weep: The Emotional Lives of Animals*. New York: Delta, 1996.

Massumi, Brian. "The Autonomy of Affect." *Cultural Critique* 31 (fall 1995): 83–109.

———. *Parables for the Virtual: Movement, Affect, Sensation*. Durham, NC: Duke University Press, 2002.

———. *What Animals Teach Us about Politics*. Durham, NC: Duke University Press, 2014.

Masuzawa, Tomoko. *The Invention of World Religions: Or, How European Universalism Was Preserved in the Language of Pluralism*. Chicago: University of Chicago Press, 2005.

Mazzarella, William. "Affect: What Is It Good For?" In *Enchantments of Modernity: Empire, Nation, Globalization*, edited by Saurabh Dube, 291–309. New York: Routledge, 2009.

———. "Mind the Gap! Or, What Does Secularism Feel Like?" In *The Sahmat Collective: Art and Activism in India Since 1989*, edited by Jessica Moss and Ram Rahman, 258–265. Chicago: Smart Museum of Art at University of Chicago, 2013.

McAlister, Melani. "What Is Your Heart For? Affect and Internationalism in the Evangelical Public Sphere." *American Literary History* 20, no. 4 (2008): 870–895.

McCutcheon, Russell T. *The Discipline of Religion: Structure, Meaning, Rhetoric*. London: Routledge, 2003.

McVay, Scott. "A Siamese Connexion with a Plurality of Other Mortals." In *The Biophilia Hypothesis*, edited by Stephen Kellert and Edward O. Wilson, 3–19. Washington, DC: Island Press, 1993.

Meillassoux, Quentin. *After Finitude*. Translated by Ray Brassier. New York: Continuum, 2008.

Merleau-Ponty, Maurice. *Phenomenology of Perception*. Translated by Colin Smith. New York: Routledge, 1962.

Meyer, Birgit, David Morgan, Crispin Paine, and S. Brent Plate. "Introduction: Key Words in Material Religion." *Material Religion* 7, no. 1 (2011): 4–9.

Midgley, Mary. *The Ethical Primate: Humans, Freedom, Morality*. London: Routledge, 1994.

———. *The Solitary Self: Darwin and the Selfish Gene*. Durham, UK: Acumen, 2010.

Miller, Patricia Cox. "Adam, Eve, and the Elephants: Asceticism and Animality." In *Ascetic Culture: Essays in Honor of Philip Rousseau*, edited by Blake Leyerle and Robin Darling Young. Notre Dame, IN: University of Notre Dame Press, 2013.

Morgan, David. *The Embodied Eye: Religious Visual Culture and the Social Life of Feeling*. Berkeley: University of California Press, 2012.

Mortensen, Eric D. "The Problem: If Subjects, Then Themselves Religious?" Paper presented at the Annual Meeting of the American Academy of Religion, Montreal, October 2009.

Moss, Cynthia J. *The Amboseli Elephants: A Long-Term Perspective on a Long-Lived Mammal*. Chicago: University of Chicago Press, 2011.

———. *Elephant Memories: Thirteen Years in the Life of an Elephant Family*. Chicago: University of Chicago Press, 2000.

Muñoz, José Esteban. "Feeling Brown: Ethnicity and Affect in Ricardo Bracho's 'The Sweetest Hangover (and Other STDs).'" *Theatre Journal* 52, no. 1 (March 2000): 67–79.

Narayanan, Vasudha. "Embodied Cosmologies: Sights of Piety, Sites of Power." *Journal of the American Academy of Religion* 71, no. 3 (September 2003): 495–520.

Nathanson, Donald L. "Prologue: Affect Imagery Consciousness." In *Affect Imagery Consciousness: The Complete Edition*, by Silvan S. Tomkins, xi–xxvi. Edited by Bertram P. Karon. New York: Springer, 2008.

———. *Shame and Pride: Affect, Sex, and the Birth of the Self*. New York: Norton, 1992.

Nelson, Lance. "Cows, Elephants, Dogs, and Other Lesser Embodiments of *Atman*: Reflections on Hindu Attitudes toward Nonhuman Animals." In *A Communion of Subjects*, edited by Paul Waldau and Kimberley Patton, 179–193. New York: Columbia University Press, 2006.

Ngai, Sianne. *Ugly Feelings*. Cambridge, MA: Harvard University Press, 2005.

Nietzsche, Friedrich. *The Gay Science (The Joyful Wisdom)*. Translated by Thomas Common. Digireads.com, 2009.

O'Neill, Kevin. "Beyond Broken: Affective Spaces and the Study of American Religion." *Journal of the American Academy of Religion* 81, no. 4 (December 2013): 1093–1116.

Otto, Rudolf. *The Idea of the Holy: An Inquiry into the Non-rational Factor in the Idea of the Divine and Its Relation to the Rational*. Translated by John W. Harvey. New York: Pelican, 1959.

Paley, Nina. *Sita Sings the Blues*. Film. Self-produced, 2008.

Panksepp, Jaak. *Affective Neuroscience: The Foundations of Human and Animal Emotions*. New York: Oxford University Press, 1998.

Papoulias, Constantina, and Felicity Callard. "Biology's Gift: Interrogating the Turn to Affect." *Body and Society* 16, no. 1 (2010): 29–56.

Patton, Kimberley C. "'He Who Sits in the Heavens Laughs': Recovering Animal Theology in the Abrahamic Traditions." *Harvard Theological Review* 93, no. 4 (October 2000): 401–434.

Pellegrini, Ann. "Movement." *Material Religion* 7, no. 1 (2011): 66–75.

———. "'Signaling through the Flames': Hell House Performance and Structures of Religious Feeling." *American Quarterly* 59 no. 3 (September 2007): 911–935.

Pettman, Dominic. *Love and Other Technologies: Retrofitting Eros for the Information Age*. New York: Fordham University Press, 2006.

Plate, S. Brent. *A History of Religion in 5½ Objects: Bringing the Spiritual to Its Senses*. Boston: Beacon, 2014.

Probyn, Elspeth. "A-ffect: Let Her RIP." *Media/Culture Journal* 8, no. 6 (December 2005). http://journal.media-culture.org.au/0512/13-probyn.php.

Protevi, John. *Political Affect: Connecting the Social and the Somatic*. Minneapolis: University of Minnesota Press, 2009.

————. *Political Physics: Deleuze, Derrida, and the Body Politic*. New York: Athlone, 2001.

Prothero, Stephen. *God Is Not One: The Eight Rival Religions That Run the World—and Why Their Differences Matter*. New York: HarperOne, 2010.

Proust, Marcel. *Remembrance of Things Past: 1*. Translated by C. K. Scott Moncrieff and Terence Kilmartin. Middlesex, UK: Penguin, 1985.

Pruetz, Jill D., and Thomas C. LaDuke. "Brief Communication: Reaction to Fire by Savanna Chimpanzees (*Pan troglodytes verus*) at Fongoli, Senegal: Conceptualization of 'Fire Behavior' and the Case for a Chimpanzee Model." *American Journal of Physical Anthropology* 141 (2010): 646–650.

Puar, Jasbir. *Terrorist Assemblages: Homonationalism in Queer Times*. Durham, NC: Duke University Press, 2007.

Pyrdum, Carl. "Professor Newt's Distorted History Lesson." Got Medieval, August 2, 2010. http://www.gotmedieval.com/2010/08/professor-newts-distorted-history-lesson.html.

Pyysiäinen, Ilkka. "Cognition, Emotion, and Religious Experience." In *Religion in Mind: Cognitive Perspectives on Religious Belief, Ritual, and Experience*, edited by Jensine Andresen, 70–93. Cambridge: Cambridge University Press, 2001.

————. "Introduction: Cognition and Culture in the Construction of Religion." In *Current Approaches in the Cognitive Science of Religion*, edited by Ilkka Pyysiäinen and Veikko Anttonen, 1–13. New York: Continuum, 2002.

Pyysiäinen, Ilkka, and Veikko Anttonen, eds. *Current Approaches in the Cognitive Science of Religion*. New York: Continuum, 2002.

Rand, Ayn. *Ayn Rand Answers: The Best of Her Q&A*, edited by Robert Mayhew. New York: New American Library, 2005.

————. "Philosophy: Who Needs It?" Address to the graduating class of the United States Military Academy at West Point, March 6, 1974.

Reber, Dierdra. "Headless Capitalism: Affect as Free-Market Episteme." *Differences: A Journal of Feminist Cultural Studies* 23, no. 1 (2012): 62–100.

Responsible for Equality and Liberty (R.E.A.L.). "NYC: Anti-Islam Hate Leads to Death Threats." Responsible for Equality and Liberty (R.E.A.L.), September 23, 2010. http://realhumanrights.wordpress.com/2010/09/23/nyc-anti-islam-death-threats/.

Rose, Steven. *Lifelines: Biology beyond Determinism*. New York: Oxford University Press, 1998.

Sagan, Dorion, and Lynn Margulis. "God, Gaia, and Biophilia." In *The Biophilia Hypothesis*, edited by Stephen R. Kellert and Edward O. Wilson, 345–364. Washington: Shearwater/Island Press, 1993.

Schaefer, Donovan O. "Blessed, Precious Mistakes: Deconstruction, Evolution, and New Atheism in America." *International Journal for Philosophy of Religion.* doi: 10.1007/s11153-014-9446-5.

———. "Do Animals Have Religion? Interdisciplinary Perspectives on Religion and Embodiment." *Anthrozoös: A Multidisciplinary Journal of the Interactions of People and Animals* 25, Supplement 1 (August 2012): 173–189.

———. "Embodied Disbelief: Poststructural Feminist Atheism." *Hypatia* 29, no. 2 (2014): 371–387. doi: 10.1111/hypa.12039.2014.

———. "Let's Be Queer about Darwin: Teleology, Desire, and Accident." Paper presented to the Evolution and Historical Explanation Conference of the Ian Ramsey Centre for Science and Religion, Oxford, 2014.

———. "On Dictionaryism: The Good News and Maledictions of Religious Literacy." *Bulletin for the Study of Religion* 40, no. 2 (2011): 3–8.

———. "*Se Plastiquer*: Freedom and Metaphysics in Catherine Malabou's *What Should We Do with Our Brain?*" Paper presented to the Society for Phenomenology and Existential Philosophy Annual Conference, Philadelphia, 2011.

———. "The Shape of the Field: Bruce Lincoln's *Discourse and the Construction of Society.*" *Council of Societies for the Study of Religion Bulletin* 38, no. 3 (2009): 58–61.

———. "Tight Genes: Feminism, Evolutionary Theory and the Dancing Religious Body." Paper presented at American Academy of Religion Annual Meeting, Atlanta, GA, 2010.

Schaller, George B. *The Year of the Gorilla.* Chicago: University of Chicago Press, 1964.

Schüler, Sebastian. "Synchronized Ritual Behavior: Religion, Cognition and the Dynamics of Embodiment." In *Religion and the Body: Modern Science and the Construction of Religious Meaning*, edited by David Cave and Rebecca Sachs Norris, 81–101. Leiden and Boston: Brill, 2012.

Sedgwick, Eve Kosofsky. "A Dialog on Love." *Critical Inquiry* 24, no. 2 (winter 1998): 611–631.

———. *Epistemology of the Closet.* Berkeley: University of California Press, 1990.

———. "Teaching/Depression." *The Scholar and Feminist Online* 4, no. 2 (spring 2006). http://sfonline.barnard.edu/heilbrun/sedgwick_01.htm.

———. *Touching Feeling: Affect, Pedagogy, Performativity.* Durham, NC: Duke University Press, 2003.

———. *The Weather in Proust.* Durham, NC: Duke University Press, 2011.

Sharf, Robert H. "Experience." In *Critical Terms for Religious Studies*, edited by Mark C. Taylor, 94–114. Chicago: University of Chicago Press, 1998.

Shouse, Eric. "Feeling, Emotion, Affect." *Media/Culture Journal* 8, no. 6 (December 2005). http://journal.media-culture.org.au/0512/03-shouse.php.

Sikka, Sonia. "The Delightful Other: Portraits of the Feminine in Kierkegaard, Nietzsche, and Levinas." In *Feminist Interpretations of Emmanuel Levinas*, edited by Tina Chanter, 96–113. State College: Pennsylvania State University Press, 2001.

Simpson, George Gaylord. *Biology and Man.* New York: Harcourt Brace Jovanovich, 1969.

Slajda, Rachel. "At TN Mosque Hearing, Plaintiffs Claim Islam Isn't a Religion." TPM, September 30, 2010. http://tpmmuckraker.talkingpointsmemo.com/2010 /09/at_tn_mosque_hearing_plaintiffs_claim_islam_isnt_a.php.

Slingerland, Edward. *What Science Offers the Humanities: Integrating Body and Culture*. Cambridge: Cambridge University Press, 2008.

Slone, D. Jason, ed. *Religion and Cognition: A Reader*. New York: Equinox, 2006.

Sloterdijk, Peter. *Rage and Time: A Psychopolitical Investigation*. New York: Columbia University Press, 2010.

Smith, Caleb. *The Prison and the American Imagination*. New Haven: Yale University Press, 2009.

Smith, Jonathan Z. *Imagining Religion: From Babylon to Jonestown*. Chicago: University of Chicago Press, 1982.

———. "Map Is Not Territory." In *Map Is Not Territory: Studies in the History of Religions*, 289–309. Chicago: University of Chicago Press, 1978.

———. *Map Is Not Territory: Studies in the History of Religions*. Chicago: University of Chicago Press, 1978.

———. *Relating Religion: Essays in the Study of Religion*. Chicago: University of Chicago Press, 2004.

Smuts, Barbara. "Encounters with Animal Minds." *Journal of Consciousness Studies* 8, no. 5–7 (2001): 293–309.

Spinoza, Benedict de. *Ethics*. Edited and translated by Edwin Curley. New York: Penguin, 1996.

Spivak, Gayatri Chakravorty. *A Critique of Postcolonial Reason: Toward a History of the Vanishing Present*. Cambridge, MA: Harvard University Press, 1999.

Staiger, Janet, Ann Cvetkovich, and Ann Reynolds, eds. *Political Emotions*. New York: Routledge, 2010.

Sterelny, Kim. *Dawkins vs. Gould: Survival of the Fittest*. Cambridge, UK: Icon: 2001.

Stewart, Kathleen. *Ordinary Affects*. Durham, NC: Duke University Press, 2007.

———. "Worlding Refrains." In *The Affect Theory Reader*, edited by Melissa Gregg and Gregory J. Seigworth, 339–353. Durham, NC: Duke University Press, 2010.

Taussig, Michael. *What Color Is the Sacred?* Chicago: University of Chicago Press, 2009.

Taves, Ann. *Religious Experience Reconsidered: A Building-Block Approach to the Study of Religion and Other Special Things*. Princeton, NJ: Princeton University Press, 2009.

Teilhard de Chardin, Pierre. *The Phenomenon of Man*. Translated by Bernard Wall. New York: Harper, 1959.

Thandeka. *The Embodied Self: Friedrich Schleiermacher's Solution to Kant's Problem of the Empirical Self*. Albany: State University of New York Press, 1995.

———. *Learning to Be White: Money, Race, and God in America*. New York: Continuum, 1999.

Thrift, Nigel. "Intensities of Feeling: Towards a Spatial Politics of Affect." *Geografiska Annaler. Series B, Human Geography* 86, no. 1 (2004): 57–78.

———. *Non-representational Theory: Space, Politics, Affect.* New York: Routledge, 2007.

Tiger, Lionel, and Michael McGuire. *God's Brain.* New York: Prometheus, 2010.

Tomkins, Silvan S. *Affect Imagery Consciousness: The Complete Edition.* Edited by Bertram P. Karon. New York: Springer, 2008.

———. *Exploring Affect: The Selected Writings of Silvan S. Tomkins.* Edited by Virginia Demos. New York: Cambridge University Press, 1995.

———. *Shame and Its Sisters: A Silvan Tomkins Reader.* Edited by Eve Kosofsky Sedgwick and Adam Frank. Durham, NC: Duke University Press, 1995.

Tweed, Thomas A. *Crossing and Dwelling: A Theory of Religion.* Cambridge, MA: Harvard University Press, 2006.

———. *Our Lady of the Exile: Diasporic Religion at a Cuban Catholic Shrine in Miami.* New York: Oxford University Press, 1997.

Ulrich, Roger S. "Biophilia, Biophobia, and Natural Landscapes." In *The Biophilia Hypothesis,* edited by Stephen R. Kellert and Edward O. Wilson, 73–137. Washington, DC: Shearwater/Island Press, 1993.

Vásquez, Manuel A. *More Than Belief: A Materialist Theory of Religion.* New York: Oxford University Press, 2011.

von Uexküll, Jakob. "A Stroll through the Worlds of Animals and Men: A Picture Book of Invisible Worlds." In *Instinctive Behavior: The Development of a Modern Concept,* edited by Claire H. Schiller, 5–80. New York: International Universities Press, 1957.

Wallace, David Foster. "Tense Present: Democracy, English, and the Wars over Usage." *Harper's Magazine,* April 2001, 39–58.

Wallis, Jim. "Jim Wallis on the Story behind Pastor Terry Jones's Change of Heart." *Washington Post,* September 19, 2010.

Wasserstrom, Steven M. *Religion after Religion.* Princeton, NJ: Princeton University Press, 1999.

Watkins, Megan. "Pedagogic Affect/Effect: Embodying a Desire to Learn." *Pedagogies: An International Journal* 1, no. 4 (2006): 269–282.

Weil, Kari. *Thinking Animals: Why Animal Studies Now?* New York: Columbia University Press, 2012.

White, Ben. "The Dolphin's Gaze." In *Between Species: Celebrating the Dolphin-Human Bond,* edited by Toni Frohoff and Brenda Petersen, 72–76. San Francisco: Sierra Club, 2003.

Whitehouse, Harvey. *Modes of Religiosity: A Cognitive Theory of Religious Transmission.* Lanham, MD: AltaMira, 2004.

———. "Terror." In *The Oxford Handbook of Religion and Emotion,* edited by John Corrigan, 259–275. New York: Oxford University Press, 2008.

Wills, David. *Dorsality: Thinking Back through Technology and Politics.* Minneapolis: University of Minnesota Press, 2008.

Wilson, David Sloan. *Darwin's Cathedral: Evolution, Religion, and the Nature of Society.* Chicago: University of Chicago Press, 2002.

Wilson, E. O. "Biophilia and the Conservation Ethic." In *The Biophilia Hypothesis,* edited by Stephen R. Kellert and Edward O. Wilson, 31–41. Washington, DC: Shearwater/Island Press, 1993.

———. *Biophilia: The Human Bond with Other Species*. Cambridge, MA: Harvard University Press, 1984.

———. *On Human Nature*. Cambridge, MA: Harvard University Press, 1978.

———. *Sociobiology: The New Synthesis*. Cambridge, MA: Belknap, 1975.

Wilson, Edward O., and Stephen R. Kellert, eds. *The Biophilia Hypothesis*. Washington, DC: Island Press, 1993.

Wilson, Elizabeth A. "Organic Empathy: Feminism, Psychopharmaceuticals, and the Embodiment of Depression." In *Material Feminisms*, edited by Stacy Alaimo and Susan Hekman, 373–399. Bloomington: Indiana University Press, 2008.

———. *Psychosomatic: Feminism and the Neurological Body*. Durham, NC: Duke University Press, 2004.

Wilson, Erika. *Emotions and Spirituality in Religions and Spiritual Movements*. Lanham, MD: University Press of America, 2012.

Wolfe, Cary. *Animal Rites: American Culture, the Discourse of Species, and Posthumanist Theory*. Chicago: University of Chicago Press, 2003.

———. *What Is Posthumanism?* Minneapolis: University of Minnesota Press, 2009.

Wolfson, Elliot R. *A Dream Interpreted within a Dream: Oneiropoiesis and the Prism of Imagination*. New York: Zone, 2011.

———. "Dreams and the Specter of Invisibility: The Role of the Oneiric in the Mystical Imagination." Lecture, Syracuse University, April 2012.

———. *Language, Eros, Being: Kabbalistic Hermeneutics and Poetic Imagination*. New York: Fordham University Press, 2005.

Jesus Camp (film), 63, 67–91, 172
Jones, Terry, 138–139, 141–143, 246n108
joy, 33, 46–47, 75, 116, 132, 175–176, 187, 204, 239n59; dance of relating and, 214–215

Kant, Immanuel, 10–12, 117, 181, 253n4
Keller, Evelyn Fox, 159
Kellert, Stephen R., 195–196, 257n107
Khan, Daisy, 135–140, 245n91
King, Barbara J., 4, 131, 194
Klassen, Pamela, 36–38, 52, 57–59, 237n3
knowledge production, 12, 50–51, 57, 61, 99, 176, 208. *See also* epistemology

LaMothe, Kimerer, 189–192, 198, 212
language: accident and, 63, 106, 149–151, 180–182, 201–202, 231n4; affect and, 7, 11, 21, 23–30, 37–45, 57–58, 85, 88–89, 137, 167, 182–184, 209–213; animality and, 2–4, 17–18, 129, 187–188, 207; biology, 167–169, 180–182; deconstruction and, 150–155; Levinas on, 179–180; power and, 7, 10–11, 22, 34–35, 103–106, 117, 150, 190, 223n5, 223n7; racialization and, 122, 132–134, 145, 243n70; religion and, 4–10, 19–20, 118, 182, 189–191, 198–200, 201–205, 207–208, 215–217, 234n41, 253–254n10. *See also* Guru English; linguistic fallacy
Latour, Bruno, 24, 118–119
lek (bowerbird den), 186–188; religion as, 192–193, 197–203, 207, 210–215, 258n126
Levinas, Emmanuel, 179–181, 189, 203–205, 208, 244n49, 252n4, 253n5, 254n13, 259n135
Levine, George, 208
Lewontin, Richard, 16, 159–160, 166, 174–175, 250n71
Leys, Ruth, 42, 225n27, 227n19, 227n25, 227n26
liberalism: citizenship and, 214; secularism and, 74, 84–86, 235; subjectivity and, 23–24, 32, 44–45, 93–96, 99, 208
lifeworld (Umwelt), 98–101, 104, 123; lek as, 186–188
Lingis, Alphonso, 89
linguistic fallacy, 4–10, 20–23, 27, 35, 57–58, 93, 117, 155, 176, 189–190, 200, 207, 216;

racialization and, 129, 143. *See also* language
logos, 92, 163–172, 182, 213; Derrida's critique of, 149–156; in Levinas, 202–205

Mahmood, Saba, 215, 221n13, 233n23
Malabou, Catherine, 151–153, 176, 223n35
Manning, Erin, 24, 26, 33, 255n21; on dance, 182–186
Massumi, Brian, 47, 78, 117, 128, 183, 227n25, 241n11; Deleuzian affect theory and, 24–32, 39–43; science in, 224n22, 225n27, 226n7, 227n13, 227n18
material feminism, 23, 38, 50–51, 161
materialist shift in religious studies, 4, 7–10, 22, 27, 189; affect theory and, 30, 34, 50, 56, 58, 209, 217; globalization and, 63, 88
material religion, 106–117, 136, 189, 196
Mazzarella, William, 32
McAlister, Melani, 71, 74, 134n51
McCutcheon, Russell T., 7, 20. *See also* social-rhetorical theory of religion
Merleau-Ponty, Maurice, 98–100, 103, 186, 188, 239n56
Midgley, Mary, 131–132, 159
morality, 2, 131–140, 145, 198, 207, 254n13
Morgan, David, 55–56, 116–117. *See also* material religion
Muñoz, José Esteban, 141n16
mysterium tremendum (Otto), 54

Narayanan, Vasudha, 189–192
Ngai, Sianne, 223n37, 229n42, 239n59

O'Neill, Kevin, 28, 65, 117, 134, 136
onto-phenomenology, 49–52, 57–59, 185, 204, 230n80, 231n107; biophilia and, 192–199; solitary confinement and, 99–102; race and, 134, 143–144. *See also* intransigence; material feminism
Otto, Rudolf, 54, 59, 76

Panksepp, Jaak, 42, 51, 236n1, 237n21, 237n22, 255n46
Papoulias, Constantina, 41–42, 47, 225n27, 227n19
Park51 controversy, 124, 135–143, 245n83

Patton, Kimberley C., 3, 4, 224n20
pedagogy: affective dimensions of,
61–62, 65–68, 232n9, 233n13, 235n81,
236n94; gender and, 79–81; globalization as, 63–65, 235n81; religion as,
68–91, 233n13; Sedgwick on, 54–56,
61, 111
Pellegrini, Ann, 21, 33–34, 76, 87–88, 119;
on secularism, 215; on theatre, 168–169,
225n45
phenomenology: affect theory and, 8,
23–24, 28–35, 37–51, 61, 66–68,
102, 107, 119, 123–125, 172, 183–185,
214–215, 226n60, 227n26, 229n42,
238n42, 241n116; critical (Guenther),
94–102; materialist (Vásquez), 7–8, 22,
37–38, 58–59, 75–76, 179, 192, 195, 200,
207–208, 212, 239n56; religious studies
and, 5–7, 18, 21, 51–55, 62, 201
Plate, Brent S., 112, 116–117
postcolonial theory, 6–10, 54–55, 189,
220n13, 223n5, 228n35, 232n17
posthumanism, 12, 18, 23, 155, 221n11
postsecularism, 10–11, 64, 68–71, 82–88,
100, 110, 215–216, 235n81
power: affect theory and, 4, 8–11, 18,
21–23, 27–28, 33–35, 37–39, 49–57, 59,
67–68, 93–94, 101–117, 149–150, 155, 165,
169–176, 182–186, 190–191, 207–208,
222n16, 239n59; animals and, 128–129,
200; ideology and, 123–130, 243n34;
language and, 10–11, 223n5; religion
and, 5–8, 19–20, 64, 75–80, 83, 87–91,
118–119, 141–145, 195–199, 212–213,
215–218, 226n69, 232n17, 235n69. See also
compulsion; linguistic fallacy
pride. See dignity
primatology, 1–4, 17, 144, 200, 207; morality and, 131–135, 207; racialization and,
123–124, 128–131
Probyn, Elspeth, 31, 45
Prothero, Stephen, 19–20, 35, 134, 223n2,
232n17
Proust, Marcel, 27, 94, 106–113, 118–119,
122, 126, 145, 239n73, 244n60; cata-
logues and (Tomkins), 229n57, 239n59;
habit and, 240n82; lifeworlds and,
186–189, 209

psychoanalysis, 19, 29, 126, 197, 221n23,
243n23, 252n123
Puar, Jasbir, 23, 122, 128, 141, 224n19

queer theory: critical race theory and,
127–128, 138–139, 243n34; material religion and, 106–111, 118, 257n107; relation
to affect theory, 8, 17, 21, 32, 35, 145, 176,
195–197, 222n29, 224n15; theater and, 28

racism, 10, 37, 53, 75, 119–124, 210, 221n21,
228n30, 235n81, 241n1, 242n16; erotic
life of (Holland), 125–128, 134–135,
138–146, 243n34; primatology and,
128–131
Reber, Dierdra, 149, 246n7
Rose, Steven, 157, 159, 163–164, 228n30,
248n51, 252n117

savages, 11, 120–124, 143–146, 241n1
secularity, 10–12, 35, 64, 70–71, 82–88, 110,
145, 215–216, 235n81
Sedgwick, Eve Kosofsky: Buddhism and,
54–57, 231n103; on paranoid and reparative reading, 21, 175, 225n45; pedagogy
and, 60–61, 232n23; phenomenological
affect theory and, 24, 35, 58, 77–78, 101,
118, 126, 150, 223n37, 227n19, 227n26;
Proust and, 107–111, 239n73; Tomkins
and, 28–32, 43–50, 59, 67, 228n30,
228n38, 229n42, 238n42, 239n59, 246n7,
252n123
sexuality, 168–169, 185, 222n29, 228n30
sexual selection, 180, 185, 201, 250n74;
Grosz's reading of, 165–169
shame, 10, 30–31, 46–49, 77–78, 90, 103,
172, 234n66; pedagogy and, 85, 236n91.
See also dignity
Simpson, George Gaylord, 156–157
Slingerland, Edward, 44, 55, 222n32
Sloterdijk, Peter, 106, 125–128, 144, 243n23,
243n27
Smith, Caleb, 94–96
Smith, Jonathan Z., 20–21, 28, 30, 106,
217, 223n7; linguistic fallacy and, 4–11,
221n20, 221n21, 223n5, 232n17
social-rhetorical theory of religion, 17,
20–22, 119, 176–177, 223n7